SAP HCM – A Complete Tutorial

Deploy and implement the diverse functionalities of SAP HCM

Ganesh Karthik S

[PACKT] enterprise 88
PUBLISHING   professional expertise distilled

BIRMINGHAM - MUMBAI

SAP HCM – A Complete Tutorial

First published: June 2014

Production reference: 1180614

Published by Packt Publishing Ltd.
Livery Place
35 Livery Street
Birmingham B3 2PB, UK.

ISBN 978-1-78217-220-8

www.packtpub.com

Cover image by Asher Wishkerman (wishkerman@hotmail.com)

Credits

Author
Ganesh Karthik S

Reviewers
Gordon Du

Vladimir Mikhaylenko

Eric Wildenstein

Commissioning Editor
Amarabha Banerjee

Acquisition Editor
Mohammad Rizvi

Content Development Editor
Shaon Basu

Technical Editors
Manan Badani

Menza Mathew

Akash Rajiv Sharma

Copy Editor
Karuna Narayanan

Project Coordinator
Venitha Cutinho

Proofreaders
Simran Bhogal

Ameesha Green

Paul Hindle

Indexers
Mehreen Deshmukh

Rekha Nair

Tejal Soni

Graphics
Ronak Dhruv

Production Coordinator
Arvindkumar Gupta

Cover Work
Arvindkumar Gupta

Disclaimer

The author would like to advice consultants, end users, and aspirants to do a scrupulous testing of the configuration/customization in the Development client before moving the objects to the Production system. The author will not be held accountable for any damage caused by using or misusing the information, code, or methods suggested in this book, and anyone using them does so at his/her own risk. The evolution of the book is from the author's own interests and book publisher's trust in the author's abilities and not necessarily from the interests of his current and former employers.

About the Author

Ganesh Karthik S, who prefers to be called Karthik, is a senior SAP HCM functional consultant with Cognizant (NASDAQ: CTSH), based in Chennai, India. He holds a Master's degree in Human Resource Management from Monash University (Go8 universities), Melbourne, Australia (2005-2006). In December 2010, he earned a certification in SAP Certified Application Associate - Human Capital Management with SAP ERP 6.0 EHP4. He has close to 120 man months of progressive IT experience, which includes working on SAP and Oracle ERP products. He has been associated with multiple end-to-end implementation projects, along with projects on rollouts, upgradation, and production support. He is also determined to share his experiences with SAP aspirants and consultants in the form of a book. He is passionate about SAP and takes joy in sharing knowledge with others. He is an avid blogger and frequently writes on his blog (http://saperphcm.blogspot.in/). He loves sports, and his favorite movie is *The Pursuit of Happiness (2006)*. This book, *SAP HCM – A Complete Tutorial*, is his first attempt at an endeavor of this kind, and he would like to wholeheartedly thank the entire team at Packt Publishing for this opportunity. He likes to network and can be contacted via his Skype ID, Dreambeckons or via his Google Talk ID, sapenjooy.

Acknowledgments

At the very outset, I am thankful to my parents, sister, athimber (ak), nieces (Ananya and Mridini), Sarayu maami, Jayaram mama, Babu mama, Saraswati manni, chittappas, grandpa (ICF) for all their support and wishes. Special thanks to my grandpa and grandma (chrompet), who aren't with me now physically, for their blessings. I would also like to thank my friends Raja, Madhan, Venki, Rajesh, Matheen, Jean, Bean, Anbu (Ramesh), Yogi, Chaks, Machan R, and Mahesh (Alwarpet) for their encouragement. I would like to thank some of my mates in the SAP sphere: Sivabalan, Eswar (Income Tax), Thomas, Arun Vajrakantham, Dinakar, Gopalraj, Arathi, Sankaraman Subramaniam, Santhosh Somasekaran, Rajesh Burra, Kamlesh, Lokesh Sharma, Lokesh, Shankar, Thaneesh, Bala, Guna, Singh, Kamba, Gyan, Prasanna, Charmi, Papri, Suneeta, Eswar (ISU), Kishore, Raju, Govind Rao, Laxmi Rao, Ashok (ABAP), Ganesh (FI), Radhey Shyam, Saravanagopal, and Vijay NR for their continuous support. It's a big list and I apologize if I have inadvertently missed mentioning any of you. I am indebted to the entire team of Packt Publishing for this opportunity and a special mention to Rahul Nair, Mohammad Rizvi, and Shaon Basu for entrusting me with the responsibility, and the technical reviewers, Alexey Tveritinov, Eric Wildenstein, Vladimir Mikhaylenko, and Gordon Du, for their invaluable suggestions and inputs.

About the Reviewers

Gordon Du has been working in the Information Technology sector for over 30 years now. He is passionate about helping others whenever he can. Being the top contributor in the SAP Community Network since 2008, he has helped thousands of users to utilize ERP package more efficiently and solve their problems. He has broad knowledge in all aspects of ERP, especially for SAP.

Gordon has worked and trained in Canada, China, Singapore, and the USA. In China, he was the first person to successfully implement an international ERP software package in a domestic company. He is the author of *Mastering SQL Queries for SAP Business One*, *Packt Publishing*.

Vladimir Mikhaylenko is a SAP developer with more than five years of development experience in various SAP modules including, but not limited to, Financials, Material Management, Sales, and Distribution. At present, Vladimir works with SAP Globalization Services in the Russian Federation, and participates in development projects for the localization of SAP Human Capital Management for CIS and Ukraine.

Eric Wildenstein is a SAP techno-functional independent consultant, and has been working on ERP implementations for blue chip companies in Western Europe and Northern Africa regions since 1997. He mainly specializes in ABAP object-oriented programming, NetWeaver XI/PI/AIF, and SAP Business Workflow, providing technical expertise across the core business modules of SAP. Prior to becoming self-employed in 2000, he worked as an in-house programmer analyst for PricewaterhouseCoopers, UK, and Andersen Consulting, France, on both SAP R/3 and C/S architectures.

Eric has already reviewed several SAP books, including the very informative *SAP ABAP Advanced Cookbook, Rehan Zaidi, Packt Publishing*.

I would like to thank my dear Laurence for her patience and understanding. While I have been away from home working on various projects for the past 19 years, she is still very supportive, although I, myself, sometimes don't have much time to share with her.

www.PacktPub.com

Support files, eBooks, discount offers, and more

You might want to visit www.PacktPub.com for support files and downloads related to your book.

Did you know that Packt offers eBook versions of every book published, with PDF and ePub files available? You can upgrade to the eBook version at www.PacktPub.com and as a print book customer, you are entitled to a discount on the eBook copy. Get in touch with us at service@packtpub.com for more details.

At www.PacktPub.com, you can also read a collection of free technical articles, sign up for a range of free newsletters and receive exclusive discounts and offers on Packt books and eBooks.

http://PacktLib.PacktPub.com

Do you need instant solutions to your IT questions? PacktLib is Packt's online digital book library. Here, you can access, read and search across Packt's entire library of books.

Why subscribe?

- Fully searchable across every book published by Packt
- Copy and paste, print and bookmark content
- On demand and accessible via web browser

Free access for Packt account holders

If you have an account with Packt at www.PacktPub.com, you can use this to access PacktLib today and view nine entirely free books. Simply use your login credentials for immediate access.

Instant updates on new Packt books

Get notified! Find out when new books are published by following @PacktEnterprise on Twitter, or the *Packt Enterprise* Facebook page.

Table of Contents

Preface   **1**

Chapter 1: End User Transactions   **5**

  Daily transactional codes   **5**

    Frequently used T-codes   7

      The Recruitment submodule   7

      The Organization Management submodule   8

      The Personnel Administration submodule   9

      The Time Management submodule   10

      The Payroll Accounting submodule   11

      The Talent Management submodule   13

      The Training and Event Management submodule   14

      The Travel Management submodule   15

  Standard reports   **15**

    Recruitment   15

    Organizational Management   19

    Personnel Administration   20

    Time Management   22

    Payroll Accounting   23

    Talent Management   25

    Training and Event Management   25

    Travel Management   26

  Creating a folder and moving the T-codes   **28**

  An overview of SAP standard reports   **29**

    Recruitment   29

    Organization Management   29

    Personnel Administration   30

    Time Management   30

    Payroll Accounting   31

    Talent Management   32

Training and Event Management	32
Travel Management	32
Summary	**33**
Chapter 2: Recruitment Configuration	**35**
Handling vacancies	**35**
Vacancy maintenance steps	37
Advertising vacancies	**39**
Channels or recruitment instruments	40
Vacant position mapping using recruitment instruments	41
Recruitment medium	41
Applicant cycle	43
Integration with personnel administration	**52**
Integration tools	54
Common error message during data transfer	57
Tips and tricks	57
Features	57
Transport requests in SAP	59
Summary	**62**
Chapter 3: SPOCK – the Building Block of OM	**63**
The concepts of Organization Management	**63**
Elucidating an organizational structure	64
Basic relationships between organizational objects	65
Building an organizational structure	66
Creating an organizational structure with different interfaces	**66**
Organization and Staffing	66
The relationship between an Org unit and Position	68
The relationship between Position and Job	69
Simple Maintenance	70
Creating a Cost Center	75
The Expert Mode	77
Creating an organizational unit object in the Expert Mode	78
Creating a position object in the Expert Mode	79
Creating a Job object in the Expert Mode	80
The concept of Number Ranges	81
Scenarios where we use external number assignment	83
The Plan Version	85
Creating an organizational structure using the Expert Mode	91
Configuring the table	96
Integrating Organization Management with Personnel Administration	**99**
Integration switches	99

Data Transfer Tools   103
RHINTE Reports   104
The purpose of the OM tool   106
Summary   **107**

Chapter 4: PA Configuration in Less Than 24 Hours   **109**
Personnel Administration infotypes   **109**
**Important infotypes that are mandatory and
their configuration steps**   **110**
Functions of infotypes   110
The 0000 (Actions) infotype   110
The 0001 (Organization Assignment) infotype   112
The 0002 (Personal Data) infotype   113
The 0006 (Address) infotype   114
The 0007 (Planned Working Time) infotype   114
The 0008 (Basic Pay) infotype   116
The 0009 (Bank Details) infotype   117
Configuration steps   118
What makes the enterprise structure?   118
What makes the personnel structure?   119
Tips and tricks that will be handy while configuring the submodule   **129**
Recommendation on number range assignment   129
Configuring mandatory infotypes   131
Customizing the infotype menu and info groups   **140**
Configuring personnel actions   **144**
Dynamic actions   148
Summary   **150**

Chapter 5: Time Management Configuration – Negative Time   **151**
Nodes for configuring the Work schedule rule and Absence Quotas   **152**
Time Management infotypes   152
The Planned Working Time infotype (0007)   152
The Absences infotype (2001)   155
The Attendances infotype (2002)   155
The Absence Quotas infotype (2006)   156
The Attendance Quotas infotype (2007)   157
The Overtime infotype (2005)   158
The Employee Remuneration infotype (2010)   158
The Quota Correction infotype (2013)   159
The Time Quota Compensation infotype (0416)   161
**Important nodes and/or customizing tables for the
Work schedule rule**   **162**
The holiday calendar   162
The daily work schedule   165
The period work schedule   167

The day type 167
The Work schedule rule 168
Important nodes and/or customizing tables for Absence Quotas **170**
Absence Quotas generation rule configuration 176
Tips to generate Absence Quotas without any hassles **184**
Frequent error message and workaround 185
Important Time Management-related tables 188
Important functions, operations, and features 189
Internal tables and cluster tables used in time evaluation 190
Tool to check the configuration settings for quota generation 192
Summary **192**
Chapter 6: Payroll Configuration **193**
Infotypes mandatory for payroll processing **193**
Payroll infotypes 194
The 0000 (Actions) infotype 194
The 0001 (Organizational Assignment) infotype 194
Payroll area 194
Control record elucidated **196**
The 0003 (Payroll Status) infotype 197
The 0007 (Planned Working Time) infotype 198
The 0008 (Basic Pay) infotype 198
The 0027 (Cost Distribution) infotype 199
The 0014 (Recurring Payment and Deduction) infotype 200
The 0015 (Additional Payments) infotype 201
The 0267 (Additional off-cycle payments) infotype 202
Steps to configure the payroll **203**
Wage types 203
The 0008 (Basic Pay) configuration 206
The 0014 (Recurring Payments and Deductions) configuration 208
The 0015 (Additional Payments) configuration 209
The 0267 (On-demand or Additional Payments) configuration 211
Writing a PCR to meet your customer's requirements **213**
Schematic payroll schema 213
Personnel calculation rule (PCR) **216**
Important payroll functions 218
Important payroll operations 219
Frequent error messages and workaround 219
Configuring a payslip **220**
Integration with the finance module **221**
Activities in the HR system 222
Activities in an accounting AC system 223

Posting payroll results to finance steps   224
Different statuses of a posting run   227
Summary   **227**
Chapter 7: Talent Management and Development Configuration **229**
Basic settings – Personnel Development   **229**
Integration aspects with other submodules of HCM   **234**
Master data for the Personnel Development component   **235**
The qualification catalogue   237
Career maintenance   240
Functions in Personnel Development   241
Standard tools in the PD component   244
Development plans   244
Objective setting and an appraisal's template configuration **246**
Category group creation   248
Category creation   250
Steps to create an appraisal template   254
Summary   **256**
Chapter 8: Training and Event Management Configuration **257**
The basic settings in TEM   **257**
Integration aspects in the Training and Event Management module **258**
Configuring a business event preparation/event catalog **262**
Time schedule   263
Physical location   264
Master data   268
Resource management   270
The business event catalog   273
Day-to-day activities   274
Booking   275
Recurring activities   279
Follow-up processing   280
Employee Self-Service (ESS)   283
Summary   **284**
Chapter 9: Travel Management Configuration   **285**
Travel Management – features and functions   **285**
Basic settings for number ranges   286
Master data required for Travel Management   287
Important transaction codes   289
Travel Request configuration steps   **290**
Configuring Travel Planning   **294**
Configuring Travel Expenses   **306**

Integration aspects with other application components   **314**
Summary   **316**
Chapter 10: Building a Report Using SAP Query Viewer   **317**
  Building an ad hoc query using the SQ01 transaction code   **317**
    Steps for creating the user group   318
    Steps for creating the infoset   324
    Steps for creating a query   326
  Executing a report using an ad hoc query   **328**
    Frequent error messages when building an ad hoc query   333
      Analysis   333
      Workaround   333
    An interesting feature to tag the T-code with the report   334
  Transport a query across clients   **338**
  Develop a report using SAP Query Viewer (SQVI)   **340**
    Converting the query view to a SAP query   345
  Summary   **345**
Index   **347**

Preface

The HR or HCM function plays the role of strategic partner/business partner in current business scenarios, and the SAP HCM module is a great plugin for SAP. This book attempts to cover most of the modules in HCM such as Payroll, Time, and Travel to mention a few. There are plenty of excellent books written by experts in SAP HCM space, but you will not come across one that covers most of the topics under this module, and that is where I got the inspiration. I hope this book will serve as a one-stop shop to learn SAP HCM module configuration. Many real-time examples are covered along with configuration steps and many snapshots for easy understanding.

What this book covers

Chapter 1, *End User Transactions*, discusses all of the SAP HCM modules' important transaction codes and standard reports that can be used for daily operations.

Chapter 2, *Recruitment Configuration*, shows how to configure the recruitment submodules.

Chapter 3, *SPOCK – the Building Block of OM*, introduces you to important concepts of OM and multiple interfaces that can be used to build an organization structure.

Chapter 4, *PA Configuration in Less Than 24 Hours*, shows how to configure the PA module and understand the standard customizing settings to map the business process.

Chapter 5, *Time Management Configuration – Negative Time*, covers negative time configuration in detail along with how to generate quotas, and error messages that occur frequently and steps to fix the errors.

Chapter 6, *Payroll Configuration*, tells you about the payroll schema and how to customize the PCR. You will also delve into posting the pay results to the FI module, which covers integration with the Finance module.

Chapter 7, Talent Management and Development Configuration, shows you how to configure the appraisal template in less time and understand its functionality in detail.

Chapter 8, Training and Event Management Configuration, helps you to understand the various features that TEM module covers in detail.

Chapter 9, Travel Management Configuration, explores the various standard configuration features that the Travel Management module offers.

Chapter 10, Building a Report Using SAP Query Viewer, enlightens you on ways to build bespoke reports without any programming skills.

What you need for this book

You are expected to have basic knowledge of computers and know-how of Enterprise Resource Planning products and domain experience.

Who this book is for

This book is for SAP HCM aspirants, end users, and consultants who are keen on learning or fine-tuning their configuration knowledge. This book will attempt to help learn concepts and apply them in real-time projects. There are plenty of screenshots for better understanding. Some of the error messages frequently raised in real-time environment are covered and solutions for the same are also proposed.

Conventions

In this book, you will find a number of styles of text that distinguish between different kinds of information. Here are some examples of these styles and an explanation of their meaning.

Code words in text, database table names, folder names, filenames, file extensions, pathnames, dummy URLs, user input, and Twitter handles are shown as follows: "They define the nature of absence such as `Sick`, `Casual`, and so on."

A block of code is set as follows:

```
ZLEN (PCR name)
  3(ESG Grouping for PCR)
  1234 (Leave encashment Wage type that holds number)
                AMT=6789(Wage type)
                AMT/30
  MULTI ANA (Multiply Amount and Number, place it in Amount field)
                ADDWT 1234(Wage type)
```

New terms and **important words** are shown in bold. Words that you see on the screen, in menus or dialog boxes for example, appear in the text like this: "The **Sort Criterion** option is very handy when we try to find the holiday that we defined in order to map it in the holiday calendar."

> Warnings or important notes appear in a box like this.

> Tips and tricks appear like this.

Reader feedback

Feedback from our readers is always welcome. Let us know what you think about this book—what you liked or may have disliked. Reader feedback is important for us to develop titles that you really get the most out of.

To send us general feedback, simply send an e-mail to `feedback@packtpub.com`, and mention the book title via the subject of your message.

If there is a topic that you have expertise in and you are interested in either writing or contributing to a book, see our author guide on `www.packtpub.com/authors`.

Customer support

Now that you are the proud owner of a Packt book, we have a number of things to help you to get the most from your purchase.

Errata

Although we have taken every care to ensure the accuracy of our content, mistakes do happen. If you find a mistake in one of our books—maybe a mistake in the text or the code—we would be grateful if you would report this to us. By doing so, you can save other readers from frustration and help us improve subsequent versions of this book. If you find any errata, please report them by visiting `http://www.packtpub.com/submit-errata`, selecting your book, clicking on the **errata submission form** link, and entering the details of your errata. Once your errata are verified, your submission will be accepted and the errata will be uploaded on our website, or added to any list of existing errata, under the Errata section of that title. Any existing errata can be viewed by selecting your title from `http://www.packtpub.com/support`.

Piracy

Piracy of copyright material on the Internet is an ongoing problem across all media. At Packt, we take the protection of our copyright and licenses very seriously. If you come across any illegal copies of our works, in any form, on the Internet, please provide us with the location address or website name immediately so that we can pursue a remedy.

Please contact us at copyright@packtpub.com with a link to the suspected pirated material.

We appreciate your help in protecting our authors, and our ability to bring you valuable content.

Questions

You can contact us at questions@packtpub.com if you are having a problem with any aspect of the book, and we will do our best to address it.

1
End User Transactions

End user transaction code or simply T-code is a functionality provided by SAP that calls a new screen to carry out day-to-day operational activities. A transaction code is a four-character command entered in SAP by the end user to perform routine tasks. It can also be a combination of characters and numbers, for example, FS01. Each module has a different T-code that is uniquely named. For instance, the FICO module's T-code is FI01, while the Project Systems module's T-code will be CJ20.

The T-code, as we will call it throughout the chapters, is a technical name that is entered in the command field to initiate a new GUI window. In this chapter, we will cover all the important T-codes that end users or administrators use on a daily basis. Further, you will also learn more about the standard reports that SAP has delivered to ease daily activities.

Daily transactional codes

On a daily basis, an end user needs to access the T-code to perform daily transactions. All the T-code is entered in a command field. A command field is a space designed by SAP for entering T-codes. There are multiple ways to enter a T-code; we will gradually learn about the different approaches.

The first approach is to enter the T-code in the command field, as shown in the following screenshot:

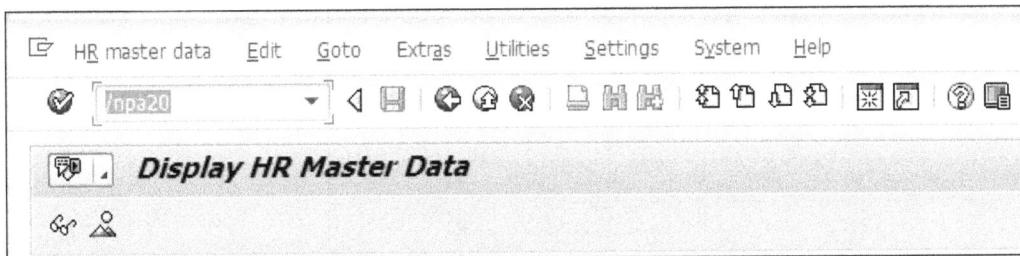

Second, the T-codes can be accessed via **SAP Easy Access**. By double-clicking on a node, the associated application is called and the start of application message is populated at the bottom of the screen. **SAP Easy Access** is the first screen you see when you log on. The following screenshot shows the **SAP Easy Access** window:

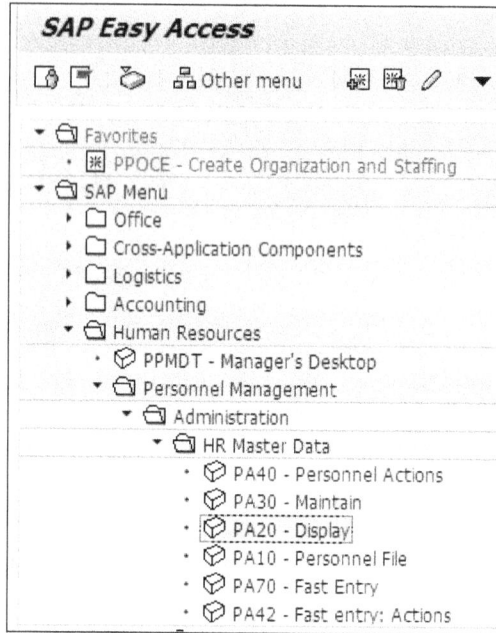

[We don't have to remember any T-codes. SAP has given a functionality to store the T-codes by adding it under **Favorites**.]

To add a T-code to **Favorites**, navigate to **Favorites | Insert transaction**, as shown in the following screenshot, or simply press *Ctrl + Shift + F4* and then enter the T-code that we wish to add as favorite:

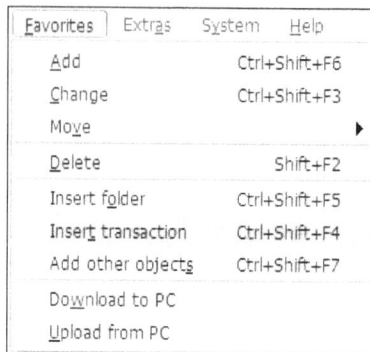

There are different ways to call a technical screen using a T-code. They are shown in the following table:

Command+T-code	Description
/n+T-code, for example, /nPA20	If we wish to call the technical screen in the same session, we may use the /n+T-code function.
/o+T-code, for example, /oFS01	If we wish to call the screen in a different session, we may use the /n+T-code function.

Frequently used T-codes

Let's look closely at the important or frequently used T-codes for administration or transactional purposes.

The Recruitment submodule

The following are the essential T-codes in the Recruitment submodule:

T-code	Description
PB10	This T-code is used for initial data entry. It performs actions similar to the PB40 T-code. The mandatory fields ought to be filled by the user to proceed to the next infotype.
PB20	This T-code is used for display purposes only.
PB30	This T-code is used to make changes to an applicant's data, for example, changing a wrongly entered date of birth or incorrect address.
PBA1	This T-code provides the functionality to bulk process an applicants' data. Multiple applicants can be processed at the same time unlike the PB30 T-code, which processes every applicant's data individually. Applicants' IDs along with their names are fetched using this T-code for easy processing.
PBA2	This T-code is useful when listing applicants based on their advertising medium for bulk processing. It helps to filter applicants based on a particular advertising channel such as a portal.
PBAW	It's used to maintain the advertisements used by the client to process an applicants' data.
PBAY	All the vacant positions can be listed using this T-code. If positions are not flagged as vacant in the **Organizational Management** (**OM**) submodule, they can be maintained via this T-code.
PBAA	A recruitment medium, such as job portal sites, that is linked with an advertisement medium is evaluated using this T-code.

T-code	Description
PBA7	This is an important T-code to transfer an applicant to employee. Applicant gets converted to an employee using this T-code. The integration between Recruitment and Personnel Administration submodules come into picture.
PBA8	To confirm whether an applicant has been transferred to employee, PBA8 needs to be executed. The system throws a message that processing has been carried out successfully for the applicants.

After PBA8 T-code is executed, we will see a message similar to the one shown in the following screenshot:

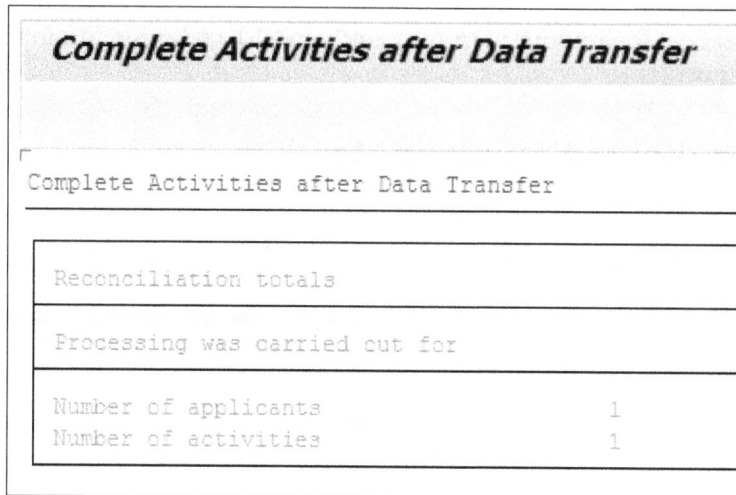

The Organization Management submodule

We will cover some of the important T-codes used to design and develop the organization structure in the following table:

T-code	Description
PPOCE	This T-code is used to create an organizational structure. It is a graphically supported interface with icons to easily differentiate between object types such as org unit and position.
PPOC_OLD	SAP provides multiple interfaces to create a structure. This T-code is one such interface that is pretty simple and easy to use.

T-code	Description
PP01	This is also referred to as the Expert Mode, because one needs to know the object types like SPOCK, where S represents position, O represents organization unit, and relationships A/B, where A is the bottom-up approach and B is the top-down approach, in depth to work in this interface.
PO10	This T-code is used to build structures using object types individually based on SPOCK. This is used to create an Org unit; this T-code creates the object type O, organization unit.
PO13	This is used to create the position object type.
POO3	This T-code is used to create the job object type.
PP03	This is an action-based T-code that helps infotypes get populated one after another. All of the infotypes such as 1000-object, 1001-relationships, and 1002-description can be created using this interface.
PO14	Tasks, which are the day-to-day activities performed by the personnel, can be maintained using this T-code.

The Personnel Administration submodule

The Personnel Administration submodule deals with everything related to the master data of employees. Some of the frequently used T-codes are listed as follows:

T-code	Description
PA20	The master data of an employee is displayed using this T-code.
PA30	The master data is maintained via this T-code. Employee details such as address and date of birth can be edited using this T-code.
PA40	Personnel actions are performed using this T-code. Personnel actions such as hiring and promotions, known as the action type, are executed for employees.
PA42	This T-code, known as the fast entry for action solution, helps a company maintain large amount of data. The information captured using this solution is highly accurate.
PA70	This T-code, known as the fast entry functionality, allows the maintenance of master data for multiple employees at the same time. For example, the recurring payments and deduction (0014) infotype can be maintained for multiple employees.

The usage of the PA70 T-code is shown in the following screenshot. Multiple employees can be entered, and the corresponding wage type, amount, currency, and so on can be provided for these employees. Using this functionality saves the administrator's time.

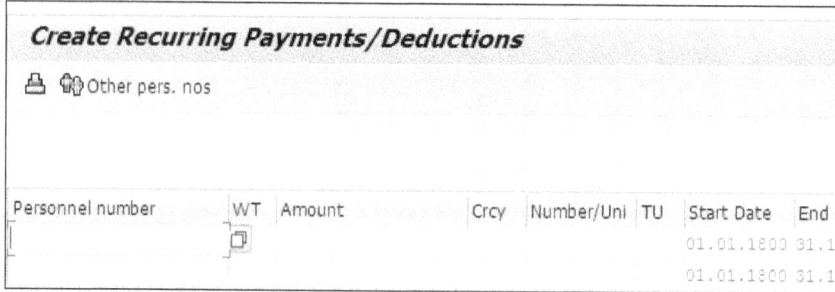

Create Recurring Payments/Deductions								
🖨 👭 Other pers. nos								
Personnel number	WT	Amount		Crcy	Number/Uni	TU	Start Date	End
	☐						01.01.1800	31.1
							01.01.1800	31.1

The Time Management submodule

The Time Management submodule is used to capture the time an employee has spent at their work place or make a note of their absenteeism. The important T-codes that maintain time data are covered in the following table:

T-code	Description
PT01	The work schedule of the employee is created using this T-code. The work schedule is simply the duration of work, say, for instance, 9 a.m. to 6 p.m.
PTMW	The time manager's workplace action allows us to have multiple views such as one-day view and multiday view. It is used to administer and manage time.
PP61	This T-code is used to change a shift plan for the employee.
PA61	This T-code, known as maintain time data, is used to maintain time data for the employees. Only time-related infotypes such as Absences, Attendances, and Overtime are maintained via this T-code.
PA71	This T-code, known as the fast entry time data action, is used to capture multiple employees' time-related data.
PT50	This T-code, known as quota overview, is used to display the quota entitlements and leave balances of an employee.
PT62	The attendance check T-code is used to create a list of employees who are absent, along with their reasons and the attendance time.
PT60	This T-code is used for time evaluation. It is a program that evaluates the time data of employee. Also, the wage types are processed using this program.
PT_ERL00	Time evaluation messages are displayed using this T-code.

T-code	Description
PT_CLSTB2	Time evaluation results can be accessed via this T-code.
CAC1	Using this T-code, data entry profile is created. Data entry profiles are maintained for employees to capture their daily working hours, absence, and so on.
CATA	This T-code is used to transfer data to target components such as PS, HR, and CO.

The Payroll Accounting submodule

The gross and net calculations of wages are performed using this submodule. We will cover all the important T-codes that are used on a daily basis in the following table:

T-code	Description
PU03	This T-code can be used to change the payroll status of an employee if necessary. It lets us change the master data that already exists, for example, locking a personnel's number. One must exercise caution when working on this T-code. It's a sensitive T-code because it is related to an employee's pay. Also, time data for the employees is controlled using this T-code.
PA03	The control record is accessed via this T-code. The control record has key characteristics of how a payroll is processed. This T-code is normally not authorized by administrators.
PC00_MXX_SIMU	This is the T-code used for the simulation run of a payroll. The test is automatically flagged when this T-code is executed.
PC00_MXX_CALC	A live payroll run can be performed using this T-code. The test flag is still available to be used if required.
PC00_MXX_PA03_RELEA	This T-code is used normally by end users to release the control record. Master data and time data is normally locked when this T-code is executed. Changes cannot be made when this T-code is executed.
PC00_MXX_PA03_CORR	This T-code is used to make any changes to the master data or time data. The status has to be reverted to "release" to run a payroll for the payroll period.
PC00_MXX_PA03_END	Once all the activities are performed for the payroll period, the control record must be exited in order to proceed for the subsequent periods.
PC00_MXX_CEDT	The remuneration statement or payslip can be displayed using this T-code.

T-code	Description
PE51	The payslip is designed using this T-code. The payments, deductions, and net can be designed using this T-code.
PC00_MXX_CDTA	The data medium exchange for banks can be achieved using this tool.
PUOC_99	The off-cycle payroll or on-demand payroll, as it's called in SAP, is used to make payments or deductions in a nonregular pay period such as in the middle of the payroll period.
PC00_M99_CIPE	The payroll results are posted to the finance department using this T-code.
PCP0	The payroll posting runs are displayed using this T-code. The release of posting documents is controlled using this T-code.
PC00_M99_CIPC	The completeness check is performed using this T-code. We can find the pay results that are not posted using this T-code.
OH11/PU30	The wage type maintenance tool is useful when creating wage type or pay components such as housing, dearness allowance.
PE01	The schema, which is the warehouse of logic, is accessed and/or maintained via this T-code.
PE02	The **Personnel Calculation Rule** is accessed via this T-code. The PCR is used to perform small calculations.
PE04	The function and operations used can be accessed via this T-code. The documentation of most of these functions and operations can also be accessed via this T-code.
PC00_M99_DLGA20	This shows the wage types used and their process class and cummulation class assignment. The wage type used in a payroll is analyzed using this T-code.
PC00_M99_DKON	The wage type mapped to general ledgers for FICO integration can be analyzed using this T-code
PCXX	Country-specific payroll can be accessed via this T-code.
PC00	Payroll of all the countries, such as Europe, Americas, and so on, can be accessed via this T-code.
PC_Payresult	The payroll results of the employee can be analyzed via this T-code. The following screenshot shows how the payroll results are shown when the T-code is executed.

> The "XX" part in PCXX denotes the country grouping. For example, its 10 for USA, 01 for Germany, and so on. SAP has localized country-specific payroll solution, and hence, each country has a specific number. The country-specific settings are enabled using **MOLGA**, which is a technical name for the country, and it needs to be activated. It is the foundation of the SAP HCM solution.
>
> It's always 99 for Offcyle run for any country grouping. It's the same for posting as well.

The following screenshot shows the output of the PC_Payresult T-code:

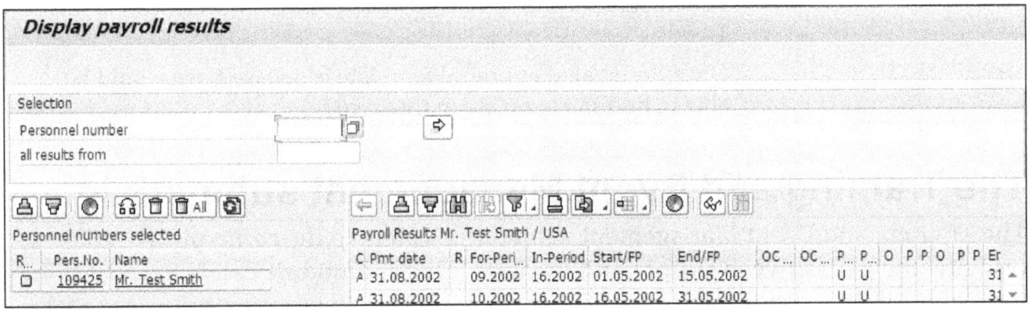

The Talent Management submodule

The Talent Management module deals with assessing the performance of the employees, such as feedback from supervisors, peers, and so on. We will explore all the T-codes used in this submodule. They are described in the following table:

T-code	Description
PHAP_CATALOG	This is used to create an appraisal template that can be filled by the respective persons, based on the **Key Result Areas** (KRA) such as attendance, certification, and performance.
PPEM	Career and succession planning for an entire org unit can be performed via this T-code.
PPCP	Career planning for a person can be performed via this T-code. The qualifications and preferences can be checked, based on which suitable persons can be shortlisted.
PPSP	Succession planning can be performed via this T-code. The successor for a particular position can be determined using this T-code. Different object types such as position and job can be used to plan the successor.

T-code	Description
OOB1	The form of appraisals is accessed via this T-code. The possible combination of appraiser and appraisee is determined based on the evaluation path.
APPSEARCH	This T-code is used to evaluate the appraisal template based on different statuses such as "in preparation" and "completed".
PHAP_CATALOG_PA	This is used to create an appraisal template that can be filled in by the respective persons based on the KRAs such as attendance, certification, and performance. The appraisers and appraisee allowed can be defined.
OOHAP_SETTINGS_PA	The integration check-related switches can be accessed via this T-code.
APPCREATE	Once the created appraisal template is released, we would be able to find the template in this T-code.

The Training and Event Management submodule

The Training and Event Management submodule caters to the company's need of bridging the gap between supply and demand. This submodule caters to identifying the right skill that needs to be provided to carry out the task successfully. Let's take a look at the important T-codes and their functionalities in the following table:

T-code	Description
S_AHR_61011845	The necessary master data needs to be set up before using the Training and Event Management submodule. The cost item T-code is used to determine and represent the cost incurred for a business event.
S_AHR_61011843	The address or physical location is maintained using this T-code.
S_AHR_61011841	The business event location is set up using this T-code, for example, Training Center, Atlanta.
PSVQ	This function lets you change/display external organizers such as your company.
S_AHR_61011893	The instructor who doesn't belong to the system, in other words, whose master data is not maintained, is captured using this function.
S_AHR_61011889	The business event group such as the language course is set up using this function.
S_AHR_61011888	The business event type is used to capture the delivery method, cost, capacity, and so on.
PSV2	This function lets you maintain the exact date on which the event is scheduled to take place. It has the start and end dates of events.

T-code	Description
PSV1	This function lets you enroll attendees for business events and, at the same time, store the relevant billing and activity allocation data.
S_PH9_46000434	The internal activity allocation for settling the fees of external instructors and also of the employees who had attended an event can be settled using this function.

The Travel Management submodule

The Travel Management submodule offers functionalities such as creating different travel expense types, processing business trip data, taking care of approvals, and entering the travel trip data into the system. Let's focus on the important T-codes related to this submodule, shown in the following table:

T-code	Description
TRIP	This T-code allows you to create a travel request, book rooms, hotel, and so on.
PR05	The travel expense functionality allows you to track the status, settlement status, amount, and so on.
PRAP	The mass approval of any number of trips is performed via this function.
PREC	The expected travel expenses cannot be determined until a trip is approved. In order to proceed further, the trip needs to be settled, and this function helps to meet the purpose.
PRFI	The posting run is performed using this function. The travel expenses that need to be settled are collected as transfer documents for posting to accounting.
PRRW	The trip transfer documents are posted to FI/CO using this function.

Standard reports

SAP has delivered many standard reports that meet business needs. For example, the SAP1 T-code can be used to display all reports module-wise in SAP. Let's look closely at some of the important reports that can be used by administrators.

Recruitment

The Recruitment standard reports can be accessed by navigating to **SAP Easy Access | Human Resources | Personnel Management | Recruitment | Infosystem | Reports | Variable Applicant List**.

The **Variable Applicant List** report, which can be accessed via the S_AHR_61015508 T-code, is very useful when fetching the flexible list of all the applicants' data. There are flexible reports that let us choose from a combination of 20 fields from different infotypes. They also allow us to sort different fields such as age.

> All of the reports can also be accessed via the SE38 or SA38 T-code, depending on user authorizations, and can be fetched by navigating to **System** | **Status** | **Program**.

The statuses of applicants along with their names can be fetched using the **applicants by name** report that can be accessed via the S_AHR_61015509 T-code. The output has the following data:

- The number of the applicants
- The applicants' names
- The text of the status, for example, in process
- The beginning date of the applicants' statuses

> The applicant action along with the status of each applicant, name, and so on can be fetched via the **applicant by action** report, and it can be accessed via the S_AHR_61015510 T-code. The output received is the action type such as initial data entry, overall applicant status, applicant name, or applicant id.
>
> The frequently fed input data such as the company code can be entered in the input selection screen and saved as a variant for saving time.

Before clicking on Save (or pressing *Ctrl + S*), we can give the variant a name and description; however, isn't mandatory. This is shown in the following screenshot:

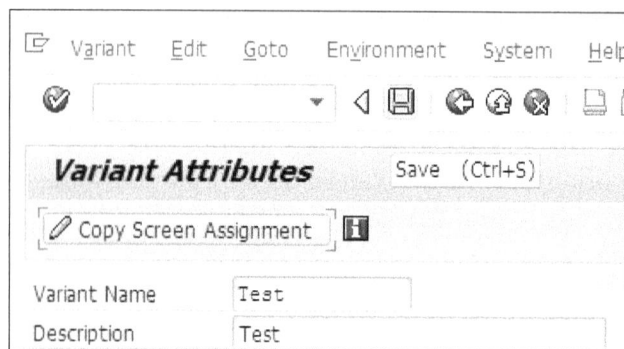

The variant can be called and it automatically feeds on the data stored using the variant. From the standard report, we can call the variant by clicking on Get Variant (or pressing *Shift + F5*) and choosing the variant name. We can do this if we want to get the **Test** variant for example. We saved this variant in the previous step. The demonstration is shown in the following screen:

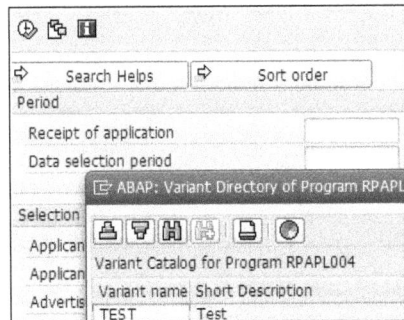

The ad hoc query is a useful tool to pull any data from tables and is accessed via the `S_PH0_48000512` T-code. The standard `/SAPQUERY/HR_APP` infoset can be used to set the selection and output. If the standard report doesn't meet the requirement of the client, this ad hoc query function can be utilized.

From the different fields available, **Selection** and **Output** need to be flagged, and the preview of the output can also be viewed at the bottom of the screen. This is demonstrated in the following screenshot. Finally, click on the Save button to access the query when required.

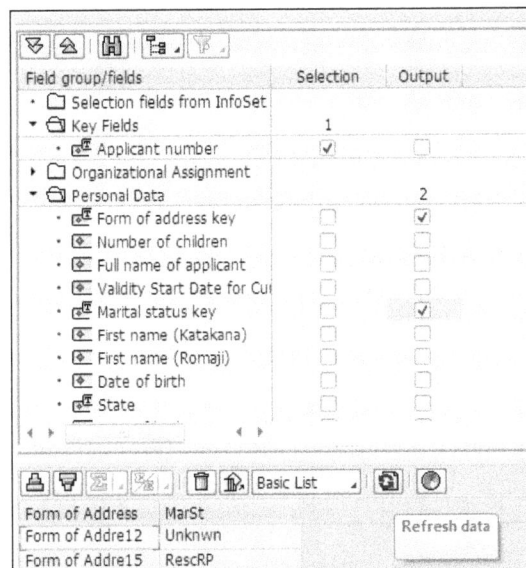

The name and title of the query need to be entered when saving. Click on **Query**, select **Open** (or press *F6*), and then select the query name to execute the saved query, as shown in the following screenshot. There is also a date and time stamp when the query is saved.

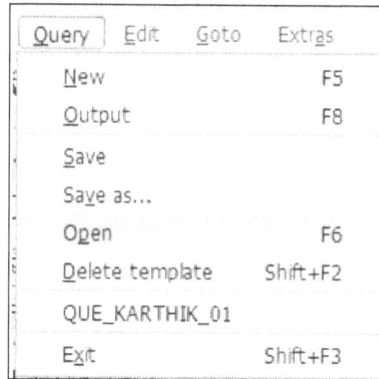

Query	Edit	Goto	Extras	
New				F5
Output				F8
Save				
Save as...				
Open				F6
Delete template				Shift+F2
QUE_KARTHIK_01				
Exit				Shift+F3

As seen in the following screenshot, the selection and the output saved in the query gets displayed automatically when we open the query.

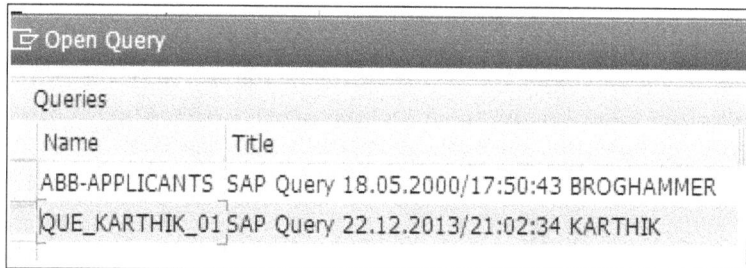

Open Query	
Queries	
Name	**Title**
ABB-APPLICANTS	SAP Query 18.05.2000/17:50:43 BROGHAMMER
QUE_KARTHIK_01	SAP Query 22.12.2013/21:02:34 KARTHIK

We can display the output by clicking on the Output button or by pressing the *F8* key.

> Transaction SERP and SARP can be used to display and maintain the standard report tree. HR00 needs to selected, then click on Display (*F5*) to start the report.

Organizational Management

The OM reports can be accessed by navigating to **SAP Easy Access | Human Resources | Organizational Management | Infosystem | Organization Unit**. The backbone of OM is the SPOCK object types, and there are plenty of standard reports to display them individually. There are many standard reports provided by SAP to display the object types and their description. The S_AHR_61016491 function is used to display the organizational units with their start and end dates, along with their object IDs and description.

The existing positions can be seen via the S_AHR_61016502 T-code. The output is similar to what is displayed for an organizational unit. All the existing jobs, along with their descriptions, are accessed via the S_AHR_61016497 T-code.

The structure hierarchy is displayed via the RHSTRU00 report. This report uses the object ID that is entered as the root of a tree structure, and using the specified evaluation path, it fetches the object and its related object type. The display depth in the report tells us how far the object and its relationship need to be displayed in the output.

> The evaluation path gives instructions to the system to look for the object types and relationships and is maintained in the T778A table or via the OOAW T-code.

The graphic interface is also supported by SAP; the structure can be displayed in a graphical format. The S_AHR_61016530 T-code is used to display the structure in a graphical form. They can be downloaded on to the system for further analysis.

The reporting infotype is a functionality given to run reports based on infotypes. Normally, 1000-1999 are OM infotypes, and in this report, we can give the infotype number and execute the report. The S_AHR_61016532 T-code is used to execute the report.

The authorization for objects based on a user can be fetched using the **Authorized Objects per User/Profile** report and is accessed via the RE_RHAUTH00 T-code. When the user ID is entered and executed, the system displays all the authorization objects to which the user has access.

Relationship is a key concept in OM; it's like A and B, where A is bottom up and B is top down. We can find the missing relationships for object types using this report. The **Display and Create Missing Inverse Relationships** report helps find the missing relationships between object types, and it is accessed via the RE_RHCHECKV T-code.

The object types and relationships can be exported to different clients using the **Manual Transport Link** report, which is accessed via the RE_RHMOVE30 T-code.

Personnel Administration

The most wanted and frequently used report is the one maintaining a record of the employees who have joined and left the company, and SAP has provided a standard report that can be accessed via the S_PH9_46000223 T-code. The output has the first and last names of the employee, start date, and leaving date, along with the Org unit and its description.

> The layout of reports can be controlled by clicking on Change layout (or pressing *Ctrl + F8*). The order of display can be sorted, or the fields can be unselected so that they are not displayed.

The education and training details of all the employees can be displayed via the S_PH9_46000224 T-code. It's mandatory that data is maintained in the respective infotypes in order to be correctly shown in the output. The output format can be set to SAP list viewer or spreadsheet, based on the requirement. This is a common functionality of all the reports.

The promotion-related activities surrounding an employee, such as the time spent in each pay scale group and level, can be fetched using the **Time spent in each pay scale area/type/group/level** report. This is accessed via the S_AHR_61016356 T-code. The output has the pay scale type, area, group, and level details along with the calculated years and months. This is shown in the following screenshot:

Time spent in pay scale group/level

Key date: 23.12.2013
The report includes 2.913 Employees

Pers.No.	ID number	Employee/app.name	PSA	Ty.	PS group	Lv	since	Years	Months
00000069	NA454444A	Mr. Horatio Holder	01	02	GR04	3	01.01.2003	10	11

If we notice, the logic to fetch the year and month is built in report that SAP uses to display in the output. If the standard report doesn't meet your requirements, only then is it recommended that you go for a new development.

The personnel numbers are normally of eight digits, and should the client wish to capture the numbers maintained in the legacy system, they can do it using the 0031 infotype. SAP provides a standard report to capture the numbers maintained for all the employees, which is accessed via the S_AHR_61016358 T-code.

The list of active employees is one of the most frequently wanted reports, along with gender details, and SAP has built a standard one that can be accessed via the S_AHR_61016369 T-code. It displays the first name, last name, position, and personnel number, along with the entry and leaving dates.

The flexible report that SAP has provided for a user to select/deselect the fields according to their business needs is the **Flexible Employee Data** report. It is accessed via the S_AHR_61016362 T-code. The advantage of using the report is that it displays all the available fields from which we can choose 20 separate fields. It's a very user friendly report that can be tweaked based on the company's needs.

The employee's nationalities can be displayed using the **Nationalities** report, which is accessed via the S_AHR_61016374 T-code.

The organizational changes made to the employee can be captured via the **Headcount changes** report, and it is accessed via the S_L9C_94000095 T-code. The action type and action reason normally adds meaning to the personnel action performed. For example, the change of position action has been performed and also the promotion action; the two actions can be listed using the standard report. The important fields such as enterprise and personnel structure can be fetched using this report.

The age and gender reports are accessed via the S_PH9_46000218 T-code. SAP also provides a standard report to display age and gender based on seniority, in other words, the duration spent in the company. This is accessed via the S_PH9_46000217 T-code. The personnel who has spent more time in the company gets prioritized and listed first.

The infotype changes have to be captured, and this is very vital for audit purposes. Any changes done intentionally or unintentionally need to be captured, and there is a report for this known as **Logged Changes in Infotype Data** provided by SAP for security purposes. This report can be accessed via the S_AHR_61016380 T-code.

> The **HR Documents: Infotypes with Documents (V_T585A)**, **HR Documents: Field Group Definition (V_T585B)**, and **HR Documents: Field Group Characteristics (V_T585C)** tables must be maintained for the effective use of this report.

A detailed log of report can be accessed via the S_AHR_61016381 T-code. The report name along with user details and date and time of access is displayed when the report is executed. This, however, is only created for a report maintained via the V_T599R (HR Report Attributes) table and also the **Record at start required online** field is flagged.

The ad hoc query report for Personnel Administration submodule with the standard `/SAPQUERY/HR_ADM` infoset can be used to build a report with your own selection and output fields. The only difference is the infoset that is chosen for the PA submodule. The infoset query is accessed via the `S_PH0_48000510` T-code.

Time Management

The work schedule, absence, and attendance of the employee are closely monitored by the administrators, and SAP has provided many standard reports to meet the demands.

The daily work schedule of an employee can be accessed via the `PT03` T-code. The personal work schedule of an employee, which can be for a week or month, for example, can be displayed via the `PT63` T-code. The employee number, name, and daily work schedule are displayed in the following screenshot:

The start and end dates, along with the holiday calendar, are also displayed, making it easy for administration.

The absence and attendance information is vital for administration, and SAP has provided standard reports to meet business demands. They can be accessed via the `PT64` T-code. This report gives us the output in the form of working hours anticipated and days.

The graphical format is supported by accessing the `PT90` T-code. The absence is displayed in a different color for easy recognition. Multiple employees can be chosen based on the organization unit, for example, and the **Attendance/Absence Data: Multiple-Employee View** report can be accessed via the `PT91` T-code.

The graphical format of absence/attendance can be displayed via the **Graphical Overview of Attendances/Absences** report and can be accessed via the `PT65` T-code. When we double-click on absence or attendance type mentioned on the screen, it will automatically take us to the master data screen.

The quota entitlements and balances can be displayed via the **display absence quota information** report, and it is accessed via the PT_QTA10 T-code. The base entitlements in number of days, for example, and the applied leave along with the available balance or the remaining total is displayed in the output. This is another one of the most frequently used report in business. The output of this report is shown in the following screenshot:

The **Cumulated Time Evaluation Results: Time Balances/Time Wage Types** report is accessed via the PT_BAL00 T-code. If we use PT60 (Time evaluation), time wage types / time balances are formed via time evaluation. These reports will be very useful to display information.

Time evaluation data can be accessed via the PT_EDT_TELU T-code; the time statement form can also be configured and used in this report. If time-evaluated data is available in time cluster, it gets displayed as the output. The standard form TEDT TF00 Time statement form (standard) is used and copied according to customer needs. This copied time form can be used in the report. This is very similar to the payslip configuration in the Payroll submodule.

The working times captured via **Cross Application Time Sheet** (CATS) can be accessed via the CATS_DA T-code. An important report of transferring data to cross modules such as HR is accessed via the CATA T-code.

The data can also be transferred individually module-wise and can be accessed via the CAT6 T-code for HR, CAT5 for project systems, and CAT7 for FICO.

Payroll Accounting

The payments and deductions of employees are displayed via the Payments and Deductions report. It's a flexible report that allows us to display data based on the wage type if necessary. This is accessed via the S_AHR_61015608 T-code.

The bank details of employees are displayed via the **Bank Details** report or accessed via the S_AHR_61015609 T-code. The data maintained in the following infotypes and subtypes can be displayed via this report:

- Bank Details (0009)
- Capital Formation (0010)
- External Transfers (0011)

Payslip or remuneration statement is displayed via the program remuneration statement that can be accessed via the S_AHR_61015606 T-code. The form name that we use is the copied version of **Remuneration statement (SAP standard) - XF01**. It's recommended that you copy the standard, rename it, and change it accordingly. The remuneration statement can also be printed using the HR smart forms. They are accessed via the PC00_M99_HRF T-code.

The wage type reporter is a useful report that displays the wage types and the corresponding amount, along with other related information of the employee such as company code and personnel area. It's accessed via the PC00_M99_CWTR T-code. The data is fetched from Cluster tables (Results table and WPBP). All the payment and deduction wage types can be displayed using this report.

The payments made on public holidays can be determined using the **Paydays on holidays or weekends** report. It's accessed via the S_AHR_61015614 T-code. The prerequisite is to have the paydays defined in the T549S table.

The payment date, end date of pay period, and so on are graphically displayed using the **Payday calendar** report, and are executed via the S_AHR_61015615 T-code. The legends used clearly indicate the meaning. For example, **X** denotes a payday in the past. This is demonstrated in the following screenshot:

Talent Management

The display profile matchup report can be accessed via the PEPM T-code. It's a comparison of the position's requirements with the person's qualifications. We can also generate a training proposal by flagging the checkbox.

Applicable career paths within an organization structure can be displayed via the **Evaluate Careers** report, and are accessed via the S_AHR_61015524 T-code. The following screenshot shows the **Evaluate Careers** report:

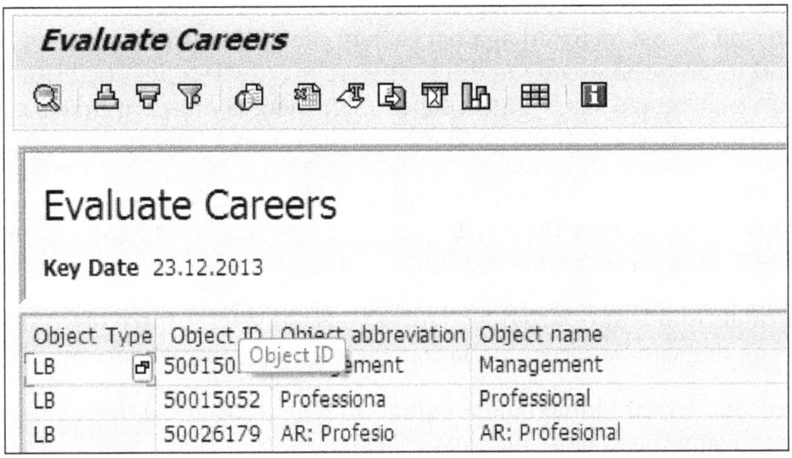

The career path and its description along with the object type, **LB**, are displayed as the output.

The object without qualification or requirement can be accessed via the S_PH9_46000019 T-code. The object type in selection can be, for example, a person, and when it is executed, it lists the IDs of people whose qualifications are not maintained. It basically takes us to the PPCP T-code.

The overview of all the qualifications maintained is accessed via the **Qualification Overview** report, and it is accessed via the S_PH9_46000016 T-code.

Training and Event Management

The standard reports help administrators capture the training cost, details about the business event, attendees, and so on. The reports can be accessed by navigating to **SAP Easy Access | Human Resources | Training and Event Management | Information Systems | Reports**.

All the attendees enrolled for a training program can be displayed via the S_PH9_46000434 T-code. The report list many fields such as the following:

- Attendee's name and abbreviation
- Booking date
- Attendance fee/price
- Business event name
- Start and end dates of the event

The comparison of cost incurred against each organization unit is a useful report for analysis, and it can be accessed via the S_PH9_46000423 T-code. The business event schedule can be accessed via S_PH9_46000438. If there is no event that is scheduled, the system throws an error message to indicate its nonavailability.

The resources to organize an event are captured via a standard resource equipment report, which is accessed via the S_AHR_61016224 T-code. This report gives details of the equipments that are available in training rooms.

The graphical format is supported by SAP. The graphical resource reservation report is a useful one that can be accessed via the S_PH9_46000441 T-code.

The Training and Event Management submodule also has an ad hoc query that can be developed using the S_PH0_48000535 T-code.

Travel Management

The Travel Management component supports all processes involved in handling business trips. Its comprehensive functionality is integrated with settlement and payment processes.

Travel Management enables you to request, plan, and book trips, create expense reports, and transfer expense results to other business function areas.

There are various standard reports that can be accessed by navigating to **SAP Easy Access | Human Resources | Information Systems | Reports | Travel Management**. They broadly cover trip expenses and planning reports.

The **General Trip Data/Trip Totals** report is very useful to evaluate the trip totals listed per trip. This report is accessed via the S_AHR_61016401 T-code. There are many branching options that can be selected from the following options:

- Trip
- Trip receipts
- Trip cost assignment
- Trip block list

The **Cost Assignment for Trip** report is very vital for a business to evaluate the cost and assignment to respective general ledger in accounting. This report is accessed via the S_AHR_61016404 T-code.

The period-wise travel expense report can be displayed using the S_AHR_61016408 T-code.

Multiple periods or period parameters can be selected so that a report can be displayed. The period could be from the following options:

- Monthly
- Bi-weekly
- Weekly

This is a very flexible report that allows up to seven periods to be represented in a single report. The different selection parameters could be from the following options:

- Personnel's number
- Cost center (employee master cost center), for example, the employee cost center maintained in 0001 infotype
- Trip expense types (see field documentation)
- Trip expense categories (see field documentation)
- Per diems/flat rates (for meals, travel costs, and accommodations)

There are plenty of tricks to save time for administrators. We will cover some of them specifically to access T-codes and reports.

Creating a folder and moving the T-codes

First, SAP provides an easy functionality to help us access T-codes easily without the need to remember them. It is done by navigating to **SAP Easy access** | **Favorites** | **Insert folder**, as shown in the following screenshot:

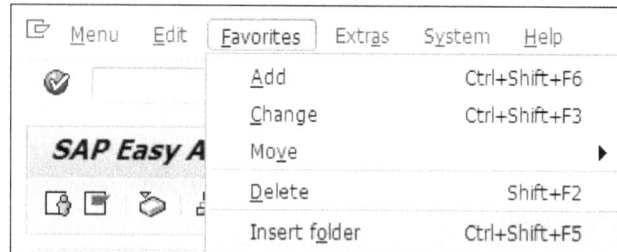

Users can create folders and insert all the T-code related to them. For example, `payroll` can be a folder, and all the T-code related to the payroll can be moved to that folder.

SAP also has the feature to add the T-codes that are frequently accessed, to the folder of our choice that we created earlier. It is done by navigating to **SAP Easy access** | **Favorites** | **Insert transaction**, as shown in the following screenshot:

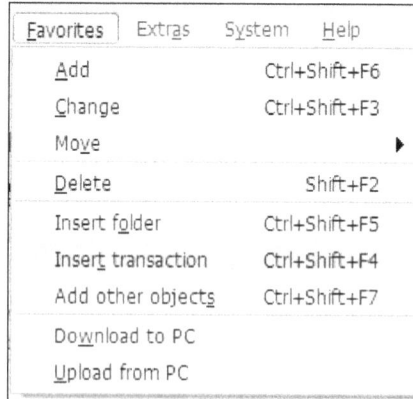

All the T-codes are moved to the respective folders, and hence, accessibility is easier for administrators. SAP has an interesting feature of downloading T-codes for easy accessibility or to share it with your teammates. It is accessed by navigating to **SAP Easy access** | **Favorites** | **Download to PC**. The format can be a text file or a word pad option of your choice.

The technical names of reports can be shown or hidden by changing the settings by navigating to **SAP Easy Access | Extras | Settings | Display Technical Names**.

When the **Display Technical Names** option is flagged, all the technical names of the reports and the T-code get displayed automatically.

An overview of SAP standard reports

SAP has developed many standard reports that normally meet business requirements. We will cover frequently used reports submodule-wise. We will see the reports along with their T-code and program name for easy understanding and can use them in a real-time environment.

Recruitment

The following are the important T-codes along with their ABAP program names:

Report	ABAP Program	T-code
Variable Applicant List	RPAPL012	S_AHR_61015508
Applicants by Name	RPAPL001	S_AHR_61015509
Applicants by action	RPAPL004	S_AHR_61015510
Ad Hoc Query	SAPLAQ_ADHOC	S_PH0_48000512

Organization Management

The Organizational Management program names are prefixed with RH and are shown in the following table along with their technical names:

Report	ABAP Program	T-code
Existing Organizational Units	RHXEXI00	S_AHR_61016491
Existing Positions	RHXEXI03	S_AHR_61016502
Existing Jobs	RHXEXI02	S_AHR_61016497
Structure Display/Maintenance	RHSTRU00	SE38
PD Graphics Interface	PDGRAPHX	S_AHR_61016530
Infotype Reporting	RHINFAW0	S_AHR_61016532
Authorized Objects	RHAUTH00	RE_RHAUTH00
Check Relationships	RHCHECKV	RE_RHCHECKV
Manual Transport Link	RHMOVE30	RE_RHMOVE30

Personnel Administration

The Personnel Administration report's program names normally start with RP. We have listed all the frequently used T-codes and their technical names in the following table:

Report	ABAP Program	T-code
EEs Who Entered And/Or Left Company	AQZZ/SAPQUERY/H2FLUCTUATIONS==	S_PH9_46000223
Education and Training	AQZZ/SAPQUERY/H2EDUCATION=====	S_PH9_46000224
Time spent in pay scale group/level	RPLTRF00	S_AHR_61016356
Reference Personnel Numbers	RPLREF00	S_AHR_61016358
Employee List	RPLMIT00	S_AHR_61016369
Flexible Employee Data	RPLICO10	S_AHR_61016362
Nationalities	RPSNAT00	S_AHR_61016374
Headcount Changes	AQZZ/SAPQUERY/H2STAFF_CHANGES2	S_L9C_94000095
Statistics: Gender Sorted By Age	AQZZ/SAPQUERY/H2GENDER_PER_AGE	S_PH9_46000218
Statistic: Gender by Service Age	AQZZ/SAPQUERY/H2GEND_P_SENIOR=	S_PH9_46000217
Logged Changes in Infotype Data	RPUAUD00	S_AHR_61016380
Log of Report Starts	RPUPROTD	S_AHR_61016381
Ad Hoc Query	SAPLAQ_ADHOC	S_PH0_48000510

Time Management

We will see all the Time Management T-codes and their technical names in the following table. We can execute the functionalities directly via the T-code or by executing the ABAP program.

Report	ABAP Program	T-code
Display Work Schedule	SAPMP51S	PT03
Personal Work Schedule	RPTPSH10	PT63

Report	ABAP Program	T-code
Attendances/Absences: Calendar View	RPTABS50	PT90
Attendances/Absences: For Multiple Employees	RPTABS60	PT91
Graphical Attendances/Abs. Overview	RPTLEA40	PT65
Absence Quota Information	RPTQTA10	PT_QTA10
Cumulated Time Evaluation Results	RPTBAL00	PT_BAL00
Time Balances Overview	RPTEDT00	PT_EDT_TELU
Display Working Times	RCATS_DISPLAY_ACTIVITIES	CATS_DA
Transfer to Target Components	RCATSTAL	CATA
Transfer External -> Time Management	RPTEXTPT	CAT6
Data Transfer CATS -> PS	RCATSTPS	CAT5
CATS: Transfer Data to CO	RCATSTCO	CAT7

Payroll Accounting

The Payroll T-codes are easy to memorize; they normally start with PC00 followed by country-grouping numbers. We will see the frequently used T-codes and their technical names in the following table:

Report	ABAP Program	T-code
Payments and Deductions	RPLPAY00	S_AHR_61015608
Bank Details	RPLBNK00	S_AHR_61015609
Remuneration Statements	RPCEDTX0	S_AHR_61015606
Wage Statement with HR Forms	H99_HRFORMS_CALL	PC00_M99_HRF
Wage type reporter	H99CWTR0	PC00_M99_CWTR
Paydays on Holidays or Weekends	RPCHCK00	S_AHR_61015614
Payday Calendar	RPCSHS00	S_AHR_61015615

Talent Management

We will cover the frequently used Talent Management T-code in the following table, which will serve as a quick reference note:

Report	ABAP Program	T-code
Profile Matchup	SAPLRHPP	PEPM
Evaluate Careers	RHPECPAS	S_AHR_61015524
Objects w/o Qualis or Requirements	RHXPEP20	S_PH9_46000019
Career Planning	RHPEPLAC	PPCP
Qualifications Overview	RHXPE_QUALI_PRO_ORGUNIT	S_PH9_46000016

Training and Event Management

The standard T-code and their technical names under the Time and Event Management report have been covered in the following table:

Report	ABAP Program	T-code
Attendee List	RHXTEILN	S_PH9_46000434
Budget Comparison	RHXBUDG0	S_PH9_46000423
Business Event Schedule	RHABLAUF	S_PH9_46000438
Resource Equipment	RHXRESA0	S_AHR_61016224
Graphical Resource Reservation	RHXRBEL1	S_PH9_46000441
Ad Hoc Query	SAPLAQ_ADHOC	S_PH0_48000535

Travel Management

We will cover the frequently used Travel Management T-code in the following table, which will serve as a quick reference note:

Report	ABAP Program	T-code
General Trip Data/Trip Totals	RPR_TRIP_HEADER_DATA	S_AHR_61016401
Cost Assignment for Trip	RPR_TRIP_COST_ASSIGNMENT_DATA	S_AHR_61016404
Travel Expense Reporting by Period	RPRSTA01	S_AHR_61016408

Summary

In this chapter, we covered all the transaction codes or simply T-codes and standard reports that are used submodule-wise. We started off by covering all the important T-codes that are used on a day-to-day basis for both master and transactional processing. Next, we covered all the standard reports along with their program names that can be executed directly instead of the T-code functionality.

In the next chapter, we will look closely at configuring the Recruitment submodule and explore the standard functionalities provided by SAP.

2
Recruitment Configuration

In this chapter, we will learn how the Recruitment submodule is configured to map the business requirements in the SAP system. We will also learn how to configure the recruitment module and also the integration aspects with other modules such as organization management. Throughout the recruitment component, data is captured in separate databases such as PBxxxx, where xxxx is the infotype number and PB denotes the applicants. Recruitment infotypes are in the range of 4000-4999. Some useful recruitment-related infotypes are as follows:

- **4000**: This refers to an applicant's action
- **4001**: This refers to the applications
- **4002**: This refers to a vacancy assignment
- **4003**: This refers to an applicant's activities
- **4004**: This refers to the status of an applicant's activity
- **4005**: This refers to an applicant's personnel number

Handling vacancies

Hypothetically, let's say there is an open position that needs to be filled by an employee.

The open positions are created in an Organization Management submodule, which you will be learning in the next chapter, *Chapter 3, SPOCK – the Building Block of OM*.

We will cover a scenario where the open position (Senior Manager HR) created in an OM component will be used in the Recruitment submodule.

We will see how an open position is created in OM, although we will cover it extensively in *Chapter 3, SPOCK – the Building Block of OM*.

We will enter the PP01 T-code in the command line. We will create an open position (Senior Manager HR) and flag it as vacant. To create open positions, we can use the PP01 T-code. This is shown in the following screenshot:

The vacant position is the one we will attempt to fill using the Recruitment submodule. Click on **Save**. We will keep this position vacant as shown in the following screenshot:

We will flag all the positions as open; they need to be filled. Click on **Create** (*F5*). You get the following screenshot:

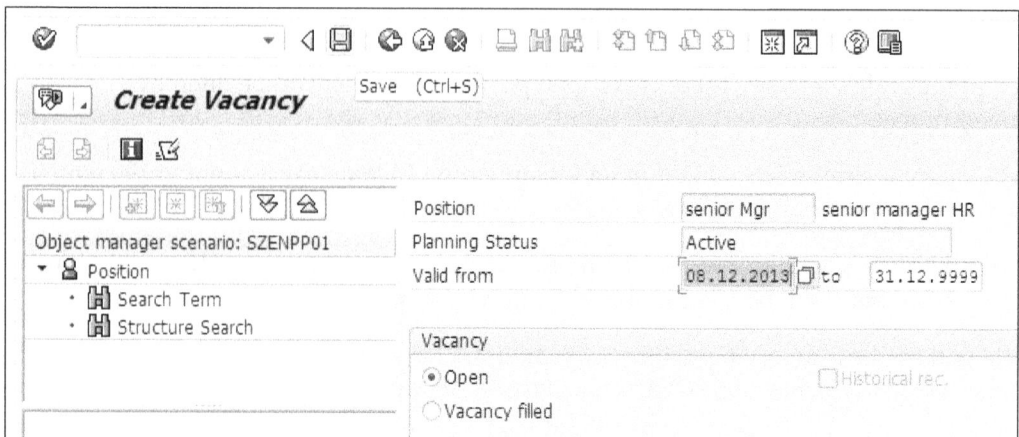

We will create the open position in the OM side of the world, and this is where the integration between recruitment and organization management comes into play:

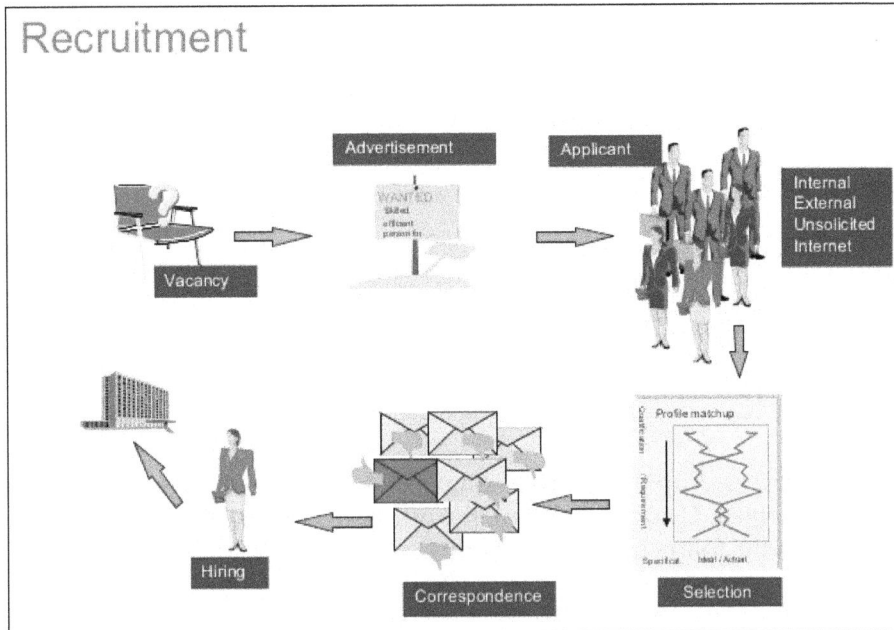

Vacancy maintenance steps

We will discuss how the vacant position created in the OM side is processed in the recruitment side of the world. Click on **Execute** or press *F8*. We can use the PPOCE/PP01/PPOC_OLD T-code to create positions in the OM as shown in the following screenshot:

A vacancy is maintained via the TCD PBAY or by navigating to **SAP easy access | Human Resources | Personnel Management | Recruitment | Advertising | Vacancy | PBAY (Maintain)**.

There is a standard report for listing out all the open positions created in the OM. When we execute the report, we can not only list all the open positions, but also assign the officer in charge of the open position. This is depicted in the following screenshot:

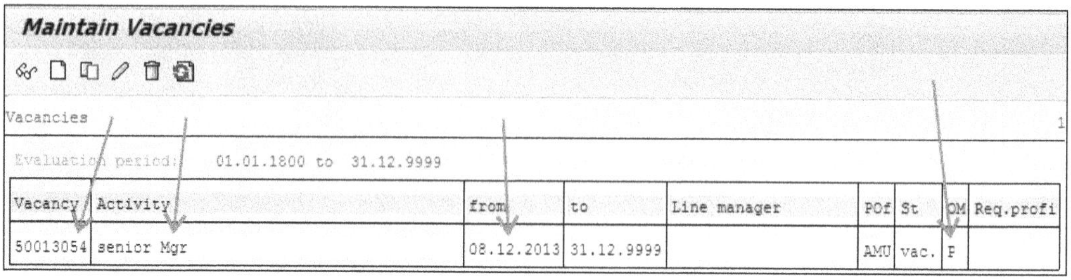

When we click on the icon that looks like a pencil (edit), the **Change vacancy** window gets enabled. Using this option, the officer in charge can be mapped. This is shown in the following screenshot:

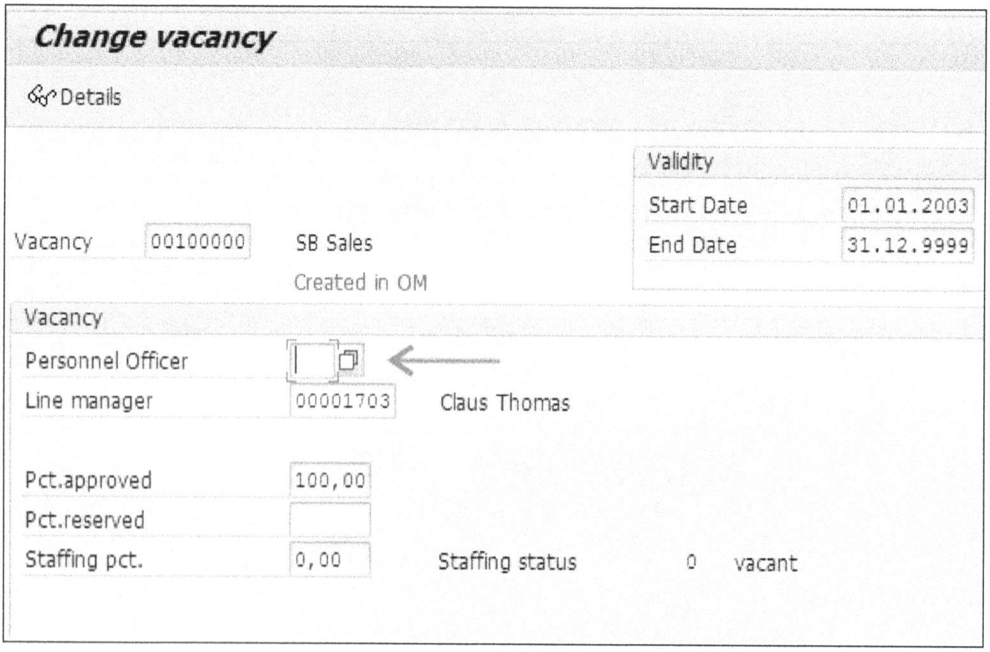

The complete administrator name gets populated, and we can choose from the list. We will see the personnel officer assigned as AMU when we click on the details button. AMU is the personnel officer in charge of the vacant position's application, and it can be maintained by navigating to **SPRO | Personnel Management | Personnel administration | Organization data | define administrators** or via the SM30/31 T-code in the T526 table. This is shown in the following screenshot:

Maintain Vacancies							

							1
Vacancies							
Evaluation period:	01.01.1800 to 31.12.9999						

Vacancy	Activity	from	to	Line manager	POf	St	OM	Req.profi
50013054	senior Mgr	08.12.2013	31.12.9999		AMU	vac.	F	

The OM column is crucial, because the indicator **P** denotes that it's created in the OM side and cannot be changed.

Advertising vacancies

The different channels that are used to fill the vacant positions are of prime importance for the stakeholders. The following are the different types of recruitment instruments that clients make use of:

Recruitment Instruments	Description
Internal postings	These are the ways to look internally for possible candidates to fill the position
Employee referral program	This is a cost-effective and efficient mode to track potential candidates
Classified advertising	These are jobs posted in newspapers
Employment agencies and search firms	These are consultancies that are tied up with companies, and they specialize in identifying the right candidate for the job
Job fairs	This is like a place where all the interested companies gather and hire the right talent
Online recruiting sites	These are free websites that let candidates upload their profiles, and companies use them as a source to identify the right candidate

Channels or recruitment instruments

Recruitment instruments or channels are classified according to the different media used. The media could be job portals, newspapers, television advertisements, employee references, and so on.

The recruitment instruments are configurable items that can be used by the end user to map the vacant position.

We will look at the configuration of applicant number ranges first. This can be accessed by navigating to **SPRO | Personnel Management | Recruitment | Basic settings | Create number ranges for applicant numbers**. The following screenshot demonstrates this:

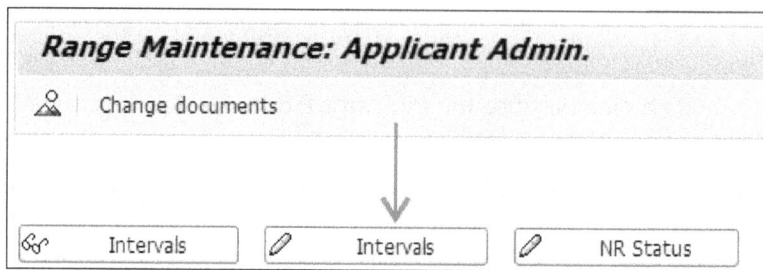

We will see three options, which are as follows:

- **Display**: This option shows a number range, which is a two-digit code, the start and end numbers (range), NR status, which has the last number assigned, and finally, the flag that indicates whether it is internal or external.

- **Change**: This option allows us to make changes to the two-digit code, start and end numbers (range), NR status, which has the last number assigned, and finally, the flag that indicates whether it is internal or external.

> To delete the number range, we need to set the NR status to 0 or else the system will throw an error message. Deletion is possible only if the status is initial.

- **Change**: This option allows us to change the current number assigned from the current choice to a number of choices. The other fields are grayed out and cannot be altered when this option is chosen.

Vacant position mapping using recruitment instruments

We will see how different recruitment instruments, such as job portal, job fair, and so on, are mapped to the vacant position.

First, the recruitment instruments such as ABC job portal and XYZ job portal are created, and they are classified as the medium to which they belong. The recruitment instruments can be accessed by navigating to **SPRO | Personnel Management | Recruitment | Workforce requirements and advertising | Create recruitment instruments**.

We can otherwise use **Table Maintenance** directly, which is common for all the configurable tables.

The T-code that can be used is SM30/SM31. This is shown in the following screenshot:

Instrument	Instrument	Medium	Name of medium	Address
00000000	Journal Interno	04	Internal Job Posti	

Change View "Recruitment Instrument": Overview

The first **Instrument** column has the unique ID, and the second instrument column has the text maintained.

Recruitment medium

The recruitment medium is configured to group the instruments into one category. We can access the recruitment medium by navigating to **SPRO | Personnel Management | Recruitment | Workforce requirements and advertising | Create media**. The following screenshot shows this:

Change View "Medium": Overview

Medium	Name of medium	Applicant class	Applicant class text
01	Job Portal	AP	External applicant

We can also maintain the address of the instrument, or the source can also be maintained by navigating to **SPRO | Personnel Management | Recruitment | Workforce requirements and advertising | Create addresses for recruitment instruments**.

The Recruitment submodule has the provision of creating applicant groups and ranges. For example, the "Senior Managers" are all grouped under Manager, the range is technical or nontechnical, and so on.

We will look at how this can be configured by navigating to **SPRO | Personnel Management | Recruitment | Applicant administration | Applicant Structure | Create applicant groups**. This is shown in the following screenshot:

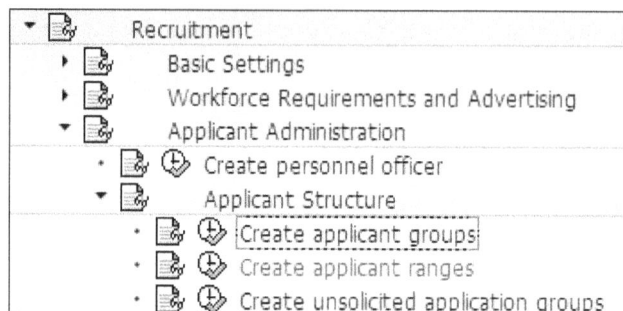

The applicant group allows us to categorize the applicants according to their business needs, which are as follows:

- Consultants
- Managers
- Freelancers

The applicant group is mapped to an applicant class. An applicant class is categorized into two classes, which are as follows:

- "P" for internal applicants
- "AP" for external applicants

The applicant group not only allows us to bifurcate the applicants based on their categories, it also has the functionality of mapping them as unsolicited and lets us see how it is handled in the system. Unsolicited application groups can be created by navigating to **SPRO | Personnel Management | Recruitment | Applicant administration | Applicant Structure | Create unsolicited application groups**.

The personnel administrators created are also used in the Personnel Administration submodule, and they serve as an integration point.

In recruitment, this is called **Create Personnel Officer**, while in personnel administration, it's called **Define Administrator**.

They can be accessed directly via the SM30/SM31 T-code and the T526 table.

The administrators are configured in the system by navigating to **SPRO | Personnel Management | Recruitment | Applicant administration | Create personnel officer**.

> The administrators defined are also used in the PA as shown in the 0001 (organization assignment) infotype.

We can use the standard template that can be captured and sent out to applicants based on their different statuses.

The standard template or text is configurable; however, mailing out to applicants is a customizable activity that requires a technical consultant's involvement. The path is **SPRO | Personnel Management | Recruitment | Applicant administration | Short profile | Create standard text**. The template can be mapped as a short profile to the applicant via **Feature SHPRO**.

> The repository documentation of features, payroll functions, and operations can be accessed via the PDSY T-code. This is a useful Tcode to memorize.

Applicant cycle

The different stages of an applicant cycle are captured via applicant actions such as in process, put on hold, and rejected. The applicant actions are performed via the PB40 TCD, and it helps capture the details of the applicant, such as initial data is captured, profile is screened, process applicant, and so on.

We will see how applicant actions are configured in the system by navigating to **SPRO | Personnel Management | Recruitment | Applicant selection | Applicant status | Change action texts**. This is shown in the following screenshot:

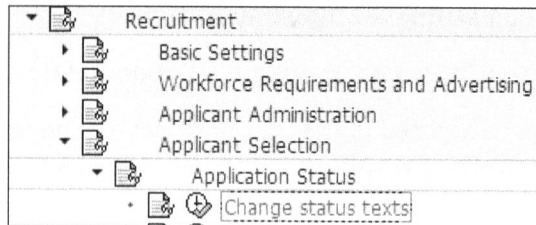

The standard statuses in SAP are as follows:

- In process
- To be hired
- On hold
- Rejected
- Contract offered
- Offer rejected
- Invite
- Invite to AC

The different reasons associated with each applicant action can be configured by navigating to **SPRO | Personnel Management | Recruitment | Applicant selection | Applicant status | Create status reasons**.

The following are the reasons why a candidate may be rejected:

- Insufficient qualifications
- Formal error
- Overqualified
- New application
- No requirement

The standard statuses will normally meet your requirements and needs and should be changed only in exceptional cases, as shown in the following screenshot:

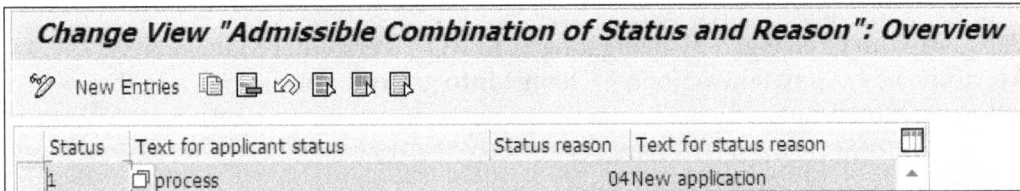

SAP also allows us to map the permissible vacancy assignment status to an overall status, and this is achieved using the STATU feature by navigating to **SPRO | Personnel Management | Recruitment | Applicant Selection | Applicant Status | Set permissible vac.assign statuses for each overall status**. This is shown in the following screenshot:

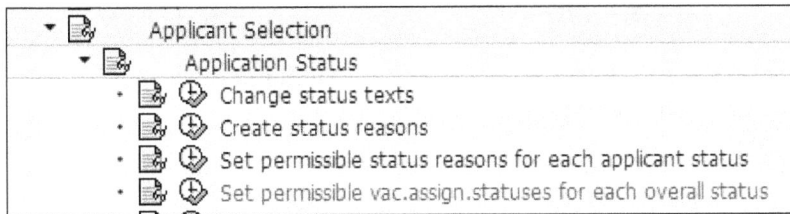

The STATU feature lets us define the overall status based on the status and return value, as shown in the following screenshot:

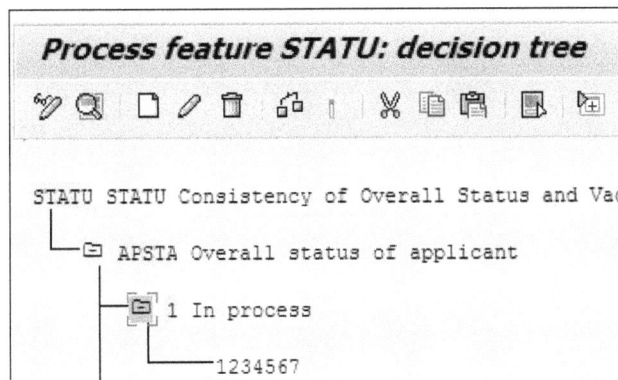

The HR administrator can process the applicant in the system via information types or infotypes. The info group is simply a collection of infotypes populating sequentially to assist the user in completing the transaction quickly.

The group can be changed by navigating to **SPRO | Personnel Management | Recruitment | Applicant actions | Change info groups**. This is shown in the following screenshot:

Double-click on the **Info Groups** option and you will get the **User Group Dependency on Menus and Info Groups** window.

Here, we define the info group and mention whether it's dependent on **user group** (**UGR**) or not. This is shown in the following screenshot:

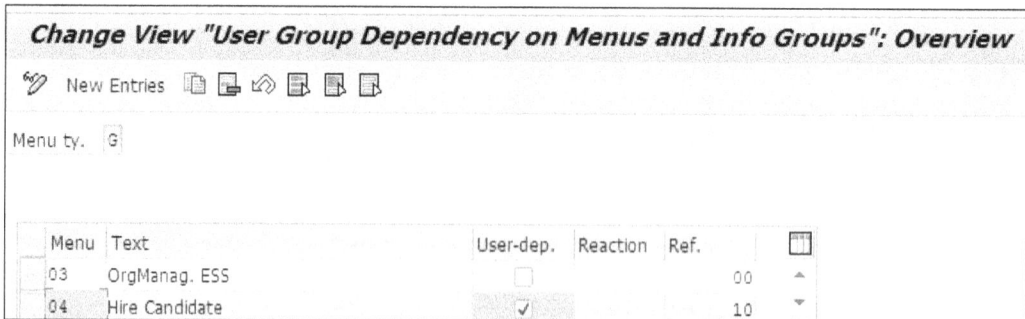

The flag controls whether the menu is dependent on the UGR parameter maintained in the user's profile, as shown in the following screenshot:

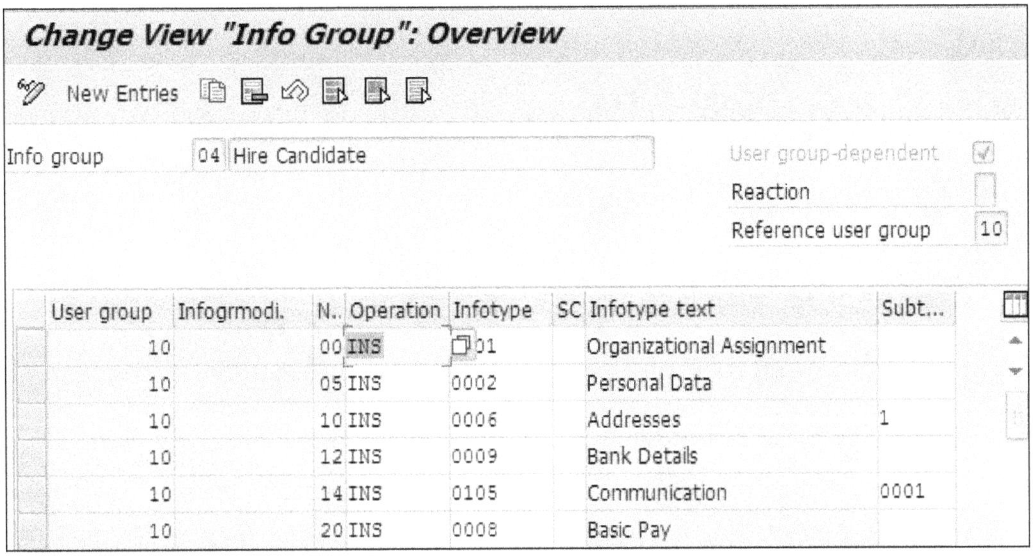

User group	Infogrmodi.	N..	Operation	Infotype	SC	Infotype text	Subt...	
10		00	INS	01		Organizational Assignment		
10		05	INS	0002		Personal Data		
10		10	INS	0006		Addresses	1	
10		12	INS	0009		Bank Details		
10		14	INS	0105		Communication	0001	
10		20	INS	0008		Basic Pay		

Change View "Info Group": Overview

New Entries

Info group 04 Hire Candidate   User group-dependent ☑
                                        Reaction
                                        Reference user group 10

The parameter value is set in the UGR parameter, and it is maintained via the SU3 or SU01 T-code.

If required, every user can be assigned a parameter value against the UGR parameter ID.

For instance, UGR is a user group parameter and MOL is country grouping.

The output of the SU3 T-code looks like the following screenshot:

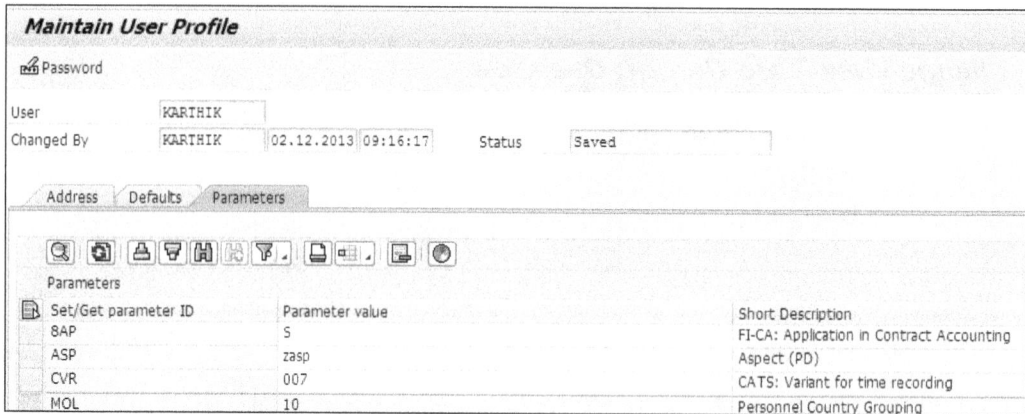

The output of the SU01 T-code looks like the following screenshot:

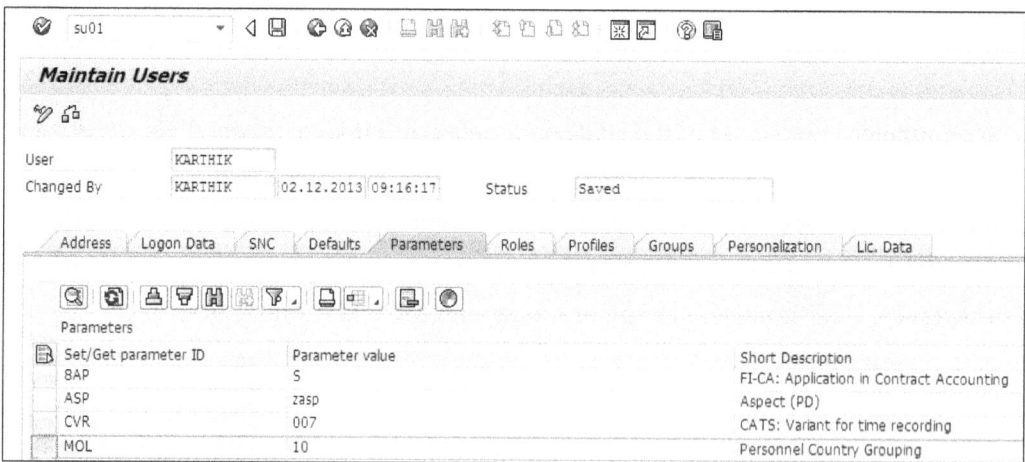

Each applicant action, such as the initial entry of basic applicant data, prepare to hire, and so on, is mapped to an applicant's status, such as in process, to be hired, and so on. We will see how the applicant action is configured by navigating to **SPRO | Personnel Management | Recruitment | Applicant selection | Applicant actions | Change applicant actions**. This is shown in the following screenshot:

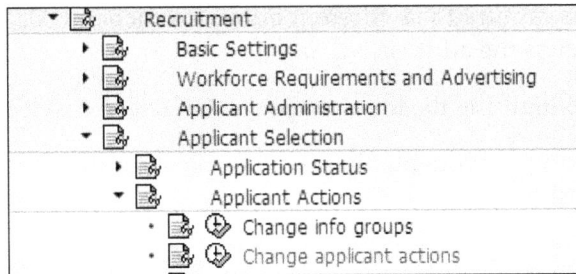

All the applicant actions, such as an applicant's initial screening, shortlisting applicants, and interviewing, are maintained as shown in the following screenshot:

Change View "Applicant Action Type": Overview

New Entries

Applicant action ...	Name of action type	Status	Applicant status
01	Process applicant	1	In process
02	Put applicant on hold	3	On hold
03	Reject applicant	4	Rejected
04	Offer applicant contract	5	Contract offered
05	Applicant rejects offer	6	Offer rejected
06	Prepare to hire	2	To be hired

The applicant actions are performed via the PB40 T-code. This is shown in the following screenshot:

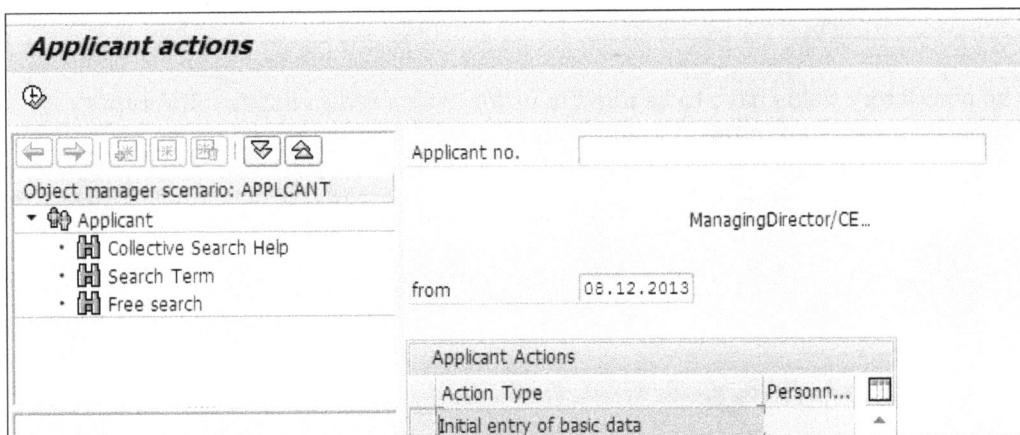

Applicant actions

Object manager scenario: APPLCANT

- Applicant
  - Collective Search Help
  - Search Term
  - Free search

Applicant no.

ManagingDirector/CE…

from   08.12.2013

Applicant Actions	
Action Type	Personn...
Initial entry of basic data	

The applicant data is captured via different infotypes such as 0002, which is personal data, and 0006, which is the address.

This is possible by configuring the info groups that we covered earlier in this chapter.

We will see how infotypes sequentially populate one after the other. This is shown in the following screenshot:

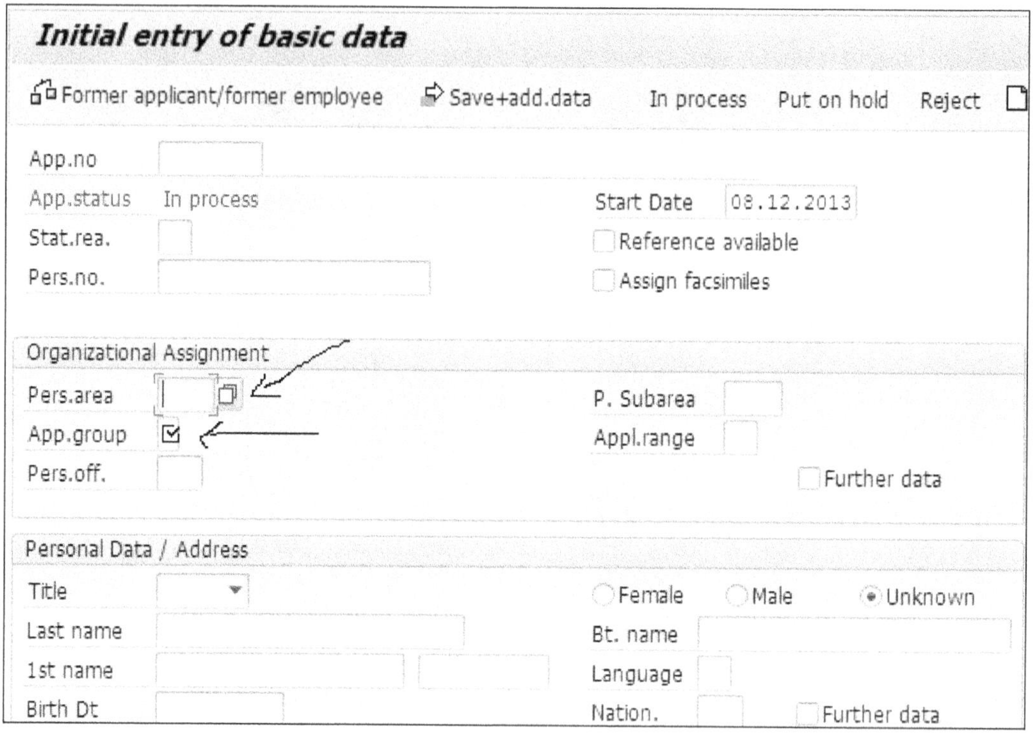

The mandatory fields have to be filled in order to proceed to the next infotype. This is demonstrated in the following screenshot:

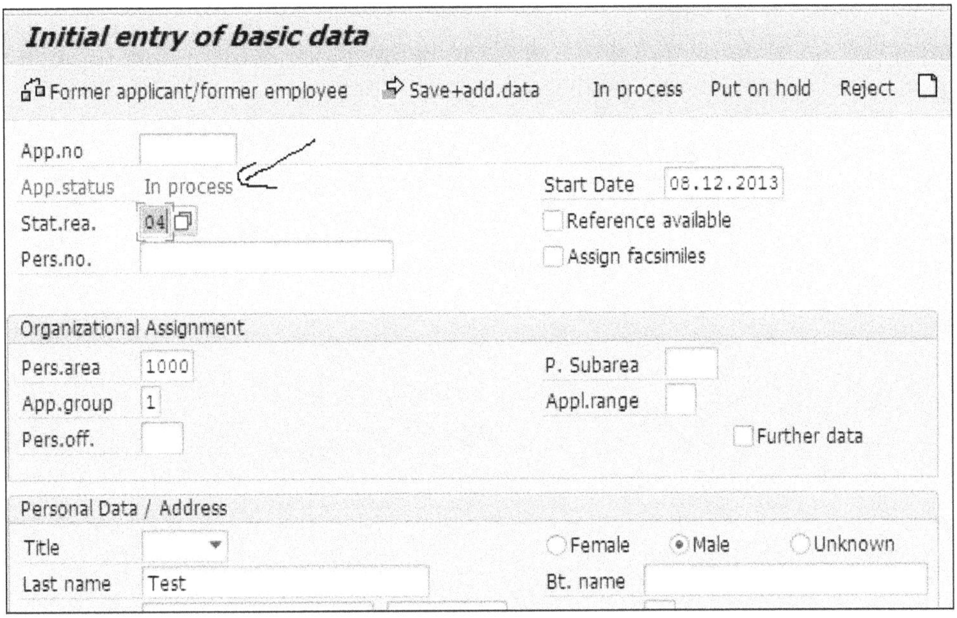

The next infotype is the personal data of the applicant, such as the first name, last name, date of birth, and so on. This is demonstrated in the following screenshot:

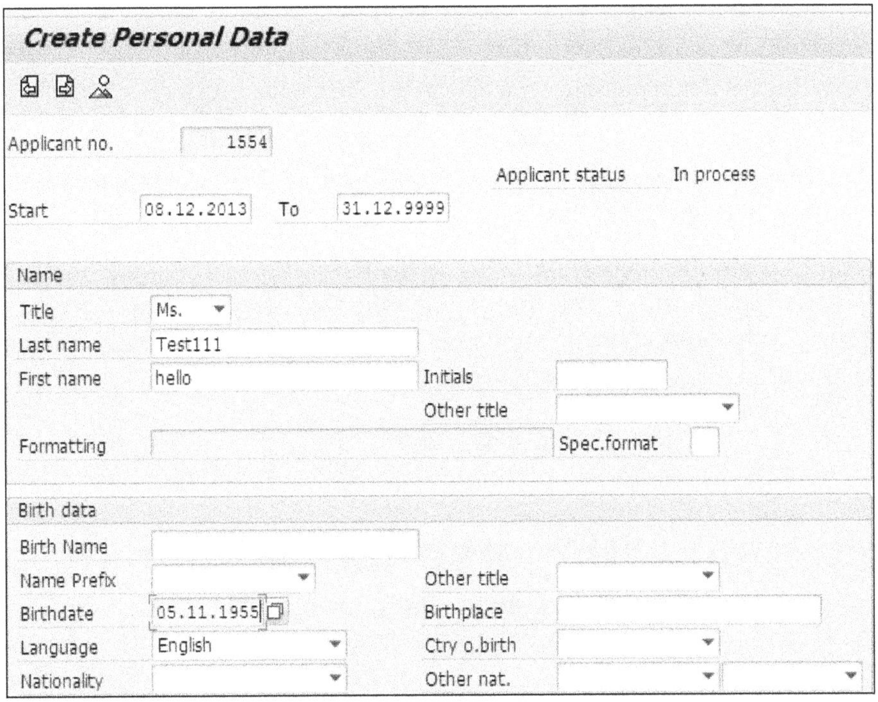

We will also find the applicant number generated automatically by the system. This is controlled via a configuration in number ranges; we covered this earlier in this chapter. This is shown in the following screenshot:

Click on the **Save** button after feeding data in to each infotype.

The system throws a message that the action for the applicant has been successfully executed.

We will discuss the integration aspects of the Recruitment submodule and Personnel Administration submodule in the next chapter.

We will find a seamless integration between the Recruitment and Personnel Administration submodules. This integration will enable the applicants from being transferred as employees.

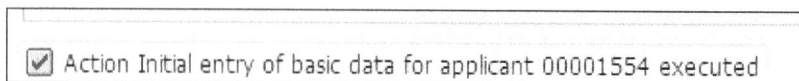

Integration with personnel administration

There is a seamless integration between the Recruitment and Personnel Administration submodules, and we will now look at how the configuration is done to achieve this.

There are two features that can be checked: the first one is **PRELI**, and the other one is **PRELR**. They are checked by navigating to **SPRO | Personnel Management | Recruitment | Basic settings | Set up integration with other components**. The following screenshot demonstrates this:

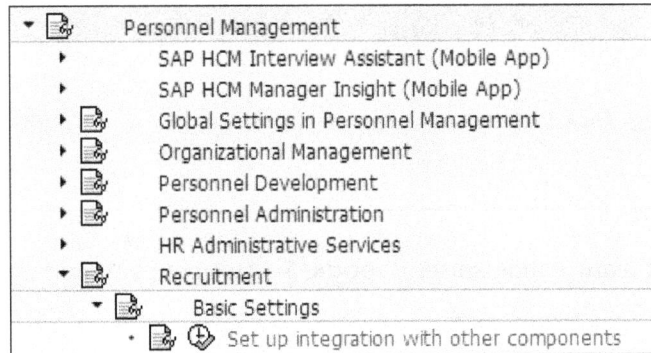

Click on **Execute**.

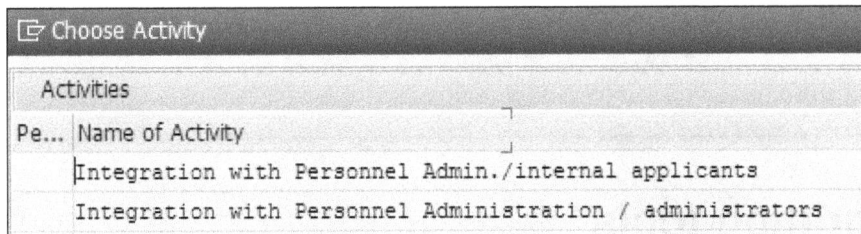

The important features related to the Recruitment submodule are PRELI and PRELR.

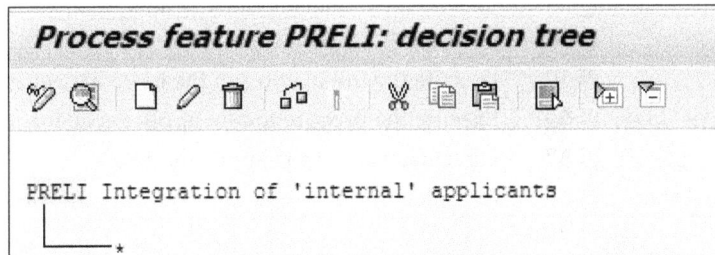

PRELI and PRELR are useful in the recruitment module to check if the number entered in the recruitment module is to be checked with the database.

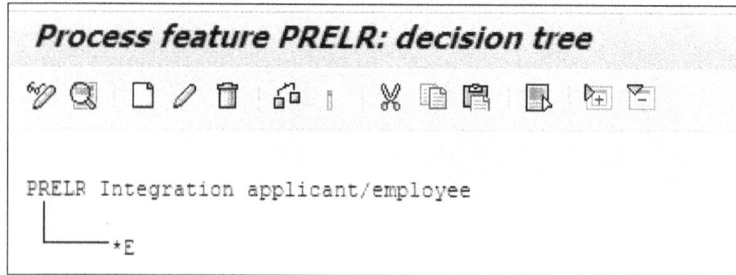

PAPLI is another feature that is useful for the Recruitment submodule.

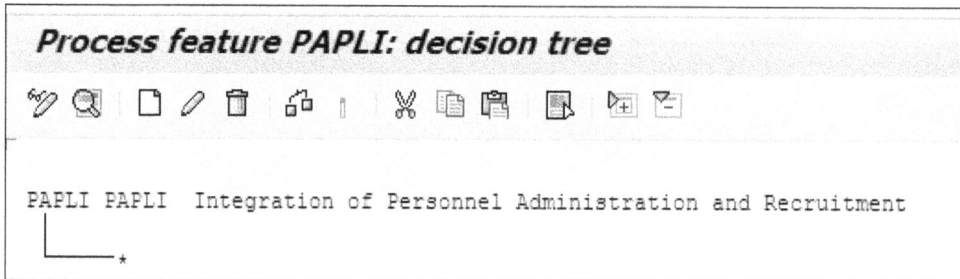

Integration tools

The procedure for transferring applicant data to Personnel Administration is listed in the following table:

Steps	Tcode	Comment
First step	PB40	Execute the initial entry of the basic data applicant action
Second step	PB40	Execute the prepare to hire applicant action
Third step	PBA7	Direct transfer of the applicant data
Fourth and final step	PBA8	Complete the activities after the data transfer

We will look at the steps in detail. The integration point between recruitment and personnel administration is controlled via **Data Transfer Tools**, and it is accessed via the PBA7 T-code.

> Do not change the action of hiring as it is hardcoded in the program (RPAPRT09) as 60.

The following screenshot shows the integration point between recruitment and personnel administration:

```
131    SELECTION-SCREEN BEGIN OF LINE.
132      SELECTION-SCREEN COMMENT 01(30) text-mas FOR FIELD massn.
133      SELECTION-SCREEN POSITION 33.
134      PARAMETERS massn LIKE t530t-massn                          "XDPK010843
135                     DEFAULT '60' OBLIGATORY.                    "XDPK010843
136    *    parameters massn like t530t-massn obligatory.           "XDPK010843
137    *    selection-screen comment 52(6) text-msg.                "XDPK017265
138    *    selection-screen position 58.                           "XDPK017265
139    *    parameters massg like t530t-massg.                      "XDPK017265
140    SELECTION-SCREEN END OF LINE.
```

To find the name of the program from the T-code, select the T-code, navigate to **System | Status**, and double-click on the program. This is shown in the following screenshot:

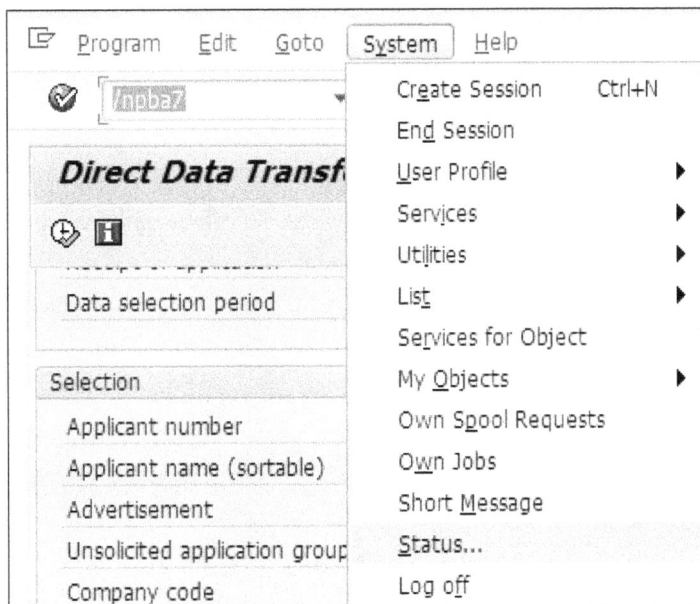

We can see the program name of any code as shown in the following screenshot:

SAP data	
Repository data	
Transaction	PBA7
Program	RPAPRT09
Program (screen)	RPAPRT09
Screen number	1000
Program (GUI)	RSSYSTDB
GUI status	$_00

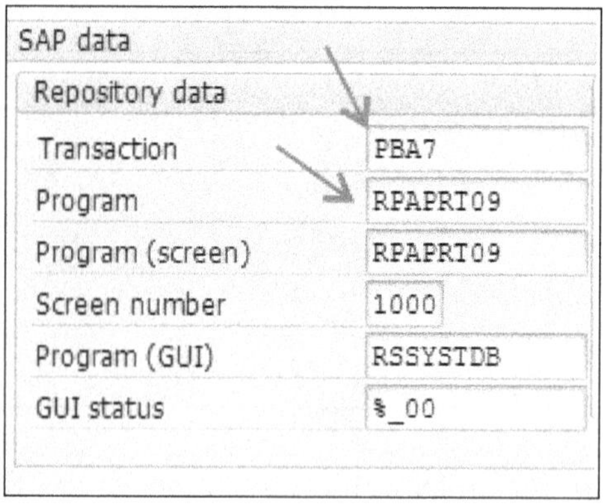

The overall status must be set to 2 (corresponds to hired) for transferring the applicant to the employee. This is shown in the following screenshot:

Status (overall)	2	⇨

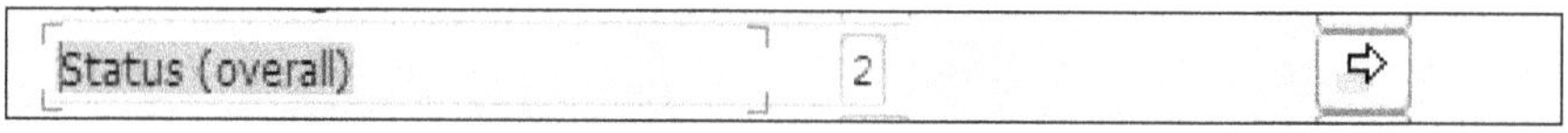

Click on **Execute**.

Finally, to complete the activity, execute the PBA8 T-code as shown in the following screenshot:

Program	Edit	Goto	System	Help

/npba8

Complete Activities after Data Transfer

Period

| Receipt of application | | To | |
| Data selection period | | To | |

Selection

| Applicant number | | ⇨ |

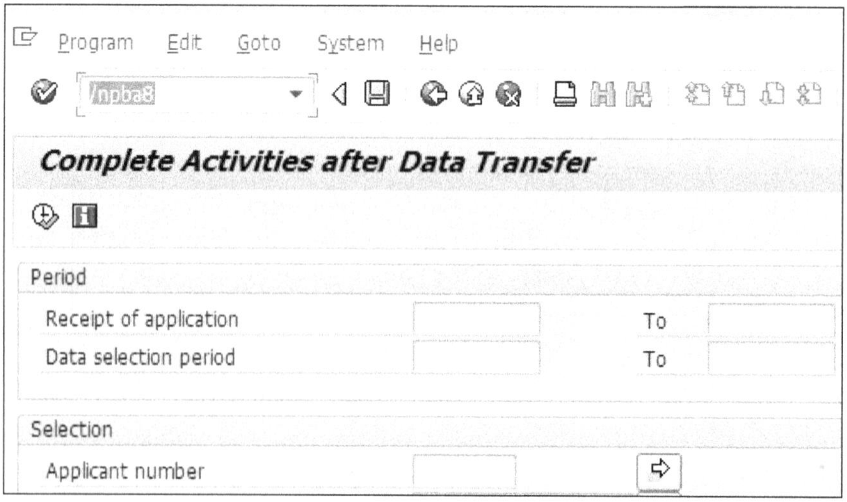

Common error message during data transfer

We normally come across the "Error during activity import" error. We might have run the initial entry of basic data and then we can execute the applicant' action. When we try to transfer the applicant data to employee data using the PBA7 T-code, the system might throw an error. We would need to check the PB60 T-code and choose transfer data; navigate to **Planned | Completed** (*F8*).

Tips and tricks

Let us take a look at certain features and transport requests in SAP which will make our work easier.

Features

SAP has certain given features to default the values based on the enterprise or personnel structure. The feature used to default an applicant number range is NUMAP (which refers to applicant number ranges). The repository of features can be maintained via the PE03 T-code. The features normally query enterprise and personnel structure fields and return the value. The features' functionality is useful, and it saves time and eradicates error while processing data. This is shown in the following screenshot:

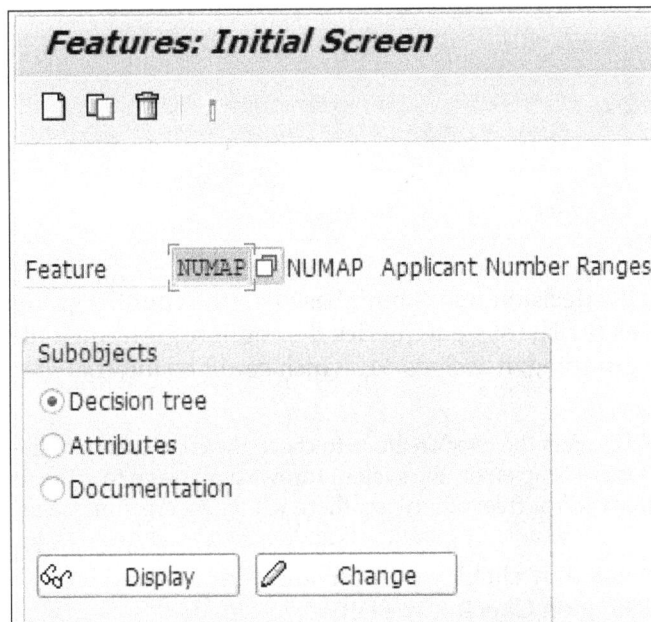

The applicant number range feature can be maintained via the PE03 T-code as shown in the preceding screenshot, or by navigating to **SPRO | Personnel Management | Recruitment | Basic Settings | Choose number ranges**.

The system determines which number range, such as external or internal, needs to be assigned to the applicant during the initial entry of the applicant data. This is in conjunction with the decision tree. The following screenshot demonstrates this:

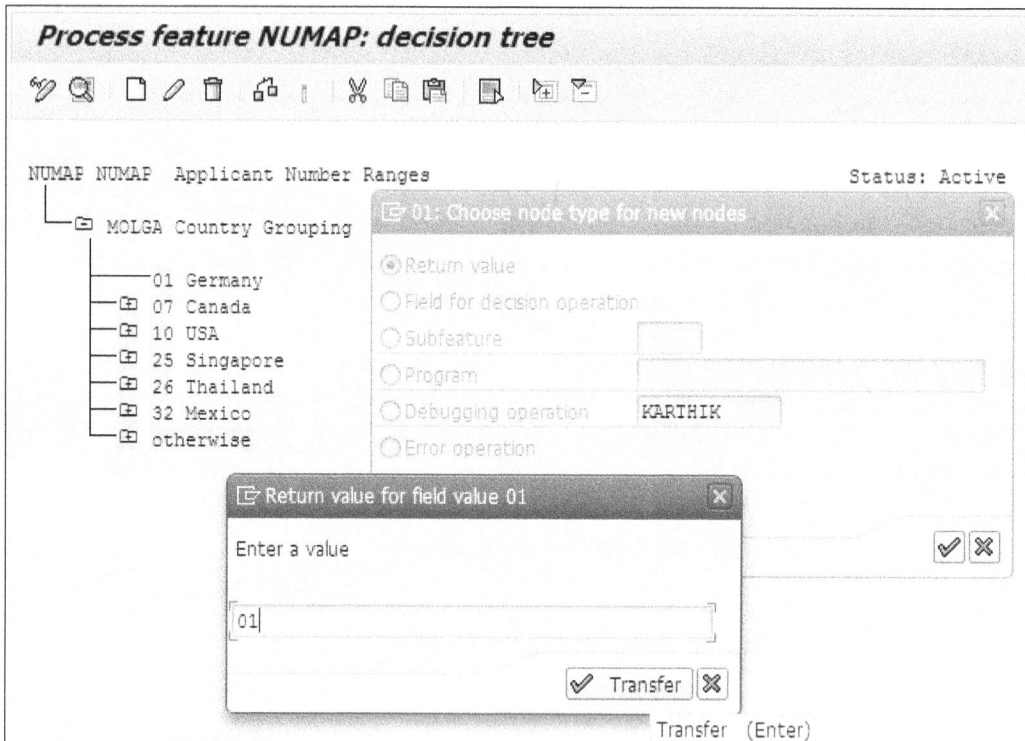

Here, we see that the decision tree is built based on the country grouping. The return value is assigned as 01. The system queries the country grouping of the applicant, and based on the grouping, it assigns 01, which could be internal or external.

> SAP offers the check feature to check the consistency of the action. If there is no error, the system throws a message that the decision tree is error free; otherwise, there will be an error message.

This feature is activated by clicking on **Activate** (*Ctrl+F3*), and it can be checked for correctness by clicking on **Check** (*Ctrl+F2*).

Normally, when a feature is activated, the system triggers a transport request, or TR. The TR is significant for moving data from one client to another without making changes separately. This is shown in the following screenshot:

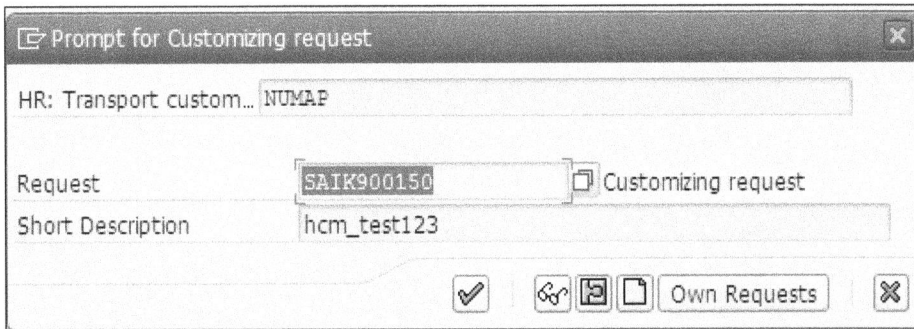

SAP offers the functionality to hide the free search help for applicants and persons. This is customized by navigating to **SPRO | Personnel Management | Recruitment | Basic settings | Hide Free Search in Search Help** or via the T77S0 system table. SAP recommends that we have SEARK and NOAHQ in the T77S0 settings (system table). The blank space in the value description field will denote that the free search is displayed, and if the field has an entity "X", then the free search is hidden. This is the control feature for free search. In the HR system, use the SM30/SM31.Type V_T77S0 T-code in the field table view and click on maintain. We will have to make sure the following parameters are set.

The following table illustrates the functionalities:

Group	Semantic short name	Value abbreviation	Description
SEARK	NOAHQ		The free search is displayed
SEARK	NOAHQ	X	The free search is hidden

Transport requests in SAP

The system generates the transport request number when you click on **Activate**.

The topic of transport requests must be known although, it is part of the basis activity.

The transport request allows the changes made in one client to be moved to a different client without any risk.

The transport request created earlier can be see by navigating to the SE09 T-code.

We won't dwell any more on the concept of transport requests, as it's a completely different topic. The output of the SE09 T-code looks like the following screenshot:

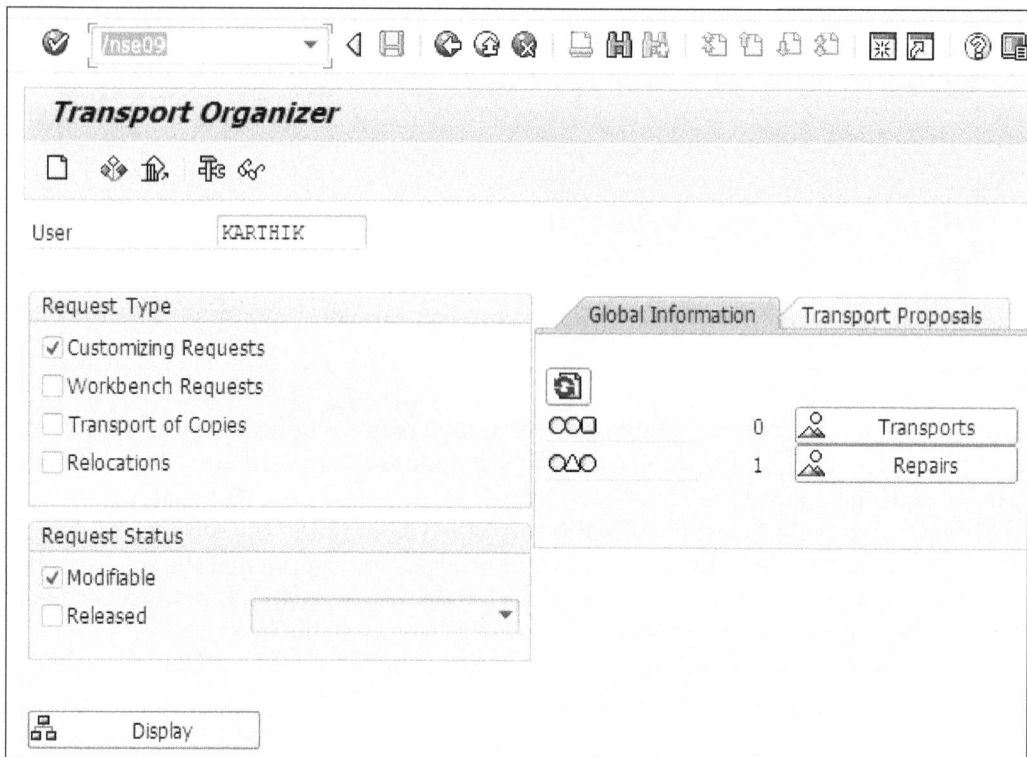

It's very important to understand the request type and request status functionalities:

- The request type has multiple options to flag such as customizing and workbench options
- The request that is created by **Functional Consultants** (FC) is collected as a customizing request
- The request that is created by technical consultants is collected as a workbench request
- The request status has modifiable and released statuses:
    - Modifiable means the request is not yet released for transport
    - Released are the ones that have been released and can be moved to different clients

Click on **Display**. Transport requests need to be released by the functional consultant, and the porting of TR to different clients is taken care of by the basis consultant.

We need to click on the **Transport bus** (*F9*) to release the request, and there will be a green flag that denotes that the request is released. When the TR is released, we will find the message populating it at the bottom of the screen, as shown in the following screenshot:

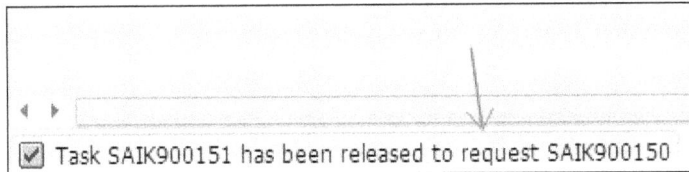

The repository of transport requests is maintained via STMS, and normal access is prohibited to those T-codes.

The following is a screenshot of the **SAP Transport Management System** (**STMS**) T-code:

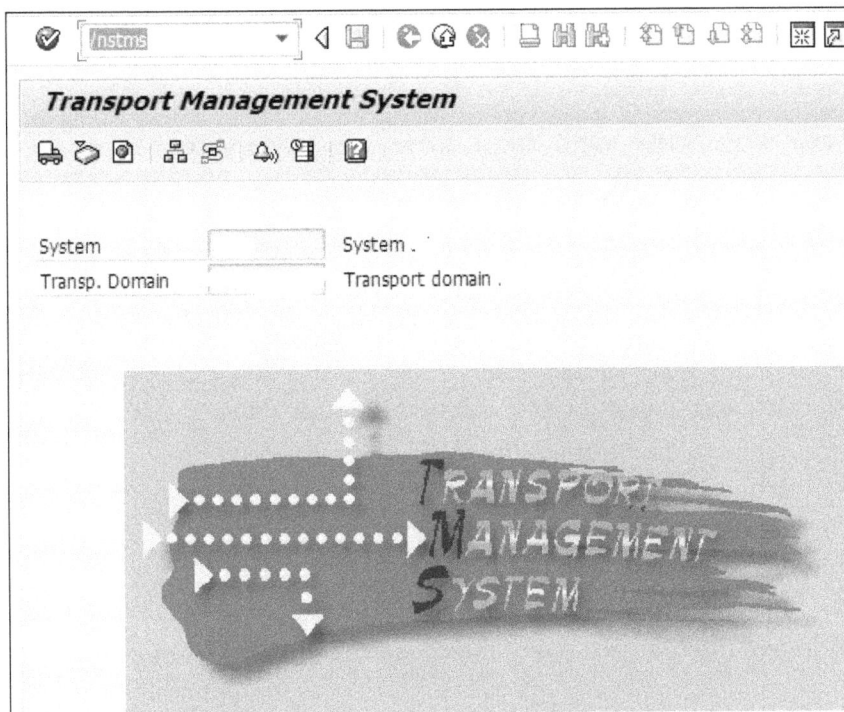

Summary

In this chapter, we have covered the standard functionalities provided by SAP to configure the Recruitment submodule. The configurable items such as recruitment instruments, media, and vacant positions have been covered. The integration points between recruitment and organization management have been discussed. The data transfer from Recruitment to Personnel Administration has been explained.

In the next chapter, we will look closely at configuring the Organizational Management submodule and explore the standard functionalities provided by SAP.

3
SPOCK – the Building Block of OM

We will now learn how the **Organizational Management** (**OM**) submodule is configured to map the business requirement in a SAP system. We will see how a functional structure is mapped into the system. In this chapter, we will cover the following topics:

- The basic concepts of OM
- Creating an organizational structure
- Integrating OM with Personnel Administration

The concepts of Organization Management

The building blocks of OM are SPOCK. They are described as follows:

- **S**: This stands for **Position** (for example, HR Manager, Marketing Director, and so on)
- **P**: This stands for **Person**
- **O**: This stands for **Organizational unit** (also known as **Org unit**; it represents the department in a company)
- **C**: This stands for **Job** (for example, manager, director, and so on)
- **K**: This stands for **Cost Center**

> Note that both K and P are external object types. The K object type, Cost Center, is maintained in the FI/CO module, and the P object type, Person, is maintained in the PA submodule. When we say external, it is simply not created in the OM submodule.

SAP has delivered multiple interfaces to design an organizational structure, and we will understand each of them separately.

Elucidating an organizational structure

An organizational structure is a functional structure. It simply represents the departmental hierarchy in a company. It identifies each Job, Position, its functions, and where it reports to within the organization. The following table is an example of an organizational structure:

Company name	Departments (suborg units)	Subordinate departments	Positions	Jobs
ABC Paper Company (Root organizational unit)	Administration		• Office Supervisor • Office Clerk • Receptionist	• Director • Manager • Analyst • Administrator • Supervisor
	Human Resources		• HR Director • Benefits Administrator • Hiring Manager • Hiring Analyst	
	Finance	• Accounts Payable • Accounts Receivable	• A/P Manager • A/P Clerk • A/R Manager • A/R Clerk	
	Manufacturing	• Pulp • Paper • Maintenance	• Plant supervisor • Technician shift 1 - 05 • Technician shift 2 - 05 • Maintenance supervisor	

Basic relationships between organizational objects

The relationships in organizational management are mostly similar to a parent-child structure in two ways. A Position can belong to an organizational unit, and inversely, can be incorporated by an organizational unit. In the following table, A indicates the bottom-up approach, while B indicates the top-down approach:

Relationship type	Related object type	Relationship name
A002	O-O	An organizational unit reports to another organizational unit
B002	O-O	This is the line supervisor of an organizational unit
A003	S-O	All the Positions that reports to an organizational unit
B003	O-S	A Position belongs to an organizational unit
A007	C-S	A Job describes a Position
B007	S-C	A Position is described by a Job
A012	S-O	The chief Position manages an organizational unit
B012	O-S	An organizational unit is managed by a chief Position
A011	K	This is the Cost Center assignment
A008	P-S	This is a Position-to-Person relationship
B008	S-P	This is a Person-to-Position relationship

It is important to note that Cost Center is always one sided unlike other object types that can have both A and B. It can be mapped either to an Org unit or to a Position, depending on the business requirement.

> Irrespective of the interface we use to create the structure, the object types are stored in the HRP1000 table, and the relationship between the two object types is stored in HRP1001.

When we discuss relationships, it is important to know the concept of the evaluation path in SAP. The evaluation path lets us create a relationship between two object types. An evaluation path can also have a sequence of object relationships. The evaluation path can be accessed by navigating to **SPRO | Personnel Management | Organizational Management | Basic Settings | Data Model Enhancement | Maintain Evaluation Paths** or via OOAW. The BOSSONLY T-code, for example, is a standard evaluation path that can be used in a report that will fetch the Org units that have the B012 relationship and the holder of the Position.

Building an organizational structure

The different methods of building an organizational structure are as follows:

- Organization and Staffing
- Simple Maintenance
- Expert Mode

Creating an organizational structure with different interfaces

There are multiple interfaces provided by SAP to build a functional structure. We will look at each of them in detail.

Organization and Staffing

The Organization and Staffing method of building organizational structure is delivered by SAP in a scenario where the company does not have an HR module, but the organizational structure is needed for the purpose of other modules, for example, workflow requirements. Using this method, the organization objects can be moved using the drag-and-drop approach. Also, we can add some extra attributes to the organizational objects.

To work in this module, you have to navigate to **SAP Easy Access | Organizational Management | Organizational Plan | Organization and Staffing | PPOCE - Create**. The following screenshot demonstrates the navigation path:

SAP Easy Access

▸ ☐ Cross-Application Components
▸ ☐ Logistics
▸ ☐ Accounting
▾ ☐ Human Resources
    · ⬡ PPMDT - Manager's Desktop
    ▸ ☐ Personnel Management
    ▸ ☐ Time Management
    ▸ ☐ Payroll
    ▸ ☐ SAP Learning Solution
    ▸ ☐ Training and Event Management
    ▸ ☐ Training Needs Management
    ▾ ☐ Organizational Management
        ▾ ☐ Organizational Plan
            ▾ ☐ Organization and Staffing
                · ⬡ PPOCE - Create
                · ⬡ PPOME - Change
                · ⬡ PPOSE - Display

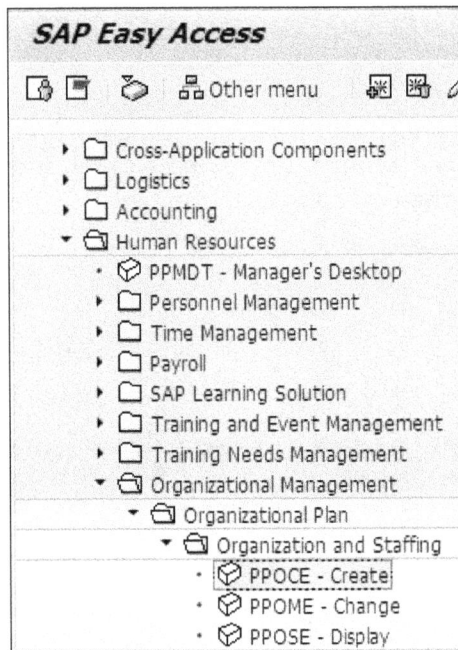

When you use the **PPOCE - Create** T-code, it prompts you to enter the start date and end date, as seen in the following screenshot. It is recommended that you have the start date as backdated as possible, say `01011900`, for instance.

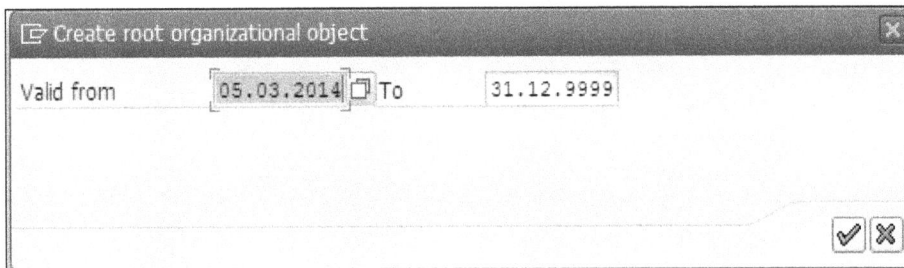

> ⬡ Create root organizational object
>
> Valid from   `05.03.2014` ☐ To   `31.12.9999`
>
>   ✔ ✖

The relationship between an Org unit and Position

We can use the PPOME T-code to use this interface via the **SAP Easy Access** screen. We can right-click on **Organizational unit**, select **Assign**, and click on **Incorporates**, as shown in the following screenshot:

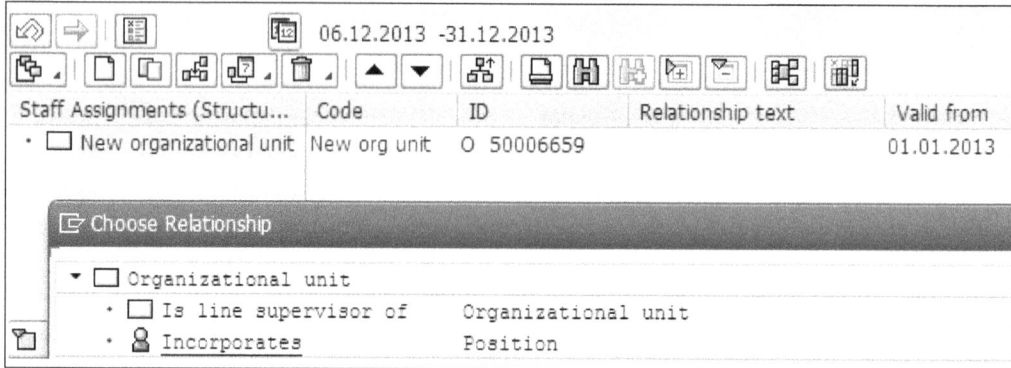

You can enter the name of the Position, as shown in the following box, and click on *Enter*. You can see that the **Asst Manager** position belongs to **New organizational unit**. Also, notice **O** and **S** under **ID**. As discussed earlier, **O** refers to the Org unit and **S** is for Position.

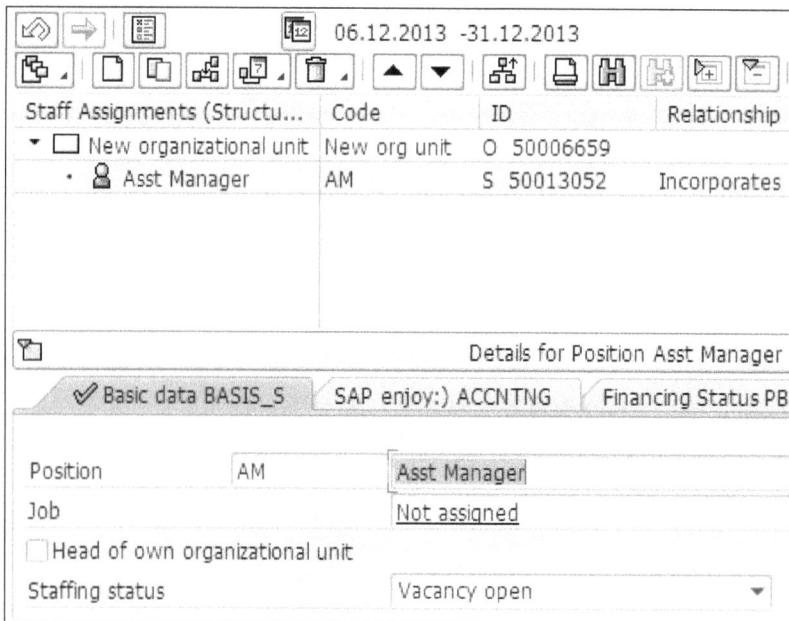

The relationship between Position and Job

We will use the PPOME T-code again, to use this interface via the SAP Easy Access screen. Click on **Edit** and select **Create Job**. When the **Create Job** window opens, enter the required fields, as shown in the following screenshot. You can create the required jobs and click on *Enter*. The jobs are saved, and we can assign them to positions by selecting the jobs that you have created for the positions.

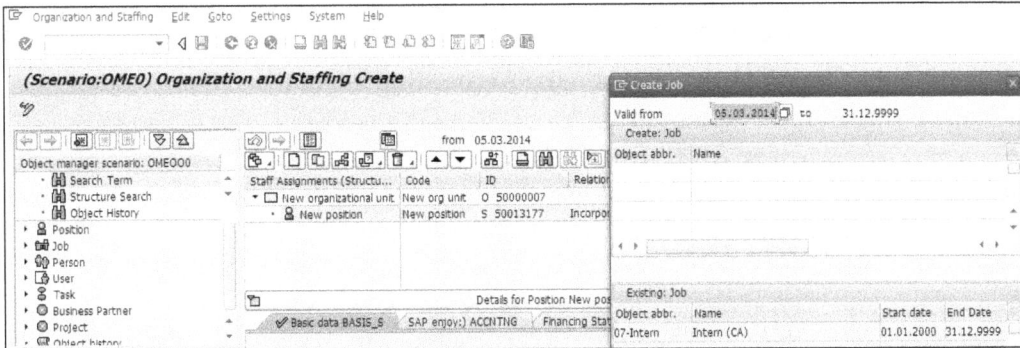

We will see how a Cost Center is mapped to an Org unit. Click on the **Accounting** tab after you execute the PPOME T-code. You can assign the Cost Center either to the position or the Org unit by entering the required details. This is demonstrated in the following screenshot:

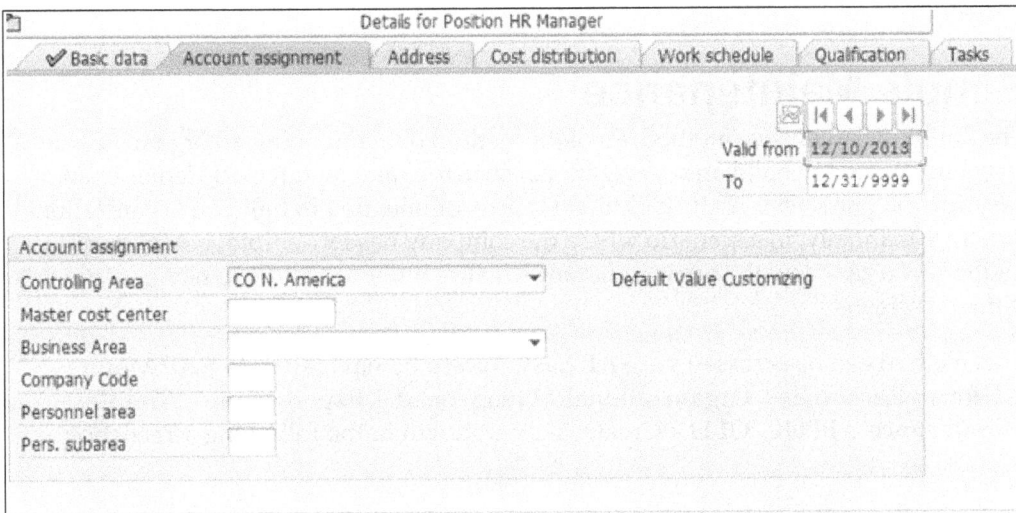

The Cost Center is an external object and can be mapped to either an Org unit or a position.

> Note that OM is strongly built on the principle of inheritance. When the Cost Center is mapped to the parent Org unit, all the other Org units or positions mapped to them will automatically have the Cost Center tagged to them.

The following screenshot is an example that shows how a Master Cost Center is mapped to the Org unit by clicking on the **Accounting** tab in the PPOME T-code:

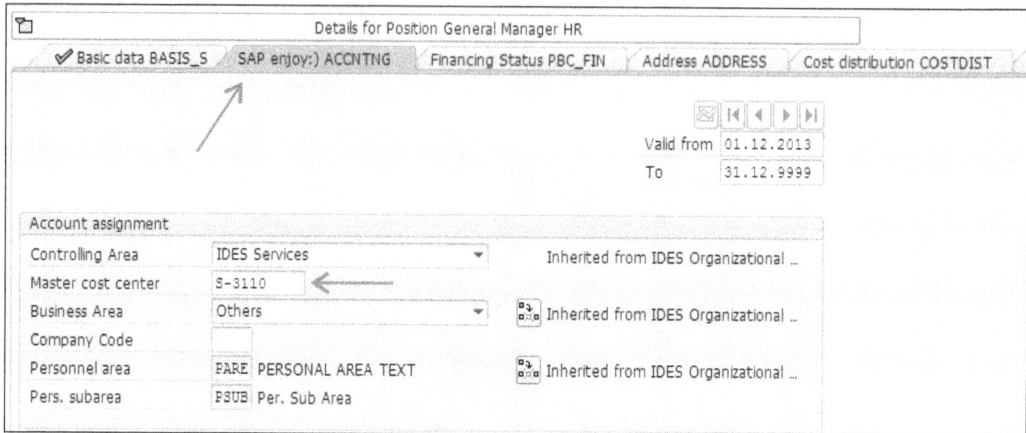

Simple Maintenance

The Simple Maintenance method, an older method of maintaining an organizational structure, is used to build an organizational structure and assign Cost Center in an easy way on one screen itself. This method is recommended to build an organizational structure manually, in a scenario where the company has few employees. In this method, you can view the organizational structure without having to navigate much to different screens.

This method can be accessed via **SAP Easy Access** by navigating to **SAP Menu | Human Resources | Organizational Management | Expert Mode | Simple Maintenance | PPOC_OLD – Create**. This is shown in the following screenshot:

```
▼ ⬡ Human Resources
    • ⬙ FPMDT - Manager's Desktop
    ▶ ☐ Personnel Management
    ▶ ☐ Time Management
    ▶ ☐ Payrol
    ▶ ☐ SAP Learning Solution
    ▶ ☐ Training and Event Management
    ▶ ☐ Training Needs Management
    ▼ ⬡ Organizational Management
        ▶ ☐ Organizational Plan
        ▼ ⬡ Expert Mode
            • ⬙ PO10 - Organizatoral Unit
            • ⬙ PO03 - Job
            • ⬙ PO13 - Position
            • ⬙ PO01 - Work center
            • ⬙ PFCT - Task Catalog
            • ⬙ PP01 - General
        ▼ ⬡ Simple Maintenance
            • ⬙ PPOC_OLD - Create
```

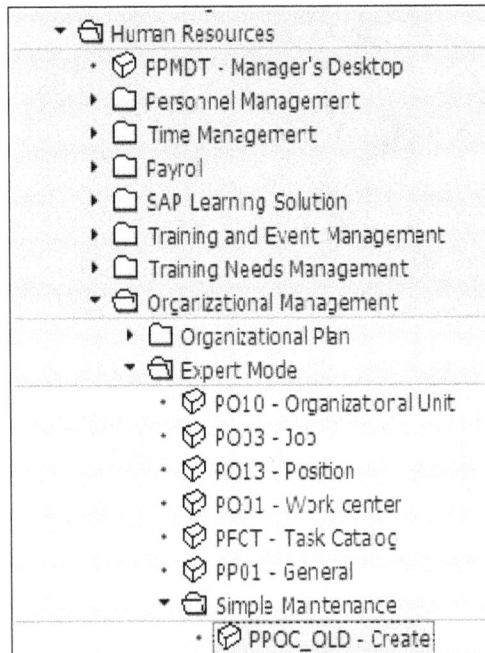

Also, we can directly access this method via the PPOC_OLD T-code, which is shown in the following screenshot:

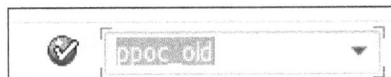

```
 ✅  │ ppoc old                              ▼ │
```

Enter the required fields in the **Create Organizational Unit** window to create the Org unit. We will be able to enter the Org unit's name, the abbreviation, as well as the long text. In the **Create Organizational Unit** window, the users will have the following two options:

- **Overall view**: In this view, the options and features cater to the users of SAP Business Workflow

- **Human Resources view**: In this view, the options and features cater to the users of HR

After this is done, click on the Create button in the top-left corner of the window, as shown in the following screenshot:

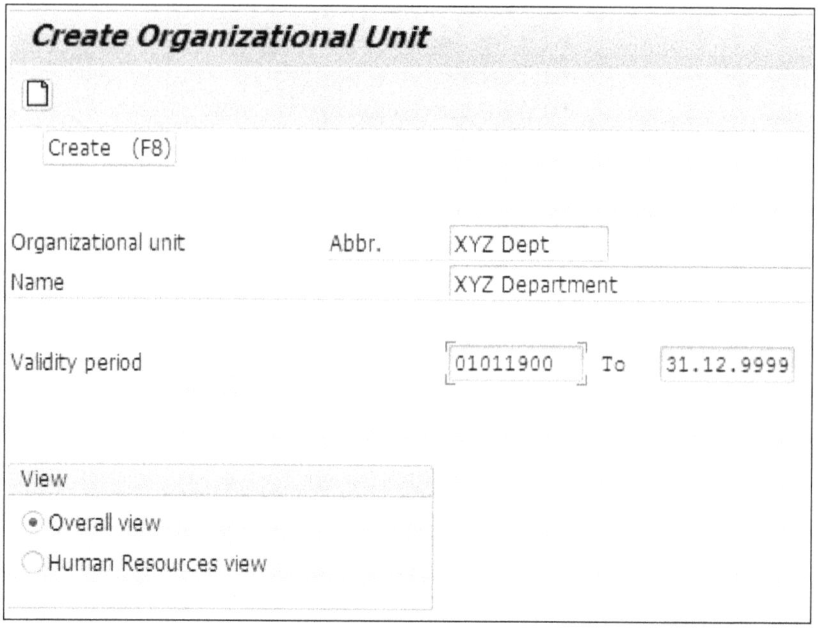

After performing the preceding steps, SAP automatically assigns an 8-digit identifier that is unique to the object. The letter o identifies the object as an organizational unit.

The positions are created by clicking on **Staff assignments**, as shown in the following screenshot:

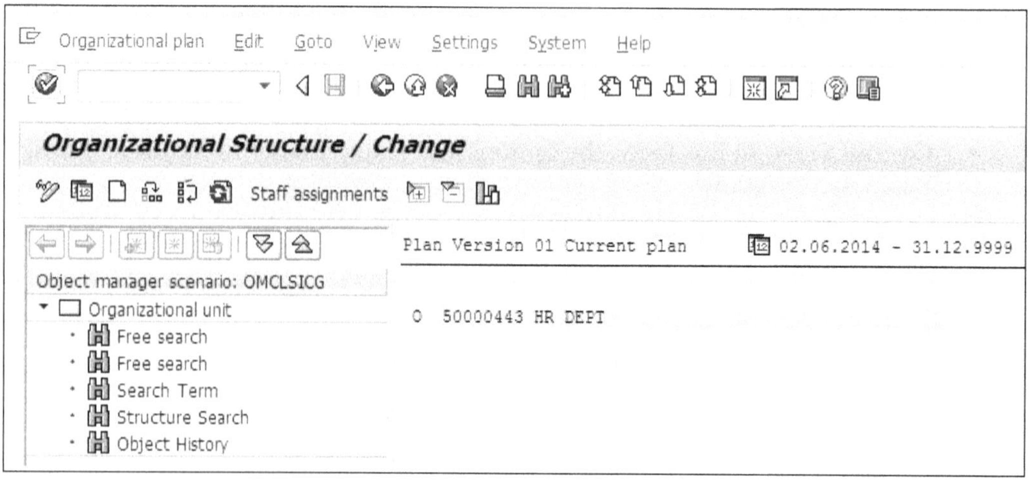

After this, click on **Positions...** and a screen pops up wherein the required fields and validity periods are entered (it's recommend that you have them backdated). SAP assigns a unique 8-digit identifier to each Position. The letter s identifies the object as a Position. The following screenshot shows a demonstration of the preceding steps:

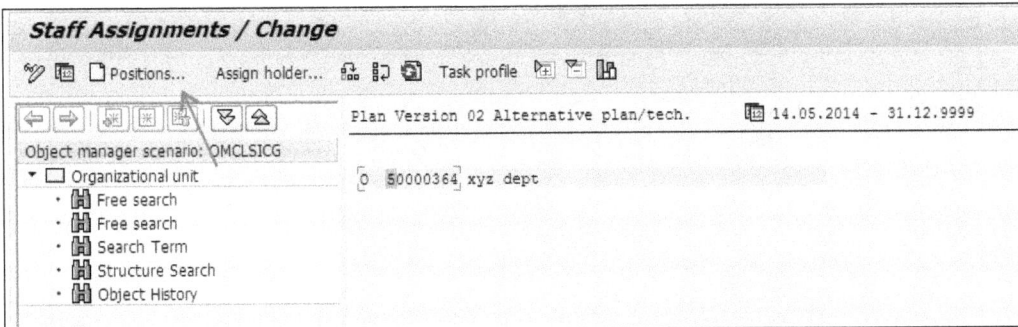

In the **Create Positions** window, we will enter the abbreviation and the long text that identifies the Position, the s object. The following screenshot shows a demonstration of the preceding steps:

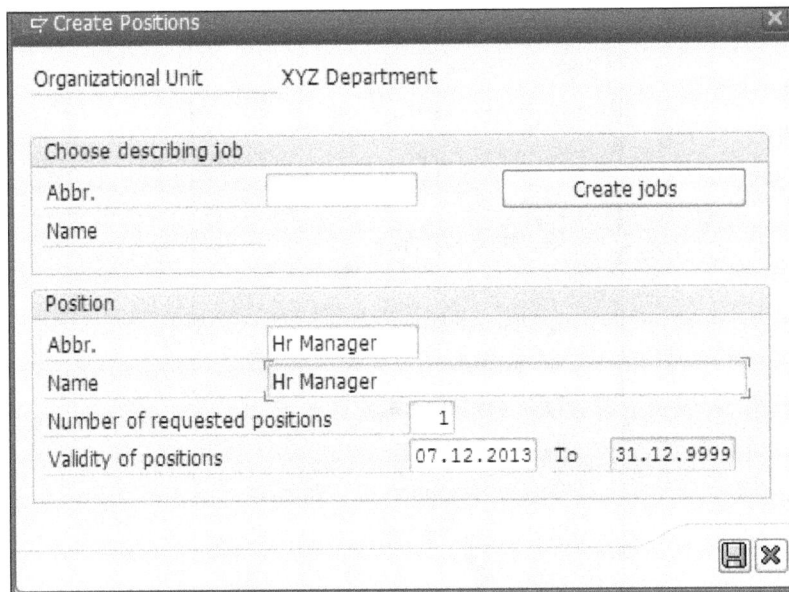

After performing the preceding steps, the jobs are created by clicking on **Create jobs**; they are then mapped to positions. We need to enter the abbreviation and its long text and then click on the Save button. After clicking on the **Create jobs** button, the **Create Jobs** window opens up, which is shown in the following screenshot:

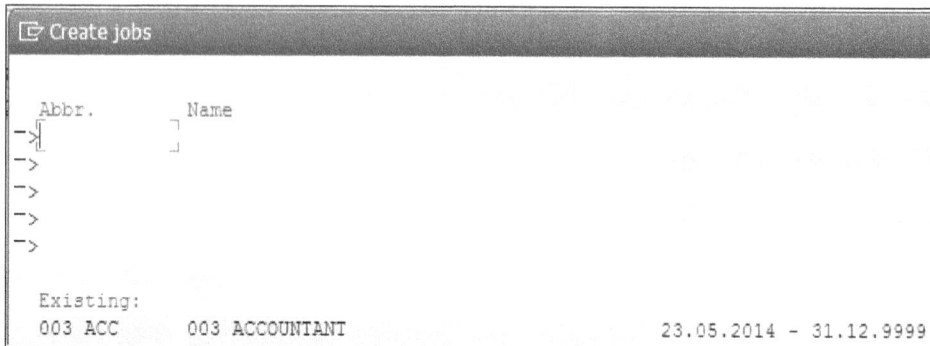

We can map the Cost Center to the Org units or Positions by navigating to **Goto | Account Assignment** and then clicking on the **Master cost center...** tab, as shown in the following two screenshots:

After clicking on the **Master cost center…** tab, choose the appropriate Cost Center and then click on the Save icon.

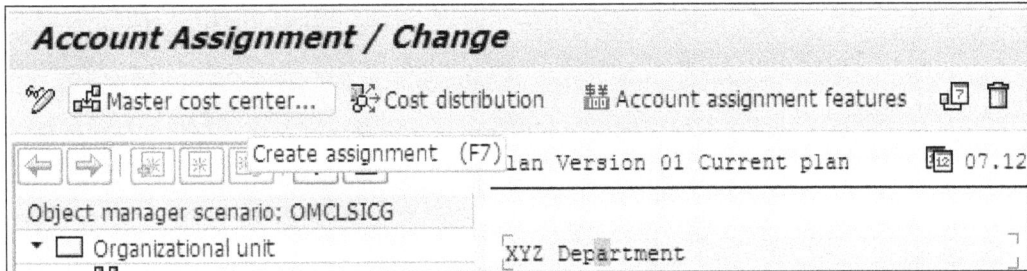

When we click on the **Account Assignment** tab, it will allow us to choose the relevant Cost Center that needs to be mapped to that Org unit. This is demonstrated in the following screenshot:

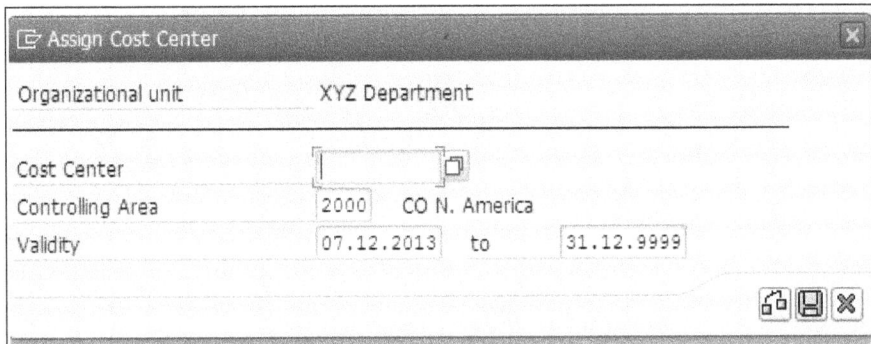

Creating a Cost Center

The Cost Center is an external object; it is created by a Finance (FI) consultant and serves as an integration point between HCM-FI modules. The Cost Center is essentially used for expense classification to know the breakup of costs according to General Ledger (G/L).

Though Cost Center belongs to the FI module, it is useful to know the navigation path. To access the Cost Center, navigate to **SAP Easy Access | SAP Menu | Accounting | Controlling | Cost center accounting | Master Data | Cost Center | Individual Processing | KS01 - Create)**, as shown in the following screenshot:

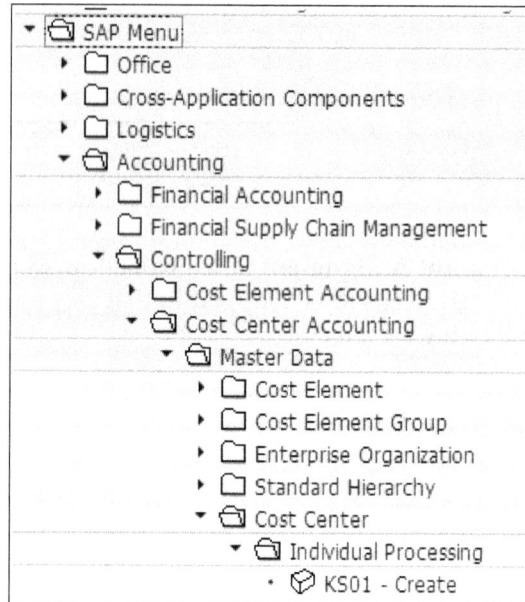

The following screenshot shows the **Create Cost Center** window that allows you to enter the Cost Center name and the validity period:

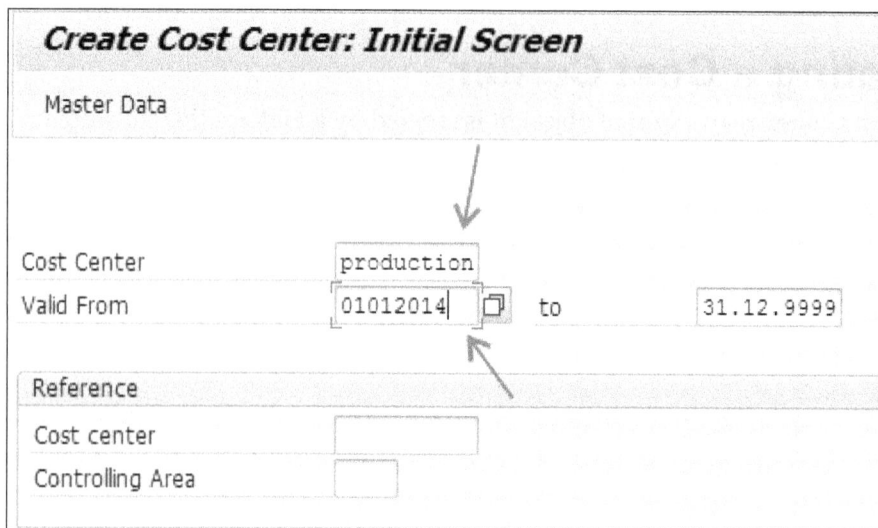

The validity period is important when assigning it to an employee. The start date of the Cost Distribution infotype 0027 must not be before the start date of the Cost Center, or else, the system will throw an error.

The Expert Mode

The next interface that we will learn to use is **PP01 - General**. Using it, we can create any of the object types such as O, S, C, and K. Using this method, we can maintain any type of attribute to any of the organizational objects. If any organizational structure needs to be built using uploaded programs, especially for large companies, the uploaded programs can use the expert method of building an organizational structure.

The Expert Mode can be accessed by navigating to **SAP Easy Access | SAP Menu | Organizational Management | Expert Mode | PP01 - General**, as shown in the following screenshot:

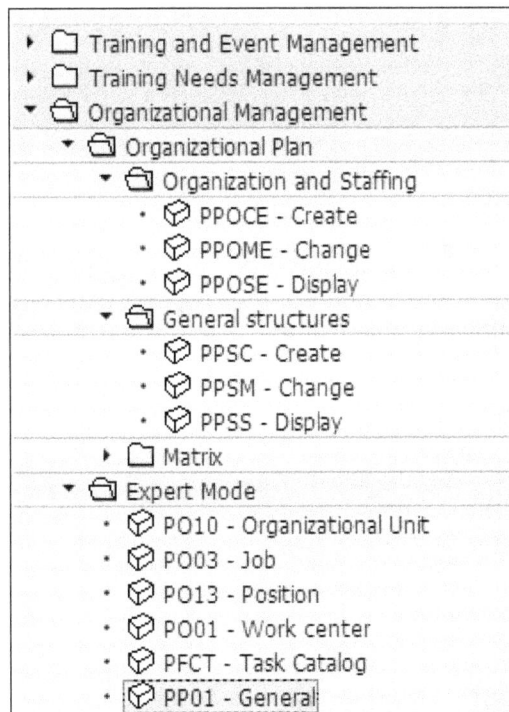

▶ ☐ Training and Event Management
▶ ☐ Training Needs Management
▼ ☐ Organizational Management
   ▼ ☐ Organizational Plan
      ▼ ☐ Organization and Staffing
         • ▽ PPOCE - Create
         • ▽ PPOME - Change
         • ▽ PPOSE - Display
      ▼ ☐ General structures
         • ▽ PPSC - Create
         • ▽ PPSM - Change
         • ▽ PPSS - Display
      ▶ ☐ Matrix
   ▼ ☐ Expert Mode
      • ▽ PO10 - Organizational Unit
      • ▽ PO03 - Job
      • ▽ PO13 - Position
      • ▽ PO01 - Work center
      • ▽ PFCT - Task Catalog
      • ▽ PP01 - General

Creating an organizational unit object in the Expert Mode

The object type and its relationships are created using the Expert Mode interface. This interface is convenient to work with if we are familiar with the object types and the relationships between them. It is normally used by functional consultants. The following screenshot shows a demonstration of the process of object creation:

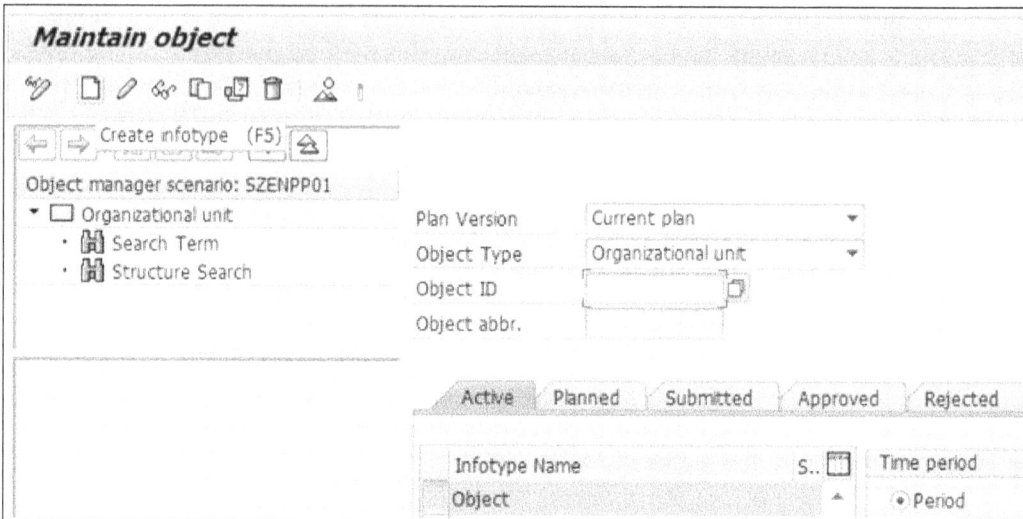

Select **Object** and click on the Create infotype button (or press *F5*). Give an object abbreviation as well as an object name for the Org unit that we are creating. This is demonstrated in the following screenshot:

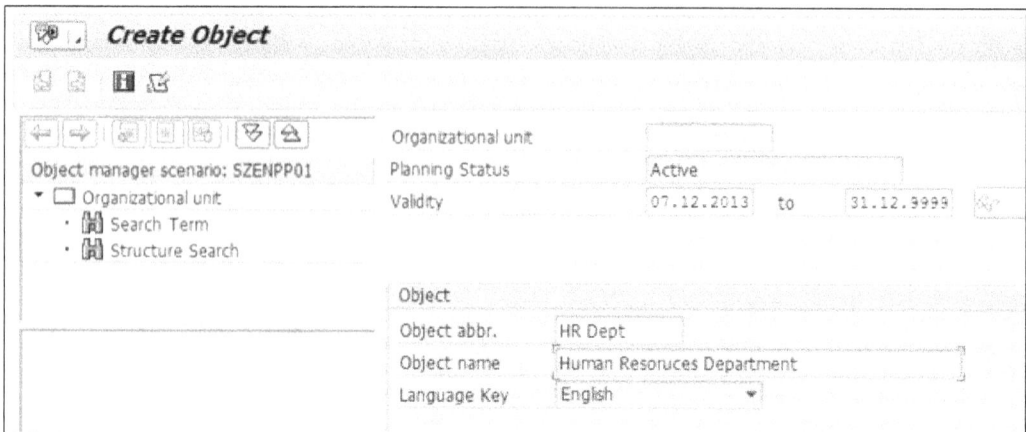

Creating a position object in the Expert Mode

We will now try to understand how a Position object is created. Follow the steps mentioned in the preceding section about creating an organizational unit. Instead of selecting **Organizational unit** as **Object Type**, select **Position**. The demonstration is shown in the following screenshot:

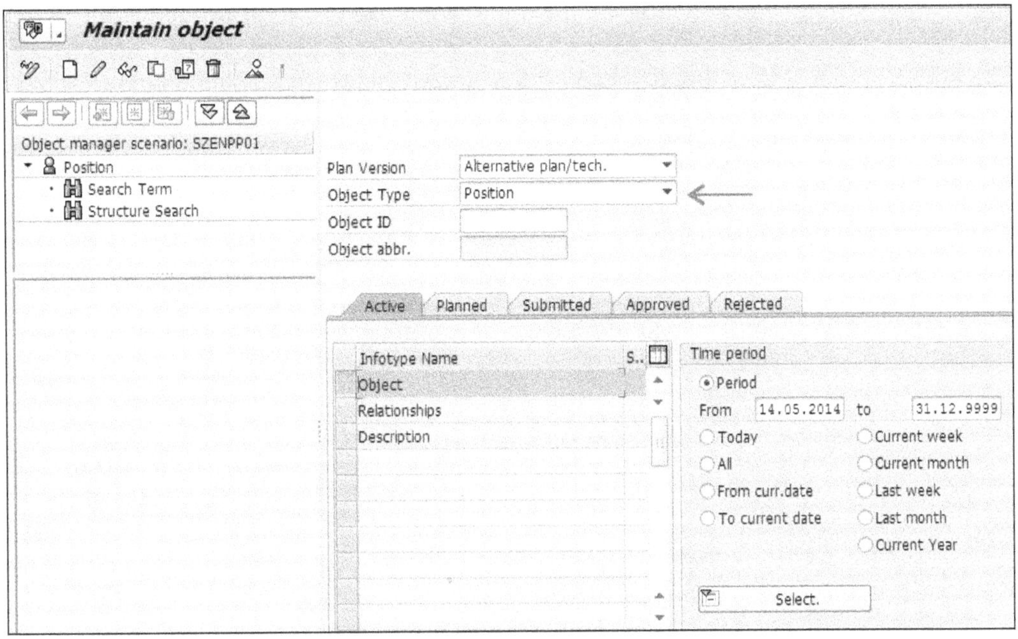

As shown in the following screenshot, enter all the fields just as it was done when creating an organizational unit:

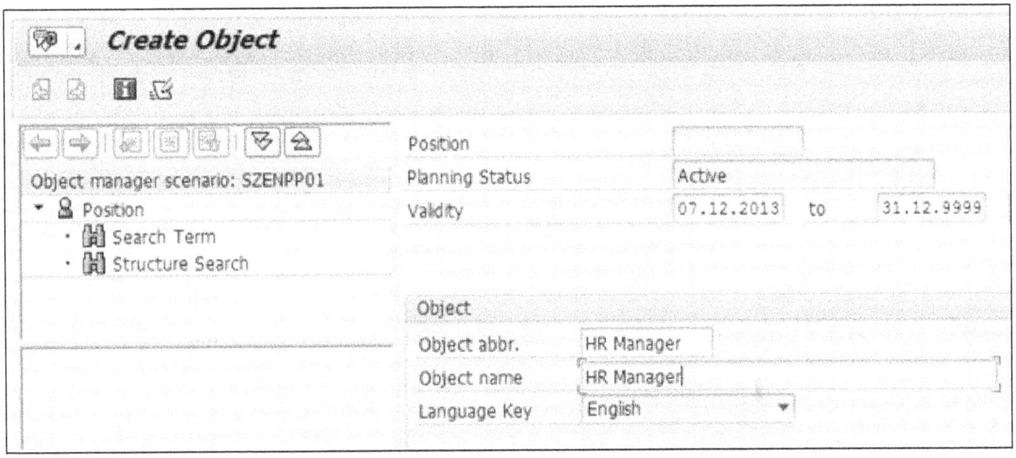

Creating a Job object in the Expert Mode

You can create a Job object in the same manner in which you created the Position object. Follow the steps mentioned in the preceding two sections. Instead of selecting **Position** as **Object Type**, select **Job**. The demonstration is shown in the following screenshot:

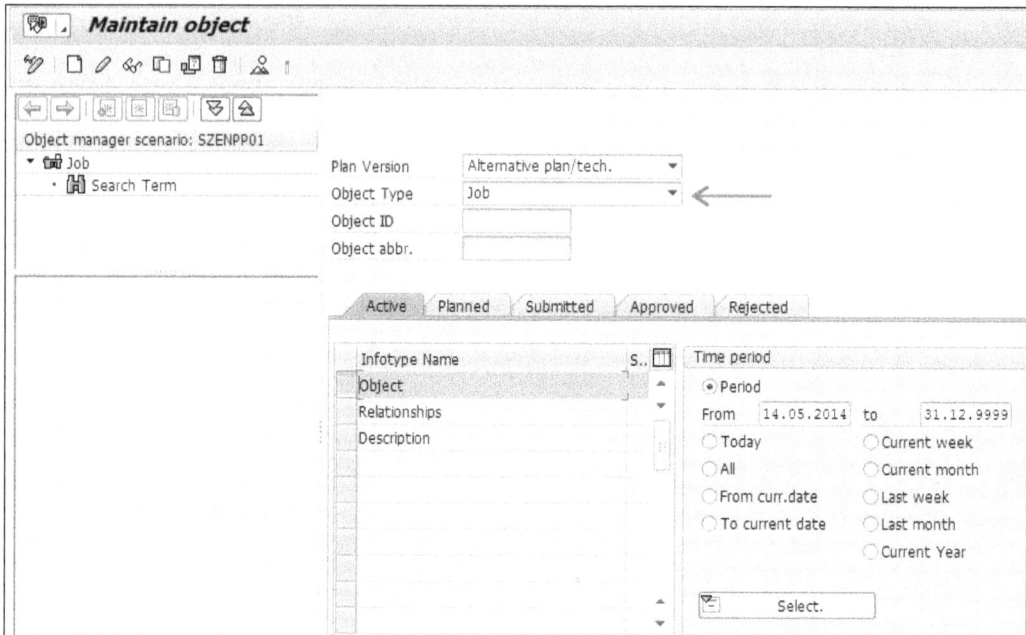

In the **Maintain object** window, the different statuses that we will find are as follows:

- **Active**
- **Planned**
- **Submitted**
- **Approved**
- **Rejected**

The statuses are useful if we want an approval-type mechanism of workflow based on different statuses. In general, all OM objects are created in the **Active** status.

When we click on **Create object**, the **Create Object** window allows you to enter the object description and name, as shown in the following screenshot:

> The object abbreviation is, by standard, 12 characters in length, and the object name is 40 characters in length. We can find the length of each field by pressing *F1* from the field and clicking on the technical information. Double click on table name in field data.

The concept of Number Ranges

It's important to know where the object IDs are actually generated from. Each object has a unique number that's associated with it.

To check what number is assigned to the different subgroups, navigate to **SPRO | Personnel Management | Organizational Management | Basic Settings | Maintain Number Ranges | Maintain Number Ranges**. The following screenshot shows the **Change View "Number Assignment": Overview** window:

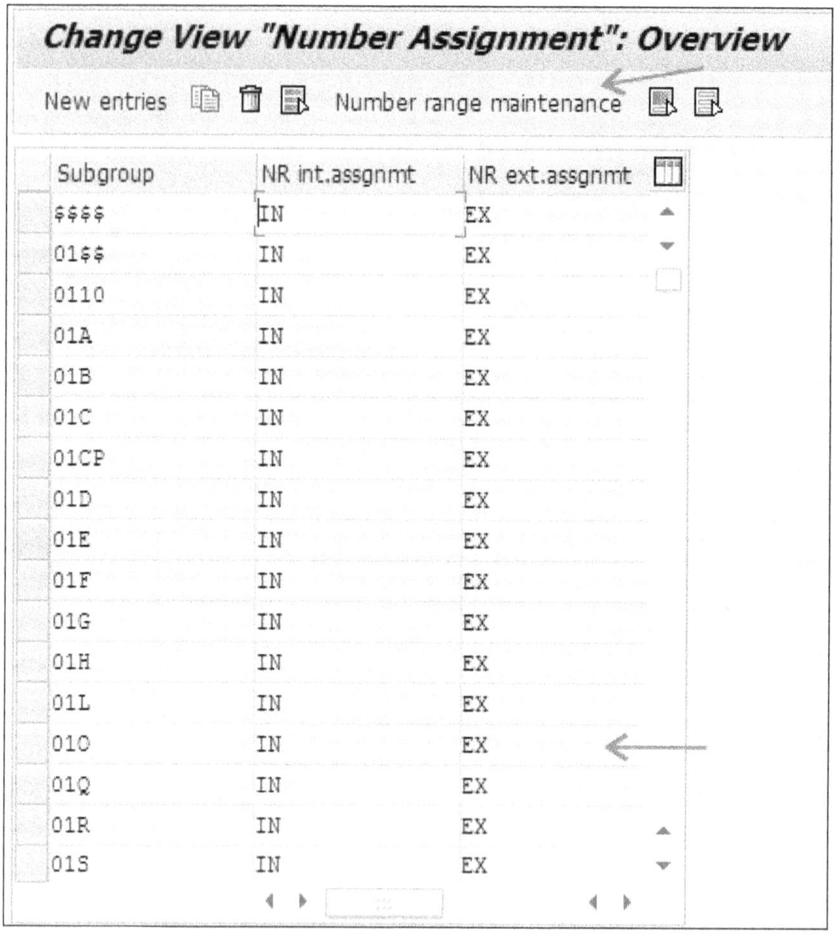

Subgroup	NR int.assgnmt	NR ext.assgnmt
$$$$	IN	EX
01$$	IN	EX
0110	IN	EX
01A	IN	EX
01B	IN	EX
01C	IN	EX
01CP	IN	EX
01D	IN	EX
01E	IN	EX
01F	IN	EX
01G	IN	EX
01H	IN	EX
01L	IN	EX
01O	IN	EX
01Q	IN	EX
01R	IN	EX
01S	IN	EX

Change View "Number Assignment": Overview — New entries — Number range maintenance

We can also access the preceding window via the OONR T-code. After clicking on the **Number range maintenance** tab in the preceding screenshot, the **Range Maintenance** window appears, as shown in the following screenshot:

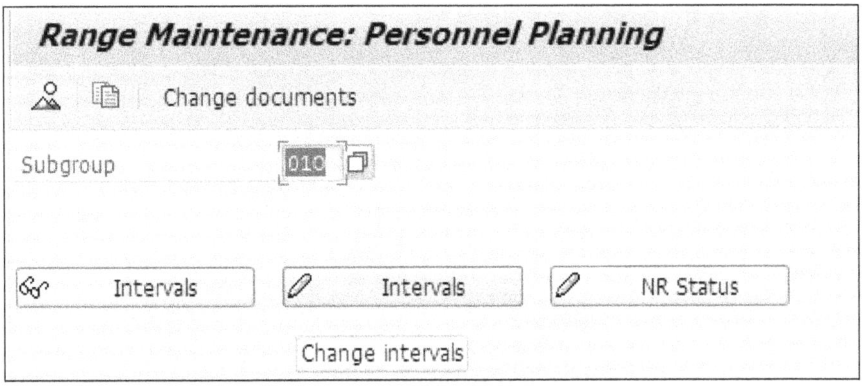

When we can click on the **Intervals** tab (the pencil icon depicts that we can change intervals), shown in the preceding screenshot, the **Interval Maintenance** window opens up, as shown in the following screenshot:

N..	From No.	To Number	NR Status	Ext	
EX	00000001	49999999	0	☑	▲
IN	50000000	99999999	50067346	☐	▼

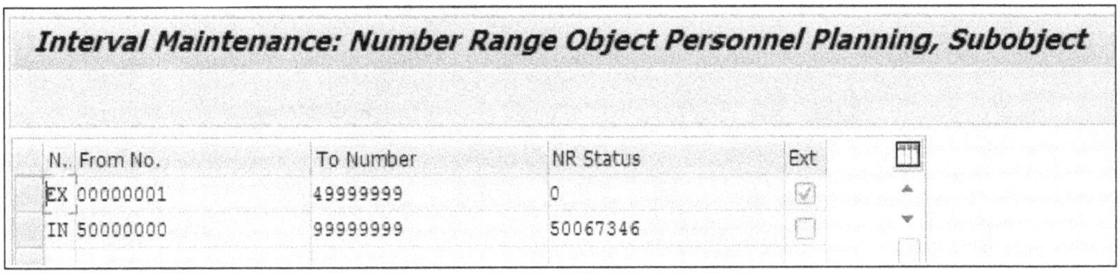

Scenarios where we use external number assignment

Let's say that the company has object keys (numbers) already defined in an existing system and would like the same numbers to be brought over to SAP too.

Consider the number range is $$$$. The first two $$ represent the **plan version** and the next two $$ represent the object type. For example, 010 refers to the number range for organizational units. No changes may be needed in this table.

We can also access the **Number Range Object Maintenance** window via the SNRO T-code. In the following screenshot, RP_PLAN is Number Ranges for Personnel Planning:

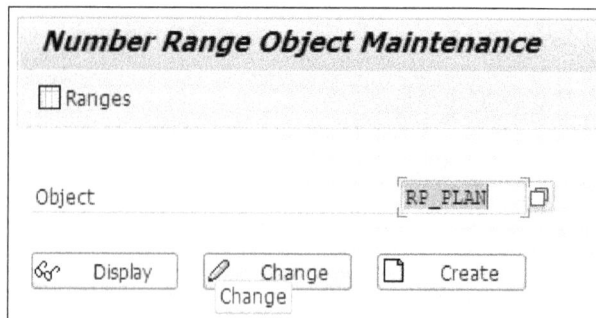

Click on the **Ranges** button in the following screenshot (or press *F7*). It leads to the Range Maintenance window for Personnel Planning:

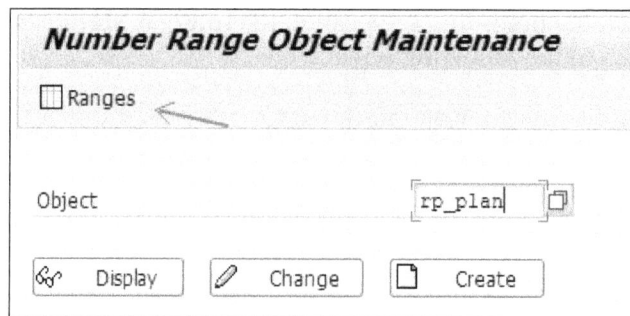

After performing the preceding step, the subgroup for Personnel Planning is displayed. In the following screenshot, RP_Plan is the object that we choose for Organization Management number ranges, 01 is the Plan version, and O denotes the object type:

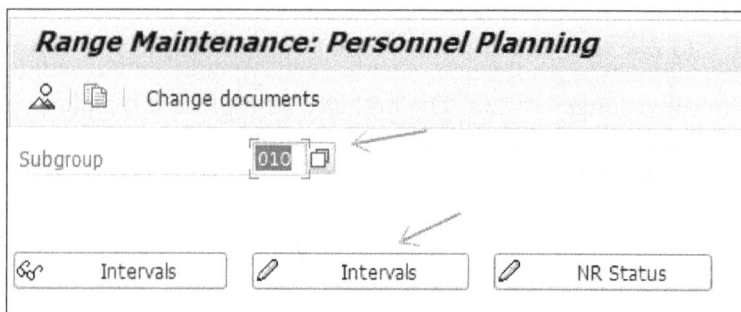

The Plan Version

The Plan Version lets us simulate multiple versions in parallel. It allows us to manage different scenarios in the OM. We can have a number of plan versions, but only one can be active and current.

Plan versions can be configured by navigating to **SPRO | Personnel Management | Global Settings in Personnel Management | Plan Version Management | Maintain Plan Version**. The following screenshot shows the **Change View "Plan Versions": Overview** window:

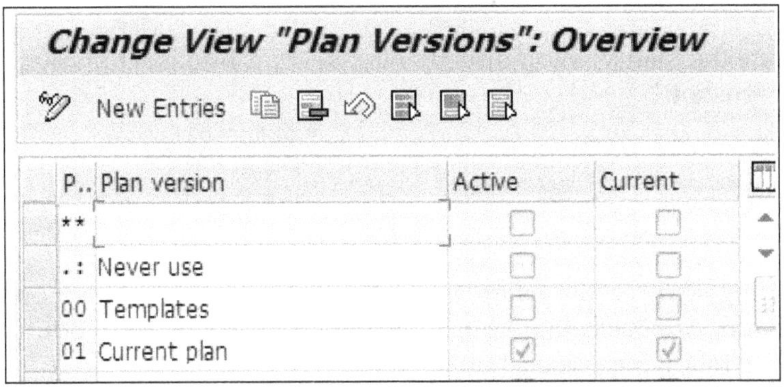

We have to set the plan version by mapping the plan version ID into the T77S0 table.

Plan versions can be activated by navigating to **SPRO | Personnel Management | Global Settings in Personnel Management | Plan Version Management | Set active Plan Version**. The following screenshot shows the **Change View "Set Active Plan Version": Overview** window:

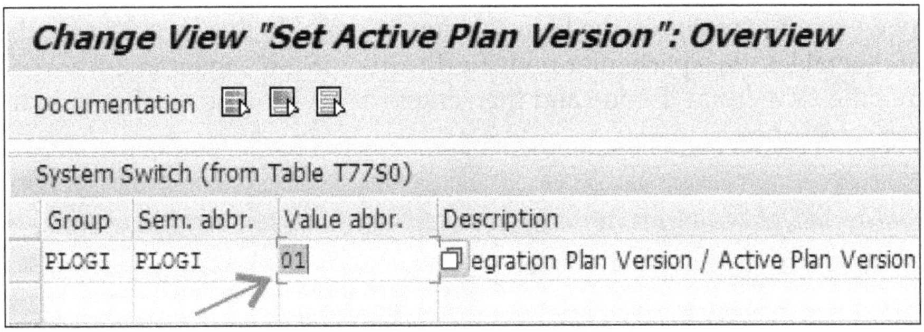

To activate the plan version, we use the **PSO0 – Set Plan Version** option, which can be found by navigating to **Organizational Management | Settings**:

We can activate the Plan Version directly via the PCO0 T-code, as shown in the following screenshot:

After performing the preceding step, a window will open up asking you to give the **Plan Version**. After selecting your **Plan Version**, click on the Continue button, as shown in the following screenshot:

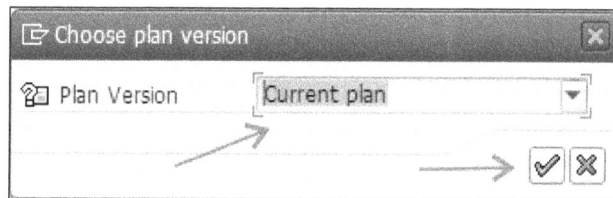

Let's say we want to maintain the Plan Version. We can do this by accessing the configurable tables via a particular node or directly via table maintenance. We have to execute the SM30/SM31 T-code and then enter the table name, as shown in the following screenshot:

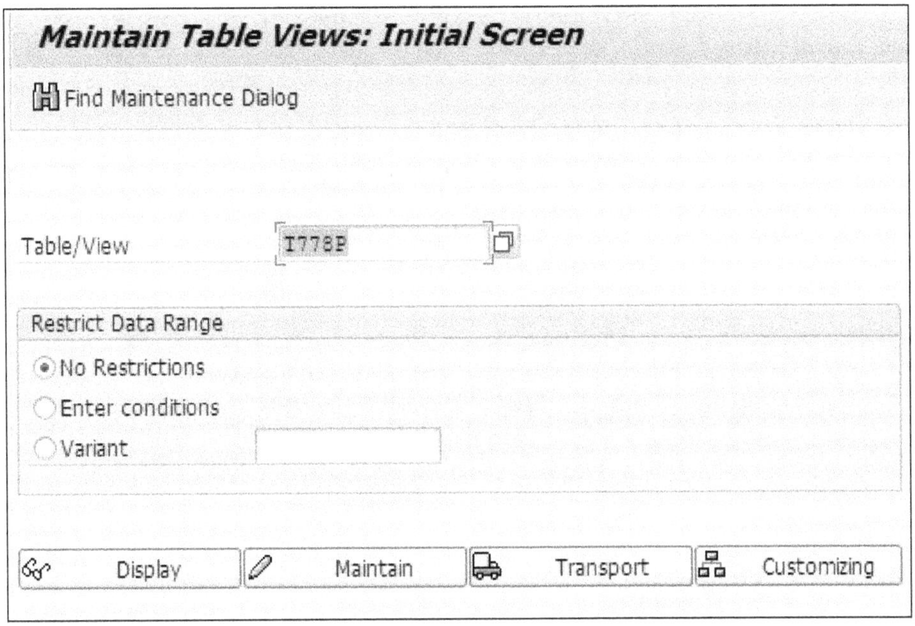

Maintain Table Views: Initial Screen

[H] Find Maintenance Dialog

Table/View   I778P [▢]

Restrict Data Range

◉ No Restrictions
○ Enter conditions
○ Variant   [   ]

| ✂ Display | / Maintain | 🚚 Transport | 品 Customizing |

Clicking on the **Maintain** button will take us to a configurable table, as shown in the following screenshot:

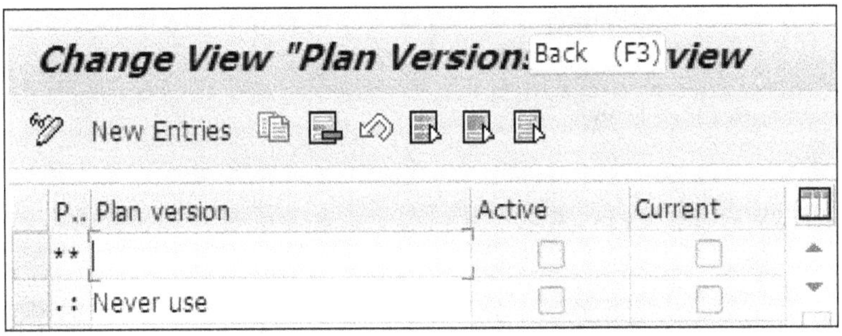

Change View "Plan Version. Back (F3) view

✏ New Entries 🗐 🖳 ◇ 🖹 🖹 🖹

P..	Plan version	Active	Current	▦
**	[ ]	☐	☐	▲
.:	Never use	☐	☐	▼

We can also go directly to the node by clicking on **Customizing**. This is shown in the following screenshot:

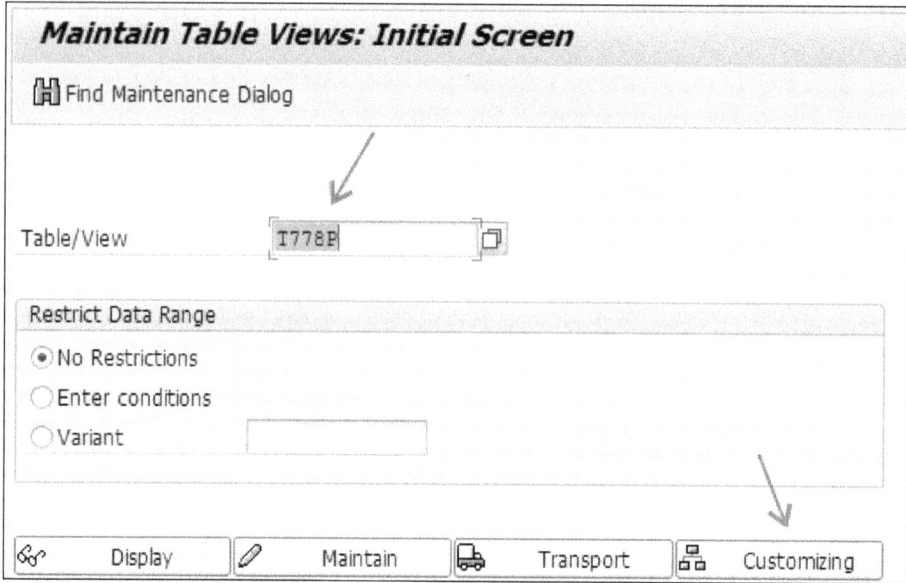

Once we click on the **Customizing** button, the following screen appears; click on **Continue w/o Specifying Project**:

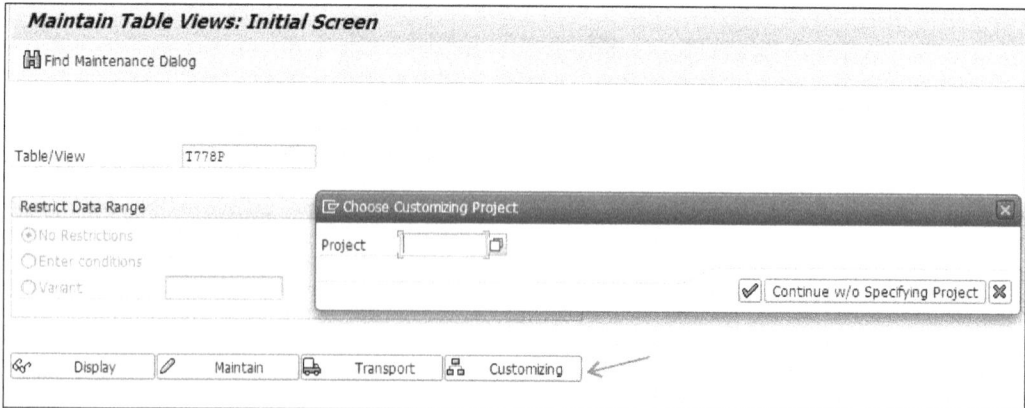

After clicking on **Continue w/o Specifying Project**, the **IMG activities overview window** appears; click on **Global Settings in Personnel Management**:

Implementation guide	IMG activity
Global Settings in Personnel Management	Maintain Plan Versions
Learning Solution	Maintain Plan Versions
Room Reservation Management (SIMG_OHP4)	Maintain plan versions
Training and Event Management (SIMG_OHP3)	Maintain Plan Versions

After clicking on **Global Settings in Personnel Management**, click on the Continue button, as shown in the following screenshot:

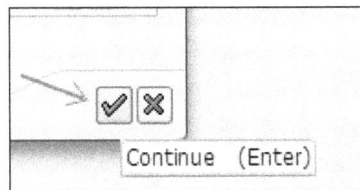

After clicking on the Continue button, we will see the **Maintain Plan Versions** node, as shown in the following screenshot:

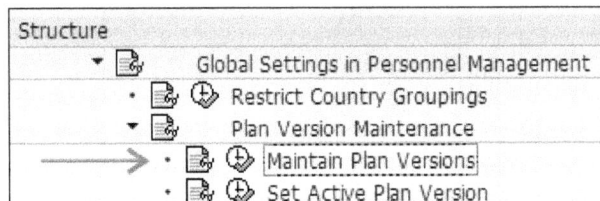

After clicking on the **Maintain Plan Versions** node, the **Plan Versions** screen will appear, as shown in the following screenshot:

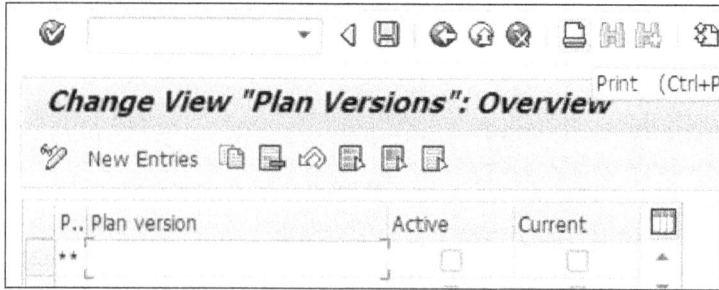

In the preceding screenshot, you'll find the Print icon; click on it or press *Ctrl + P*. The following screenshot appears:

Creating an organizational structure using the Expert Mode

We will now see how the organizational structure is created via **Expert Mode** by navigating to **SAP Easy Access | Human Resources | Organizational Management | Expert Mode | PO10 – Organizational Unit**. The following screenshot shows how this is done:

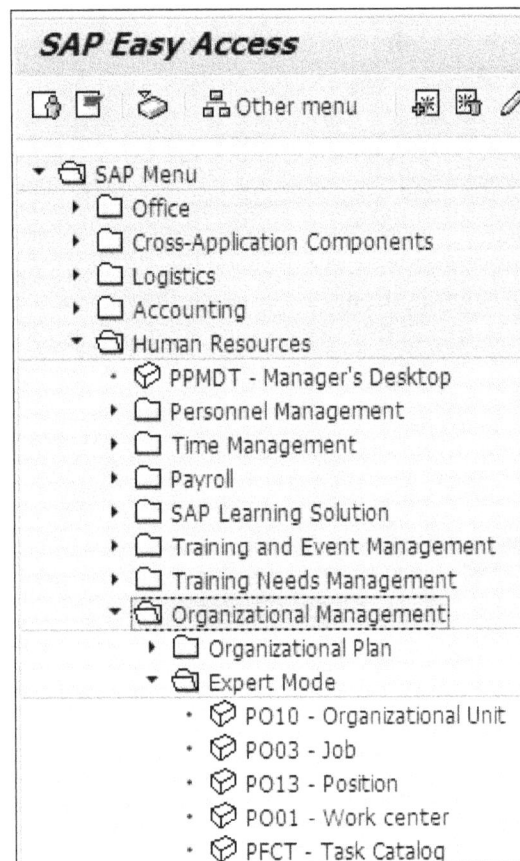

We can perform the preceding steps directly via the PO10 T-code.

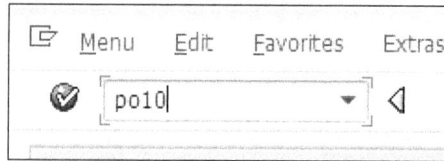

It's known as "Expert Mode" simply because you must have a good understanding of the object types and relationships to build the structure using this interface. The following screenshot shows the status of the structure:

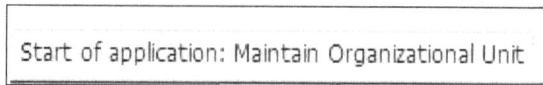

Start of application: Maintain Organizational Unit

As seen in the preceding screenshot, we will see the status indicating that it starts the application to build the organizational unit. The following screenshot shows how an object is created:

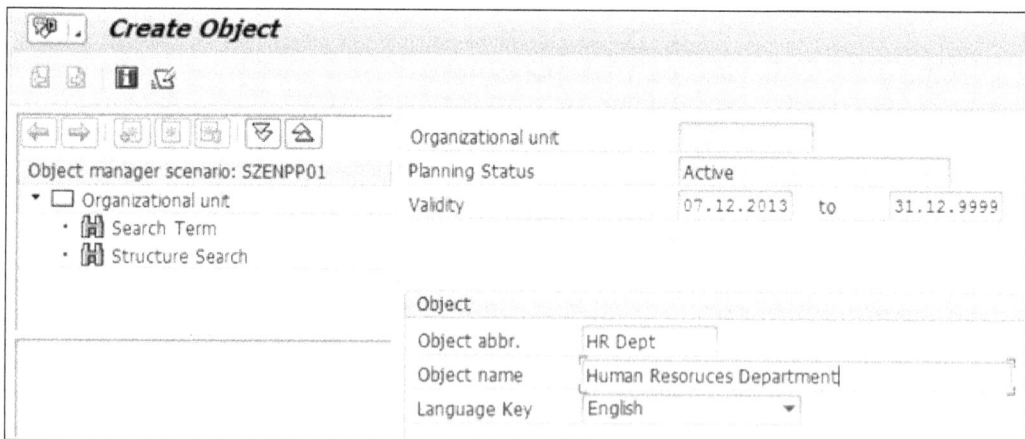

To create positions, we navigate to **SAP Easy Access | Human Resources | Organizational Management | Expert Mode | PO13 - Positions**. This is demonstrated in the following screenshot:

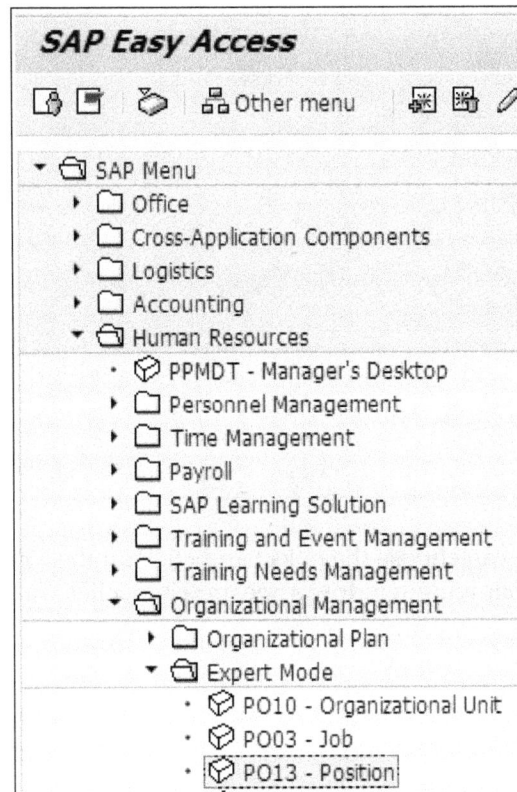

We can perform the preceding steps directly via the PO13 T-code. The following screenshot shows the **Maintain Position** window that appears after creating a Position:

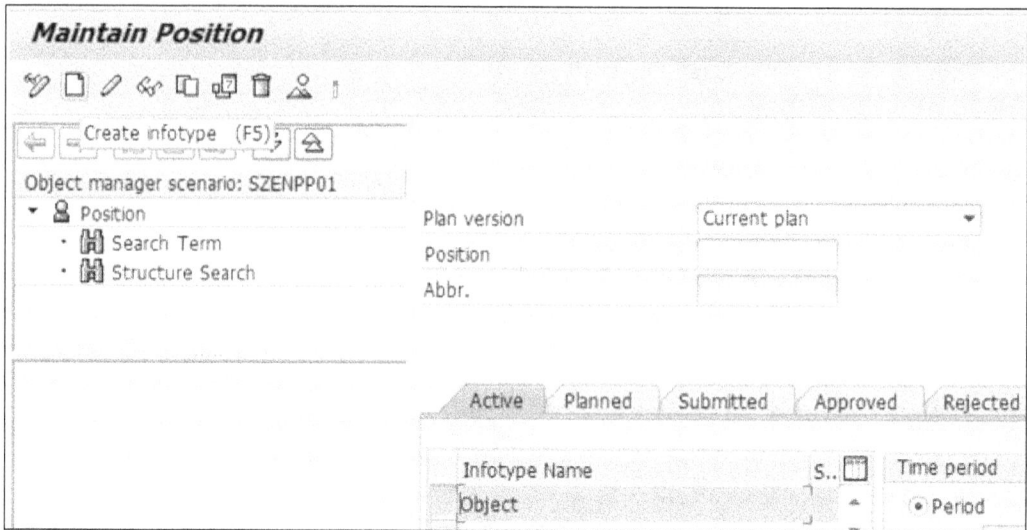

To create an object, we can choose the object and click on the Create infotype (or press *F5*) and the following window appears. Then, click on the Save:

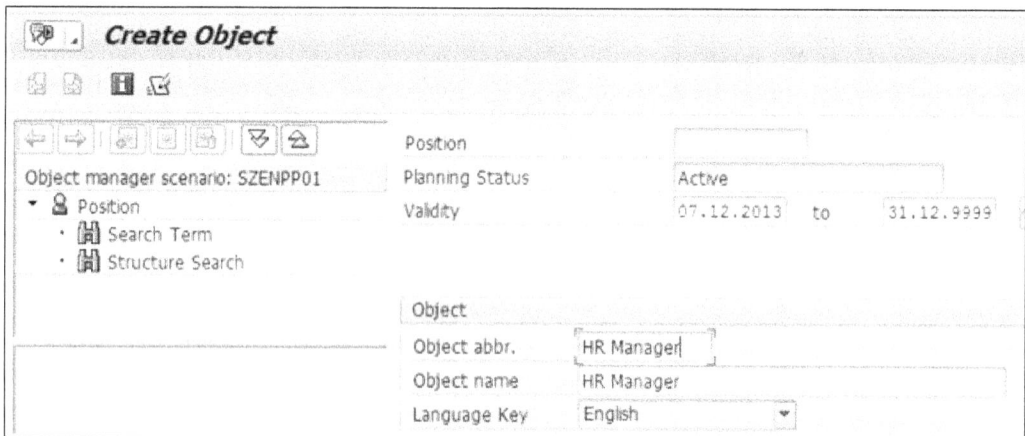

To create Jobs, we navigate to **SAP Easy Access | Human Resources | Organizational Management | Expert Mode | PO03 - Jobs**, as shown in the following screenshot:

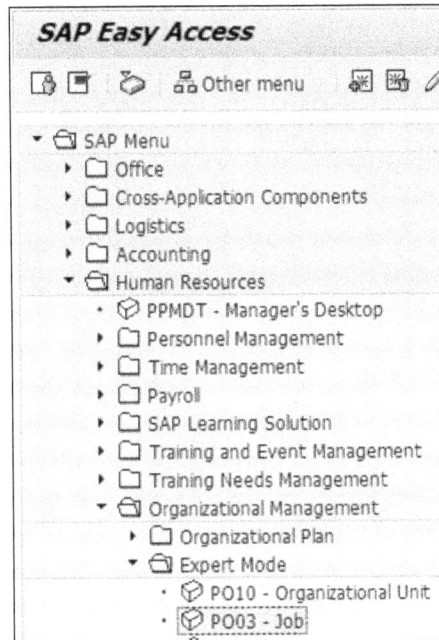

We can perform the preceding steps directly via the PO03 T-code. The following window appears after creating an object:

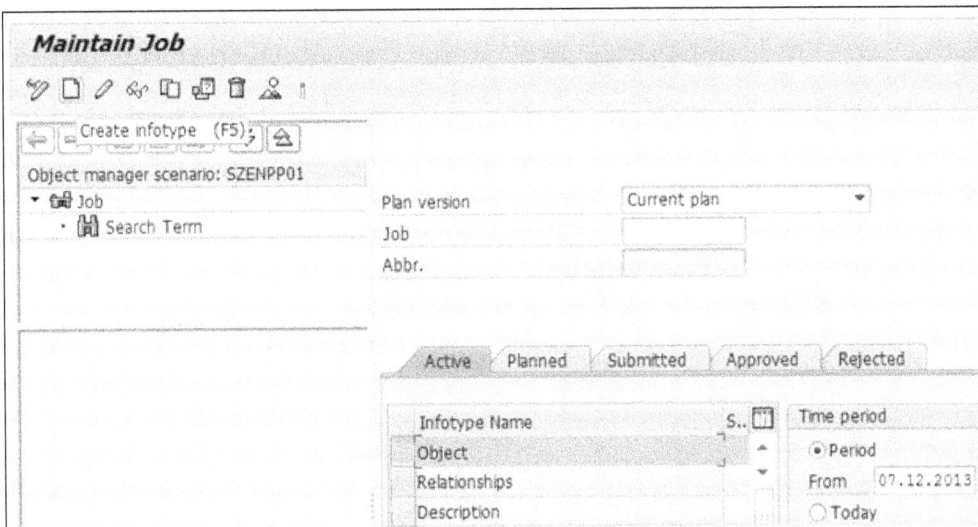

Choose an object, click on the Create infotype button seen in the preceding screenshot, then enter the required fields in the following **Create Object** window, and click on the Save button:

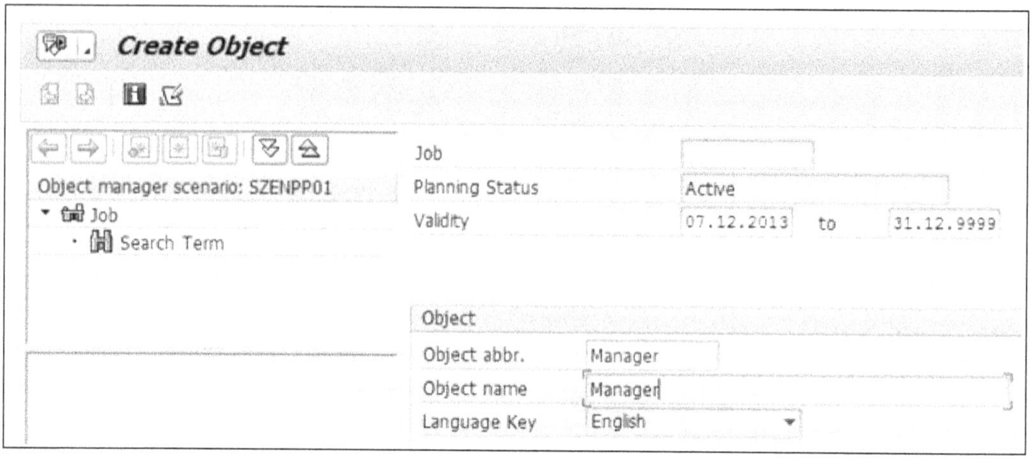

Configuring the table

For the table configuration steps, the **Data Browser** screen needs to be used. Then, enter the table name (for example, hrp1000), as seen in the following screenshot:

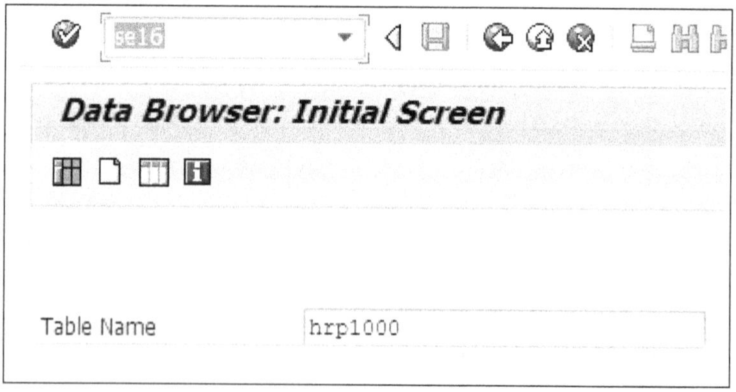

Once we enter the table name, the respective table comes up, as seen in the following screenshot:

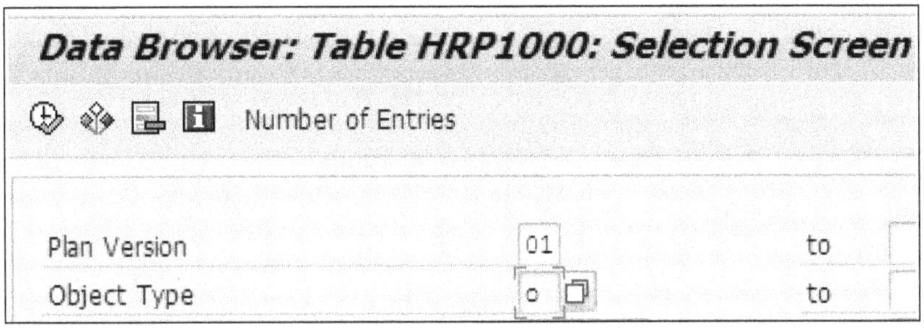

Data Browser: Table HRP1000: Selection Screen

Number of Entries

Plan Version	01	to
Object Type	o	to

The relationship between objects is always two-sided such as A/B, where A is the bottom-up approach and B is the top-down approach. The relationship with Cost Center is always one side; it is represented by A011.

The relationship between object types is maintained in the HRP1001 table. This can be seen in the following screenshot:

Data Browser: Table HRP1001: Selection Screen

Number of Entries

Object Type	O	to
Object ID	1	to
Plan Version	01	to
Relationship	B	to
Relat'ship	002	to

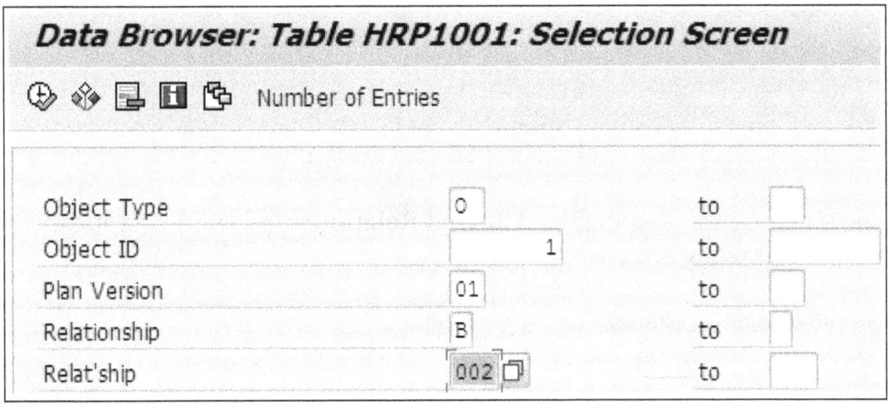

The permitted relationships are stored in the T777E table. The OOVK T-code gives us the completed view of the Relationship between Objects. We can check using the SM30 or SM31 T-code, as seen in the following screenshot:

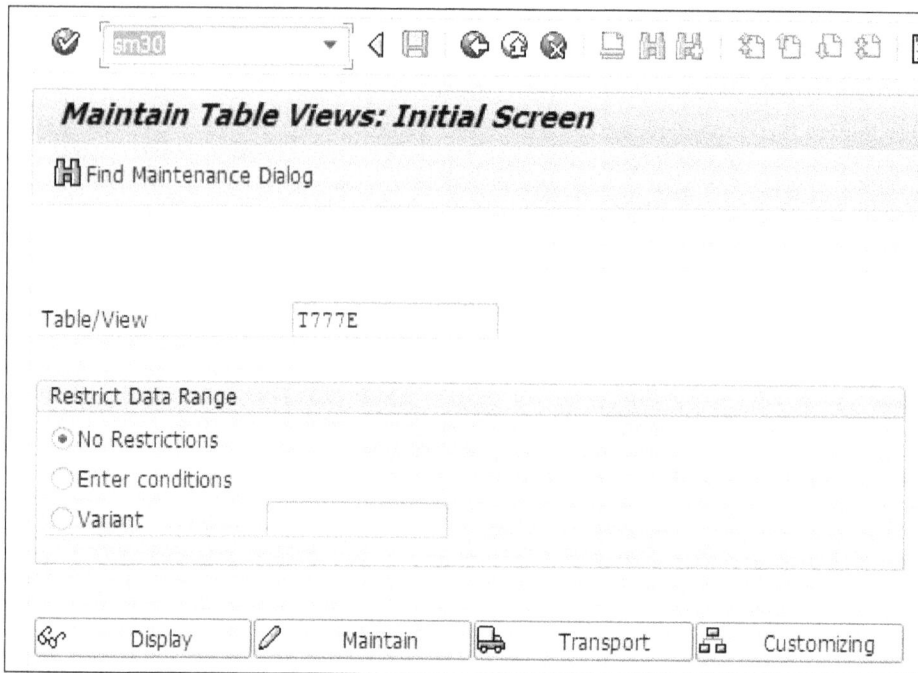

Using the SM30 or SM31 T-code, the **Allowed Relationships** window appears as shown in the following screenshot:

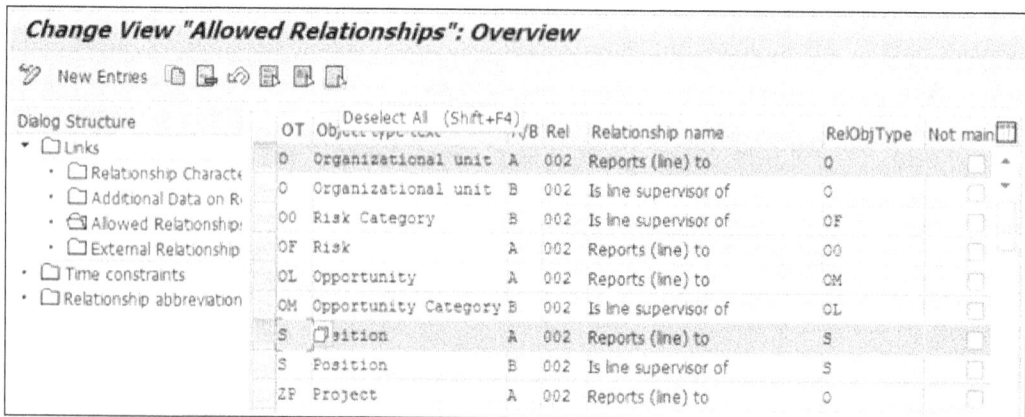

Integrating Organization Management with Personnel Administration

The dataflow between the Organizational Management and Personnel Administration submodules is controlled via a system table.

Integration switches

A system table can be accessed via multiple ways, directly via **SPRO**, T-code, or via table maintenance. We will explore all the methods in detail.

First, we will access a system table by navigating to **SPRO | Personnel Management | Organizational Management | Integration | Integration with Personnel Administration | Set up Integration with Personnel Administration**. The navigation path is shown in the following screenshot:

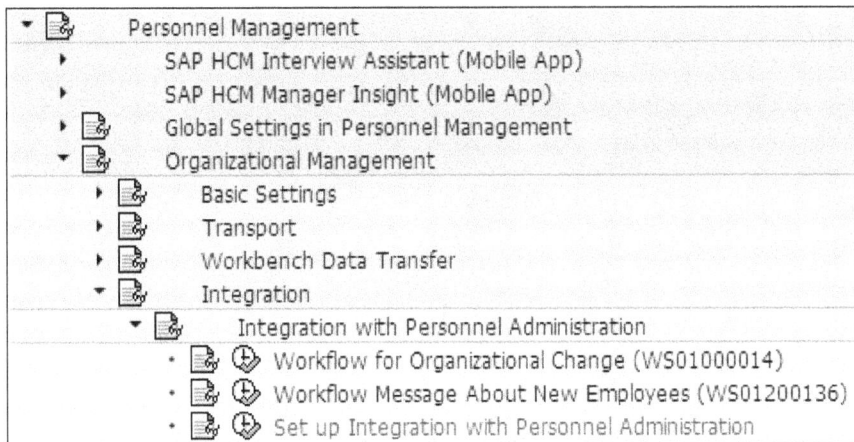

Secondly, we will access the system table via the SM30/SM31 table maintenance T-code. The following screenshot appears after executing the T-code:

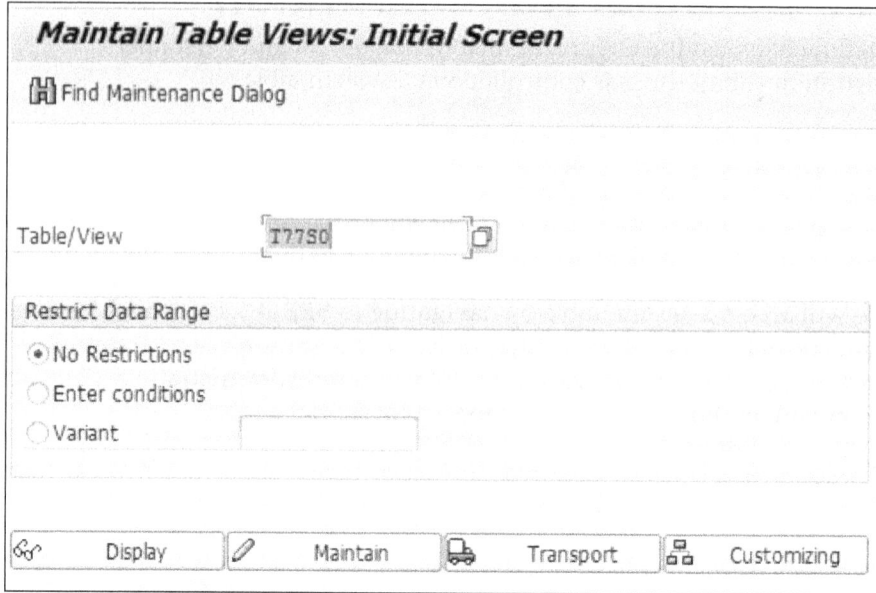

Finally, we will access the system table via the OOPS T-code, as shown in the following screenshot:

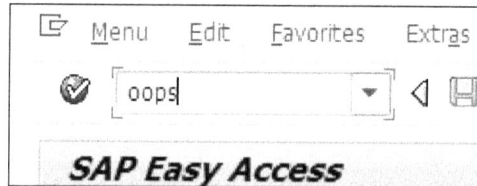

After executing the OOPS T-code, the HR Master Data Integration window in the following screenshot appears:

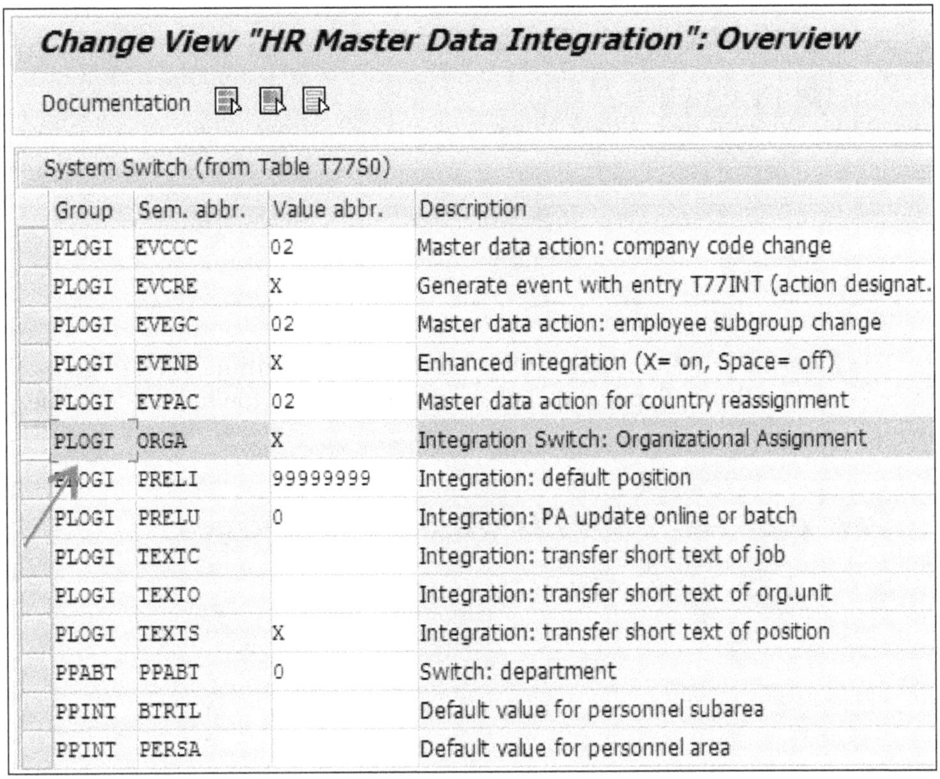

Change View "HR Master Data Integration": Overview

Documentation 🗎 🗎 🗎

System Switch (from Table T77S0)

Group	Sem. abbr.	Value abbr.	Description
PLOGI	EVCCC	02	Master data action: company code change
PLOGI	EVCRE	X	Generate event with entry T77INT (action designat.
PLOGI	EVEGC	02	Master data action: employee subgroup change
PLOGI	EVENB	X	Enhanced integration (X= on, Space= off)
PLOGI	EVPAC	02	Master data action for country reassignment
PLOGI	ORGA	X	Integration Switch: Organizational Assignment
PLOGI	PRELI	99999999	Integration: default position
PLOGI	PRELU	0	Integration: PA update online or batch
PLOGI	TEXTC		Integration: transfer short text of job
PLOGI	TEXTO		Integration: transfer short text of org.unit
PLOGI	TEXTS	X	Integration: transfer short text of position
PPABT	PPABT	0	Switch: department
PPINT	BTRTL		Default value for personnel subarea
PPINT	PERSA		Default value for personnel area

In the preceding screenshot, X denotes that data transfer from OM and PA is active. The changes made in the PA side of the world can be transferred to the OM side using Data Transfer reports that we will see in the following section.

The PLOGI table actually holds the object types and object IDs that can be accessed via the SE16 table, which is the **Data Browser** window:

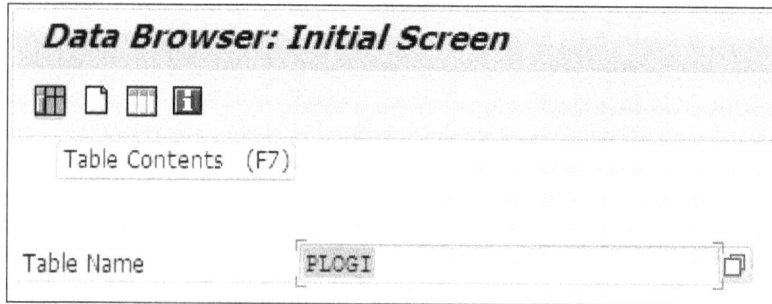

In the **Data Browser** window, click on the Table Contents button. We can give the **Plan Version**, **Object Type**, and click on the Execute button as shown in the following screenshot:

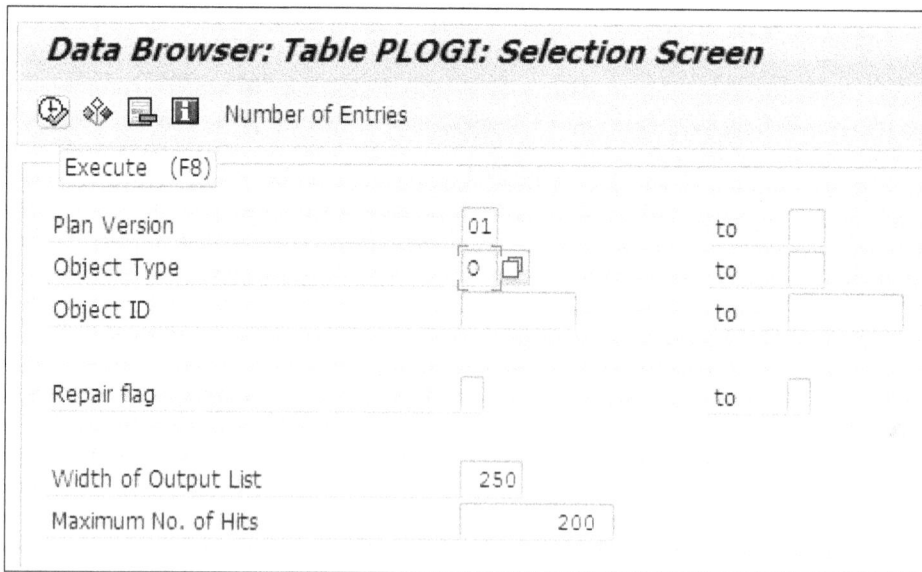

The following screenshot shows the next window that shows the selected entries:

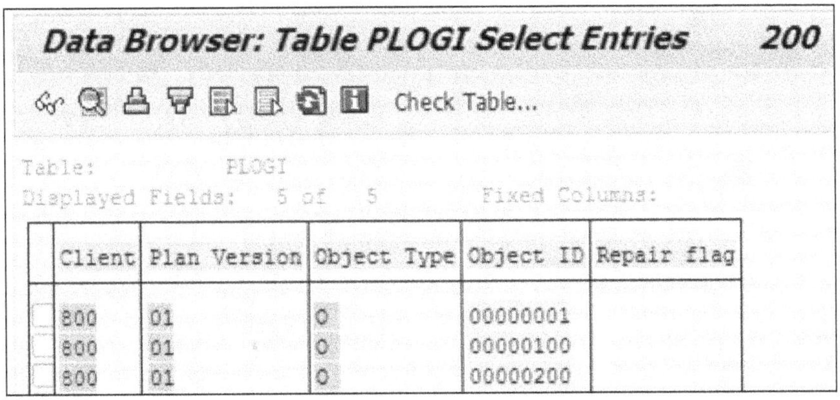

Data Browser: Table PLOGI Select Entries   200

             Check Table...

Table: PLOGI
Displayed Fields: 5 of   5   Fixed Columns:

	Client	Plan Version	Object Type	Object ID	Repair flag
	800	01	O	00000001	
	800	01	O	00000100	
	800	01	O	00000200	

Data Transfer Tools

There are standard data transfer reports provided by SAP; these reports facilitate the transfer of objects between the OM and PA submodules. They help the PA and OM submodules to be in sync after they are executed. The reports can be accessed via the SE38 or SA38 T-code, which opens the **ABAP Editor** window wherein you can enter the **Program** T-code as shown in the following screenshot:

ABAP Editor: Initial Screen

                Debugging   With Variant   Variants

Program   rhinte00   Create

Subobjects

● Source Code
○ Variants
○ Attributes
○ Documentation
○ Text elements

  Display   Change

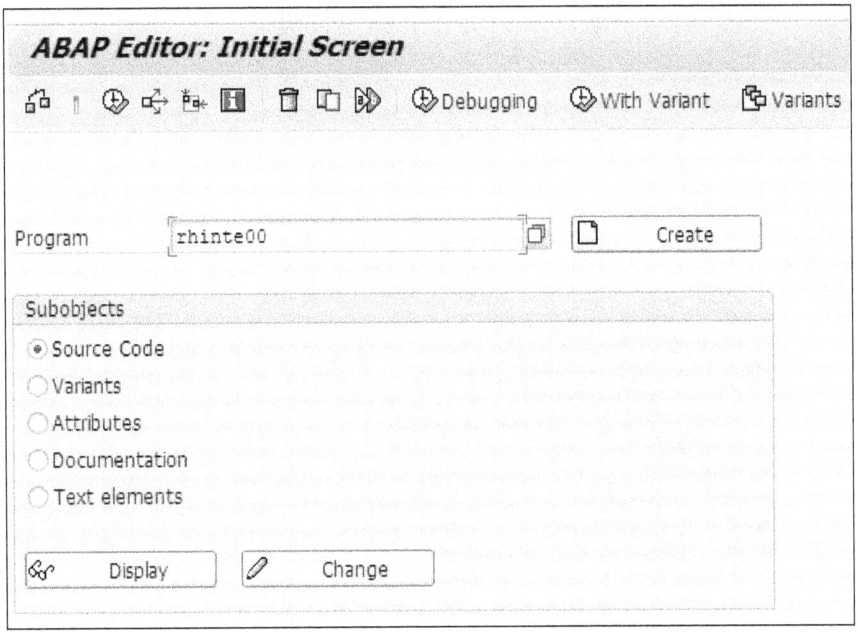

RHINTE Reports

The RHINTE00, RHINTE10, RHINTE20, and RHINTE30 tools facilitate data transfer from OM to PA and vice versa.

Let's explore RHINTE00 with a scenario. Say, we have uploaded Master in the Personnel Administration side, and we see the Org data in the 0001 infotype. However, we don't find the Position and Person mapping in the OM side. In this case, we will make use of RHINTE00, which opens the following window after it is executed.

After selecting the **Personnel Number**, the **Report-Specific Settings** window appears as follows:

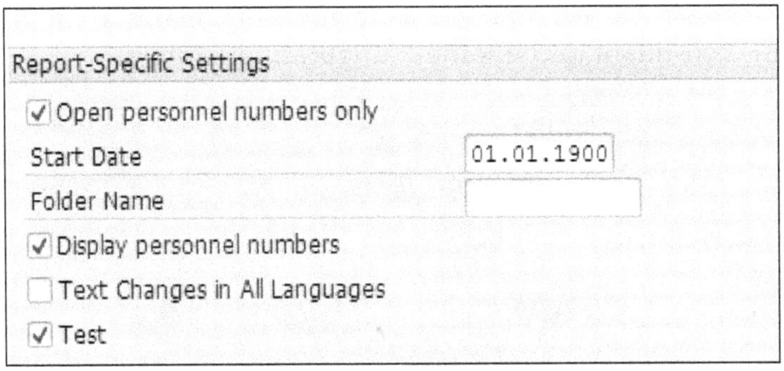

Report-Specific Settings	
☑ Open personnel numbers only	
Start Date	01.01.1900
Folder Name	
☑ Display personnel numbers	
☐ Text Changes in All Languages	
☑ Test	

We will unflag the **Test** run and execute RHINTE00. Then, we will execute the SM37 T-code to check the scheduled Job as shown in the following screenshot:

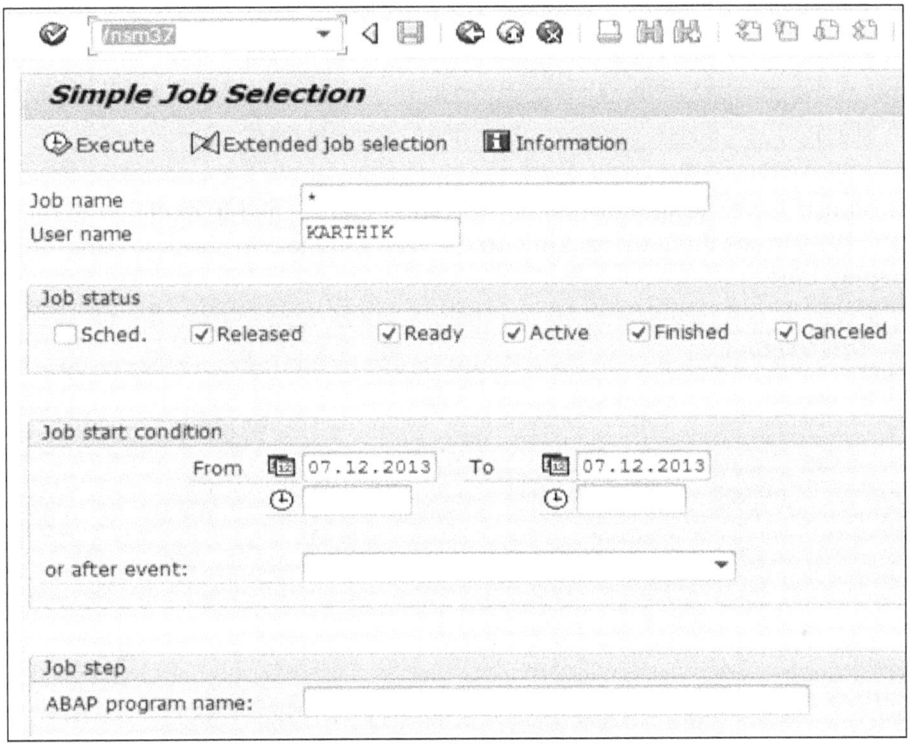

Once we process the Job, we will be able to execute the T-code. The Job will be listed with the name of the Job and the user ID.

The purpose of the OM tool

The **RHINTECHECK** tool is a very useful tool to use to check inconsistencies in integration. The missing object type and its relationship, if any, are highlighted, and it allows the consultant to check the configuration settings.

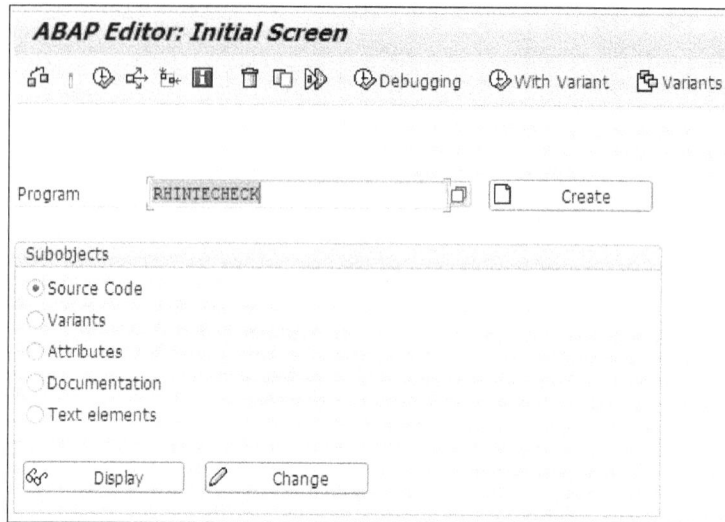

All the reports have the standard documentation maintained to explain the report purpose. We can see them by clicking on the **Documentation** checkbox and then on the **Display** button.

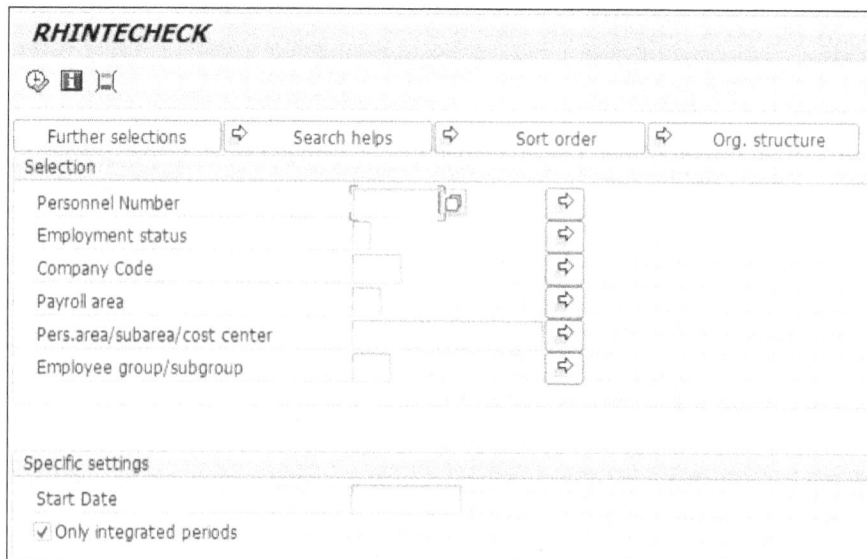

Summary

In this chapter, we have covered all the interfaces provided by SAP to design and develop the organizational structure. We have learned various T-codes and table names to configure the OM submodule. We have also covered the data-transfer tools provided that serve as an integration point between the OM and PA submodules.

In the next chapter, we will closely look at configuring the Personnel Administration submodule and explore the standard functionalities provided by SAP.

4
PA Configuration in Less Than 24 Hours

In this chapter, we will explore how **Personnel Administration** (**PA**) is configured to meet a client's requirements. We will see how different infotypes are configured to meet the business requirements.

In this chapter, we are going to cover the following topics:

- Personnel Administration infotypes
- Important infotypes and their configuration
- Configuring the submodule
- Configuring personnel action

Personnel Administration infotypes

Infotype is a four-digit number, and nnnn is assigned to each infotype. The number range 9,000 to 9,999 is reserved for customer and not standard SAP. Personnel administration is everything to do with the master data of an employee. The details of the employee are captured in infotypes.

The details of an employee such as personal data, bank details, and address are all captured in infotypes. The employee details such as which associated department he or she belong to, his or her current position, and his or her personal details such as date of birth, residential address, pay details, bank details, and so on, are captured using this submodule.

Standard PA infotypes are in the range of 0000-0999. Each number has a name associated with it. For instance, 0002 is personal data. We will cover all the mandatory infotypes in the following chapters. Customer or customized infotypes are in the range of 9,000-9,999. There are some country-specific infotypes such as court orders/student loans GB (infotype 0070), which is specific to Great Britain.

Important infotypes that are mandatory and their configuration steps

There are some important infotypes that need to be maintained for processing the payroll and time. They are as follows:

- **0000** (Actions)
- **0001** (Organization Assignment)
- **0002** (Personal Data)
- **0006** (Address)
- **0007** (Planned Working Time)
- **0008** (Basic Pay)
- **0009** (Bank Details)

> The 0003 infotype (Payroll Status) is created automatically when the hiring action is performed; we will learn about this infotype in the following chapters.

Functions of infotypes

Let's quickly cover the functionalities of each infotype in detail.

The 0000 (Actions) infotype

The Actions infotype is an important infotype that captures the activities surrounding an employee from, say, hiring to separation.

When the employee is hired, the action type is "hire", and when there is another activity such as promotion or reassignment that needs to be performed, then again there is a different action type.

Each action has a start and end date to capture the history of the activities. Let's say the hire action is performed on January 01, 2013 (the start date). Another action is performed, for example, the employee is promoted on December 01, 2013. In this scenario, there will be two line items to capture the history.

The Actions infotype also clearly illustrates the reason for performing a particular action. For example, hire can be an action type, and the reason for performing the hiring action could be replacement. These fields are very useful for reporting and administrative purposes, as demonstrated in the following screenshot:

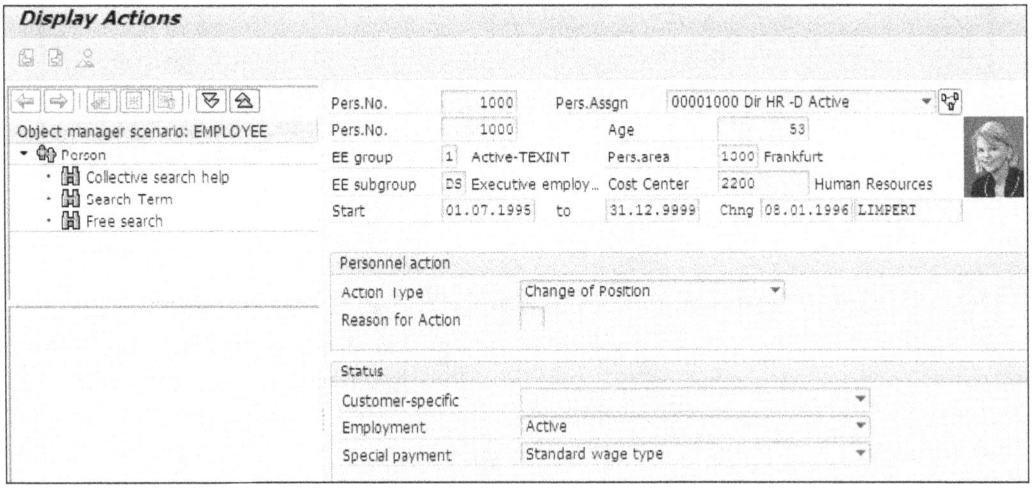

> Important activities such as change of address, addition of a family member, change in bank details, and so on, are not considered as actions but as part of the master data maintenance.

The Actions infotype also has an important configurable field that shows the employment status of an employee with the company. They are standard SAP values, and each one has a meaning. The standard employment statuses are as follows:

- Active
- Inactive
- Retiree
- Withdrawn

The status is maintained in the T529U table, and it can be accessed via SE16 or V_T529U in the SM30/31 T-code, as demonstrated in the following screenshot:

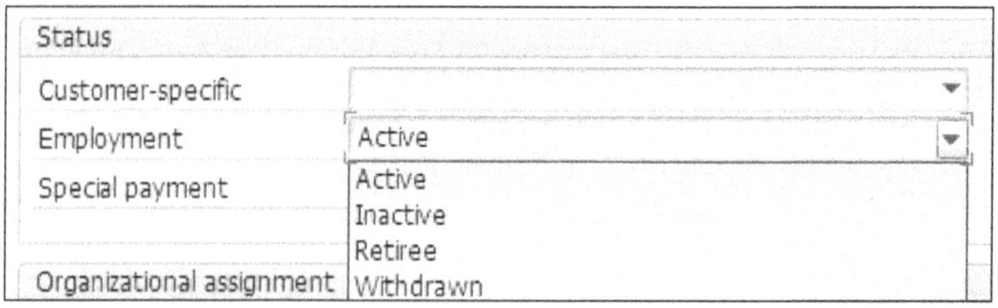

Multiple actions can be performed in a single day. However, the status of the employee cannot be changed from active to inactive on the same day. Virtual infotype and Additional Actions infotype 0302 are used to take advantage of the functionality of capturing multiple actions on the same day.

The 0001 (Organization Assignment) infotype

The Organizational Assignment infotype is of prime importance, because it holds key employee information such as the geographical location, position, department, and so on. It's one of the key infotypes for both organizational and administrative purposes. This is an important infotype for the control of payroll and for authorization purposes. This infotype has employee integration in the following structures:

- Enterprise structure
- Personnel structure
- Organizational structure

The enterprise structure is the connection between the company and company code (legal entity or profit and loss) level. The personnel structure demonstrates the connection between the employee and employer. The organization structure is the functional connection of the employee or, in other words, the employee positioned in the company.

The integration point between PA and OM applies in this infotype, as demonstrated in the following screenshot:

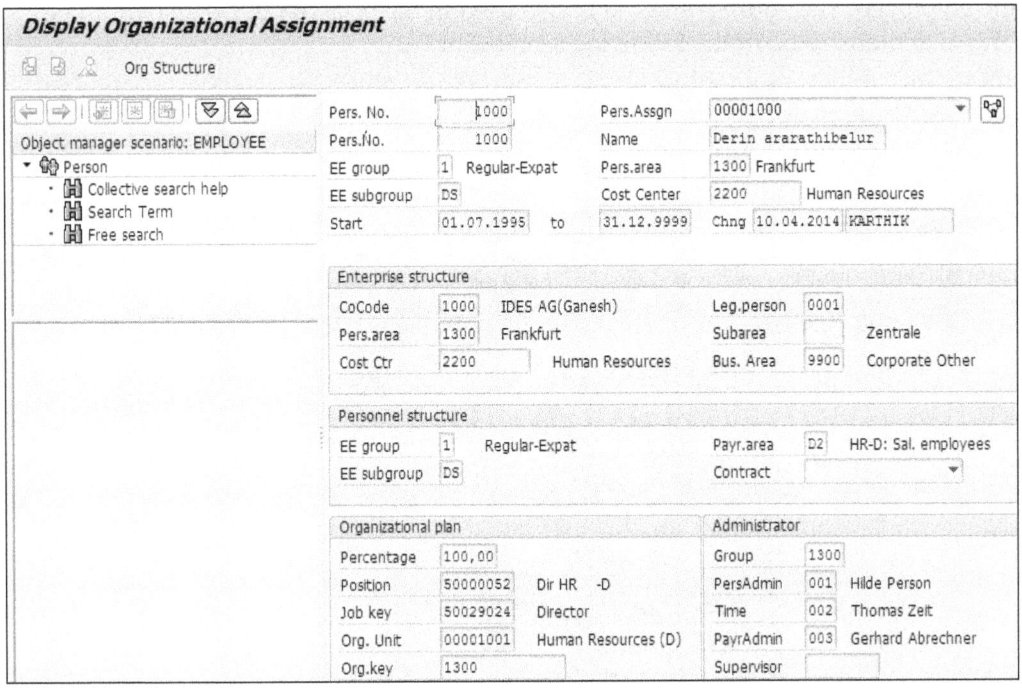

The important payroll-related control feature, payroll area, is captured in these infotypes. This helps all the employees to be grouped together when the payroll is processed. The master cost center is default in this infotype. This infotype also holds the key to an organization; this key can be used for authorization purposes, if necessary.

The 0002 (Personal Data) infotype

The Personal Data infotype is used to capture an employee's first name, last name, marital status, and date of birth.

> The start date of Personal Data infotype is the birth date. If we note, in this case, the date of birth of the employee is September 05, 1960, and the start date of the employee is September 05, 1960.

The 0006 (Address) infotype

The Address infotype is used to capture the permanent and temporary addresses of the employee. The address entered is also used in the 0009 (Bank Details) infotype. This is demonstrated in the following screenshot:

The 0007 (Planned Working Time) infotype

The Planned Working Time infotype is used to capture the work schedule of the employee. Using this infotype, the employee's stipulated working time can be captured. This is a crucial infotype that is useful for payroll. The holiday calendar is linked directly/indirectly through this infotype.

The daily/weekly work pattern is captured in this infotype. We can also get the total amount of work done on a daily, weekly, and monthly basis through this infotype. This is customized by navigating to **IMG | Time Management | Work Schedule Rule | Work Schedule Rules and Work Schedules**. We will cover this exhaustively in *Chapter 5, Time Management Configuration – Negative Time*. The following screenshot demonstrates this infotype:

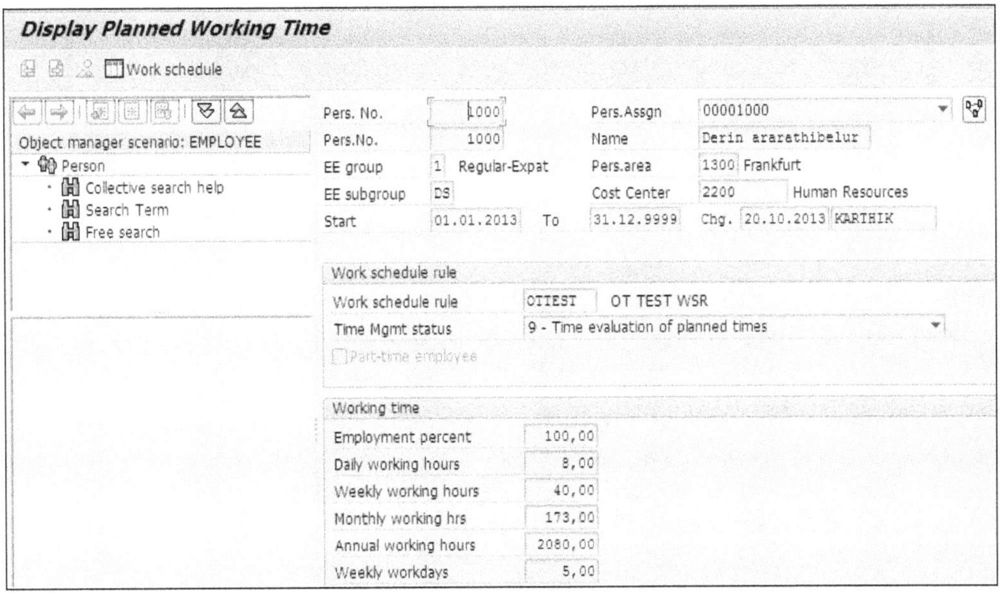

Display Planned Working Time

The work schedule will give us a detailed planned working time of the employee. The employment percentage is passed on to the Basic Pay infotype as capacity utilization level. The data flows from the Time Management submodule to the Personnel Administration submodule when the Basic Pay infotype details are maintained in the system, as shown in the following screenshot:

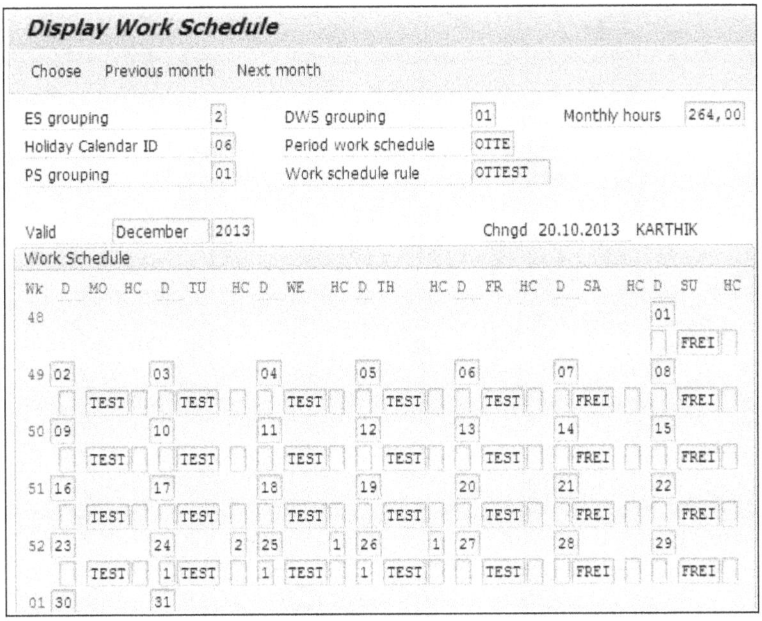

Display Work Schedule

> The T588M infotype screen control has the feature of hiding or maintaining the required fields of an infotype. It can also be accessed by navigating to **SPRO | Personnel Management | Personnel Administration | Customising user interfaces | Change Screen Modifications**.

The 0008 (Basic Pay) infotype

The Basic Pay infotype is used to capture the fixed pay components/earnings drawn by the employee. The employee industry type and physical location-specific details are captured in the form of payscale type and area.

The components captured in the Basic Pay infotype are referred to as wage types, and we will cover them exhaustively in *Chapter 6, Payroll Configuration*. For example, housing allowance and conveyance allowance are referred to as wage types, and they have a number and text to identify them.

The integration point between time and payroll is also evident in this infotype. We will see the capacity utilization level fed from the value stored in the 0007 (Planned Working Time) infotype. The following screenshot shows the Basic Pay infotype:

The basic pay infotype can also be used to see the payslip. The configuration steps will be covered in the forthcoming chapters. The payroll driver program needs the Basic Pay (0008) infotype and the 0007 (Planned Working Time) infotype for calculating the salary gross to net.

The 0009 (Bank Details) infotype

The Bank Details infotype has the payment method of salary for the employee. The different payment methods that can be maintained are as follows:

- Cash
- Check
- Bank transfer

The following screenshot gives us a clear picture of the Bank Details infotype:

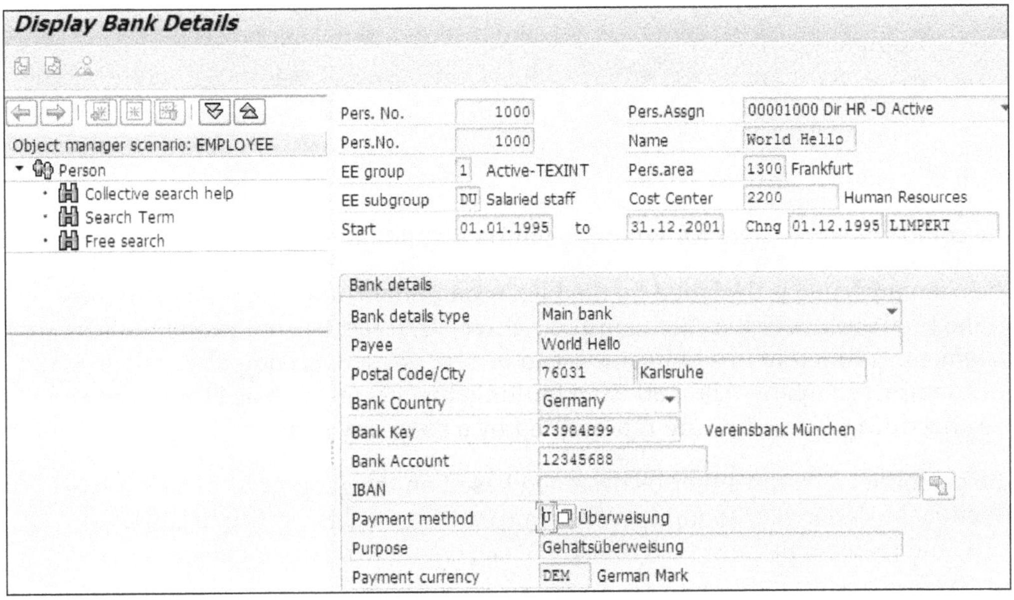

The name of the employee is populated from the 0002 (Personal Data) infotype, and the address populates from the 0006 (Address) infotype. The standard bank detail types provided by SAP are as follows:

- Main bank
- Other bank details
- Travel expenses

The account number is mandatory if the payment method is bank transfer.

> The payment is configured normally through the FICO module. However, it can also be done by an HCM consultant in liaison with a FICO consultant.

Configuration steps

The backbone of PA is a design of best practice enterprise and personnel structure. The design of the enterprise and personnel structure is crucial for both reporting and administrative purposes. It is also critical for processing the payroll and time functionalities. Let's look at the configuration steps of enterprise and personnel structure in detail.

What makes the enterprise structure?

The following components make up an enterprise structure:

- Company
- Company code
- Personnel area
- Personnel subarea

The company is the client for whom the implementation is done.

The company code is designed by the FICO component, and it actually depends on the legal entities of the client, or in other words, it has its own profit and loss statement. A different line of business can be represented as company code in SAP. For example, company ABC can have multiple businesses such as IT services and manufacturing. These two are represented by a company code.

The personnel area can either be designed based on the geographical location or functional location. For example, ABC company has its head office in Chicago, USA, and its plant in New York, USA. We can create two personnel areas.

The factors that influence the number of personnel areas needed are as follows:

- At least one personnel area is needed for each country
- The number of personnel areas needed depends on the reporting requirements
- It may depend on the number of plants, the number of states in which the company has offices, and so on
- It may depend on the authorization needs
- It may depend on the business needs in time management, payroll, and in benefits modules

> Personnel areas and subareas are four-digit alphanumeric code identifiers with long text.

Personnel subareas are a further bifurcation of personnel areas. The business characteristics are normally stored at the personnel subarea level. We will see groupings done in payroll and time management at personnel subareas and employee subgrouping levels.

What makes the personnel structure?

The following components make up the personnel structure:

- Employee group
- Employee subgroup
- Payroll area
- Organization key

The personnel structure can be designed for the purposes of both administrative and organization perspectives.

The employee group and subgroup define the relationship of the employee with the company. Say, for example, a full-time employee can be designed as employee group, and the different grades can be designed as employee subgroups such as grade A.

The payroll area allows us to group employees for whom the payroll is processed at the same time and in the same frequency, for example, monthly, bi-weekly, and so on.

Organization key is useful for authorization purpose, and its is a 14-digit key that also defines the enterprise and personnel structure.

The Organizational Assignment infotype (0001), as discussed earlier, holds the enterprise and personnel structure data of an employee, as seen in the following screenshot:

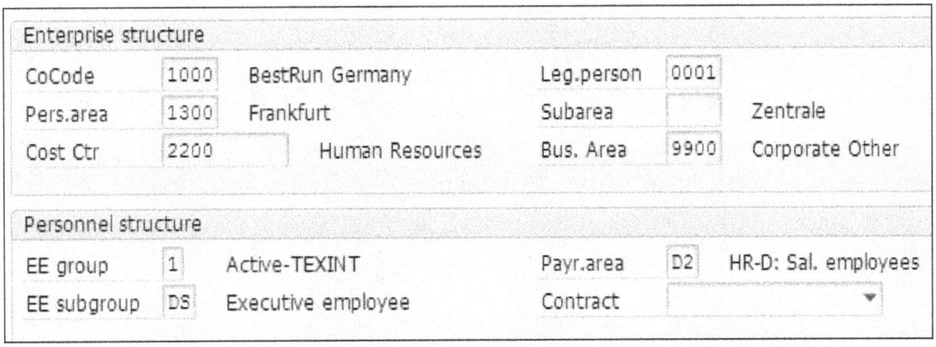

Enterprise structure					
CoCode	1000	BestRun Germany	Leg.person	0001	
Pers.area	1300	Frankfurt	Subarea		Zentrale
Cost Ctr	2200	Human Resources	Bus. Area	9900	Corporate Other

Personnel structure					
EE group	1	Active-TEXINT	Payr.area	D2	HR-D: Sal. employees
EE subgroup	DS	Executive employee	Contract		▼

Now, let's look at the configuration of enterprise and personnel structure in detail. The company and company code is created by a FICO consultant. However, we will see the steps for understanding it better.

The company is defined by a four-digit alphanumeric code, which represents the unit designed according to commercial and labor law. A company can have "N" number of company code (legal entities) that can be accessed by navigating to **SPRO | Enterprise Structure | Definition | Financial Accounting | Define company**. The following screenshot demonstrates this:

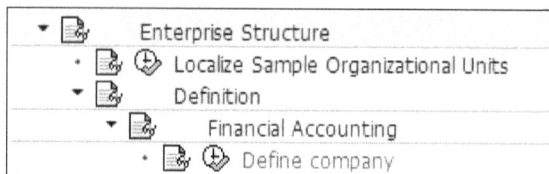

The company is defined by using a six-digit code. The long text is of 30 characters, and it can be alphanumeric.

> The best practice is to copy entries and rename entries (click on copy or press *F6*).

The following screenshot shows the list of entries for the company:

The next step is the creation of the company code. It can be accessed by navigating to **SPRO | Enterprise Structure | Definition | Financial Accounting | Edit, Copy, Delete, Check Company Code**.

The company code is below the company, and there can be "N" number of company codes mapped to a company, as shown in the following screenshot:

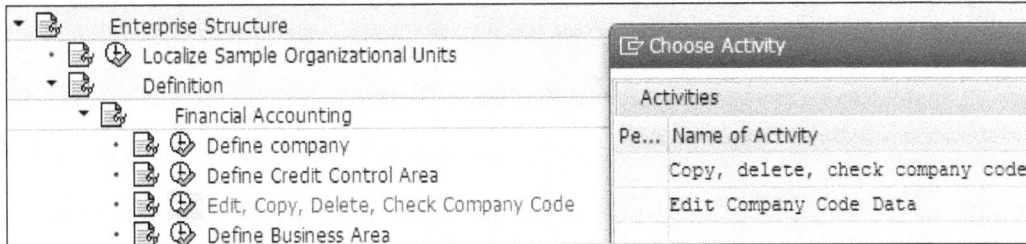

When the copy option is chosen, the related tables are automatically filled with entries, so it is advisable and the best practice in order to prevent a "No entry in table" error while performing a configuration. This is shown in the following screenshot:

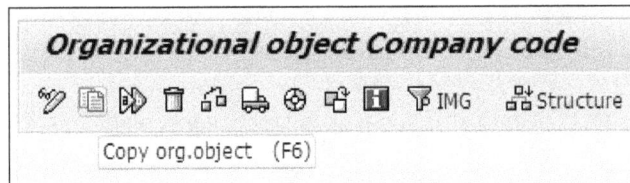

There will be many associated tables when an object is copied. The frequent pit falls while configuring could be "Customizing Error" or "No entry in table" error messages. Now, when we click on copy, it will ask us to enter the company code, as shown in the following screenshot:

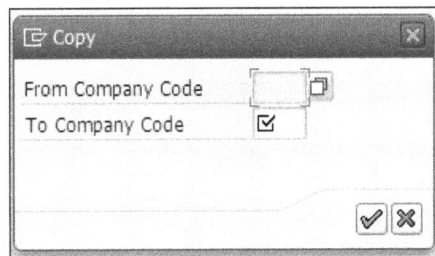

We need to give from the company code say, 1,000, and the company code is the one FI consultant creates which is, 9,000. The system throws a warning message; we need to click on **Yes** to proceed and confirm.

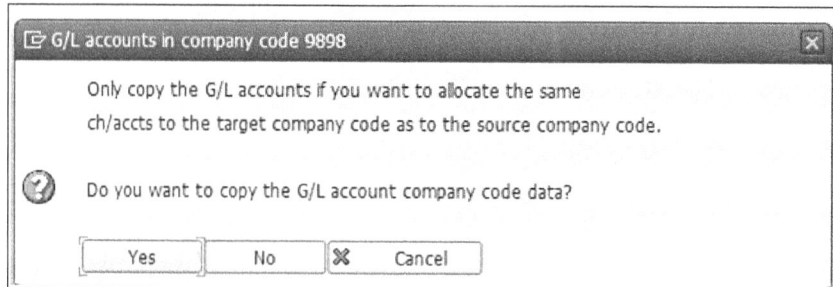

If we wish to allocate the same chart of accounts to the new company that we are defining, then we can click on **Yes**, or we can click on **No**, as shown in the following screenshot:

All the associated tables get copied when the action is performed. The objective here is to assign a different currency to the target company code we copied. Say, the reference company currency is Euro, while the target company code currency is USD. The system prompts a message that the copy action has been successfully carried out, as demonstrated in the following screenshot:

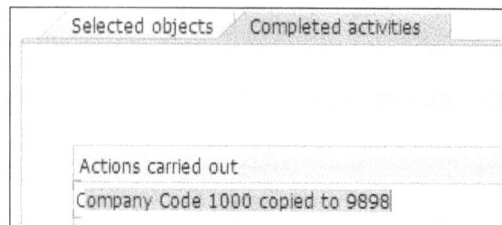

The other details about the company code such as the address, phone number, and so on can be entered by clicking on address (*Shift + F5*). The details that we enter here will be useful for reporting purpose. The following screenshot shows the various fields that are to be filled:

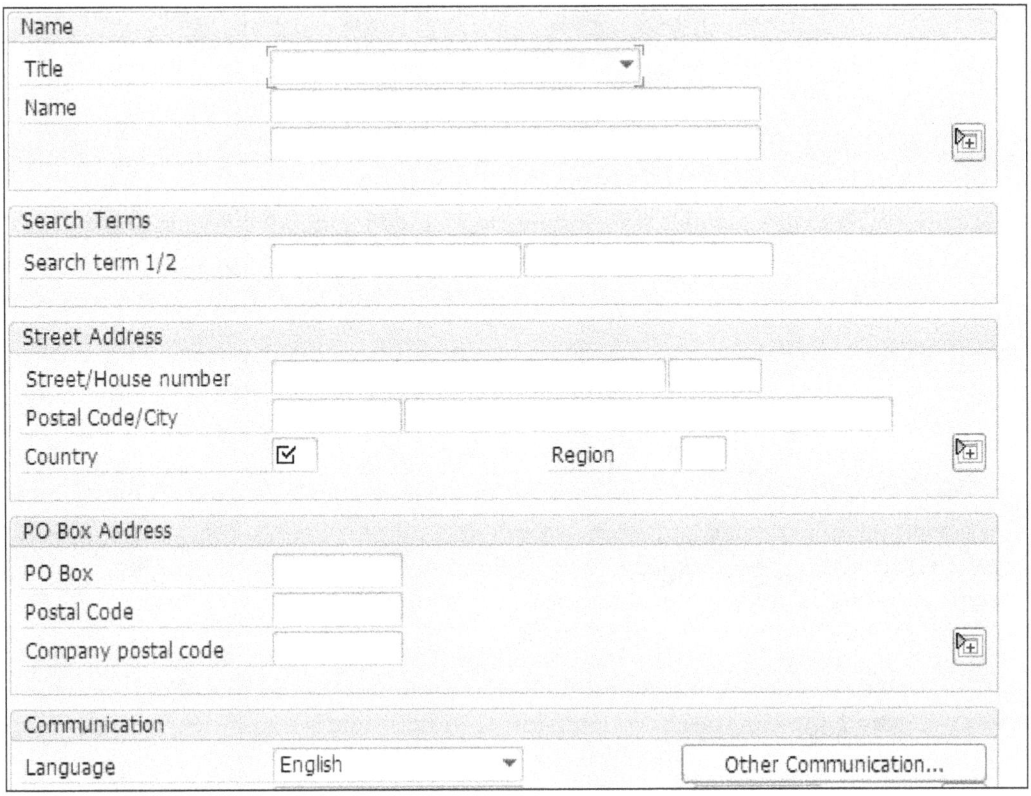

We have to define the personnel areas, subareas, employee group, and subgroups to do the assignment.

The design of enterprise and personnel structure is critical for the successful implementation of the project and mapping the client process in SAP. The best practice is to try out multiple designs before the blueprint is submitted to the client for execution.

The personnel area and subareas are defined by navigating to **SPRO | Enterprise Structure | Definition | Human Resource Management | Personnel Areas**. This is shown in the following screenshot:

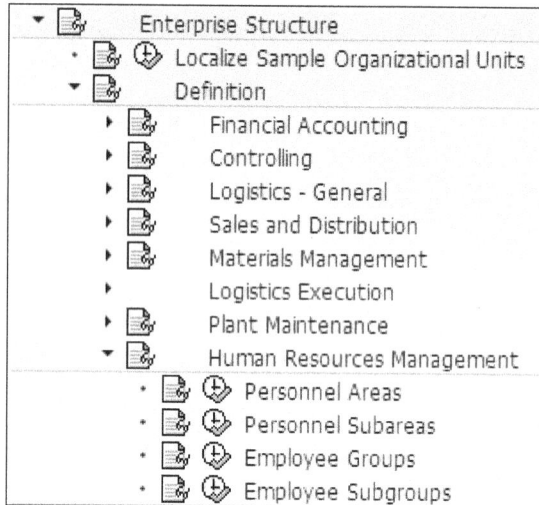

The personnel area defined can be used for reporting purpose, and they are organized according to the aspects of payroll, time, and personnel. It can be specific either to the geographical location or functional location. It is based on the client-business process and setup.

We can copy the entries from the existing SAP standard delivered personnel area and rename these entries to your customer-specific entries, as shown in the following screenshot:

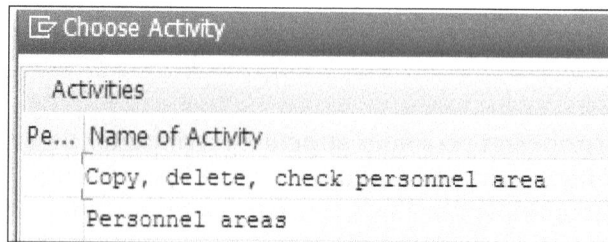

Click on **Copy**, **delete**, **check personnel area**, and give the form to the personnel area. "From" is basically the SAP standard personnel area, while" To" is the customer-specific entry. It is a four-digit alphanumeric code with the text name, as shown in the following screenshot:

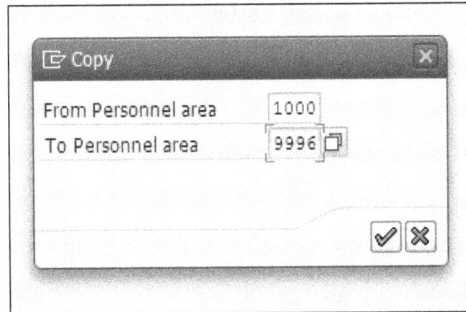

The personnel subarea holds the business characteristics. We use it for payroll and time, hence, it's critical that we get our design of the personnel area and subareas correct to have a smooth configuration and mapping of the business process in SAP.

A personnel area can have "N" number of personnel subareas.

The personnel subarea is defined by navigating to **SPRO** | **Enterprise Structure** | **Definition** | **Human Resource Management** | **Personnel Subareas**. This is shown in the following screenshot:

> The best practice is to prepare a **Key Data Structure** (KDS) in Excel. Copy and paste it in a table; it can save a lot of time and effort.

Click on **Create Personnel Subarea** and choose the personnel area for which the personnel subareas are mapped. This is demonstrated in the following screenshot:

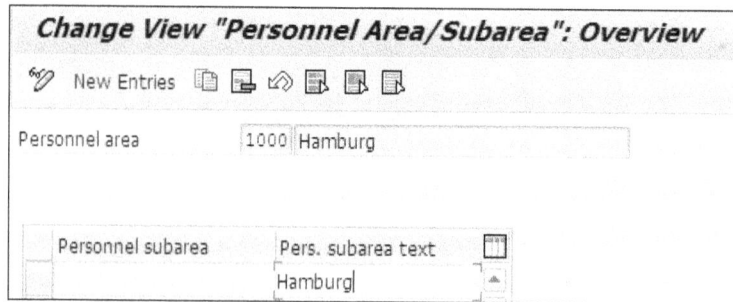

When we start defining the employee group and employee subgroups, we are ready with the personnel structure. The employee group is defined by navigating to **SPRO | Enterprise Structure | Definition | Human Resources Management | Employee Groups**. This is shown in the following screenshot:

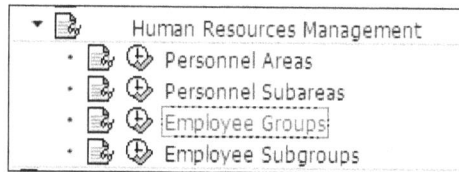

The employee group can also be defined directly via the T501 table. It is a one-digit alphanumeric code. It can also be a special character, as shown in the following screenshot:

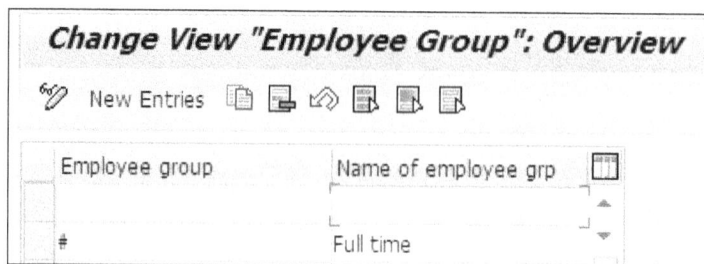

The employee subgroup is defined by navigating to **SPRO | Enterprise Structure | Definition | Human Resource Management | Employee Subgroups**.

It's a two-digit alphanumeric code and is mapped to employee group created in the earlier step. It is shown in the following screenshot:

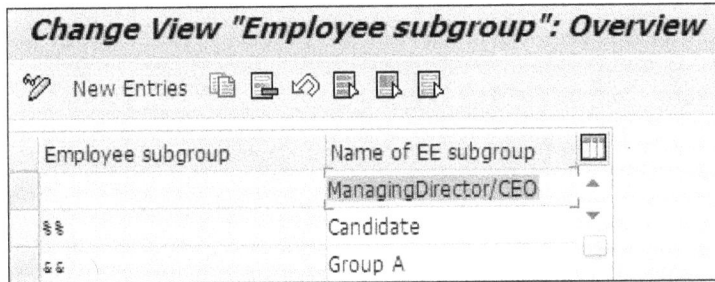

The configuration of enterprise and personnel structure is complete only when the mapping is done between company code, personnel area, employee group, and employee subgroups.

The assignment of company code to the company is done by navigating to **SPRO | Enterprise Structure | Assignment | Assign company code to company**. It is demonstrated in the following screenshot:

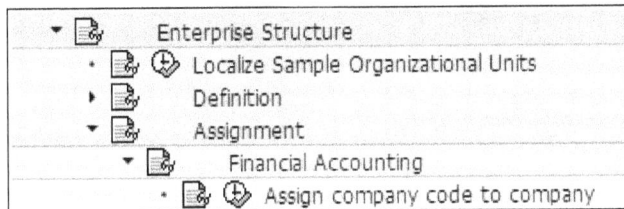

When the employee is hired, the company and the company code, by default, are automatically based on the mapping or assignment that is done in this step. This is shown in the following screenshot:

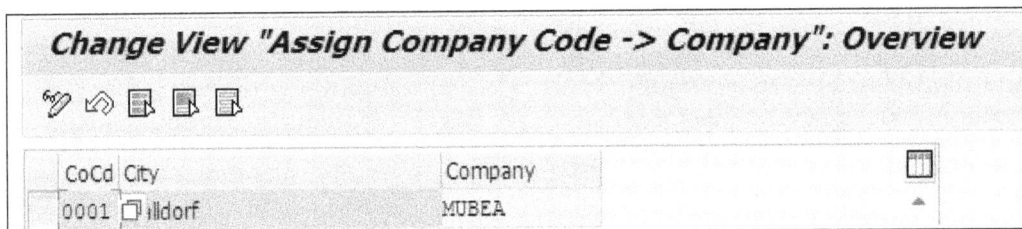

The personnel area is assigned to the company code. The mapping of the employee group and subgroup is done in the next step, as shown in the following screenshot:

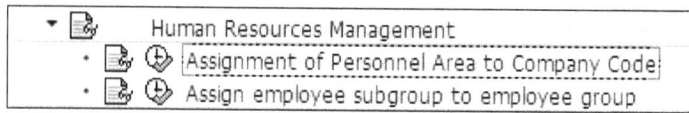

This assignment determines the employee company code mapping that happens through personnel area, as shown in the following screenshot:

The employee group and employee subgroups have an added feature of maintaining the permissibility-per-country grouping. The standard country (Molga) grouping numbers in SAP are, for example, USA-10 and Germany-01. This is shown in the following screenshot:

The allowed flag serves as an input check when the employee grouping is mapped to the employee. The flag denotes that it's permissible for country grouping, while unflag means that it's not permitted.

Tips and tricks that will be handy while configuring the submodule

We will learn the configuration steps for the PA mandatory infotypes. The first thing that is required is customizing of a number range. It's an eight-digit numeric code and is created by navigating to **SPRO | Personnel Management | Personnel Administration | Basic Settings** or directly via the PA04 T-code.

Recommendation on number range assignment

We will now see the recommendation on number assignment. The following key ideas need to be adhered to:

- During the hiring process, if the system generates an employee number, then it is called "internal number assignment". This method is recommended as part of the SAP implementation when a company wants to have uniformity of number assignment with more digits.

- A company has a number of third-party systems where employee numbers are maintained and used in lot of interfaced programs. In such cases, it is important and necessary that we maintain the same employee numbers in SAP as well. In this case, we use the concept of external number assignment.

- In some cases where a company has multiple office locations, we may use external number assignment for some locations, and we may use internal number assignment for other locations.

- As a PA consultant, you have to discuss the number range and the number of digits to be used with the client.

The following screenshot shows the number range assignment:

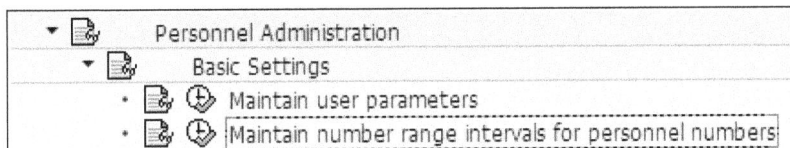

The OM and PA number range concepts are the same. We flag whether it's external (manually inputted by the user) or internal (system generated). This is shown in the following screenshot:

Maintain Intervals: Human resources

N..	From No.	To Number	NR Status	Ext
01	00000001	00000100	0	☑
02	00070000	00079999	70307	☐

The feature used for default number ranges is NUMKR. The return value is the two-digit code that is maintained in the NRIV table via the SE16 T-code.

> The number ranges are maintained in the NRIV table and are accessed via the SE16 T-code. The RP_PREL object name is for PA and RP_PLAN is for OM.

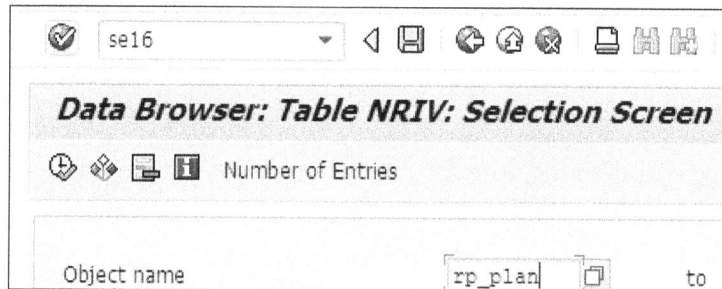

Data Browser: Table NRIV: Selection Screen

Number of Entries

Object name	rp_plan	to

The preceding table has the number range code and number range series based on which it gets executed when the hiring action is performed for an employee.

Configuring mandatory infotypes

First, let's look at personal data by navigating to **SPRO | Personnel Management | Personal Data | Personal Data | Create forms of address**. This is shown in the following screenshot:

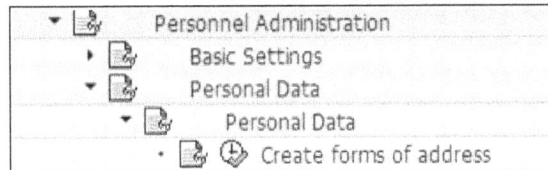

The address table T522G also has the gender category that is configurable. The standard possible entries provided are as follows:

- Permitted for males only
- Permitted for females only
- Permitted for males and females

The address table T522G is shown in the following screenshot:

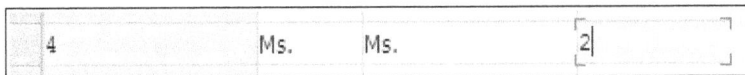

The marital status of the employee can also be configured by navigating to **SPRO | Personnel Management | Personal Data | Personal Data | Create marital status** or via the V_T502_T T-code, as shown in the following screenshot:

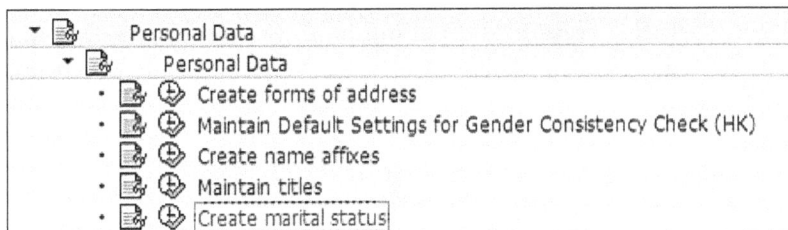

This table is freely configurable according to the client's requirement, as shown in the following screenshot:

The Addresses infotype is accessed by navigating to **SPRO | Personnel Management | Personal Data | Addresses | Create address types**. The following screenshot demonstrates this:

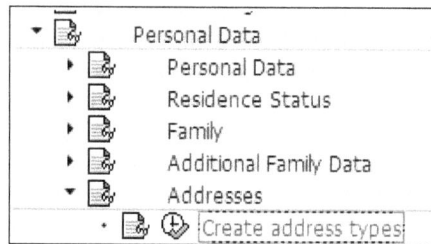

The 0006 Addresses infotype can be used to capture the temporary and permanent addresses of the employee.

The subtypes are a further classification of infotype, and in this case, the different address types are mapped as subtypes in SAP. This concept is demonstrated in the following screenshot:

The regions and countries are standard SAP-delivered entries, and it is recommended that you retain the same and not make any changes. This is demonstrated in the following screenshot:

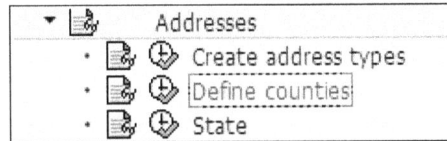

The country key in Addresses (0006) infotype is maintained by navigating to **SPRO | Basic settings | Create countries /countries of birth/nationalities**. The country global parameters table, V_T005, has the standard entries maintained. For instance, The United States of America is maintained as **US**.

Every employee master data must contain the Addresses infotype with subtypes and the permanent address.

During payroll processing, in the "preprogram DME" step, the system checks the permanent address of the employee master data. If the permanent address is not maintained, the preprogram DME will generate error messages.

The employee mode of payment is captured in the Bank Details infotype (0009). The countrywise standard SAP entries are as follows:

- C check
- T bank transfer
- Cash

The payment method is normally configured by an FI consultant and is defaulted using the ZLSCH feature. The payment method gets defaulted in 0009, and the infotype is maintained.

The standard entry is "main bank", and this is configured by navigating to **SPRO | Personnel Administration | Personal Data | Bank Details | Create bank connection types**. The following screenshot demonstrates this:

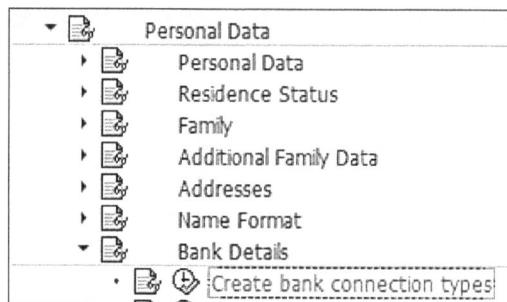

The Organizational Assignment infotype (0001) is an important infotype that holds the key characteristics of an employee, such as personnel area, subarea, employee group, and employee subgroup.

The Organizational Assignment infotype is configured by navigating to **SPRO | Personnel Management | Organizational Data | Define employee attributes** or via the V_503_H T-code.

The employment status, raining status, and activity status are standard entries, and only if necessary, SAP recommends customizing them. This is shown in the following screenshot:

The standard entries in SAP are for the status of an activity. They are as follows:

- Active employee
- Retiree
- Early retiree
- Others
- Part-time work for retirees

The standard entries in SAP for employment status are as follows:

- Industrial worker/hourly paid worker
- Salaried employee
- Civil servant
- Others

The control record and payroll area are critical customizable objects for payroll and reporting purposes. The payroll is created for mapping an employee whose payroll is processed in the same frequency and on the same date, say, monthly or biweekly for that matter.

Every payroll area must have a control record. The control record controls how the payroll is processed.

They are configured by navigating to **SPRO | Personnel Administration | Organizational Data | Organizational Assignment | Create payroll area** or via the V_T549A T-code. The following screenshot shows this:

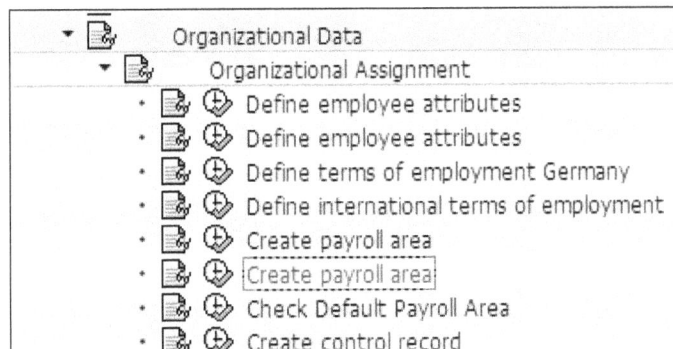

We can group the employees together and map them to a payroll area so that it is easy to process for a group of employees in one shot.

The control record determines the current period for which the payroll is processed. It also determines the payroll period past date, up to which the system allows you to make changes to the master and time data and is called as Retro in SAP.

Payroll control record

Payroll area	D2 HR-D: Sal. employees

Payroll status

✖	Released f. Payroll
✖	Rel. f. Correction
✖	Exit Payroll
✖	Check Payroll Results

Payroll period	01 2002 01.01.2002 – 31.01.2002
Run	0

Earliest retro acctg period	01 2002 01.01.2002

There are multiple statuses in control record such as "released" for payroll, which means master and time data is locked, and the correction of master data is not possible.

The release of correction implies that the system allows us to make corrections to the master and time data, and exit payroll means that we are done with processing the current payroll period, and it can be exited.

The incorrect personnel numbers are captured in match code "W". The system captures incorrectly processed employees during payroll. This needs to be corrected, and we need to rerun the payroll for the same.

The earliest retro period in control record determines how far back in time the system can allow us to make corrections to processed payroll periods.

The Basic Pay (0008) infotype is crucial for processing the payroll and is configured by navigating to **SPRO | Personnel Management | Personnel Administration | Payroll Data | Basic Pay**. The following screenshot demonstrates this:

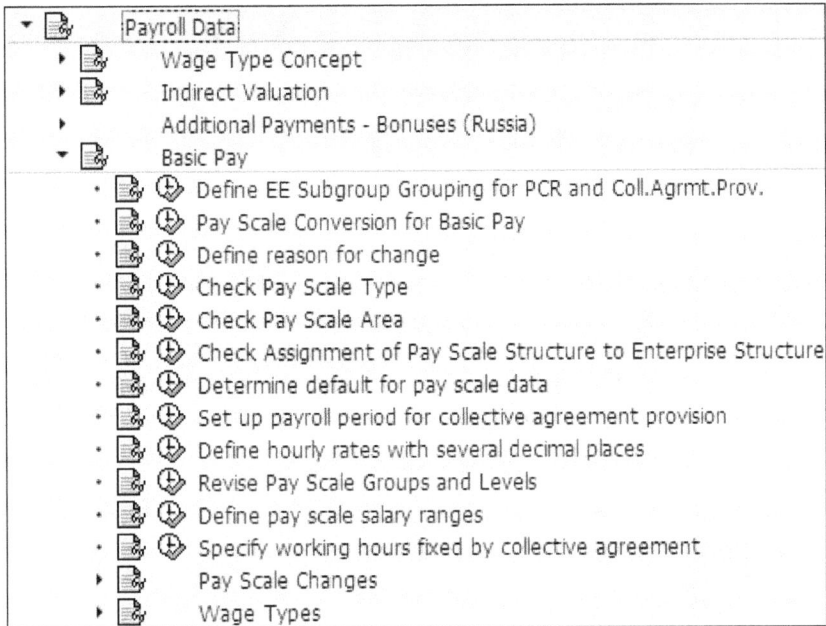

The employee subgroup grouping for **personnel calculation rule (PCR)** and **collective agreement provision (CAP)** is the cornerstone for processing payroll PCR. We can group employees based on different rules and regulations set.

They are maintained by navigating to **SPRO | Personnel Management | Personnel administration | Payroll Data | Basic Pay | Define EE Subgroup Grouping for PCR and Coll.Agrmt.Prov** or directly via the V_503_B table. This is shown in the following screenshot:

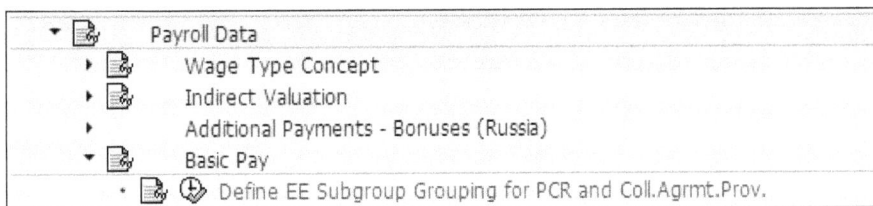

The payscale type, area, groups, and levels are configured by navigating to **SPRO | Personnel Management | Personnel Administration | Payroll Data | Basic Pay | Check PayScale Type/Area** or via the T510G/T510A T-code.

A payscale type defines the industry in which the client is operating, such as metal for example, while the pay scale area defines the physical work location of the client. This is shown in the following screenshot:

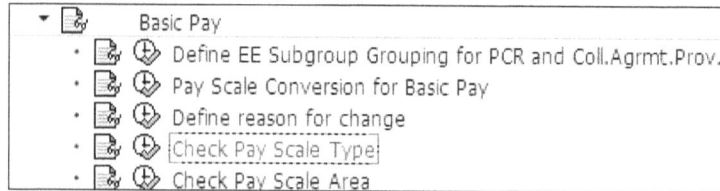

The pay components are defined as wage types in SAP. For example, housing allowance is defined as the "8888" wage type number followed by text to identify the same. Wage types are created using the tool that SAP has provided. This tool is accessed via the PU30 or OH11 T-code or by navigating to **SPRO | Personnel Management | Personnel Administration | Payroll Data | Basic Pay | Wage Types**. This is shown in the following screenshot:

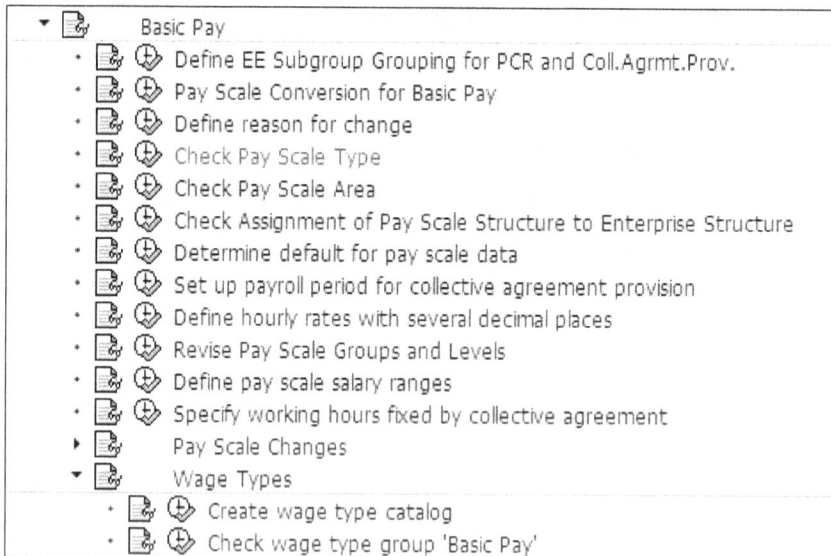

There are many associated table entries that get copied when the tool is used. We see the associated table entries in the following screenshot:

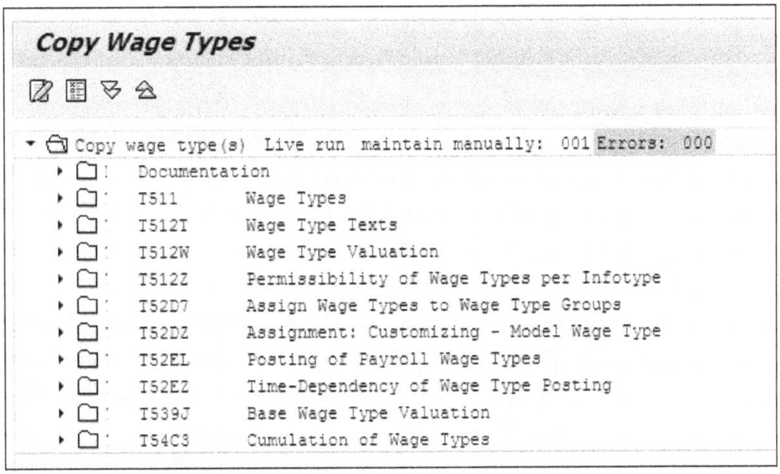

```
Copy Wage Types

📝 📇 ▽ 🔺

▼ 🗁 Copy wage type(s)  Live run  maintain manually: 001 Errors: 000
   ▸ 🗀 ¦  Documentation
   ▸ 🗀 ¦  T511      Wage Types
   ▸ 🗀 ¦  T512T     Wage Type Texts
   ▸ 🗀 ¦  T512W     Wage Type Valuation
   ▸ 🗀 ¦  T512Z     Permissibility of Wage Types per Infotype
   ▸ 🗀 ¦  T52D7     Assign Wage Types to Wage Type Groups
   ▸ 🗀 ¦  T52DZ     Assignment: Customizing - Model Wage Type
   ▸ 🗀 ¦  T52EL     Posting of Payroll Wage Types
   ▸ 🗀 ¦  T52EZ     Time-Dependency of Wage Type Posting
   ▸ 🗀 ¦  T539J     Base Wage Type Valuation
   ▸ 🗀 ¦  T54C3     Cumulation of Wage Types
```

The wage type texts are normally stored in the T511 and T512 series tables, while the assignment of wage type grouping, base type valuation, and so on are stored in T52 series tables. The Planned Working Time (0007) infotype serves as an integration point between the Time Management and Payroll submodules.

Planned Working Time has the work schedule of the employee. This is entangled with public holidays and the working time for a week, month, and so on.

It is configured via the Time Management submodule that we will be covering in the next chapter. The work schedule rule that we generate becomes the default one in the Planned Working Time (0007) infotype.

The Planned Working Time (007) infotype is configured by navigating to **SPRO | Time Management | Work Schedules | Work Schedule Rules and Work Schedules**, and is shown in the following screenshot:

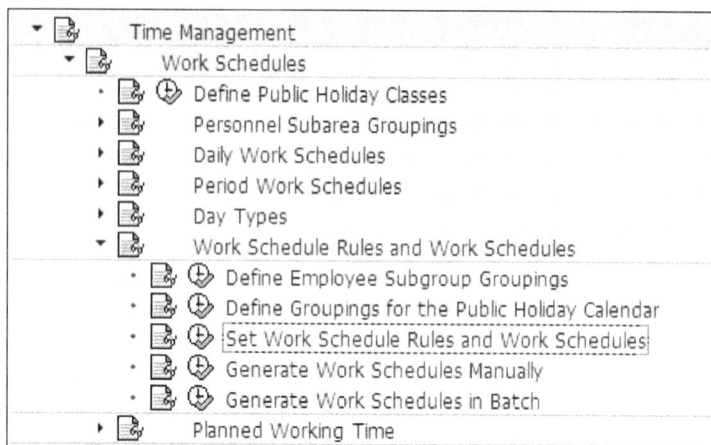

Customizing the infotype menu and info groups

The infotype menu is the one that the user sees in PA30. There are different tabs that can be maintained and different infotypes can be defaulted under each tab. This functionality is provided for simplifying the user maintenance of master data of the employees.

Infotype menus are configured by navigating to **SPRO | Personnel Management | Personnel Administration | Customizing Procedures | Infotype Menus | Infotype Menu**. This is shown in the following screenshot:

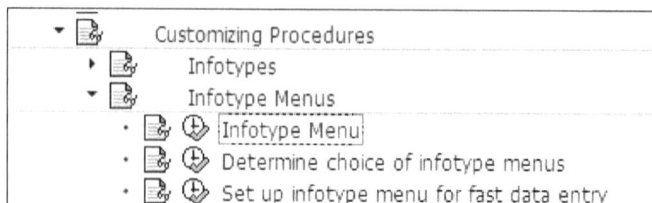

The menu can be or cannot be maintained based on the user group of the user.

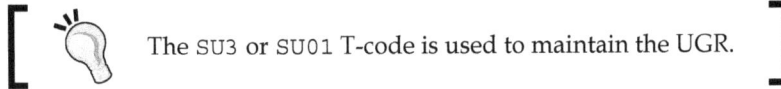

> The SU3 or SU01 T-code is used to maintain the UGR.

If we would like to have the menus dependent on a particular user group, SAP has a functionality to meet this requirement. Say, a particular menu is applicable for only a group of users mapped as UGR 10; in this case we have to configure the settings by navigating to **SPRO | Personnel Management | Personnel Administration | Customizing Procedures | Infotype Menus | Infotype Menu | User Group Dependency on Menus and Info Groups**. Should the **User-dep.** field be flagged, it means the menu is dependent on UGR parameter that is maintained in the SU3 transaction code for the user. This is shown in the following screenshot:

Change View "User Group Dependency on Menus and Info Groups": Overview

New Entries

Menu ty. I

Menu	Text		User-dep.	Reaction	Ref.	
01	Core Employee Info.		✓		10	

The advantage of using this functionality is when there are multiple client operators in multiple countries. If you would like the users to have enough control and authorization to specific infotype, for specific country infotype, this feature comes in very handy.

It is important to know the different menu types provided by SAP. Each character has a specific meaning associated with it. The different menu types are as follows:

- **B**: This refers to applicant action menu
- **G**: This refers to info group menu
- **I**: This refers to infotype menu
- **M**: This refers to personnel action menu
- **S**: This refers to infotype menu

"I" denotes that it is the infotype menu or the header tab of the PA30 or PA20 screen. The infotypes are grouped under each infotype menu. For example, a payroll tab can have the Basic Pay (0008), Recurring Payments and Deductions (0014), and Additional Payments (0015) infotypes grouped, as demonstrated in the following screenshot:

Personnel No.	1000	Pers.Assgn 00001000 Dir HR -D Active
Name	World Hello	
EE group	1 Active-TEXINT	Pers.area 1300 Frankfurt
EE subgroup	DS Executive employ…	Cost Center 2200 Human Resources

Core Employee Info. | Empl. contract data | Gross/net payroll | Net payroll

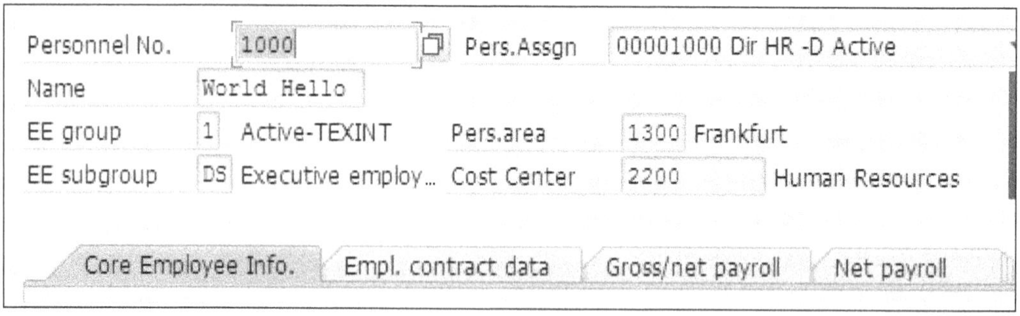

The infotype listed under each menu is controlled by navigating to **SPRO | Personnel Management | Personnel Administration | Customizing Procedures | Infotype Menus | Infotype Menu**.

The infotypes such as time-related Planned Working Time time (0007), Absences (2001), and Absence Quotas (2006), can be grouped under **Time Menu** or tab, as shown in the following screenshot:

Change View "Infotype Menu": Overview

New Entries

Menu	XY Personal-vijay		☑ User group-dependent
			Reaction
			Reference user group 94

User group	N..	Infotype	Scr...	Infotype text	
	94	01 0002		Personal Data infotype	
	94	02 0014		Recurring Payments/Deductions	

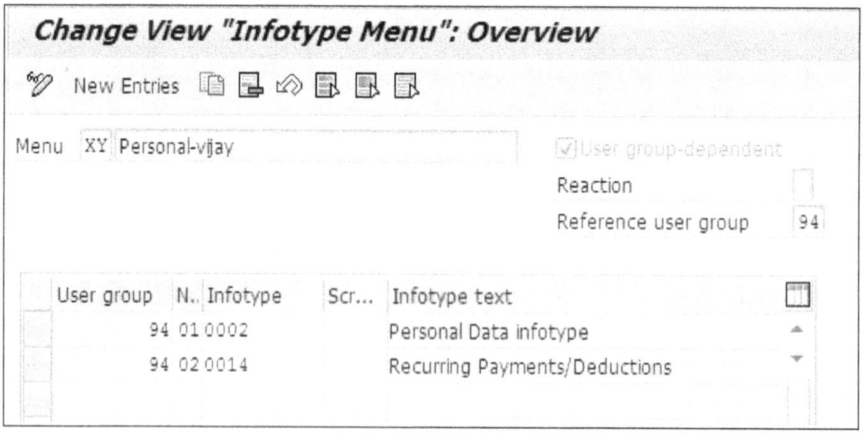

Infogroups group together infotypes that populate sequentially one after another. Let's say, in order to perform a hiring action, the infotypes such as actions (0000), organizational assignment (0001), and basic pay (0008) need to be filled in by the user. Infogroups can also be based on user grouping such as info menu. They are configured by navigating to **SPRO** | **Personnel Management** | **Personnel Administration** | **Customizing Procedures** | **Actions** | **Define infogroups**. This is shown in the following screenshot:

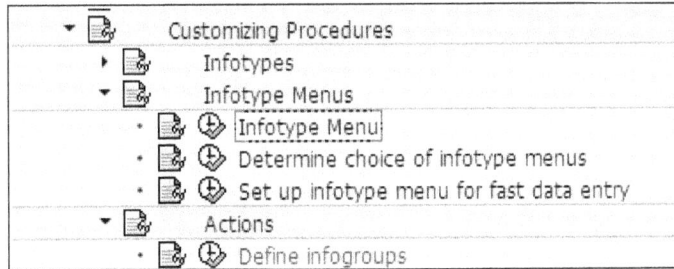

The menu type of the infogroup that needs to be configured is "G". This infogroup can also be made dependent on the user by flagging the user-dependent check box and mentioning the reference user group number maintained in the SU3/SU01 T-code. It is shown in the following screenshot:

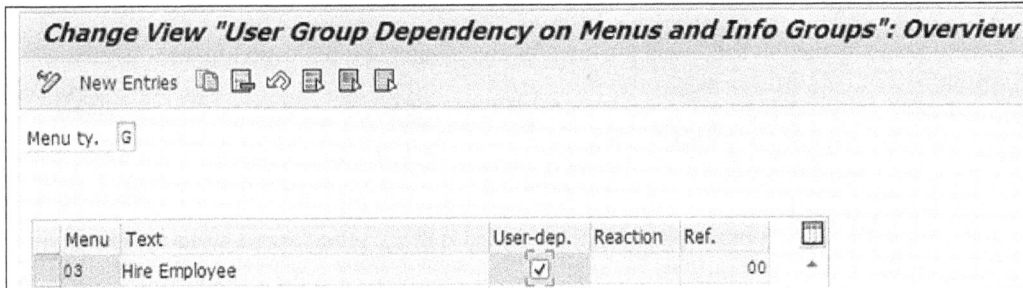

The infogroup **03** can be used to map all the related infotypes that need to be captured for a hiring action. We will see how the mapping is done in the table via the info menu. The infotypes are configured by navigating to **SPRO | Personnel Management | Personnel Administration | Customizing Procedures | Actions | Info Group**. This is shown in the following screenshot:

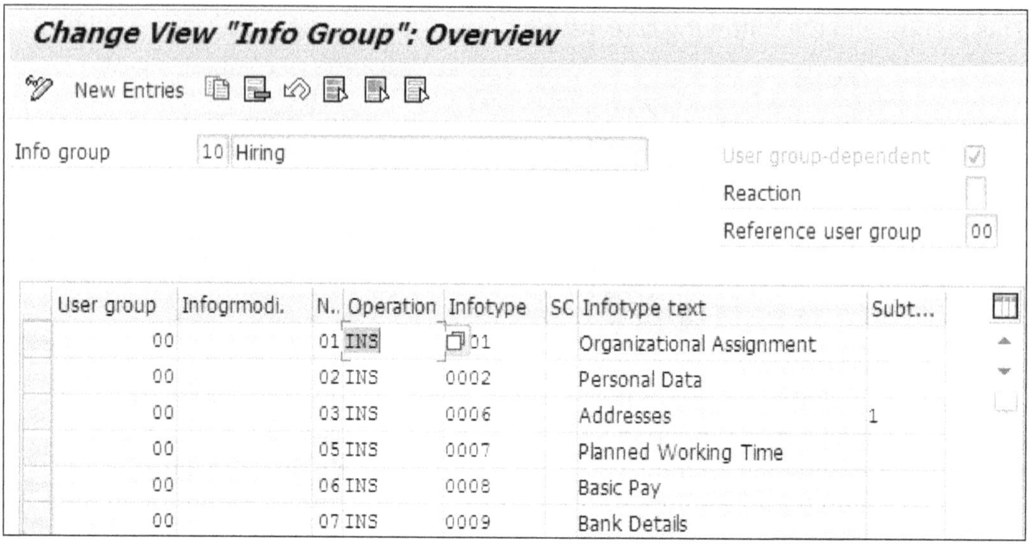

Here, the user group is the UGR parameter that has to be in congruence with the parameter that is maintained in the SU3/SU01 T-code. There are standard operations provided by SAP that can be referenced. They are as follows:

- Create (Ins)
- Change (Mod)
- Delimit (LIS9LIS) LIS9
- Lock/Unlock (EDQ)

Configuring personnel actions

The personnel actions are all the activities surrounding the employee life cycle, such as hiring, promotion, change in pay, and separation. They are called personnel actions in SAP. Each action will have the infotype populating sequentially based on the infogroups mapped to the action infotype.

The personnel actions in SAP are configured by navigating to **SPRO | Personnel Management | Personnel Administration | Customizing Procedures | Actions | Set up personnel actions | Personnel Action Types**. This is shown in the following screenshot:

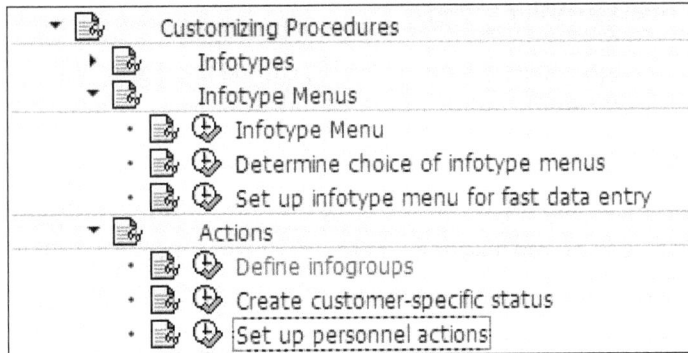

Customizing procedures is an important node where infogroups, menus, and personnel actions all can be customized.The personnel action table looks like the one shown in the following screenshot:

The action type is a two-digit alphanumeric code with text such as hire, change of position, and so on associated with it. Each action type will have the infogroup code mapped to it, and based on the personnel action chosen by the user, the infotype defaults sequentially. The FC denotes the function character for the personnel action. For example, for hiring, we can use **01**, which is the first hiring, and for other actions, we can use 0.

SAP-delivered function codes can be used and don't require customizing. They are as follows:

- **'1'**: This refers to first hiring
- **'7'**: This refers to first hiring and transfer of data from recruitment

- **'8'**: This refers to activation of personnel assignment in the host country (for global employees)

- **'9'**: This refers to activation of personnel assignment in the home country (for global employees)

- **'0'**: This refers to other actions

The SAP standard employment status (STAT2) can be used and will normally fulfill the requirements. The standard entries are as follows:

- **0**: This refers to an employee not with the company

- **1**: This refers to an employee working with the company, but inactive

- **2**: This refers to an employee working with the company, but as a retiree

- **3**: This refers to an employee who is active in the company

Based on the personnel action, we can map the status number accordingly. For example, we can use 3 for hiring personnel action and 0 for resignation or separation of personnel action.

This is how the PA40 T-code looks when the user executes to maintain the master data:

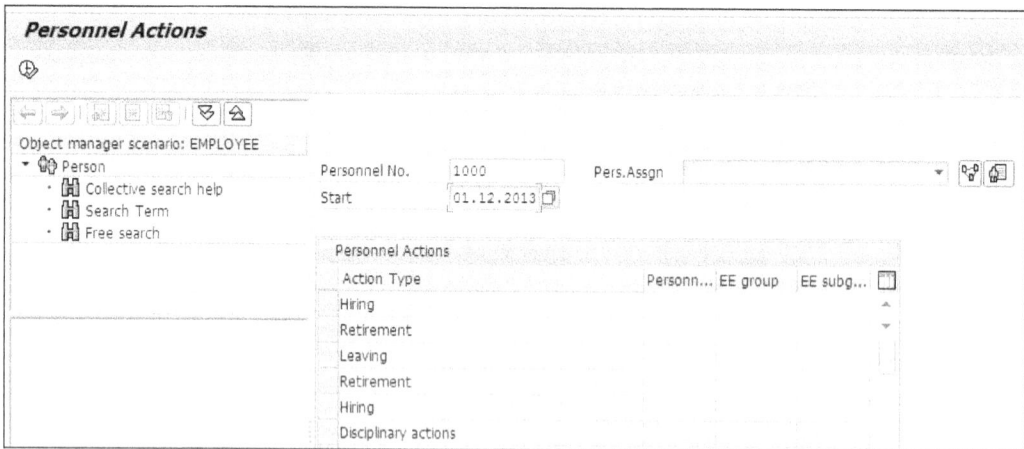

SAP also has the functionally of defining the reason for each personnel action. For instance, the hiring personnel action can be executed based on multiple reasons such as ramp up, replacement, and so on.

They are configured by navigating to **SPRO | Personnel Management | Personnel Administration | Customizing Procedures | Actions | Create reasons for personnel actions** or directly or via the V_T530 T-code. This is shown in the following screenshot:

- 📝 🕐 Determine choice of infotype menus
- 📝 🕐 Set up infotype menu for fast data entry
▼ 📝   Actions
   - 📝 🕐 Define infogroups
   - 📝 🕐 Create customer-specific status
   - 📝 🕐 Set up personnel actions
   - 📝 🕐 Create reasons for personnel actions
   - 📝 🕐 Create reasons for personnel actions

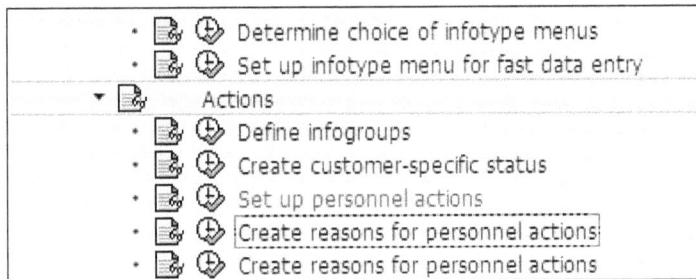

The possible reasons for each personnel action are maintained in the table and can be used in the PA40 T-code. This will be very useful for reporting purposes, and is shown in the following screenshot:

Change View "Reason for Action": Overview

🖉 New Entries 🗐 🖫 🖎 🗎 🗎 🗎

Action	Name of Action Type	Act.Reason	Name of reason for action
		04	Attrition
01	Hire		Attrition
01	Hire	01	Expansion
01	🗇 e	02	New Product Line

The menu created needs to be mapped to the standard menu provided by SAP.01, which needs to be used. The following screenshot demonstrates this:

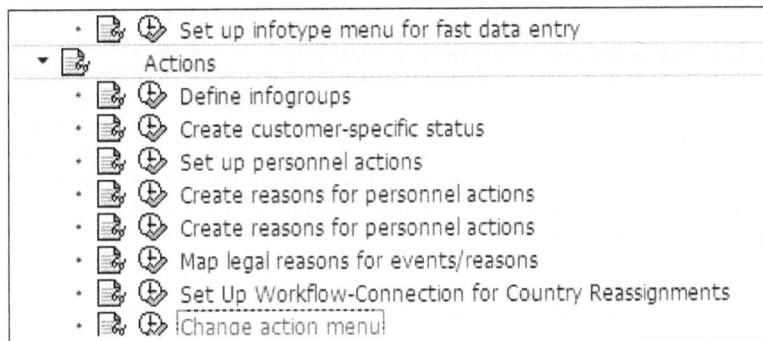

- 📝 🕐 Set up infotype menu for fast data entry
▼ 📝   Actions
   - 📝 🕐 Define infogroups
   - 📝 🕐 Create customer-specific status
   - 📝 🕐 Set up personnel actions
   - 📝 🕐 Create reasons for personnel actions
   - 📝 🕐 Create reasons for personnel actions
   - 📝 🕐 Map legal reasons for events/reasons
   - 📝 🕐 Set Up Workflow-Connection for Country Reassignments
   - 📝 🕐 Change action menu

The standard menu can be configured by navigating to **SPRO | Personnel Management | Personnel Administration | Customizing Procedures | Actions | Change action menu | User Group Dependency on Menus and Info Groups.**

The menu can be made dependent on the user maintained in the SU3/SU01 T-code. This is shown in the following screenshot:

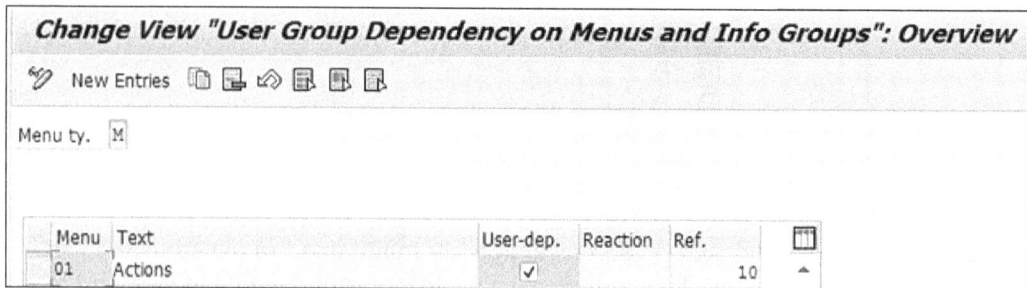

All the personnel actions are mapped to the standard **01** menu. This is shown in the following screenshot:

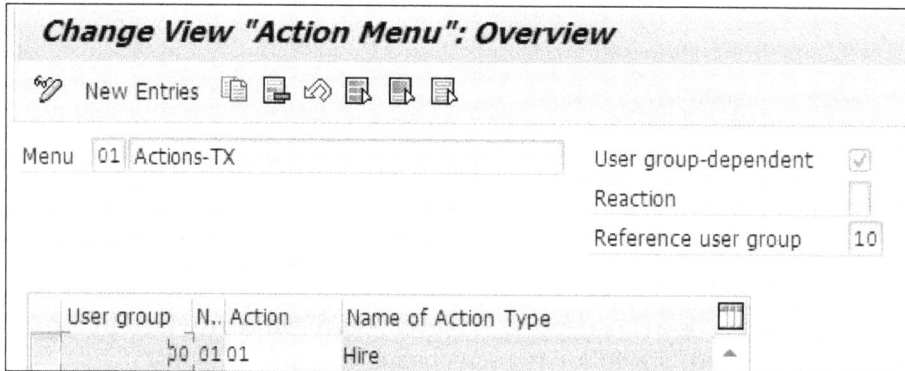

Dynamic actions

These are very useful for the maintenance of infotypes. They are triggered automatically when a particular change of an infotype is performed. They are configured by navigating to **SPRO** | **Personnel Management** | **Personnel Administration** | **Customizing Procedures** | **Dynamic Actions** or directly via T588Z. This is shown in the following screenshot:

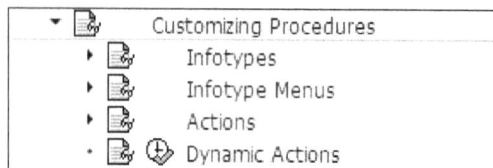

[🔆 For more information on configuring personnel action, there is an excellent reference guide, *Unleash the Power of Dynamic Actions: Tips and Tricks to Get the Best Results,* by Rehan Zaidi.]

The following screenshot demonstrates an overview of the dynamic action:

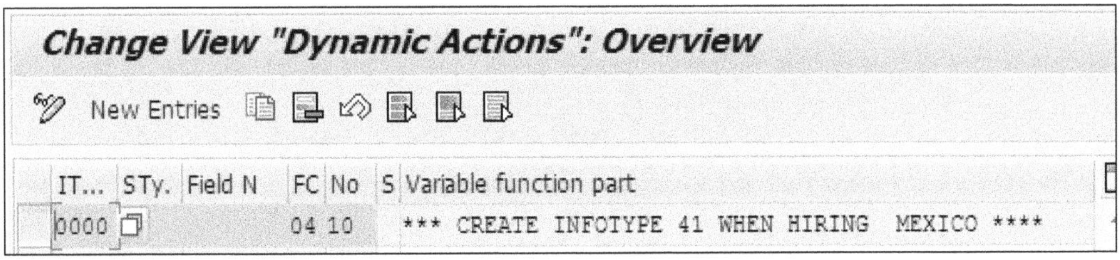

Change View "Dynamic Actions": Overview

🖉 New Entries 🗐 🖫 🖎 🖫 🖫 🖫

IT...	STy.	Field N	FC	No	S	Variable function part
0000			04	10		*** CREATE INFOTYPE 41 WHEN HIRING MEXICO ****

The infotype and subtype are used to maintain the infotype number for which we want the dynamic action to be triggered. We can also use a specific field name if we want dynamic action to trigger on the changes made to them. There are standard function characters that SAP has delivered, and we can use them in the table. They are as follows:

- **00**: This is used if it is independent of the current function carried out
- **02**: This is used for change
- **04**: This is used for create
- **06**: This is used for change and create
- **08**: This is used for delete
- **10**: This is used for change and delete
- **12**: This is used for create and delete

The standard function characters, along with the indicator for step, form the key for dynamic action. The standard SAP-delivered indicators for steps are as follows:

- **P**: This is used to check conditions
- **I**: This is used to maintain the record of infotypes
- **W**: This is used to set the default values when creating a new record
- **V**: This is used to reference to another step
- **F**: This is used to call routine
- **M**: This is used to send mail

Finally, the variable function has to be maintained.

Summary

In this chapter, we covered how to configure master data for employees. We have also covered how to customize info groups, menus, and dynamic actions.

In the next chapter, we will closely look at configuring the Time Management submodule and explore the standard functionalities provided by SAP.

5
Time Management Configuration – Negative Time

We will explore how the Time Management submodule is configured to meet the client's requirements. Time Management deals with recording, reporting, and evaluating the attendance and absenteeism of an employee. Evaluation could be the number of hours worked extra by an employee, and this is determined using the Time Management submodule. The absence and attendance entitlements or quotas are also captured. The Absence Quotas are buckets to collect the leave entitlements. We will cover the important configuration steps, infotypes, and tips to configure the submodule.

In this chapter, we will cover the following topics:

- Various nodes for configuring the Work schedule rule
- Absence Quotas
- Customizing tables for the Work schedule rule
- Customizing tables for Absence Quotas
- Generating hassle-free Absence Quotas

Nodes for configuring the Work schedule rule and Absence Quotas

Before we start to cover the important configuration points, let's closely look at the Time Management infotypes in detail. It's important for us to be familiar with the functionalities of Time Management infotypes before starting with the configuration steps.

Time Management infotypes

The important Time Management infotypes are listed in the following table:

Infotypes	Infotype text
0007	Planned Working Time
2001	Absences
2002	Attendances
2006	Absence Quotas
2007	Attendance Quotas
2005	Overtime
2010	Employee Remuneration Info
2013	Quota Correction
0416	Time Quota Compensation

The Planned Working Time infotype (0007)

The **Planned Working Time** infotype has the key details about an employee's work pattern. The work schedule is tagged to the employee based on the configuration, and it gives us details about the daily work schedule, holiday class, and day type. The **Time Management Status** (P0007-ZTERF) controls whether an employee participates in time evaluation. The following screenshot shows the **Work schedule rule** section:

Work schedule rule		
Work schedule rule	OTTEST	OT TEST WSR
Time Mgmt status	9 - Time evaluation of planned times	
☐ Part-time employee		

Working time	
Employment percent	100,00
Daily working hours	8,00
Weekly working hours	40,00
Monthly working hrs	173,00
Annual working hours	2080,00

The following table shows the related text for various indicator values:

Indicator	Text
0	No time evaluation
1	Time evaluation (Actual times)
2	Time evaluation (PDC)
7	Time evaluation without integration to Payroll
8	External services
9	Evaluation of planned times

If we are not going to use the **Time Evaluation** (RPTIME00) program for accounting time data, we can mention the employee status as 0.

If we are not going to integrate time with payroll, then the status can be set to 7, or it is advisable to set the status to 9.When the clock in and clock out time is going to be recorded, the status needs to be set to 1. **Plant Data Collection** (PDC) is useful to transfer data from the following application components to Time Management:

- **SAP Project Systems (PS)**
- **SAP Plant Maintenance and Customer Service (PM/CS)**
- **SAP Production Planning (PP) and Process Control (PP/PI)**

The TMSTA DEFAULT VALUE FOR TIME MANAGEMENT STATUS feature is configured to the default Time Management status based on different parameters. It can be accessed via the PE03 T-code.

The **Working time** details such as the daily working hours, monthly working hours, and so on are also captured in the Planned Working Time infotype. The integration point between time and payroll is the monthly working hours that flows from the Planned Working Time to Basic Pay infotype when personnel action is run for the employee. The daily hours, monthly hours, weekly hours, and weekly work days are configurable items, and when the Work schedule rule is selected, it gets displayed automatically.

The following table shows us the fields and values used in the 0007 infotype:

Working time	Field data
Employment percent	100
Daily working hours	8
Weekly working hours	40
Monthly working hours	173
Annual working hours	2080
Weekly workdays	5

From the work schedule, we can see the employee's daily, weekly, and monthly working hours. The Time Management status indicates whether the time data of an employee is processed in the following categories:

- Time evaluation
- Processed data passed to Payroll for further processing

The Absences infotype (2001)

The Absences infotype is used to capture the absence type based on the grouping. It defines the nature of absence such as Sick, Casual, and so on. The absence type is a four-character code that specifies the absence text. The following screenshot shows the **Change Absences** window:

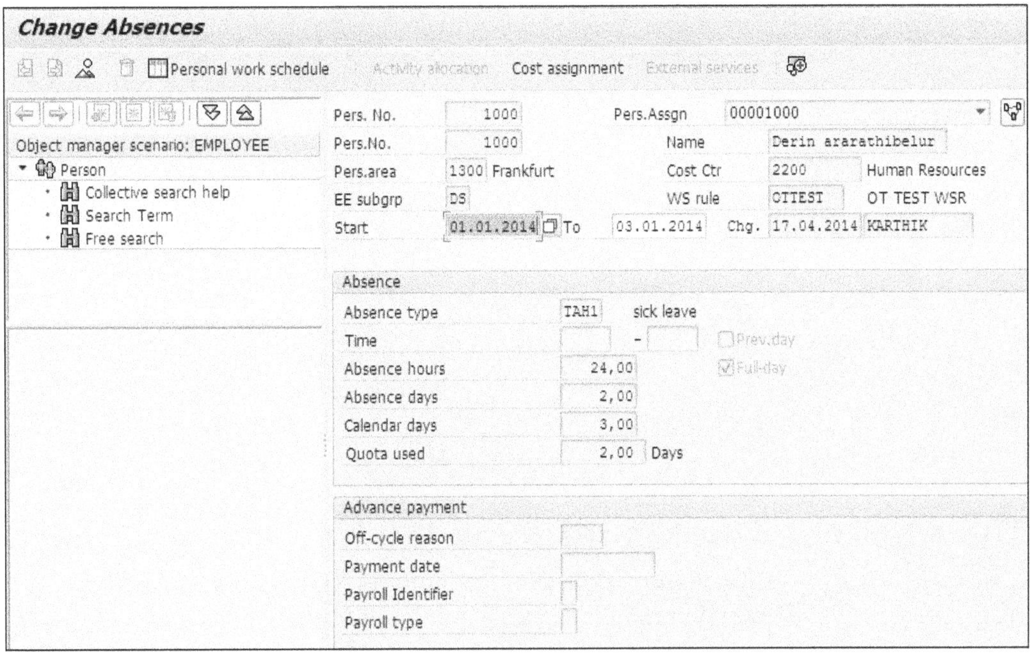

The Attendances infotype (2002)

The Attendances infotype is used to capture the special attendance reasons such as business trip or training needs, for instance, in addition to the normal work pattern. There is also a special feature for entry screen such as general attendance and attendance with quota deduction. This is controlled in customizing, and we can define the attendance quota from which a specific attendance type must be deducted.

The payment data other than the normal cost that is associated with the attendance type maintained for an employee is done in one of the following two ways:

- Using wage type, the amount can be directly entered and queried in payroll or time evaluation

- By navigating to **Goto | Different payment**, where we can enter the amount in the **Valuation basis** field, as seen in the following screenshot:

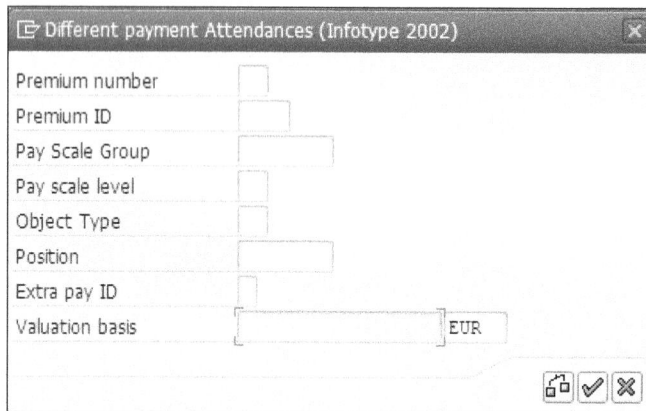

The Absence Quotas infotype (2006)

Absence Quotas are entitlements or buckets that contain the number of days an employee can avail leave. When the absence is recorded in the Absences infotype (2001), the absence gets reduced from the quota automatically. The Absence Quotas infotype has different fields, which are shown in the following screenshot:

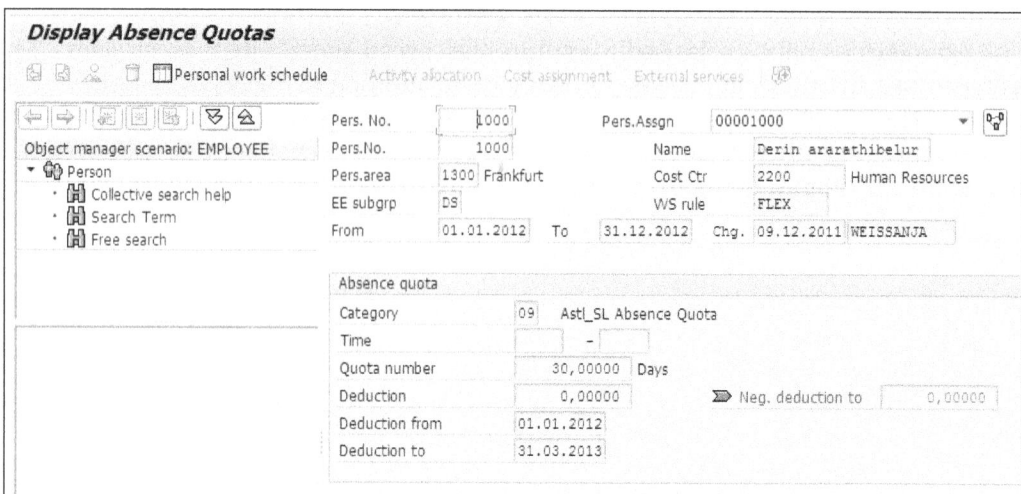

The following table contains a description of the various Absence Quotas:

Field	Description
Category	The absence quota type that includes sick leave, annual leave, and so on.
Quota number	The number of days or hours an employee is entitled to take leave.
Deduction	The **Deduction** field has the number of leaves that has been availed or used.
Deduction from	The date from which quota can be deducted when an absence is recorded.
Deduction to	The date up to which quota can be deducted when an absence is recorded.
Neg. deduction to	The value going over and beyond the entitlements days can be mentioned here. Say, the entitlement is 40 days and 50 days needs to be recorded; then, we can insert 50 here.

The Attendance Quotas infotype (2007)

The special attendance of employees that is approved using the 2002 infotype is stored in the Attendance Quotas infotypes. The following screenshot shows the **Create Attendance Quotas** window:

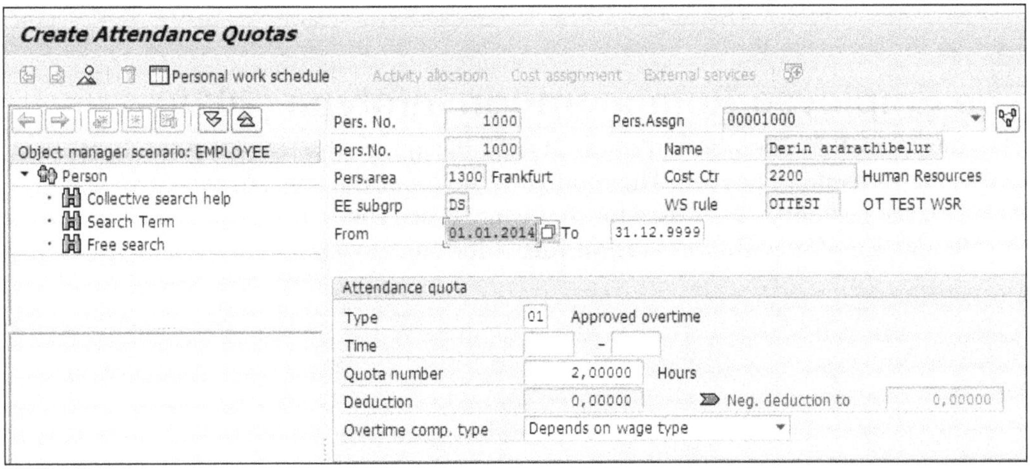

The Overtime infotype (2005)

The Overtime infotype is used to capture the additional number of hours an employee works in addition to the normal working hours. The hours are queried in payroll and compensated accordingly. The following screenshot shows the **Change Overtime** window:

The Employee Remuneration infotype (2010)

The Employee Remuneration infotype is used to capture the wage type and amount that gets processed in payroll. The number of hours or the amount can be specified based on the customized settings for that wage type. The following screenshot shows the **Change Employee Remuneration Info** window:

The Quota Correction infotype (2013)

The decrease or increase of entitlements can be controlled using the Quota Correction infotype. Let's say we would like to reduce the number of days generated in the 2006 infotype by 2. We can specify the number of days to be increased or decreased in the **Quota number** field. There are multiple options provided, and we can make use of them accordingly to meet the requirement.

Let's have a look at these options in the following screenshot:

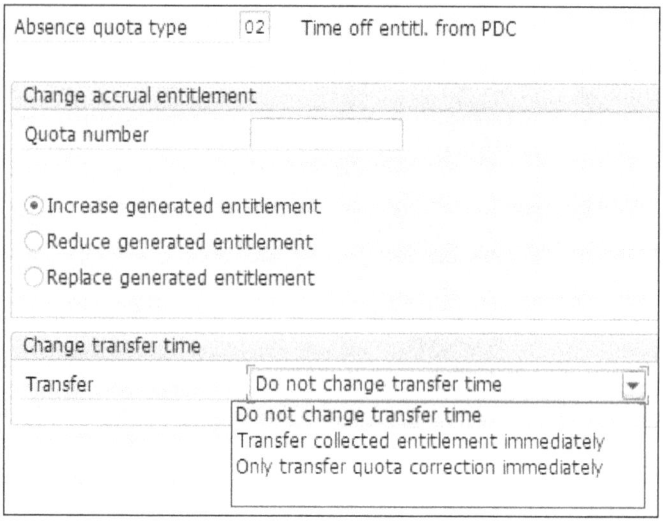

Absence quota type	02	Time off entitl. from PDC

Change accrual entitlement

Quota number

⦿ Increase generated entitlement
○ Reduce generated entitlement
○ Replace generated entitlement

Change transfer time

Transfer | Do not change transfer time ▾

Do not change transfer time
Transfer collected entitlement immediately
Only transfer quota correction immediately

The following table lists the meanings of the three options available for accrual entitlements:

Accrual entitlements option	Meaning
Increase generated entitlement	The number specified in the **Quota number** field gets added to the existing quotas in the 2006 infotype.
Reduce generated entitlement	The number specified in the **Quota number** field gets reduced from the existing quotas in the 2006 infotype.
Replace generated entitlement	The number specified in the **Quota number** field gets replaced with the existing quotas in the 2006 infotype.

The transfer of entitlements can be controlled, and there are multiple options provided by SAP. The **Transfer** options are as follows:

- **Do not change transfer time**: The quota correction does not happen immediately and does not reflect in the 2006 infotype instantly

- **Transfer collected entitlement immediately**: The correction reflects in the 2006 infotype instantly when the time evaluation is run for the employee

- **Only transfer quota correction immediately**: The correction is effective in Absence Quotas (2006) only in the next evaluation run

The Time Quota Compensation infotype (0416)

The unused entitlements can be remunerated using this infotype. The **No. to compensate** field is used to enter the absence entitlements that need to be remunerated, in days or hours. There is also a functionality to control whether the entitlement needs to be remunerated or not. This is done by flagging the **Do not account** checkbox.

There are two specifications provided by SAP that can be used to compensate the entitlements. They are as follows:

- **Automatic compensation**
- **Manual compensation**

In the **Automatic compensation** method, we mention the quota type and quota number to be compensated. In the **Manual compensation** method, the quota number that needs to be compensated has to be specified along with the wage type, amount, and currency.

If we use the **Automatic compensation** option to remunerate the quota number, we need to build the PCR and use it in the schema after running the P0416 function.

The PCR used for running the P0416 function can be used as follows:

```
ZLEN (PCR name)
  3(ESG Grouping for PCR)
  1234 (Leave encashment Wage type that holds number)
                  AMT=6789(Wage type)
                  AMT/30
  MULTI ANA (Multiply Amount and Number, place it in Amount field)
                  ADDWT 1234(Wage type)
```

The following table explains the logic built for the PCR. The business requirement is that the days used in P0416 need to be multiplied with one day's basic pay and remunerated for the employee. The following table shows the PCR operations with their explanations:

PCR Operation	Explanation
ZLEN	This checks whether the PCR is customized to map the business requirement.
3	This is the value of the Employee subgroup grouping for PCR. Please use the number used in **SPRO	Personnel Management	Personnel administration	Payroll data	Basic Pay	Define EE subgroup grouping for PCR and CAP** (V_503_B-ABART).

PCR Operation	Explanation
1234	The wage type number that has the unused quota number to be remunerated.
AMT=6789	The amount in the Basic Pay wage type in **Input Table** (**IT**) is assigned for calculation.
AMT/30	The Basic Pay wage type amount is divided by 30.
MULTI ANA	The derived amount is multiplied with the number and stored in the amount field.
ADDWT	This adds the wage type amount to the subsequent wage type, and if an asterisk is used, it moves to the output table.

Important nodes and/or customizing tables for the Work schedule rule

The fixed planned working time of an employee for a particular period of time is captured in the Planned Working Time infotype (0007), and we will closely look at the configuration of the Work schedule rule.

> The backbone of Time Management is the Personnel subarea grouping and Employee subgroup grouping.

The period work schedule has the daily work schedule mapped for 7 days, and the period work schedule is tagged with the Work schedule rule. The daily work schedule is a fixed pattern of work such as 9 a.m. to 5 p.m. The period work schedule is the work pattern followed for the number of days, say 4 weeks.

The holiday calendar

The holiday calendar must be created by navigating to **SPRO | Time Management | Work Schedule | Define Public Holiday Classes**.

Public holidays need to be defined first and then mapped to a holiday calendar. There are different types of public holidays that can be defined. They are as follows:

- With a fixed date
- With a fixed date from a particular date
- Distance to Easter
- Easter Sunday
- Floating public holiday

There are plenty of features that can be used while defining the holidays. We can mention whether the holiday falls on a particular day such as Sunday or **Not Guaranteed**. The **Sort Criterion** option is very handy when we try to find the holiday that we defined in order to map in the holiday calendar. The **Public Holiday Class** option has a standard meaning defined and the key for counting absences, the time wage type selection, and the daily work schedule variants.

The following table will shows us the meaning of the different holiday classes provided by SAP:

Public Holiday Class	Meaning
Blank	Normal working day
1	Full day off
2	Half day off
3-9	Customer specific

The short name and long name define the name of the public holiday. The short name is 10 characters in length and long name is 30 characters in length. The following screenshot shows the **Create/Change Public Holidays: Floating Public Holidays** window:

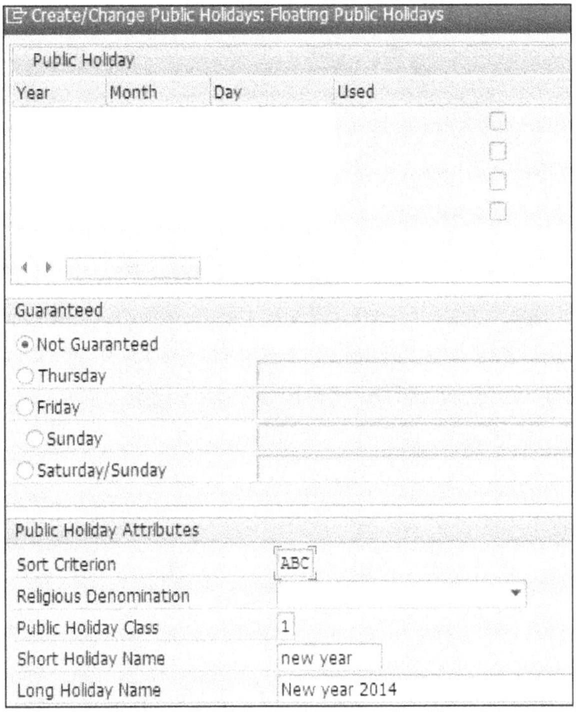

After entering the year, month, day, and choosing options in **Guaranteed** and **Public Holiday Attributes**, we need to click on the **Insert Date** button. The created public holiday needs to be inserted in the holiday calendar. We click on the **Holiday calendar** button and then on **Edit**. After performing the necessary actions, click on Create (or press *Shift + F4*) as shown in the following screenshot:

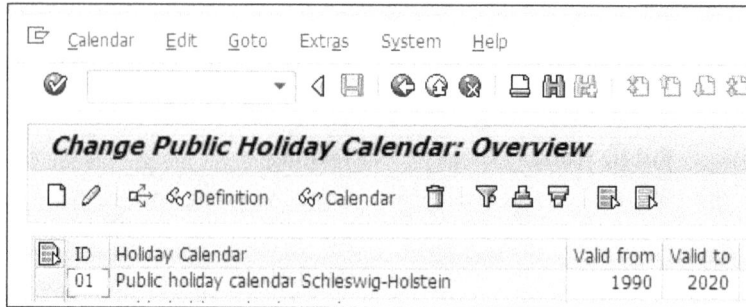

Enter the holiday **Calendar ID** and text, followed by validity, and the **From** and **To** dates. To insert the public holidays created in the previous step, we need to click on **Assign Holiday**. The public holidays created get listed so that we can choose and filter them based on the sort criterion we selected. This is demonstrated in the following screenshot:

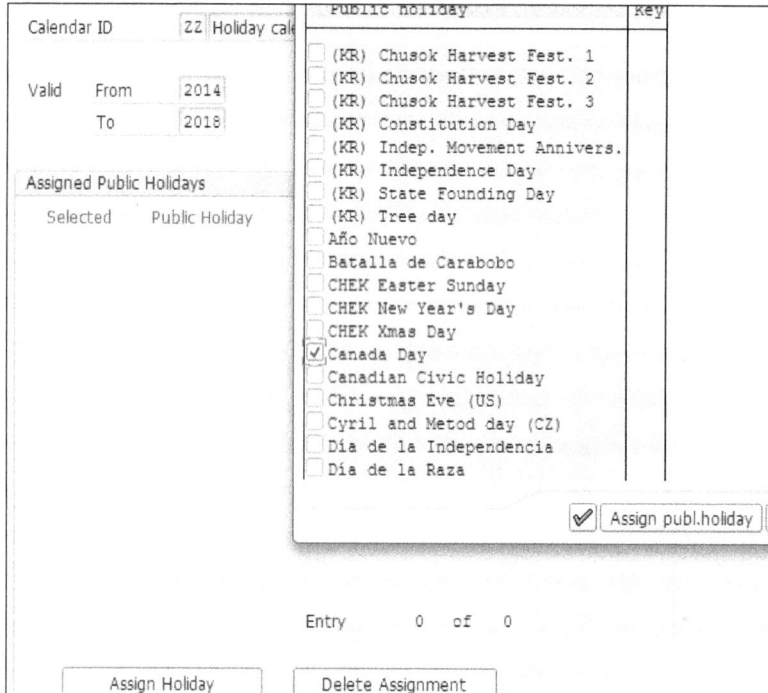

In our case, we have chosen **Canada Day** as a public holiday. When we click on **Assign publ.holiday**, as seen in the preceding screenshot, the holiday gets assigned to the holiday calendar, and it looks like the following screenshot:

The daily work schedule

We can say that the personnel subarea grouping field is the key for generating the work schedule. It's done by navigating to **SPRO** | **Time Management** | **Work Schedules** | **Personnel Subarea Groupings** | **Group Personnel Subareas for the Work Schedule**. It's a two-digit code that is mapped to the **personnel area** (**PA**) and **personnel subarea** (**PSA**). The PA and PSA that have the same working policies can be grouped together for easy processing. In the next step, we map the PS grouping with the **daily work schedule** (**DWS**) grouping. Say, if 99 is a personnel subarea PS grouping, then we will map 99 with the DWS grouping by navigating to **SPRO** | **Time Management** | **Work Schedules** | **Personnel Subarea Groupings** | **Group Personnel Subareas for the Daily Work Schedule**.

The actual working pattern of the employee on a given day is defined in the DWS, and it also includes the break schedule. The DWS can be 9 a.m. to 5 p.m. with a 30-minute break as the break schedule, for example. First, we define the break schedule and then map the break schedule in the DWS. It is configured by navigating to **SPRO** | **Time Management** | **Work Schedules** | **Daily Work Schedules** | **Define Break Schedules**. We mention the start and end time and the stipulated time as paid or unpaid. The break schedule is a four-digit alphanumeric code along with the PS grouping for the daily work schedule that we defined in the previous table.

The following screenshot shows the **Change View "Work Break Schedule":
Overview** window:

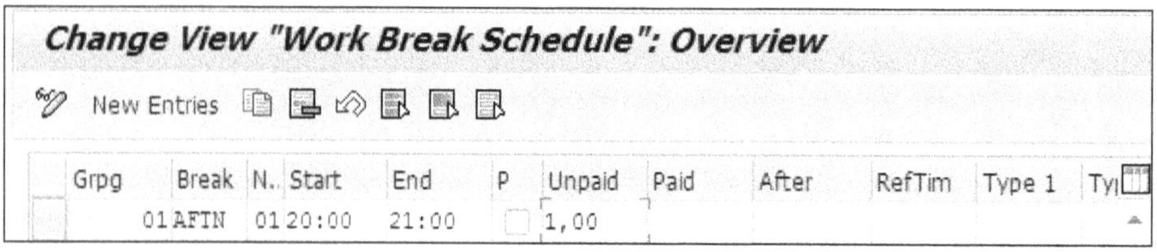

Change View "Work Break Schedule": Overview

New Entries

Grpg	Break	N.	Start	End	P	Unpaid	Paid	After	RefTim	Type 1	Tyｐ
	01 AFTN	01	20:00	21:00		1,00					

The unpaid break is the one that is not remunerated, while a paid one is part of
the remuneration.

The DWS is configured by navigating to **SPRO | Time Management | Work
Schedules | Daily Work Schedules | Define Daily Work Schedules**. The DWS is a
four-digit alphanumeric code along with some text. The **Planned working hours** field
has the total number of working hours per day (9 hours, for example) along with the
break times. In the **Work break schedule** field, the break schedule is mapped. The
following screenshot shows the details of the **Daily Work Schedule** window:

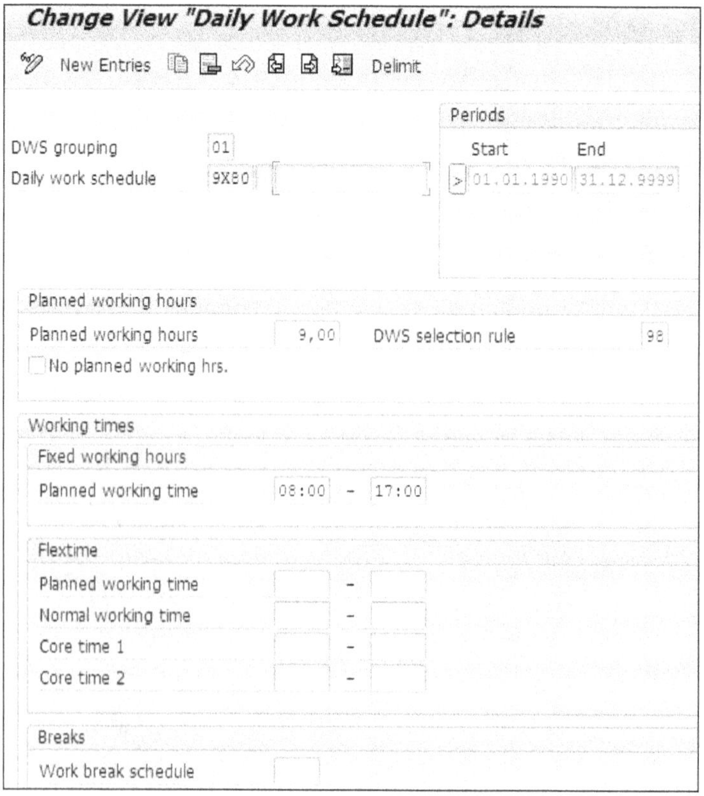

Change View "Daily Work Schedule": Details

New Entries · · · · · Delimit

DWS grouping	01
Daily work schedule	9X80

Periods

	Start	End
>	01.01.1990	31.12.9999

Planned working hours

| Planned working hours | 9,00 | DWS selection rule | 98 |

☐ No planned working hrs.

Working times

Fixed working hours

| Planned working time | 08:00 | – | 17:00 |

Flextime

Planned working time		–	
Normal working time		–	
Core time 1		–	
Core time 2		–	

Breaks

| Work break schedule | |

If the **No planned working hrs.** checkbox is flagged, it means that it's a non-working day. The best practice is to copy a DWS and rename it. We can flag the **No planned working hrs** checkbox to use it in a non-working day such as Saturday or Sunday. The system considers it as zero working hours irrespective of whether the working time, fixed or flexible, is maintained or not. This is one of the improvements made in SAP time recording and evaluation. Earlier, the **Daily work schedule** class was set to 0 to indicate that it was a day off.

The period work schedule

The period work schedule represents the weekly work pattern followed by the employee. It could be for a week or month depending on the business. The daily work schedule is mapped to the period work schedule by navigating to **SPRO | Time Management | Work Schedules | Period Work Schedules**.

The period work schedule is a four-digit alphanumeric code, and the week number represents the number of the week followed by the daily work schedule.

The day type

The day type has a defined standard meaning and is used for payment purpose. It can be customized by navigating to **SPRO | Time Management | Work Schedules | Day Types | Define Day Types**.

The standard system has 4 day types defined, and only if required, new day types need to be defined. The standard day types and their text are shown in the following table:

Day type	Text
0	Work paid
1	Time off paid
2	Time off unpaid
3	Special day
4-9	Customer specific

The Work schedule rule

The employee subgroup grouping, holiday calendar grouping, and personnel subarea grouping form the key when defining the work schedule rule, and this gets populated automatically in the 0007 infotype based on this grouping. First, the employee subgroup grouping is done by navigating to **SPRO | Time Management | Work Schedules | Define Work Schedule Rules and Work Schedule | Define Employee Subgroup Grouping**.

Next is the holiday calendar grouping; this is done by navigating to **SPRO | Time Management | Work Schedules | Define Work Schedule Rules and Work Schedule | Define Groupings for the Public Holiday Calendar**.

The key fields for the work schedule rule generation are the ES, PS, Holiday calendar grouping, and the working time. We define the daily working hours, monthly working hours, and daily working hours in configurable tables. In the work schedule generation, we map the period work schedule. The reference date indicates the date from which we would like to generate the work schedule, and the start point refers to 001 to 007, where 001 is Monday and 007 is Sunday here. Say, if we wish to generate the work schedule from 01-01-2014, which falls on a Wednesday, we will assign the start point in PWS as 003 (Wednesday).

The work schedule is customized by navigating to **SPRO | Time Management | Work Schedules | Define Work Schedule Rules and Work Schedule | Set Work Schedule Rules and Work Schedules**.

The work schedule can be generated manually or in a batch by navigating to **SPRO | Time Management | Work Schedules | Define Work Schedule Rules and Work Schedule | Generate Work Schedules Manually/Batch**.

SAP has delivered a standard feature called SCHKZ to default the work schedule rule. The return value based on the different fields based on the enterprise and personnel structure fields forms the default value for the work schedule rule. The TMSTA feature is used to default the Time Management status in the Planned Working Time infotype (0007). The different statuses and their meanings have been covered earlier in this chapter.

We will see the customizing tables that can be accessed for table maintenance using SM30/SM31:

Table	Node Text
V_001P_N	**Group Personnel Subareas for the Work Schedule**
T508Z	**Assignment of PS Grouping for Work Schedules to Daily WS**
V_T550P	**Work Break Schedule**

Table	Node Text
V_T550A	Daily Work Schedule
V_T551A	Period Work Schedule
V_T553T	Day Types Text
V_503_D	Employee Subgroup Grouping for Work Schedule
V_001P_M	Assign Personnel Subarea to Public Holiday Calendar
V_T508A	Work Schedule Rule

We will ideally be using many Employee subgroups and Personnel subarea groupings in the following nodes:

Personnel subarea grouping – V_0001_P_ALL	Employee sub group grouping – V_503_ALL
Group Personnel Subareas for the Work Schedule	Define Employee Subgroup Groupings for work schedule
Group Personnel Subareas for the Daily Work Schedule	Group Employee Subgroups for Time Quotas
Personnel area and personnel subarea grouping for the public holiday calendar	Primary Wage type
Personnel area and personnel subarea grouping for absence/attendance	Personnel Calculation Rule
Group Personnel Subareas for Time Quotas	
Personnel area and personnel subarea grouping for Substitution/Availability	
Personnel area and personnel subarea grouping for Absence/Attendance counting	

MODT is an important PCR that sets the employee subgrouping for PCR. The "where is used" feature (*Ctrl* + *Shift* + *F3*) will show us where the PCR is actually used in the schema. The PAYTP operation can be used to re-assign the value based on the Org assignment that is based on settings in the employee subgroup grouping for PCR/CAP or employee grouping for the time evaluation rule. The operation is followed by one of the two variables, X or Y.

For variable X (the generalized wage type), there are two standard values, G and V, which are defined as follows:

- G: The wage/time type is set to "****"
- V: The employee subgroup grouping is set

Variable Y (determines the employee subgroup) takes three values that can be assigned, that is S, A, and other (represented by *n*). They are defined as follows:

- S: The employee subgroup grouping from the Time Recording infotype (0050) is set

- A: The employee subgroup grouping from the employee subgroup grouping table (T503) is set

- *n*: The employee subgroup grouping is set to *n* irrespective of the current value assigned

The MODT rule is defined as follows:

```
MODT (Determine groupings)
  *
    ****
        PAYTP A Set ESG for PCR
          3
            ****
                MODIF W=01
                MODIF T=01
                MODIF A=01
                MODIF L=01
```

Thus, based on the ESG grouping for PCR, the rule processes the conditions further.

Important nodes and/or customizing tables for Absence Quotas

We have learned, from previous chapters, about absence being recorded in the 2001 infotype and Absence Quotas being captured in the 2006 infotype. When the absence is created automatically, it reflects in the entitlements getting reduced proportionately.

We will cover the important customizing steps for the generation of Absence Quotas and automatic deduction of absences.

Absences are simply the unavailability of employees to work for various reasons such as sickness, personal reasons, and so on. First, the catalog for absences is created by navigating to **SPRO | Time Management | Absences | Absence Catalog | Group Personnel Subareas for Attendances and Absences**.

This is useful in cases where multiple personnel areas and personnel subareas have the same absences. In the next step, we define the absences such as sick leave, for example. We do it by navigating to **SPRO | Time Management | Absences | Absence Catalog | Define Absence Types**.

There are multiple options provided by SAP for the input checks of absences; we can choose from these options. The standard values are given as follows:

- **First day is day off**
- **Minimum duration**
- **Last day is day off**
- **Maximum duration**
- **Non-working period**
- **Unit**

For the **First day is an off** option, we can choose one of the following options. For example, if we select W, a warning message populates when an absence is created in the 2001 infotype:

- No message
- W: Warning
- I: Information
- E: Error message

The preceding options are applicable for the absence entered on the last day and on a non-working day, for instance, on New Year's Eve.

The minimum and maximum duration is the number of days that an employee can apply in the 2001 infotype. The absence can be recorded in different units, and they are as follows:

Unit	Short description
Blank	Calendar Days
K	Calendar Days
A	Attendance and absence days
R	Payroll days

The following screenshot shows the **Absence: Input Checks** window, which shows the different nodes that were discussed earlier in this section:

When the **Second date required** option is flagged, it indicates that the **Start** date and **End** date has to be entered when an absence is recorded for an employee in the 2001 infotype.

We will cover the important customizing nodes used to count absences. We do so by navigating to **SPRO | Time Management | Time Data Recording and Administration | Absences | Absence Catalog | Absence Counting | Define Counting Classes for the Period Work Schedule**.

The counting class for the period work schedule is useful in the counting rule step. For each separate class maintained, we need to create a counting rule and this is how we can have different sets of counting rules, depending on the business requirement.

The rules set for the counting class is a very important step for counting the recorded absences based on the different conditions that get satisfied. First, we group employees and personnel subgroups for time quotas by navigating to **SPRO | Time Management | Time Data Recording and Administration | Absences | Absence Catalog | Absence Counting | Rules for Absence Counting (New) | Group Employee Subgroups for Time Quotas**. Thus, employee groups and subgroups for which the same absence quota type is applicable are grouped together for easy maintenance.

In the next node, we group personnel areas and subareas for which the same absence quota type is applicable. We do this by navigating to **SPRO | Time Management | Time Data Recording and Administration | Absences | Absence Catalog | Absence Counting | Rules for Absence Counting (New) | Group Personnel Subareas for Time Quotas**.

The rounding absence step can be used to round absences that fall in the upper and lower limit for the purpose of precision, and the rounding rule is mapped to the counting rule. We create a rounding rule by navigating to **SPRO | Time Management | Time Data Recording and Administration | Absences | Absence Catalog | Absence Counting | Rules for Absence Counting (New) | Define Rules for Rounding Counted Absences**. Say, for example, if the absence calculated is in the range of 1.5 to 2.5, then it needs to be rounded off to 2.

The counting rule is an important table that is used to define the different set of rules for calculating payroll days and hours for an absence or recorded absence. It is also useful for quota purpose. We customize this rule by navigating to **SPRO | Time Management | Time data recording and administration | Absences | Absence Catalog | Absence Counting | Rules for Absence Counting (New) | Define Counting Rules**. Once we do this, the following window appears:

The applicability of rules works on different conditions set and met. The counting rule is a three-digit alphanumeric code and sequence number. We can set different conditions and accordingly assign the sequence number; the system checks the conditions one after another until a particular condition is met. The conditions of the current day are checked, for example, if this rule is applicable on a particular day between Monday to Sunday based on the day that we flag. We need to flag all the days if we want the rule to be applicable irrespective of the day in question.

The **Holiday class** option is checked against the public holidays that are defined in the SCAL T-code (Holiday calendar). Say, there's an absence created on January 1, 2014, and we have created a holiday on the same day and flagged it as **Holiday class 1**, which is a normal public holiday. Now, the system compares this with the holiday created and doesn't count it as an absence. We are actually instructing the system to also check on a public holiday based on the flag. If all of them are flagged, then the system checks all the days.

The day type's functionality is specifically for the purpose of payment, and day type rules are used in work schedule rules. This again can be queried using different flags set. The following screenshot shows the conditions for the work schedule:

The **Counting class 0** checkbox has been previously used to check planned non-working days, and we have also seen the improvements made. Hence, it's redundant now. The recommended practice is to check all the entries and uncheck the ones that we feel won't be required. This helps in preventing attendance/absences from not being counted by mistake.

If planned hours such as Sunday need to be counted, then we use the **Planned hours = 0** flag. We have to flag both the entries to satisfy the condition.

If we want the absences that are lesser than a full day to also be counted, then we need to flag the **< 1 day** option; or, both the entries must be flagged. The rounding rule is used for rounding absences and is mapped in the counting rule, while the **Quota multiplier** option is used to satisfy two of the following conditions:

- To determine the payroll hours and days
- To count the absences and attendances for quota deduction

Based on the counting rule defined, we map it to the related absence type. The connection flows from the counting rule to the absence type to the deduction rule that holds the quotas that are mapped to the counting rule.

Finally, the counting rule is mapped to the absence type by navigating to **SPRO | Time Management | Time Data Recording and Administration | Absences | Absence Catalog | Absence Counting | Assign Counting Rules to Absence Types**. The following screenshot shows the **Absence: Counting and Quota Deduction** window:

If we would like the quota to be deducted when an absence is recorded, we need to check the **Quota deduction** flag. The **Deduction over interval end** option indicates that the system allows us to deduct absences more than the entitlement, instead of throwing an error. There are multiple tables that control quota that can be deducted over and beyond the entitlements.

Absence Quotas generation rule configuration

We will see how the Absence Quotas entitlements and generation rules are configured in the following steps. There are three important customizing steps that need to be performed to generate quotas. They are as follows:

- Base entitlements that give us the number of days an employee can avail for a particular period such as a calendar year
- Validity and deduction intervals
- Generation rules for quotas

We will see them in this chapter as we move along. The prerequisite to Absence Quotas is the grouping of personnel subarea and employee subgroup, and it's done by navigating to **SPRO | Time Management | Time Data Recording and Administration | Managing Time Accounts Using Attendance/Absence Quotas | Setting Groupings for Time Quotas | Group Employee Subgroups for Time Quotas**.

Just as we maintained employee groups and subgroups earlier, similarly, we group the employee groups and subgroups here.

Similarly, the personnel areas and subareas are grouped together, thus having the same Absence Quotas. They are customized by navigating to **SPRO | Time Management | Time Data Recording and Administration | Managing Time Accounts Using Attendance/Absence Quotas | Setting Groupings for Time Quotas | Group Personnel Subareas for Time Quotas**.

The quota types (entitlements) such as sick leave and annual leave must be defined first by navigating to **SPRO | Time Management | Time Data Recording and Administration | Managing Time Accounts Using Attendance/Absence Quotas | Time Quota Types | Define Absence Quota Types**.

The different measures of time that SAP has provided are Hours and Days. The entitlements over and above this can be defined in the **Neg. ded. to** field, as shown in the following screenshot:

ESG Time quota types				Start	End
PS Grpg Tm Quota Typ	13			> 01.01.1900	31.12.9999
Absence quota type	60	Annual Leave			

Absence Quota Type

Recording

Time/measurement unit	Hours		Start time	00:00
Time constraint class	01		End time	00:00
Transfer rem. entitlement	☐			

Deduction

Neg. ded. to		Rounding	☐

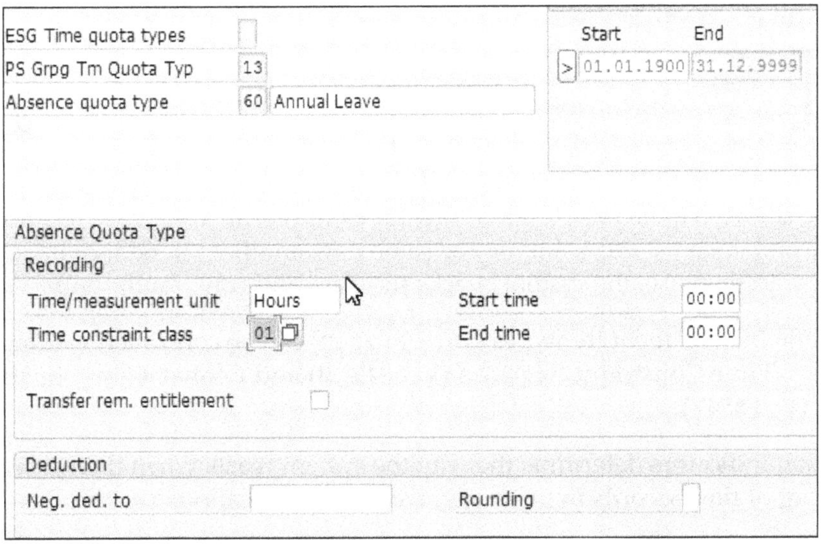

The input for the **Absence quota type** field is a two-digit alphanumeric code. The Absence Quotas are accrued based on the customization. SAP has provided multiple ways of accruing quotas, and they are as follows:

- When not considering time evaluation, use the RPTQTA00 report
- When considering time evaluation, use the time evaluation driver PT60 T-code

In order to generate quota without time evaluation, that is, using the RPTQTA00 report, we use the **No generation** radio button to control it. If we would like to generate quota using the time evaluation driver, we use the **Increase** or **Replace** radio button. We customize it by navigating to **SPRO | Time Management | Time Data Recording and Administration | Managing Time Accounts Using Attendance/Absence Quotas | Calculating Absence Entitlements | Automatic Accrual of Absence Quotas | Permit Generation of Quotas in Time Evaluation**. The following screenshot shows the **Absence Quota Type** window:

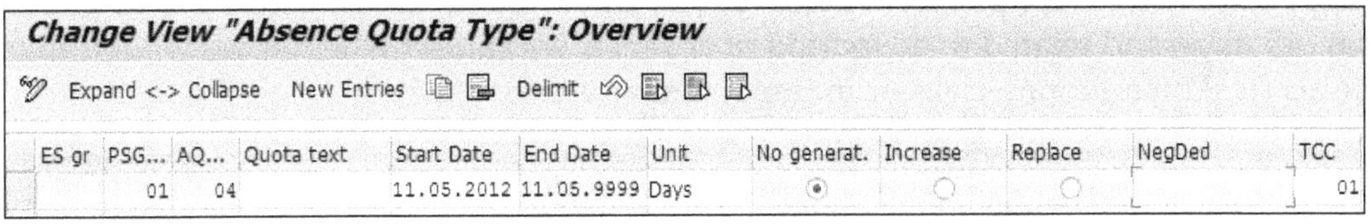

Change View "Absence Quota Type": Overview

Expand <-> Collapse   New Entries   Delimit

ES gr	PSG...	AQ...	Quota text	Start Date	End Date	Unit	No generat.	Increase	Replace	NegDed	TCC
	01	04		11.05.2012	11.05.9999	Days	⦿	○	○		01

The entitlements over and above this can be defined in the **NegDed** (Negative deduction) field. The **No generation, Increase,** and **Replace** fields have a specific functionality associated with it. The **No generation** flag indicates that the Absence Quotas are maintained manually or using a report.

> If we have the **Increase** or **Replace** flag checked, the quotas cannot be generated using the RPTQTA00 report.

The **Time Constraint** (**TC**) class has specific meaning associated with it. The collision checks are controlled via the TC class. Say, for example, an absence is recorded for an employee on January 1, 2014, and on the same day, another attendance or substation is recorded. In this case, the system checks the class and controls the entry.

All the Time Management infotypes (2001 to 2012) can be controlled via the table views, **Time Constraint Reaction (V_554Y_B)** and **Global Time Constraint Reaction (V_T554Y)**.

The reaction indicators determine the way the system reacts when there is an overlapping of time records in infotypes, and the specifications are as follows:

Specification	Text
A	The records get delimited
E	The system doesn't allow us to create a new record
W	The old record remains unchanged, and the system allows us to create a new record
N	Same as W, and collision checks are not displayed

The important rules that control the generation of quotas are defined later on. The maximum limits or entitlements are defined by navigating to **SPRO** | **Time Management** | **Time Data Recording and Administration** | **Managing Time Accounts Using Attendance/Absence Quotas** | **Calculating Absence Entitlements** | **Rules for Generating Absence Quotas** | **Set Base Entitlements**.

We can define the rules for constant in days or hours for each leave quota that serves as a prorating absence for the accrual period. It's a three-digit code that has the quota mapped to it, for example, for sick leave. The entitlements can be defined as constant, say, 15 days, and related to the period of absence, we can set whether we want it to be accrued on a prorate basis or in lump sum advance.

The base entitlement also has the additional feature of defining it based on two of the following options:

- Seniority
- Age

Seniority is the duration of stay in the company/client based on which the quotas get accrued, say, for example, for 1 to 2 years it's 10 days, while for 2 to 3 years it's 20 days.

If we would like the rule to be set based on the Age feature, say 20 to 30 years, a certain amount of leave needs to be accrued. Then, we can make use of this provision. The following screenshot shows the **Base Entitlement for Absence Quota Generation** window:

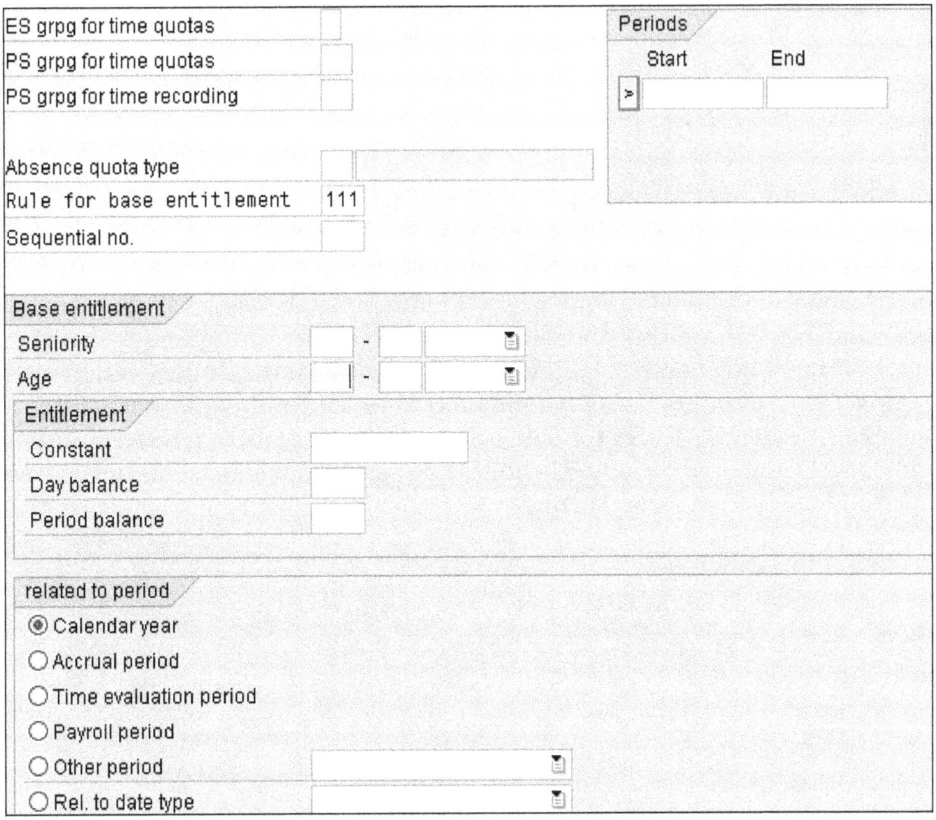

		Periods	
ES grpg for time quotas		Start	End
PS grpg for time quotas		>	
PS grpg for time recording			
Absence quota type			
Rule for base entitlement	111		
Sequential no.			

Base entitlement

Seniority		-	
Age		-	

Entitlement

Constant	
Day balance	
Period balance	

related to period

- ● Calendar year
- ○ Accrual period
- ○ Time evaluation period
- ○ Payroll period
- ○ Other period
- ○ Rel. to date type

The base entitlement related to period is as follows:

- **Calendar year**: One full year from `0101XXX` to `3112XXXX`

- **Accrual period**: The period based on which the accrual must take place

- **Time evaluation period**: The period is specified by navigating to **SPRO | Personnel Time Management | Time Evaluation | General Settings | Determine Time Evaluation Period** and is queried when this option is flagged

- **Payroll period**: Based on the payroll area, the payroll period that is valid for the current period is queried

- **Other period**: This is based on period parameters defined in customizing

- **Rel. to date type**: This is referenced to the `0041` date specification, and the length can be defined by defining the period of time more specifically

> The Base entitlement (V_T559E), Determine validity and deduction intervals (V_T559D), Reduction rules (T559M), and Rounding rules (V_T559R) can also be defined directly by going to the Selection rule table (V_T559L).

The validity and deduction periods for Absence Quotas define the "from" and "to" periods for which the quotas are valid and the period in which the quotas can be deducted. Say, between `01/Jan/XXXX` and `31/12/XXXX`, the quotas can be deducted. The validity intervals are defined more precisely using the standard options available. The validity and deduction intervals are configured by navigating to **SPRO | Time Management | Time Data Recording and Administration | Managing Time Accounts Using Attendance/Absence Quotas | Calculating Absence Entitlements | Rules for Generating Absence Quotas | Determine Validity and Deduction Periods**. The following screenshot shows the **Determine Validity and Deduction Periods** window:

Absence quota type		

Validity interval

Valid from				Valid to			
⦿ Calendar year				⦿ Calendar year			
○ Time evaluation period				○ Time evaluation period			
○ Payroll period				○ Payroll period			
○ Accrual period				○ Accrual period			
○ Base period				○ Base period			
○ Transfer time				○ Transfer time			
○ Other period				○ Other period			
○ Date type				○ Date type			
⦿ Start	○ End			⦿ Start	○ End		
Relative position				Relative position			

Deduction interval

Deduction from	Deduction to
⦿ Start of validity interval	⦿ Start of validity interval
○ End of validity interval	○ End of validity interval

There are a couple of more options to choose from, which are different from the Base entitlements period that we saw, and they are as follows:

- Base period
- Transfer Time

The rounding rule is a two-digit alphanumeric code and is used to round off the generated quota entitlements. We can define the values of **Lower limit**, **Upper limit**, and **Target value**, for example, if we would like the quotas between 1.5 and 1.75 to be rounded off to 2. The Rounding rule is customized by navigating to **SPRO | Time Management | Time Data Recording and Administration | Managing Time Accounts Using Attendance/Absence Quotas | Calculating Absence Entitlements | Rules for Generating Absence Quotas | Define Rules for Rounding Quota Entitlements**. The following screenshot shows the **Rounding Rule** window:

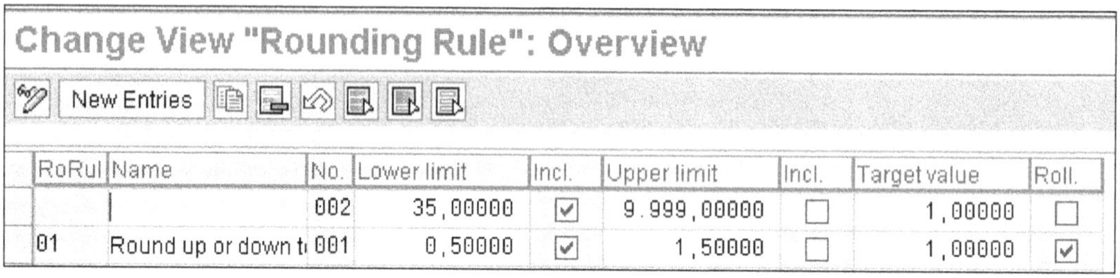

Change View "Rounding Rule": Overview

New Entries

RoRul	Name	No.	Lower limit	Incl.	Upper limit	Incl.	Target value	Roll.
		002	35,00000	☑	9.999,00000	☐	1,00000	☐
01	Round up or down t	001	0,50000	☑	1,50000	☐	1,00000	☑

The **Roll.** field indicates that the rule is applicable for all the intervals defined in the table. When the **Incl.** field is flagged, it indicates that the upper or lower limit is included in the calculation.

Finally, we define the selection rule by navigating to **SPRO | Time Management | Time Data Recording and Administration | Managing Time Accounts Using Attendance/Absence Quotas | Calculating Absence Entitlements | Rules for Generating Absence Quotas | Define Generation Rules for Quota Type Selection**. The following screenshot shows the **Generation Rules for Quota Type Selection** window:

ESG for time quotas	1			Periods	
PSG for time quotas	01			Start	End
PSG for time rec.	01			> 01.01.1990	31.12.9999

Quota type sel. grp	01	
Selection rule	002	Time off from overtime
Absence quota type	02	Time off entitl.from PDC

| Applicability | Accrual period | Base entitl. | Accrual entitl. | Transfer time | Total entitl. |

Rule for base entitlement   001

Base Entitlement

Number	Day bal.	PeriodBalance	Unit	Base Period	From
0,00000			Hours		
0,00000			Hours		
0,00000			Hours		

Calculation of Seniority

Calculation Process

Key Date for Determining Seniority	Key Date for Determining Age
⦿ For Exact Day	⦿ For Exact Day
○ Start ... ○ End of Accrual Period	○ Start ... ○ End of Accrual Period
○ Start ... ○ End of Base Period	○ Start ... ○ End of Base Period
○ Date Type	○ Date Type

The prerequisites are the Base Entitlements, Absence Quotas, and validity and deduction periods that are defined before customizing the selection rule table.

We will find multiple tabs for customization; they are as follows:

- **Applicability**
- **Accrual Period**
- **Base Entitlements**
- **Accrual Entitlements**
- **Total Entitlements**

The entry date is defined in the **Applicability** tab. For example, we can give `01011900` to `31129999` as the entry date.

The **Accrual Period** tab we defined will be used if the entitlements are prorated on the following basis:

- **Daily**: In this case, the entitlements are divided by 365 days
- **Month**: The base entitlements are divided by 12 calendar months
- **Calendar year**: The entitlements are accrued for the calendar year
- **Time evaluation period**: It's according to the customizing step in `SPRO`
- **Payroll period**: It's according to the period parameter
- **Other period**: It's according to the period parameter
- **Rel. to date type**: It's according to `0041`; the accrual period varies

The **Base Entitlements** tab is used to map the rule defined earlier, for which the prerequisites for the selection rule are also the same. The **Limit** field is defined using this tab. If we would like to generate the quota based on seniority or age, the **Key Date for Determining Seniority** subtab needs to be customized.

The **Accrual Entitlements** tab indicates whether the quotas need to be prorated or nonprorated. There is also the provision to multiply with day or period balances.

There are many options to choose from in the **Transfer time** tab:

- **Upon accrual**
- **Per calendar year**
- **Per time evaluation period**
- **Per payroll period**
- **Other period**
- **Date type**
- **Transfer rule** (this is not applicable for all the countries)

Tips to generate Absence Quotas without any hassles

The key to customizing absence quota configuration is employee subgroup grouping and personnel subarea grouping. Most of the configuration gets simplified if we use the correct grouping. We have reiterated this throughout the chapter.

Frequent error message and workaround

Most of the time, we come across the infamous `You have not selected any generation rules error` error. This error occurs when we use both `RPTQTA00` report and the `PT60` time evaluation driver T-code. To address this issue, we need to check the following tables via `SM30`/`SM31` or via SPRO:

Table	Text
V_001P_H	Personnel subarea grouping for time recording
V_T559E	Base entitlement for absence quota generation
V_T559L	Selection rules
V_T559D	Validity / Deduction intervals for Absence Quotas
V_001P_ALL	Personnel area / subarea complete view
V_503_ALL	Employee group / subgroup complete view

We come across errors such as `Not enough quota for attendance/absence 1000 on 29.03.2011 for personnel no. 00030010, Message no. HRTIM00REC014`.

There is a note released with the correction instruction; it says `OSS 601872 - Error message displays incorrect quota type`. We also need to check whether the configuration settings are correct.

We also frequently receive errors such as `Time evaluation PT60 error STOP: No rule under key $ TP20*****2 S ***`. This error clearly suggests that in `TP20`, the PCR doesn't have the `***` absence type added in the rule. This is shown in the following screenshot:

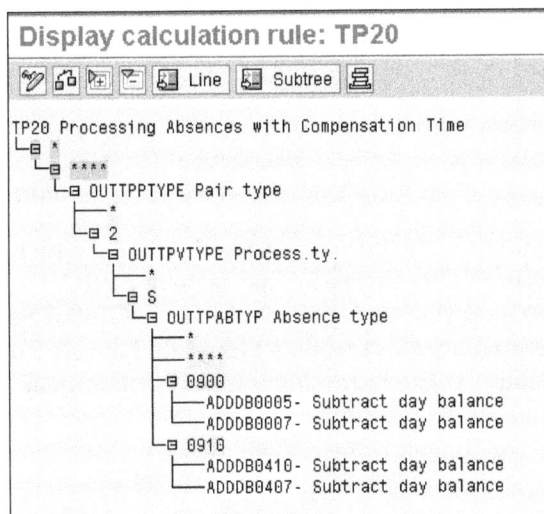

The best practice is to copy the rule and rename it, for example, to ZP20. As we can see in the following screenshot, there is a pair type 2 and a process type S for which a decision tree is built. The error, as discussed earlier, is trying to query the Absence type with the *** condition, which is missing in the standard rule, and hence, the system is throwing the error.

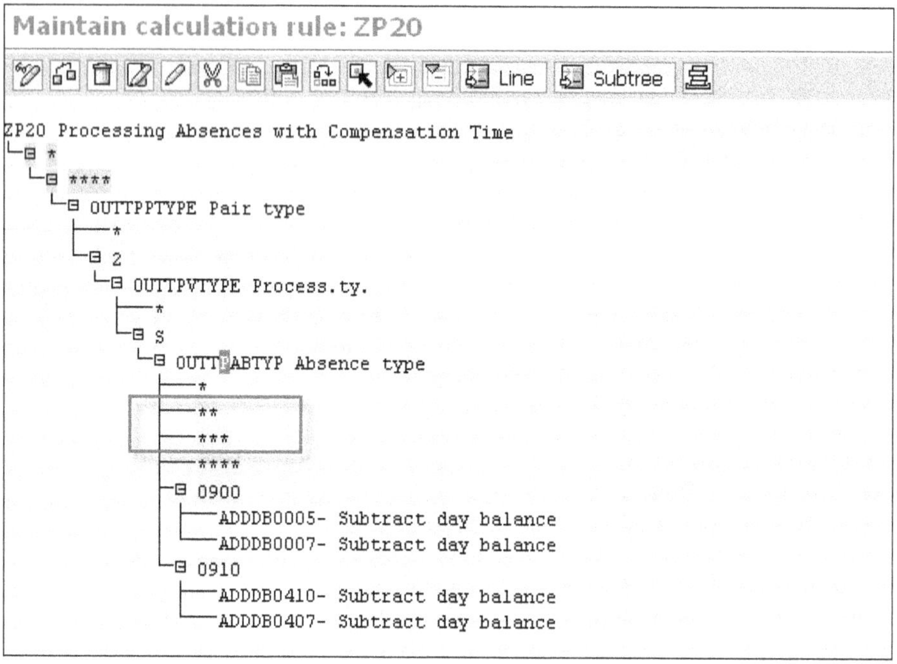

Now, when the ZP20 rule is inserted in the schema, the system won't throw the error message. The system is able to query single, double, and triple asteriskes that were missing in the standard PCR.

Another error that we bump into is entry no. 83 Error when creating absence quota General information, Rule: 001 quota type 01 Casual Leave, No payroll period for key 19 20100131 when we run a time evaluation.

The T549Q tables might not have the start and end date for which the time evaluation is actually run. To fix this issue, navigate to **SPRO | Payroll | Payroll XX** (XX-localized country like USA for example) | **Global Settings | Payroll Organization | Generate Payroll Periods | Generate Payroll Run Period** or simply execute the RPUCTP00 report. The following window will appear:

The RPUCTP00 report is significant for both Payroll and Time purposes. The parameters included in this report are as follows:

- **Period Parameter**: This determines the frequency of payroll such as monthly, weekly, and so on.
- **Date modifier**: We can use the following standard ones provided:
    - 00: Standard modifier
    - 01: Standard modifier
- **Start Date**: This is the period start date, such as 01012014.
- **Final year**: This is the year until which the periods need to be generated.
- **Start date of fiscal year**: This is based on the country legal settings. It varies between countries (such as in the Middle East, it's January to December; in India, its April to March).
- **Payday rule**: This has the following standard meanings:
    - 1: This adds the number of days to the period start date
    - 2: This deducts the number of days from the period end date
    - 3: This adds the number of days to the period end date
    - 4: This is used only for monthly periods and the number of days is used as the payment day

This field works in conjunction with the **Number of days** field.

- **Number of days**: This is based on the number assigned in the **Payday rule** field. The days are calculated. For example, if we assign 1 in **Payday rule** and 1 in **Number of days**, the system would pick the period end date, say, December. It will pick 31 and add one day to it. So, the payday becomes January 1.

- **Determine period number**: This is an indicator to map the period number based on the standard settings provided by SAP, which are as follows:
    - Payment day for period
    - Start date for period
    - End date for period

Important Time Management-related tables

We will see the important tables that control the Time Management module in the following table:

Table	Table Name
V_T552V	Dynamic Assignment of Daily Work Schedule Assignment
V_T554C	Employee Grouping for Absence Valuation
V_T555A	Time Types
V_T555E	Error Messages
V_T555Z	Time Type Determination (TIMTP)
V_T559P	Time Balance Rule Group
V_T559L	Quotas
V_T559P	Limits
V_T510V	Processing Types
V_T705A	Absence Reasons
V_554S_E	Absence, Processing, and Time Type classes

Important functions, operations, and features

Functions are technical code or **Advanced Business Application Programming (ABAP)** code, a logical block used to perform a bigger calculation, and logic is built into it to perform the task. Operations, on the other hand, are used to perform a little bit of calculation, and they can be called as PCR's control behavior. Some of the important functions are given in the following table:

Function	Text
QUOTA	The Generate Absence Quotas function is used in the RPTQTA00 report and the Time schema (TM04/TM00). Quota function is called in the 000810 line of the standard TM00 schema and the 000730 line of the TM04 schema. It's based on the T559L settings function quota that generates Absence Quotas. If time evaluation is used, the results are stored in the QTACC and QTTRANS table clusters.
CUMBT	This function is used to cumulate the results in the Results table (RT).
P2001	This function is used to import absence in the internal table TIP for further processing.
GWT	This function generates wage type from time pairs.
P2006	The Process Absence Quotas function is used to query the values in the ABWKONTI internal table for further processing.

We will explore some important operations that will be very handy to map the business process in SAP. Operations are very useful to change the data stored in the input table during processing.

The common types of operations are given as follows:

- Decision operations
- Operations that initiate one or more actions
- Branch operations
- Operations to update internal tables
- Operations to read internal tables
- Operations to manipulate hours

> For additional information, refer to *The building blocks of SAP Time Evaluation*, Dirk Liepold.

Some of the important operations are given in the following table:

Operation	Text
COLER	Transfer to error table
ADDDB	Cumulate in day balance table
ADDMB	Cumulate in monthly balance table
ADDZL	Cumulate in time wage types tables
COLOP	Transfer data to internal table TOP
HRS	Edit Number of Hours Field
ROUND	Round Clock Times or Number of Hours Field
VARST	Provide General Fields

Features, as we have seen earlier, are used to query fields and return the value. We will learn about some important features related to Time Management; they are as follows:

- QUOMO: This feature is used to determine the absence quota selection based on the organization assignment. This is queried in the V_T559L-QUOMO selection rule table.

- MASEX: This feature is used to determine the infotype admissibility for employees. The following turn values are the standard ones defined in SAP:
    - 0: This is allowed for female and male employees
    - 1: This is allowed for female employees only
    - 2: This is allowed for male employees only

Internal tables and cluster tables used in time evaluation

Internal tables are structured data types in ABAP. They are specified completely by the table type, key, and line type. Some of the important tables are given in the following table:

Table	Text
ERT	Error message table
DZL	Generated day types
ZML	Overtime wage types
ZL	Time wage types
TIP	Daily Input
TOP	Daily Output

Cluster tables are not manageable directly using database system tools. In other words, they are data from different tables packed together as a cluster, and they can be accessed via function modules. The function modules can be accessed via the SE37 T-code.

Table	Text
ZES	Daily time balances
PT	Time Pairs
AB	Absences
ZL	Time wage types

RPTERL00 and RPTERR00 are useful reports to check the predefined error messages, or we can also include our own error messages in T555E (Time Evaluation Errors). The category of error messages are standard and provided by SAP as follows:

- 1: The error set by the COLER operation in time evaluation
- 2: (No longer used) User-specific message from pair formation
- 3: A technical error from pair formation
- 4: A technical error from time evaluation
- 5: Warnings and notes generated by time evaluation

The different messages generated during time evaluation is processed and stored in clusters B1 and B2 as follows:

Message	Table	Cluster
Errors, notes, and information from the last run	ERT	B1
Information that has not been confirmed	ERT	B1
Notes and information from previous runs	FEHLER	B2

Tool to check the configuration settings for quota generation

SAP has delivered a standard report to check the customizing settings in SPRO for absence quota generation. The RPTQUOTA_CHECK report is accessed via SE38/SA38. The document for the report can be found by navigating to **SPRO | Time Management | Time Data Recording and Administration | Managing Time Accounts Using Attendance/Absence Quotas | Calculating Absence Entitlements | Rules for Generating Absence Quotas | Check Customizing Settings for Quota Generation**.

The report is very useful as it displays the customizing settings used for absence quota generation. It displays the list in a tree structure, which helps to figure out the missing table entries. It doesn't, however, simulate the time evaluation, but the setting is actually displayed.

There are three options to choose from when selecting quotas:

- All the generation methods (with/without time evaluation)
- Generation during time evaluation (PT60)
- Generation by the RPTQTA00 report

Summary

In this chapter, we covered all the important Time Management infotypes, from 2001 to 2999. We started off by discussing infotypes. Next, we covered the important customizing steps used to configure Absence Quotas. We also covered frequently occurring error messages and ways to address them. Finally, we learned a few tips to configure the time module.

In the next chapter, we will closely look at configuring the Payroll submodule and explore the standard functionalities provided by SAP.

6
Payroll Configuration

Payroll may not be as complicated as it is assumed to be. This chapter will attempt to enlighten you and correct your notion. We will explore how the Payroll submodule is configured to meet the client's requirements. We will cover the important configuration steps, infotypes, posting payroll results to finance, and the tips and tricks to configure the submodule in depth.

The following topics will be covered in this chapter:

- Infotypes that are mandatory for payroll processing
- The control record
- Payroll configuration
- Writing a **Personnel Calculation Rules** (PCR)
- Integration of payroll processing with the finance module

Infotypes mandatory for payroll processing

Before we start to cover the important configuration points, let's closely look at the mandatory infotypes that need to be maintained to process the payroll for an employee. It's imperative to be familiar with the functionality of payroll-related infotypes before starting the configuration steps.

Payroll infotypes

The **work centre basic pay (WPBP)** infotype is a critical one, so let's closely look at it:

Infotype	Infotype text
0000	Actions
0001	Organizational assignment
0003	Payroll status
0007	Planned working time
0008	Basic pay
0027	Cost distribution

We will cover the infotype's functionalities in detail in this chapter.

The 0000 (Actions) infotype

The Action infotype is the first infotype that gets updated when a personnel action is performed for an employee. Actions that affect payroll could be promotion, demotion, and so on. There is a standard function, WPBP-FUWPBP, in the INBD subschema. This function reads the master data and transfers the data to the internal WPBP table. If there is any change in the work centre and basic pay data due to splits, they are indicated by split indicators. The Actions infotype was covered in *Chapter 4, PA Configuration in Less Than 24 Hours*.

The 0001 (Organizational Assignment) infotype

The Organizational Assignment infotype holds the key characteristics of the employee, for example, company code, personnel area, personnel subarea, employee group, employee subgroup, payroll area, and so on. The enterprise and personnel structure was covered in *Chapter 4, PA Configuration in Less Than 24 Hours*. We will learn the functionality of the payroll area and control record in detail in this chapter.

Payroll area

The personnel area is grouped together and processed in the payroll area. The payroll accounting area or simply payroll area is a two-digit alphanumeric code. The payroll area has the following functionalities:

- To determine the specific payroll dates.
- To determine the specific periods that the payroll is processed for. For example, 01.01.2014 is the start period and 31.01.2013 is the end period.

- To define the earliest retro accounting period that is possible.

- To define retroactive accounting, that can be recognized.

The payroll area is configured by navigating to **SPRO | Personnel Management | Personnel Administration | Organizational Data | Organizational Assignment | Create payroll area** or via the SM30/31 T-code in the V_T549A table.

The Payroll area table has the following fields:

Payroll area	Payroll area text	Period parameter	Period parameter text	Run flag	Date modifier
XX	Monthly payroll area	Code of the frequency of the payroll such as 01	Text of the period parameter, for example, 01 is monthly	Needs to be flagged. Click on **Yes** to run the payroll.	Standard entries are 0 and 1; we can use them to differentiate between the different payment dates

Let's look at the functionalities of the fields in the payroll table. The payroll area table has the period parameter mentioned; this parameter determines the frequency of the payroll period such as monthly, weekly, and biweekly, which is defined by navigating to **SPRO | Payroll | Basic Settings | Payroll Organization | Define period parameters** or via the SM30/31 T-code in the V_T549R table. The period parameter table also has the standard time units defined as follows:

Time unit	Description
01	Monthly
02	Semi-monthly
03	Weekly
04	Biweekly
05	Every four weeks
06	Annually
07	Quarterly
08	Half-yearly

The date modifier, on the other hand, has standard entries defined and can be used to differentiate the payroll run based on different dates. In cases where the payroll periodicity is the same (for example, monthly) but the pay dates are different (for example, for one group of personnel, the pay date is the 15th, and for another group, it's the 20th), then the system will need two different date modifiers.

Date modifier code	Date modifier text
00	Standard modifier
01	Standard modifier 01

The payroll area is defaulted via the ABKRS feature and is configured by navigating to **SPRO | Personnel Management | Personnel Administration | Organizational Data | Organizational Assignment | Check default payroll area**. The return value is the default payroll area based on the different fields for the decision operation.

Control record elucidated

The control record controls how a payroll is processed, and every payroll must have one control record created in the system. The control record is defined by navigating to **SPRO | Personnel Management | Personnel Administration | Organizational Data | Organizational Assignment | Create control record** or via the PA03 T-code.

The control record performs the following functionalities in the system:

- Determines the status of the payroll, for example, if it is in released or exit state, and determines the current period for which the payroll is processed
- Determines the earliest, retro accounting period

It's important to understand the different statuses and their meaning. We will learn them from the following table:

Control record status	Meaning
Released for payroll	The master data and time data are locked and changes cannot be performed
Released for correction	Allows us to make any correction to the master data and time data
Exit payroll	The control record is exited once the payroll is performed for the particular period
Check payroll results	Checks whether the payroll has run correctly

There is also a sort field in the control record that is useful to store the payroll run. Every time the payroll is corrected and rerun, it gets incremented. The control record is sensitive, and access is normally restricted to the PA03 T-code. There are also fields to capture the time stamp that can be helpful for audit purposes. These fields are as follows:

- User ID
- Date
- Time
- Status

The control record was also touched upon in *Chapter 4, PA Configuration in Less Than 24 Hours*.

The 0003 (Payroll Status) infotype

The Payroll Status infotype is created automatically when an employee is hired. It's an important infotype that needs to be understood clearly, as it controls how the payroll is processed if there is any change in the master or time data. Retro calculation is an important concept that needs to be understood in payroll. Retro is any change triggered due to the master or time data changes made to an employee's record when the period payroll is run. The Payroll Status infotype looks like the following screenshot. PU03 is the T-code used for changing the payroll status, only if it's required. This is shown in the following screenshot:

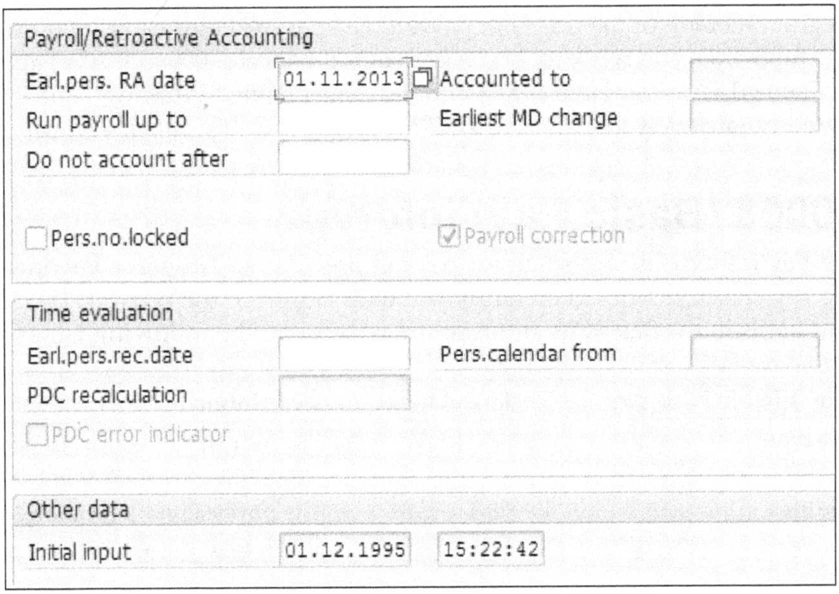

Let's closely look at the fields and their functionalities:

Field	Description
Earl pers RA date	This date is the one up to which the system will allow us to make changes to employee's master data
Accounted to	The period up to which the payroll has actually run
Run payroll up to	The period up to which we want the system to process the payroll for an employee
Earliest MD change	This refers to the master data change period stamp
Do not account after	The period after which we would not want the payroll to be processed for an employee
Payroll correction	This is the system's automatic correction indicator when the payroll rejects an employee or changes are made during the correction
Pers no locked	Personnel number won't be processed by payroll
Earl pers rec date	This is related to time evaluation

> Employees who are rejected during the payroll process are captured in the match code "W" functionality (*Shift+F8*).

The 0007 (Planned Working Time) infotype

The Planned Working Time data serves as an input for the 0008 (Basic Pay) infotype. The employment percentage (P0007-EMPCT) and monthly hours (P0007-MOSTD) serve as an integration point for the time and payroll. The payroll fields capacity utilization level (P0008-BSGRD) and working hours per payroll period (P0008-DIVGV) get filled from the Planned Working Time (0007) infotype. The Planned Working Time infotype was covered exhaustively in *Chapter 5, Time Management Configuration – Negative Time*.

The 0008 (Basic Pay) infotype

The Basic Pay infotype is important for payroll processing. The Basic Pay infotype holds the key characteristics of an employee with regard to the payroll. The important fields in the Basic Pay infotype are covered in the following table:

Important filed in basic pay	Technical name	Description
Pay scale type	P0008-TRFAR	The industry in which the client is operating, such as manufacturing
Pay scale area	P0008-TRFGB	The physical work location of the client, such as California

Important filed in basic pay	Technical name	Description
Pay scale group	P0008-TRFGR	This is used to determine different grades for pay scale distinction
Pay scale level	P0008-TRFST	The pay scale levels are a further bifurcation of the pay scale groups
Annual salary	P0008-ANSAL	This just serves as an input field and is not taken into consideration when the payroll is processed by the payroll driver
Short text for EE subgroup grouping for personnel calc rules	T546T-ATEXT	This is grayed, out and it is a control feature for processing the personnel calculation rule

> The annual salary is configured by navigating to **SPRO | Personnel Administration | Payroll Data | Basic Pay | Define annual salary | Relevant wage types for annual salary valuation**.

The 0027 (Cost Distribution) infotype

The Cost Distribution infotype is designed for the purpose of distributing costs to different Cost Centers other than the master Cost Centre of the employee. The master Cost Centre is normally mapped in Organizational Assignment infotype (0001), and it's overridden when Cost Distribution infotype (0027) is maintained for an employee. This infotype has the provision to mention the breakup percentage between cost centers. However, the percentage cannot exceed 100. Let's look at the important fields that can be maintained in the infotype. The infotype can be accessed via the PA30 or PA20 T-code. The following screenshot demonstrates this:

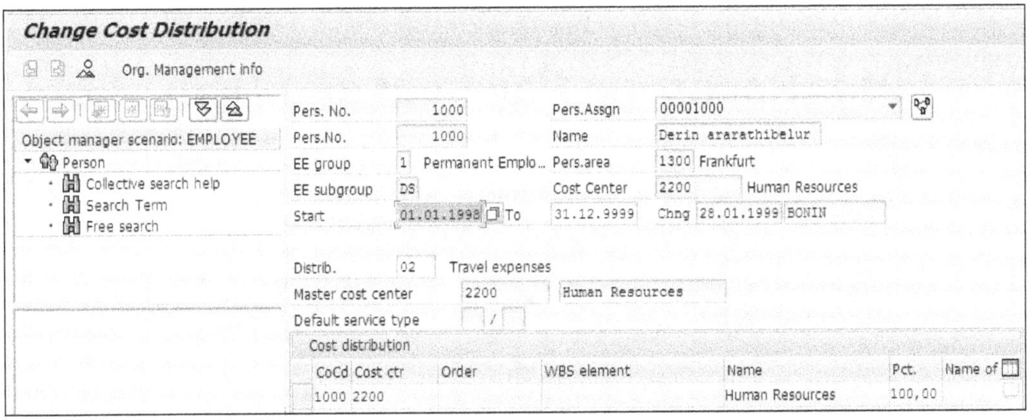

The following table gives information about the various infotypes and a description of them:

Field in infotype	Technical name	Description
Costs to be distributed	P0027-KSTAR	This describes the cost to which the distribution is actually performed. The standard entries are as follows: • Wage/salary • Travel expenses
Company code	RHCD_TAB-BUKRS	This is defined in FI module, and it's defined as per the profit and loss statements for different entities by the client
Cost Centre	RHCD_TAB-KOSTL	This uniquely identifies the Cost Centre
Pct	RHCD_TAB-PROZT	This refers to the weighting percentage of different Cost Centers

> The Cost Distribution infotype is only maintained if there is a requirement of distributing costs across different cost centers, else its master Cost Centre is maintained in 0001I. The Cost Centre is created by an FI consultant, which was explained in *Chapter 3, SPOCK – the Building Block of OM*.

In addition to mandatory infotypes that need to be maintained for payroll processing, it is necessary to know a few other infotypes. They are as follows:

• Recurring Payment and Deduction infotype (0014)

• Additional Payments (0015)

• Additional off-cycle payments (0267)

The 0014 (Recurring Payment and Deduction) infotype

The Recurring Payment and Deduction infotype is used to maintain the deductions and payments made to the employee for a particular period of time.

If you notice, wage types maintained in the Basic Pay (0008) infotype do not have the provision to delimit the wage type processing for a particular period, say, just one month.

In cases where payments or deductions are only for a particular period of time, we can use this infotype. The infotype can be accessed via the PA30 or PA20 T-code. This is demonstrated in the following screenshot:

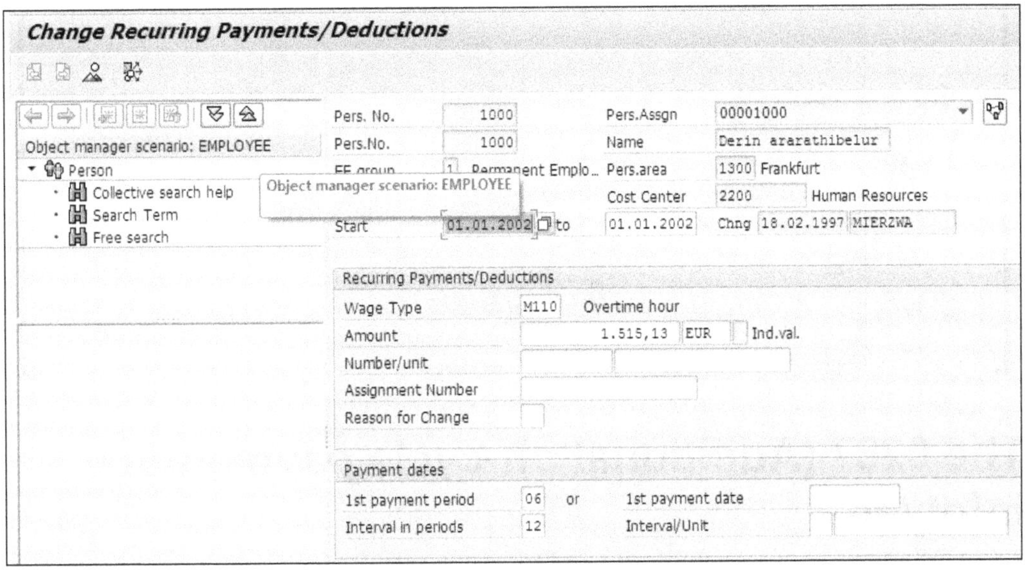

The 0015 (Additional Payments) infotype

The Additional Payments infotype is used for one-time payment purposes. It doesn't have a start date and end date but it does have the date of origin, that is, the date on which the payment must be processed for an employee. The infotype can be accessed via the PA30 or PA20 T-code.

The fields that this infotype have are shown in the following table:

Fields	Technical name	Description
Wage types	P0015-LGART	This refers to the components such as basic pay that are displayed in the paystub
Amount	Q0015-BETRG	This refers to the wage type amount for payment purposes, such as 50 USD
Date of origin	P0015-BEGDA	This refers to the date on which this wage type needs to be processed

We can maintain a different Cost Centre using the functionality maintain cost assignment (*Ctrl+F2*). This is shown in the following screenshot:

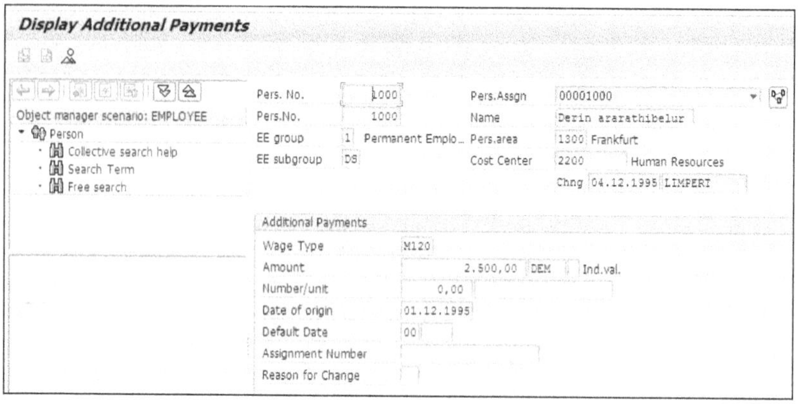

The 0267 (Additional off-cycle payments) infotype

The Additional off-cycle activity is used for payments during irregular payment periods, for example, in the middle of the payroll period. The off-cycle payroll workbench is used to process these scenarios, and the wage type processed using that off-cycle payroll workbench gets stored in the 0267 infotype. The off-cycle configuration steps will be covered in the forthcoming chapters. The infotype can be accessed via the PA30 or PA20 T-code, as shown in the following screenshot:

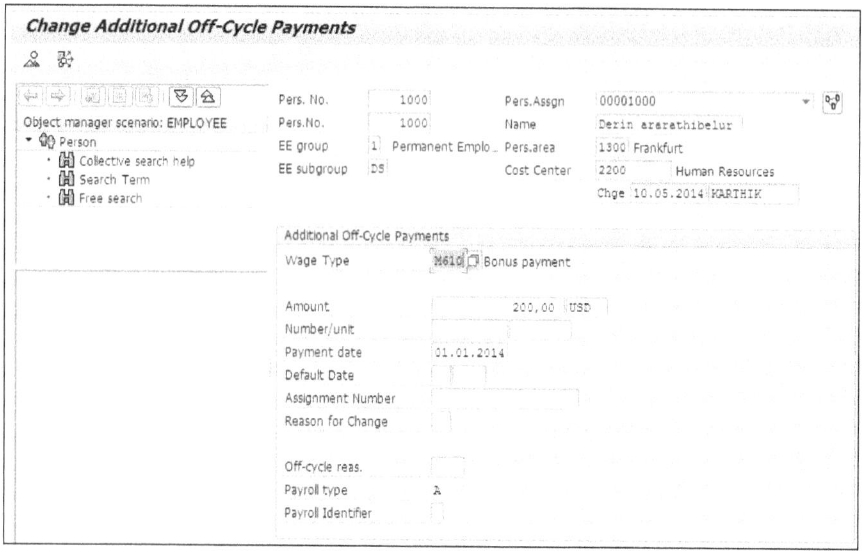

Steps to configure the payroll

We have already covered the important infotypes mandatory for payroll processing. We will look at the configuration steps involved to perform the gross and net calculation.

SAP has a payroll solution for country-specific versions and generic versions as well. There are localized payroll schemas and international schemas for which localization is not yet released by SAP. Each country has its own payroll driver program and payroll schema that covers various statutory requirements for each country.

Wage types

When we talk about payroll in SAP, it's very important to understand the functionalities of wage types. Wage types are components or allowances that we see in our paystub, such as basic pay, conveyance allowance, and so on. SAP has provided a tool to create customer-specific wage types. The best practice is to copy model wage types delivered by SAP and rename it to customer-specific wage types. When a new **service pack** (**SP**) is released by SAP, it ensures that it does not affect customer wage types. The wage types are created by navigating to **SPRO | Personnel Management | Personnel Administration | Payroll Data | Wage Types | Create Wage Type Catalog** or using the OH11 or PU30 T-code.

> Model wage types are prefixed with letters, while customer wage types are prefixed with numbers.

The system prompts us to choose a particular method for maintenance. First, we can select **Copy** and click on **Continue** (*Enter*). The three methods available are as follows:

- Copy
- Delete
- Completeness check

The best practice is to choose a model wage type from the original wage type column and enter a new wage type such as 9000 in the customizing wage type column, as shown in the following screenshot:

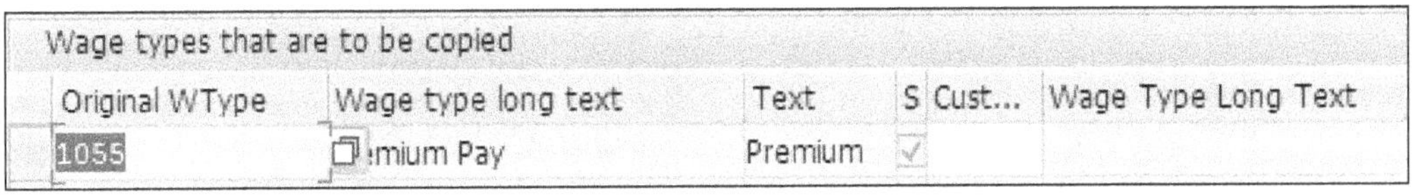

Wage types that are to be copied					
Original WType	Wage type long text	Text	S	Cust...	Wage Type Long Text
1055	:mium Pay	Premium	✓		

The wage types are grouped in the Basic Pay (0008) infotype by navigating to **SPRO | Personnel Management | Personnel Administration | Payroll Data | Wage Types | Check wage type group ' Basic Pay'** or via the SM30/31 T-code in the VV_52D7_B_0008_AL0 table. The rationale is that by assigning the wage type in this group, the administrator will be able to restrict the wage type used for different infotype groups such as 0008, 0014, 0015 and so on.

The wage type text can be checked and corrected if required by navigating to **SPRO | Personnel Management | Personnel Administration | Payroll Data | Wage Types | Check wage type catalog | Check wage type text** or via the SM30/31 T-code in the V_512W_T table.

The wage type's applicability for a particular group of employees can be controlled by navigating to **SPRO | Personnel Management | Personnel Administration | Payroll Data | Wage Types | Check wage type catalog | Define Wage Type Permissibility for each PS and ESG** or via the SM30/31 T-code in the V_511_B table. This just serves as an input to check which wage type is permissible for certain groups, as shown in the following screenshot:

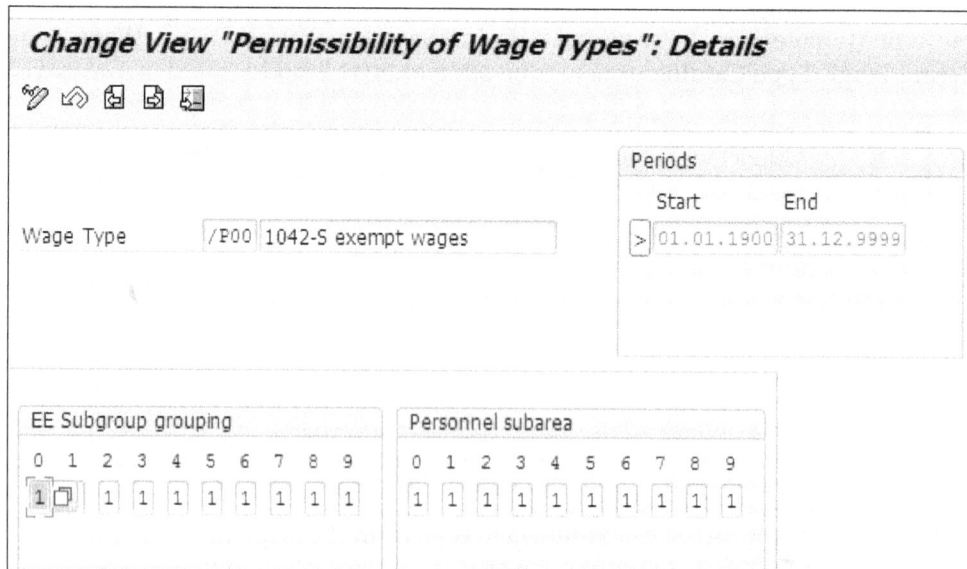

There are three standard options that we can assign from, and they are as follows:

- Wage type for employee subgroup grouping not permissible
- Wage type for employee subgroup grouping permissible
- Wage type for EE subgroup grouping permissible with warning

Let's hypothetically say that we assign a blank space for 1 in employee sub group (ESG) grouping. The personnel subarea (PSA) grouping system will throw us an error message when the wage type is mapped for this group.

This is performed in conjunction with another two steps: employee subgroups for the primary wage type and personnel subareas for the primary wage type. Let's say that we assign a 1 to 9 number range for both EE grouping and personnel subarea grouping for a wage type. This can be viewed by the following path:

- **SPRO | Personnel Management | Personnel Administration | Payroll Data | Wage Types | Employee Subgroups for Primary Wage Type** or via the SM30/31 T-code in the V_503_G table

- **SPRO | Personnel Management | Personnel Administration | Payroll Data | Wage Types | Personnel Subareas for Primary Wage Type** or via the SM30/31 T-code in the V_001P_K table.

There is a feature provided by SAP to default the wage types in the Basic Pay infotype based on the grouping, which is based on LGMST, the Enterprise structure for a wage type model. The return value used in the feature is configured by navigating to **SPRO | Personnel Management | Personnel Administration | Payroll Data | Wage Types | Revise Default Wage Types** or via the SM30/31 T-code in the V_T539A table. The following parameters are for wages:

- **F**: This does not allow the wage types assigned in 0008 to be overwritten

- **O**: This allows the wage types entered in 0008 to be overwritten

The following screenshot shows the **Default Wage Types for Basic Pay** screen:

The 0008 (Basic Pay) configuration

Let's explore the configuration required to maintain basic pay in employee's master data. The 0008 (Basic Pay) infotype holds the wage types that are paid regularly month on month. It includes the wage types that can be evaluated directly or indirectly, and this gets affected when loss of payment method is created. It is also useful when making a distinction between employees, based on the **collective agreement provision (CAP)**.

> The Basic Pay infotype can hold only a maximum of 40 wage types.

First, it's important that we define the groupings for personnel calculation rule and CAP, which is done by navigating to **SPRO | Personnel Management | Personnel Administration | Payroll Data | Basic Pay | Define EE Subgroup Grouping for PCR and Coll.Agrmt.Prov** or via the SM30/31 T-code in the V_503_B table. This grouping is very crucial as it serves as a check when a PCR is created. The groupings refer to the same rule that is applicable for a group of employees. This is shown in the following screenshot:

The standard values can be used and only changed if necessary, and are maintained in the T546A table via the SM30/31 T-code. The standard delivered values are as follows:

- **1**: This refers to the hourly wage earners
- **2**: This refers to periodic payments (for example, monthly wage earners)
- **3**: This refers to salaried employees

The value that we map to employee group and subgroups is default in the 0008 (Basic Pay) infotype and cannot be edited, as shown in the following screenshot:

Pay scale			Further Information		
Type	40	Metall	Capacity Util. Level	100,00	%
Area	02	Hessen	EESubgroupGrpg.	PER	Periodic (salar...
Group	AT	Level	Work hours/period	156,48	Monthly
			Ann.salary		EUR

The **collective agreement provision (CAP)** also has SAP standard delivered entries that can be used. They need to be changed only if the entries don't meet the requirement. The requirements are as follows:

- **1**: This refers to industrial workers/hourly wages
- **2**: This refers to industrial workers/monthly wages
- **3**: This refers to salaried employees
- **4**: This refers to employees in the non pay scale band

The **CAP** are defined by navigating to **SPRO | Personnel Management | Personnel Administration | Payroll Data | Basic Pay | Check pay scale type** or via the SM30/31 T-code in the V_T510A table, and **SPRO | Personnel Management | Personnel Administration | Payroll Data | Basic Pay | Check pay scale area** or via the SM30/31 T-code in the V_T510G table respectively.

The defined pay scale type and area can be mapped to the enterprise structure by navigating to **SPRO | Personnel Management | Personnel Administration | Payroll Data | Basic Pay | Check Assignment of Pay Scale Structure to Enterprise Structure**.

If the monthly period does not apply to an employee, we have to maintain this step by navigating to **SPRO | Personnel Management | Personnel Administration | Payroll Data | Basic Pay | Set up payroll period for collective agreement provision** or via the SM30/31 T-code in the V_T510W table.

After we set up the CAP and pay scale area, we can also further distinguish among the employees based on their groups and levels. We define this by navigating to **SPRO | Personnel Management | Personnel Administration | Payroll Data | Basic Pay | Revise Pay Scale Groups and Levels** or via the SM30/31 T-code in the V_T510 table. The prequisite is that we must maintain the pay scale type, areas, and wage types.

The 0014 (Recurring Payments and Deductions) configuration

The wage types that are to be frequently paid or deducted are defined via the 0014 infotype. Let's look at the configuration steps followed for the 0014 infotype. The configuration is very similar to the one followed for basic pay. The steps involved in this are as follows:

1. The wage type catalog can be accessed via **SPRO | Personnel Management | Personnel Administration | Payroll Data | Recurring payments and deductions | Wagetypes | Create wage type catalog**.

2. The recurring payments and deduction can be accessed via **SPRO | Personnel Management | Personnel Administration | Payroll Data | Recurring payments and deductions | Wagetypes | Check wage type group Recurring payments and deductions**.

    Here, we group the wage types in the **0014, Recurring payments/deducts** category. This is shown in the following screenshot:

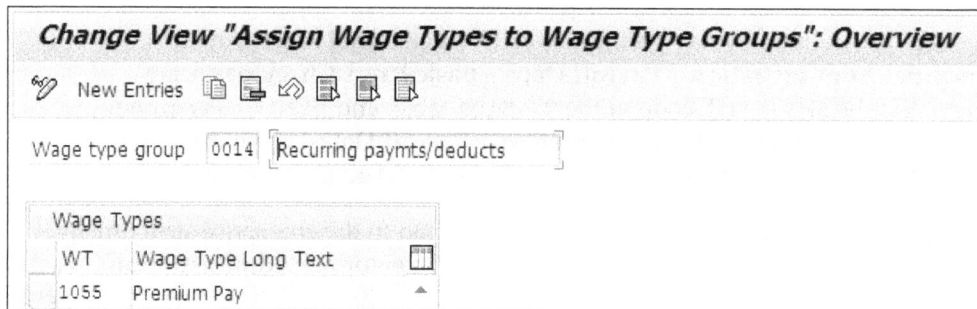

3. The wage type text can be checked and amended by navigating to **SPRO | Personnel Management | Personnel Administration | Payroll Data | Recurring payments and deductions | Wagetypes | Check Wage Type Catalog | Check wage type text**.

4. We can define the wage type permissibility by navigating to **SPRO | Personnel Management | Personnel Administration | Payroll Data | Recurring payments and deductions | Wage types | Check Wage Type Catalog | Check entry permissibility per infotype**. There is also a provision to define whether the wage type is going to be used once or multiple times.

5. We can define the personnel subarea and employee subgroup that the wage type is accessible for by navigating to **SPRO | Personnel Management | Personnel Administration | Payroll Data | Recurring payments and deductions | Wagetypes | Check Wage Type Catalog | Define Wage Type Permissibility for each PS and ESG**. We can click on details (*Ctrl+Shift+F2*) to choose the wage type and make the necessary changes.

6. We can define the wage type characteristics such as payment or deduction wage type by navigating to **SPRO | Personnel Management | Personnel Administration | Payroll Data | Recurring payments and deductions | Wagetypes | Check Wage Type Catalog | Check wage type characteristics** or via the SM30/SM31 T-code in the V_T511 table.

7. The steps work in conjunction with the values defined in the permissibility of wage types. We define the subgroup wage type for each employee. This is permissible by navigating to **SPRO | Personnel Management | Personnel Administration | Payroll Data | Recurring payments and deductions | Wagetypes | Define employee subgroup grouping for primary wage type**.

8. We define the wage type for each personnel subarea. This is permissible via **SPRO | Personnel Management | Personnel Administration | Payroll Data | Recurring payments and deductions | Wagetypes | Define personnel subarea grouping for primary wage type**.

The 0015 (Additional Payments) configuration

One-time payment that needs to be settled are paid via the 0015 infotype to the employees. Let's look at the configuration steps followed for the 0015 infotype. The configuration is very similar to one followed for the Basic Pay infotype and recurring payments/deduction. The steps involved in this are as follows:

1. The wage type catalog can be accessed via **SPRO | Personnel Management | Personnel administration | Payroll data | Additional payments | Wagetypes | Create wage type catalog**.

2. The additional payments option can be accessed via **SPRO | Personnel Management | Personnel administration | Payroll data | Additional payments | Wagetypes | Check wage type group Additional payments**.

Here, we group the wage types in the **0015, Additional payments** category, as shown in the following screenshot:

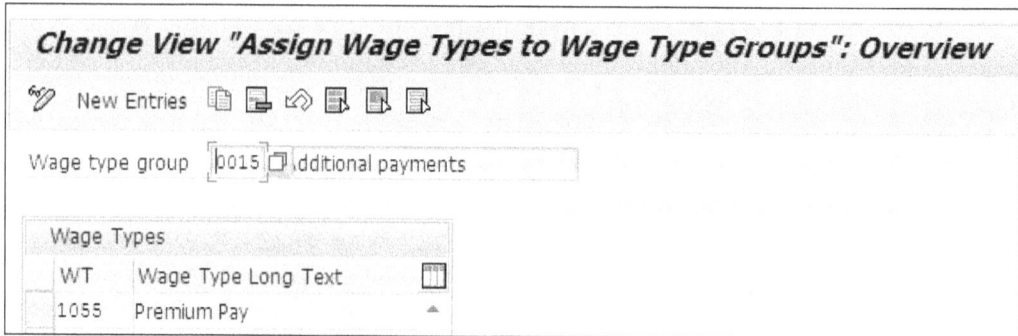

The following steps define the various wage type characteristics:

1. The wage type text can be checked and amended by navigating to **SPRO | Personnel Management | Personnel Administration | Payroll Data | Additional payments | Wagetypes | Check Wage Type Catalog | Check wage type text**.

2. We can define the wage type permissibility by navigating to **SPRO | Personnel Management | Personnel Administration | Payroll Data | Additional payments | Wagetypes | Check Wage Type Catalog | Check entry permissibility per infotype**. There is also a provision to define whether the wage type is going to be used once or multiple times.

3. We can define the personnel subarea and employee subgroup that the wage type is accessible for by navigating to **SPRO | Personnel Management | Personnel Administration | Payroll Data | Additional payments | Wagetypes | Check Wage Type Catalog | Define Wage Type Permissibility for each PS and ESG**. We can choose the wage type and click on details (*Ctrl+Shift+F2*) to choose the wage type and make the necessary changes.

4. We can define the wage type characteristics such as the payment or deduction wage type by navigating to **SPRO | Personnel Management | Personnel Administration | Payroll Data | Additional payments | Wagetypes | Check Wage Type Catalog | Check wage type characteristics**.

5. The preceding steps work in conjunction with the values defined with the permissibility of the wage types. We define the wage type for each employee subgroup. This is permissible by navigating to **SPRO | Personnel Management | Personnel Administration | Payroll Data | Additional payments | Wagetypes | Define employee subgroup grouping for primary wage type**.

6. We define for the wage type each personnel subarea. This is permissible by navigating to **SPRO | Personnel Management | Personnel Administration | Payroll Data | Additional payments | Wagetypes | Define personnel subarea grouping for primary wage type**.

The 0267 (On-demand or Additional Payments) configuration

The payment made during the middle of the payroll period or simply on a on-demand basis is maintained in the 0267 infotype. Let's look at the configuration steps followed for the 0267 infotype. The configuration is very similar to the one followed for the basic pay infotype. The steps involved are as follows:

1. The wage type catalog is accessed via **SPRO | Personnel Management | Personnel Administration | Payroll Data | Additional payments: Off-Cycle | Wagetypes | Create wage type catalog**.

2. The wage type group is accessed via **SPRO | Personnel Management | Personnel Administration | Payroll Data | Additional payments: Off-Cycle | Wagetypes | Check wage type group Additional payments**.

   ° Here, we group the wage types in the **0267**, **Additional off-cycle Pymt** category, as shown in the following screenshot:

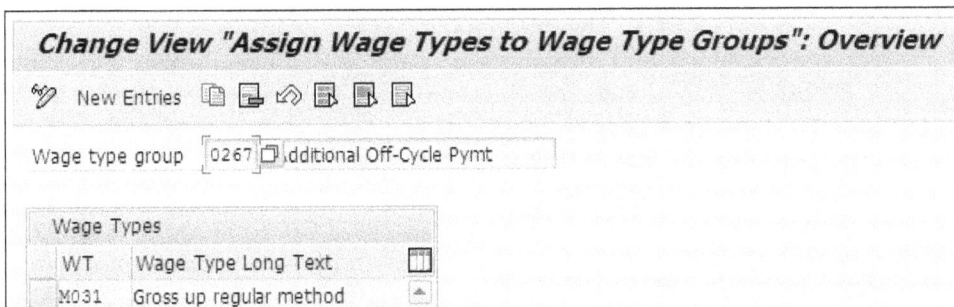

3. The wage type text can be checked and amended by navigating to **SPRO | Personnel Management | Personnel Administration | Payroll Data | Additional payments: Off-cycle | Wagetypes | Check Wage Type Catalog | Check wage type text**.

4. We can define the wage type permissibility by navigating to **SPRO | Personnel Management | Personnel Administration | Payroll Data | Additional payments: Off-cycle | Wagetypes | Check Wage Type Catalog | Check entry permissibility per infotype**. There is also a provision to define whether the wage type is going to be used once or multiple times.

5. We can define personnel who the subarea and employee subgroup, wage type is accessible for. It is accessible by navigating to **SPRO | Personnel Management | Personnel Administration | Payroll Data | Additional payments: Off-cycle | Wagetypes | Check Wage Type Catalog | Define Wage Type Permissibility for each PS and ESG**. We can choose the wage type and click on details (*Ctrl+Shift+F2*) to choose the wage type and make the necessary changes.

6. We can define the wage type characteristics such as the payment or deduction wage type by navigating to **SPRO | Personnel Management | Personnel Administration | Payroll Data | Additional payments: Off-cycle | Wagetypes | Check Wage Type Catalog | Check wage type characteristics**.

7. The steps work in conjunction with the values defined in permissibility of the wage types. We define for each employee subgroup wage type, which is permissible by navigating to **SPRO | Personnel Management | Personnel Administration | Payroll Data | Additional payments: Off-cycle | Wagetypes | Define employee subgroup grouping for primary wage type**.

8. We define the wage type for the personnel subarea, which is permissible by navigating to **SPRO | Personnel Management | Personnel Administration | Payroll Data | Additional payments: Off-cycle | Wagetypes | Define personnel subarea grouping for primary wage type**.

   ° The transaction code used to run the on-demand payroll or off-cycle work bench is PUOC_XX, where XX is country grouping, such as 10 for USA, 08 for UK. The on-demand payroll is processed via the off-cycle work bench, and the program's name is SAPLHRPAY99_OC. The off-cycle work bench is shown in the following screenshot.

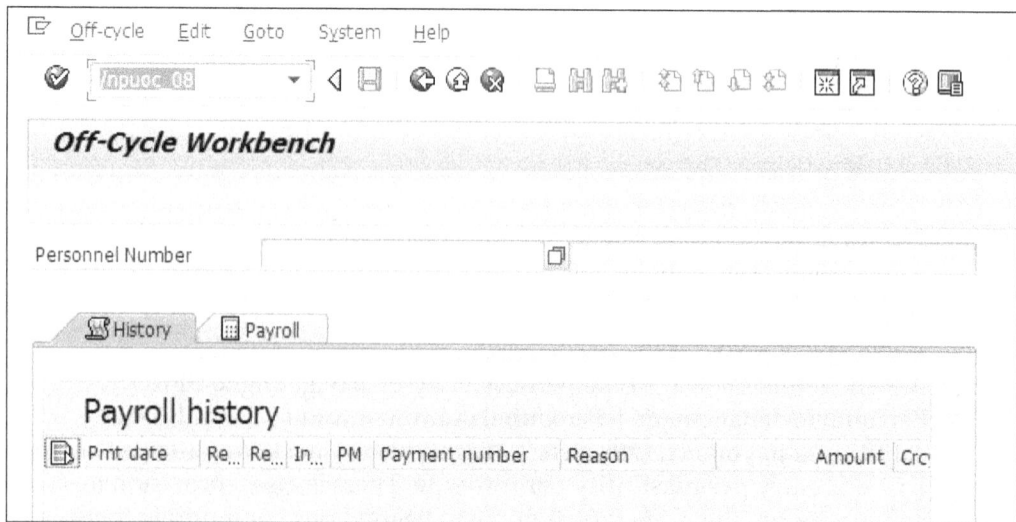

Writing a PCR to meet your customer's requirements

In the previous chapters, we covered the configuration steps required to maintain the master data of the employee in relevant infotypes such as 0008, 0014, 0015, and 0267. In this chapter, we will cover the functionality of schema and PCR.

Schematic payroll schema

The schematic payroll schema is a collection of subschemas that can be logically used for the purpose of calculation. The schemas can be accessed via the PE01 T-code. They can be accessed via the SE11 or SE16 T-code, and they are maintained in T52C0. They are displayed as rows in the table. The schema has the following three subobjects:

- Source text
- Attributes
- Documentation

The source text will have the subschemas, and we will be able to see them by clicking on the **Display** button.

The schema can be defined as payroll or time, and it is controlled in the attributes subobject. The program class has the provision to define itself as payroll or time schema. The following list defines this:

- **C**: This refers to payroll
- **T**: This refers to time management

The country-grouping attributes allow us to mention the country for which we are using the payroll, and there are localized country payroll drivers provided by SAP. If the localized solution is not available, we can use the **99** grouping.

The schema can be executed; for this, the indicator needs to be flagged. This will generate and run the schema. There is a control mechanism, and if we would like the schema to be changed only by a particular user, we can mention the user ID in the **Person responsible** field and flag **Changes only by person responsible**. Any changes made to the schema can also be captured for audit purpose. The **Administrative info** tab has the details about the user and date stamp. The following screenshot demonstrates this process:

It is always recommended that the standard schema is copied to the customer name space before being used. The schema can be copied by clicking on **Copy** (*Shift+F4*). We can click on the **Where-used** list (*Ctrl+Shift+F3*). The documentation subobject is there for us to write details about each object and schema if required.

The standard tool to generate or check schema consistency is the RPUSCG00 report. It can be executed via the SE38 or SA38 T-code or by clicking on **Generate** (*F6*). The following are two modes that are available:

- **1**: This is chosen to generate the schemas
- **2**: This is chosen for syntax errors or consistencies

There are four options that are available to be flagged. They are as follows:

- Test run
- Force generation
- Display clusters
- Print active

Some important functions to know when working on a schema are given in the following table:

Function	Description
COM	The meaning of the schema line can be mentioned using this function. We don't need to use a parameter when working on this function.
COPY	The subschema called in par 1 is called dynamically using the COPY function. For example, the main schema is X000, and in that, we can call a subschema, XIN0, using the COPY function.

It's important to understand the design and functionalities that are available in the schema. The following screenshot shows what the payroll schema screen parameter looks like:

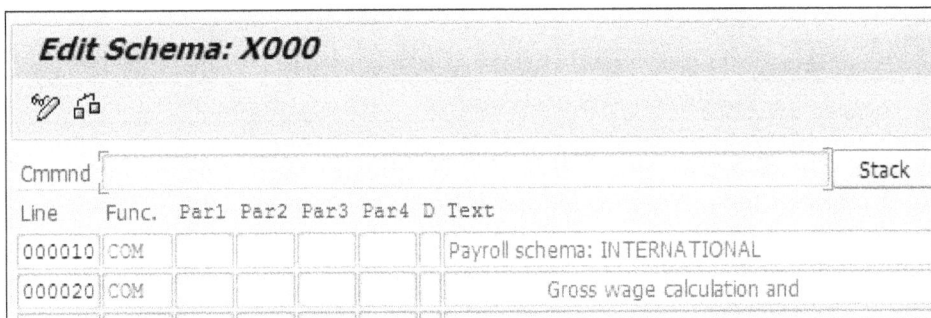

Let's look at the different functionalities of the fields of the schema editor in the following table:

Field	Description
Line	We can use this to mention the number, or many commands can be entered at the end of the number. For instance, I is used for inserting a new line.
Func	Function is code of logic developed to perform a major chunk of work. For instance, COPY is a function used to call the subschema.
Par1	A more detailed definition of functions can be used by par 1, for example, what the significance is of the function or whether we can make entries or not.

Field	Description
Par 2	A more detailed definition of functions can be used by par 2, for example, what the significance is of the function or whether we can make entries or not.
Par 3	A more detailed definition of functions can be used by par 3, for example, what the significance is of the function or whether we can make entries or not.
Par 4	A more detailed definition of functions can be used by par 4, for example, what the significance is of the function or whether we can make entries or not.
D	We can use * to have a function deactivated. This determines whether or not a function is to be included when the subschemas are executed during a payroll run.
Text	This is a free text field to describe the function by adding comments about the schemas.

The line number field we covered earlier in the chapter has more functionality. Let's look at it in detail. The possible combination is as follows:

Commands	Description
I	This is used to insert a new line
D	This deletes the line
R	This repeats the same line
Rn	Number of lines gets repeated, where *n* is a number
>	Explodes the subschema and is only used in the COPY function
<	The explosion of a schema

The payroll schema has the functions and PCR. The function calls the function modules, and rule has operations that refer to operation modules.

> Schemas and PCR can be exploded using the RPDASC00 program. This program refers to the T-codes T52C0 and T52C5 and lists the entries as maintained in the table.

Personnel calculation rule (PCR)

Personnel calculation rules are maintained via the PE02 T-code. The important functionality is to determine PCR based on employee subgroup grouping. Let's see how a sample PCR is written and maintained in the schema. The following screenshot demonstrates this:

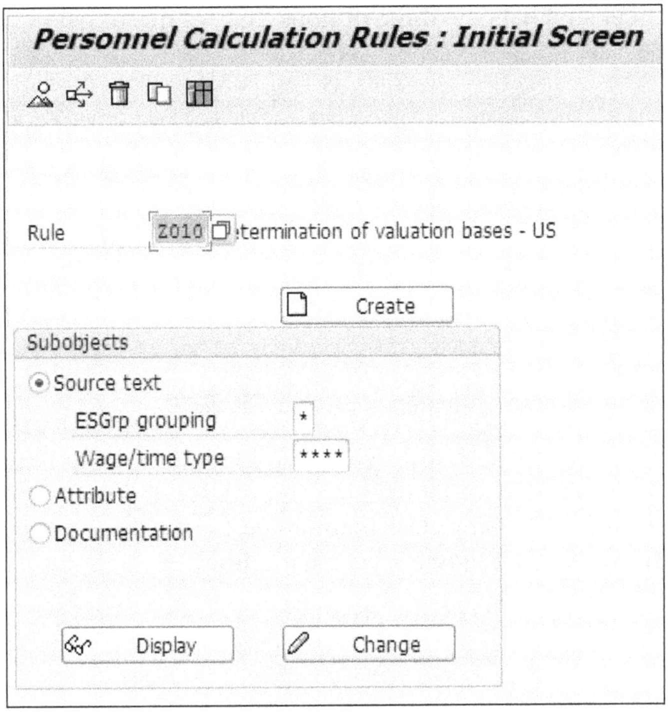

Personnel Calculation Rules : Initial Screen

Rule   Z010   :termination of valuation bases - US

Create

Subobjects

⦿ Source text

     ESGrp grouping   *

     Wage/time type   ****

◯ Attribute

◯ Documentation

Display   Change

It's recommended that we always select the standard PCR delivered by SAP, and rename it to a customer-specific PCR. The source text has the ESGrp grouping and wage type. The ESGrp is what we defined in V_503_B, and the wage type is defined if the rule is applicable for a particular wage type. We can also use the * and **** function, which means the function is applicable for all the wage types; however, it doesn't work for all ESGrp.

We can click on create or edit the PCR. When we click on **Create** (*Ctrl+F3*), it will list three options to insert objects. The three options are as follows:

- **same level**
- **Sub-level**
- **Cancel**

The following screenshot lists the three options that we discussed in the preceding bullet list:

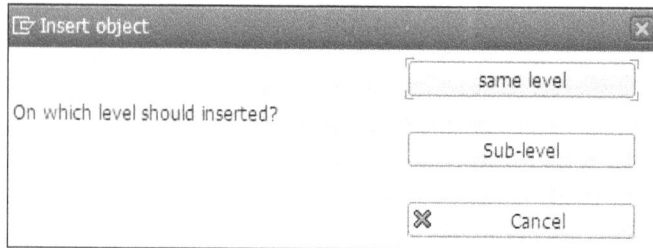

We will learn the functionality of the program **PCR Z010**.

Here, the PCR checks for EE subgroup grouping for PCR, say if it finds the option 2 2, and it's applicable for all the wage type 2. Next, it uses the VWTCL operation to check the processing class maintained for the wage type; in this case, it checks 01, as shown in the following command line:

```
****
VWTCL 01
1
   ADDWT   *    OT Output table
   ELIMI        ZEliminate time period ID
   Zero=        N    amtnumrtetime=0
   ADDWT /001   OT Output Table
```

Processing class, cummulation class, and evaluation class are maintained for wage types in the `v_512w_d` table.

If the wage type specification is 1 for `pclass 01`, then it pushes the amount to the output table. It then eliminates the number and assign it as 0, and adds the amount to valuation basis wage type 001.

Important payroll functions

The function, in general, is a piece of code developed to perform a major chunk of tasks. The following is a list of some important payroll functions that will be very handy:

Function	Meaning
COPY	If we want to insert the subschema into the main schema, we can make use of the COPY function.

Function	Meaning
WPBP	The **work centre basic pay function** (**WPBP**) is useful to import master data from 0, 1, 7, 8, and 27 infotypes to the IT and WPBP internal tables.
PGM	The PGM function is used to provide information about the type of program.
UPD	This function can be used to control whether results can be stored in databases. We can set **No** in par 1 if we would like to test a payroll run.
PIT	The **process input table** (**PIT**)is the function that is used to call a personnel calculation rule.
PRT	This function calls the PCR for different wage types from the result table.

Important payroll operations

Operations are developed to perform a small piece of a task. The following is a list of some important payroll operations that will be very handy:

Operation	Meaning
VWTCL	The set processing class value is a decision operation based on a specification set in the v_512w_d table.
AMT	This evaluates the amt field value. It can also be used as a decision operation.
NUM	This operation evaluates the **num** field.
RTE	The data is entered in the **rte** field by this operation, and it also evaluates the rte field.
ADDWT	This operation adds the value in the wage type to the subsequent wage type

> The RPDSYS00 program or the PDSY/PE04 T-code can be used to refer to the documentation for functions and operations.

Frequent error messages and workaround

During post-implementation support, there can be frequent issues that we come across. Let's discuss some of them and workarounds to address them.

The infamous posting error that we frequently get is "Posting balance is not cleared" (period 06/2011 A).

To resolve this issue, we will refer to the following table:

V_T52EK	This refers to the symbolic account and its **MOMAG** field account assignment
V_T52EZ	This includes wage type overview plus/minus sign to post a positive amount as debit and a negative amount as credit, respectively
OBYE	This T-code is used if the symbolic account has been mapped to the correct general ledger

The payroll result has already been evaluated in run 0000002259.

The workaround is that the posting run PP 0000002259 has to be deleted and a simulation has to be run instead of a live run.

Configuring a payslip

The remuneration statement or payslip is customized by navigating to **SPRO |
Payroll (XX) | Forms | Remuneration Statement | Set up Remuneration
statement** or via the PE51 T-code.

The form class chosen is CEDT, and we copy it and rename it to the customer name, and make adjustments. The important subobject that needs to be changed is a single field where we add the fields that need to be included in the paystub. We choose a single field and click on change. We click on **Create** (*F5*), and on the **Insert Single Field** screen, we mention the **Table** and **Table field** and click on **Transfer** (*F8*). This process is demonstrated in the following screenshot:

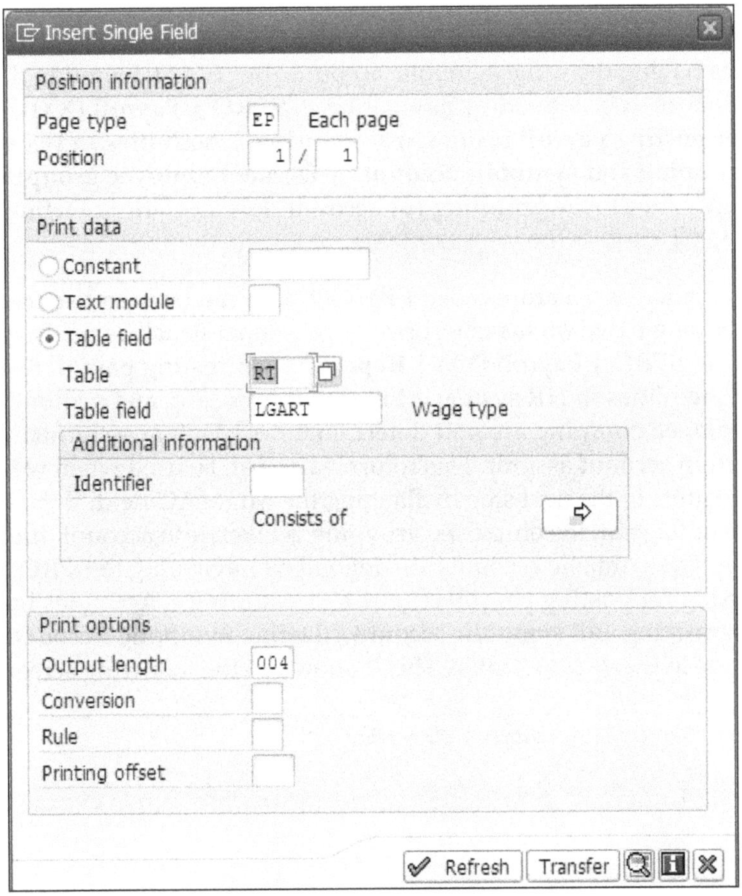

Integration with the finance module

There is a close integration between the payroll and finance modules. Payroll results are posted directly to the finance module to respective general ledgers. Symbolic accounts serve as an integration point between the payroll and finance modules. We will explore the configuration steps required to post payroll results to the finance module. There are configurations required for activities in the HR system and finance system.

Activities in the HR system

The determination of accounts while posting to the finance module is broken down into the following two steps:

- On the payroll side, the symbolic account is mapped to the wage type
- On the finance side, the symbolic account is mapped with the general ledger

The grouping of employee for account determination helps to actively group the employees having the same symbolic accounts but is distributed to different accounts in finance. It is defined by navigating to **SPRO | Payroll (XX) | Reporting for posting payroll results to accounting | Activities in HR system | Employee grouping and symbolic accounts | Define Employee grouping account determination | Employee grouping for account determination: Define values** or via the SM30/31 T-code in the V_T52EM table.

In the next step, there is a feature called **PPMOD.** This can be used to default the employee grouping based on the enterprise or personnel structure fields. It is defined by navigating to **SPRO | Payroll (XX) | Reporting for posting payroll results to accounting | Activities in HR system | Employee grouping and symbolic accounts | Define Employee grouping account determination | Define assignment of EE char. to EE group account assgmt.** This return value can be used when we define the **Symbolic Accounts** in the next step by flagging the **MOMAG** field. If the **MOMAG** field, is active or flagged, the employee grouping is taken into account during account determination. The symbolic accounts are defined by navigating to **SPRO | Payroll (XX) | Reporting for posting payroll results to accounting | Activities in HR system | Employee grouping and symbolic account | Define Symbolic Accounts** or via the SM30/31 T-code in the V_T52EK table. This is shown in the following screenshot:

Change View "Symbolic Accounts": Overview

New Entries

Symbolic Accounts

SymAc	Description	AATyp	MOMAG	Fixed MOM	Negative Postg	Neg. Posting Debit	
0120	Wages/salaries	C	☐	☐	☐	☐	

The symbolic account is a four-digit alphanumeric code with account assignment types. The account determination types determine the type of account to be posted in finance. The account assignment also determines the account mapped on the finance side.

Let's look at the different account assignment types and their functionality in the following table:

Account assignment type	Meaning
C	This refers to posting to an expense account
F	This refers to posting to a balance sheet account
K	This refers to posting to personal vendor accounts
KF	This refers to posting to fixed vendor accounts
FC	This refers to posting to a balance sheet account (NewGL)

The symbolic account defined in the preceding step can be mapped to the wage types by navigating to **SPRO | Payroll (XX) | Reporting for Posting Payroll Results to Accounting | Activities in the HR system | Maintain Wage Types | Define Posting Characteristics of Wage Types** or via the `SM30/31` T-code in the `V_T52EL_NOFM` table.

The plus and minus signs are defined along with the symbolic account, and they have specific meanings, as shown in the following list:

- +: The positive amounts from the wage types are posted as debits and negative amounts are posted as credits

- -: The positive amounts are posted as credits and negative amounts are posted as debits

Activities in an accounting AC system

The symbolic accounts that are defined are mapped to the general ledger on the accounting side. Based on the account assignment defined for the symbolic account, we have to choose the accounts as follows:

- Assign balance sheet accounts

- Assign expense accounts

- Assign technical accounts

- Assign customer accounts

- Assign vendor accounts

- Assign customer accounts for specific loan posting

Hypothetically, if we have defined a symbolic account with the account assignment type as "C", then we have to map that symbolic account to assign an expense account. If it's "FC", then we have to map it to assign balance sheet accounts. This is depicted in the following screenshot:

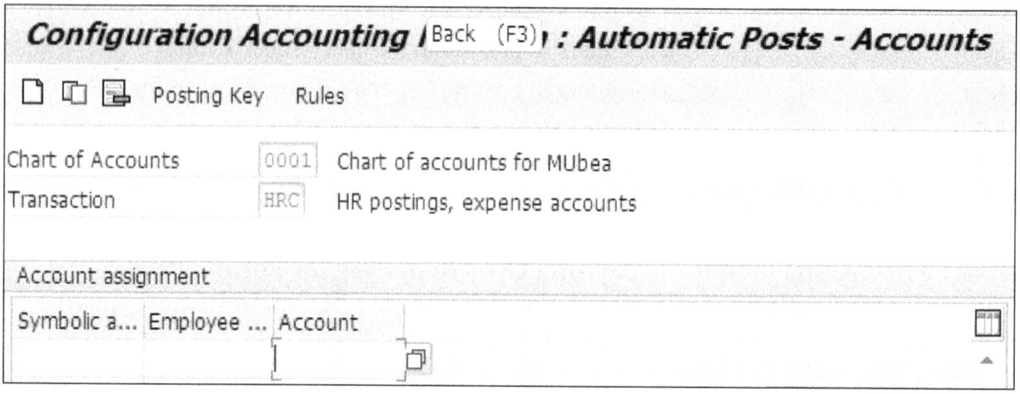

Only, if the **MOMAG** field is flagged, the employee grouping for account determination, will be active to be assigned.

> **Wage type assignment**: The G/L Accounts report RPDKON00 is useful when customizing settings of wage types, symbolic accounts, and general ledgers.

Posting payroll results to finance steps

We will look at the steps to be followed to post the payroll results to the finance steps.

The first step is executing the PC00_M99_CIPE T-code. This is shown in the following screenshot:

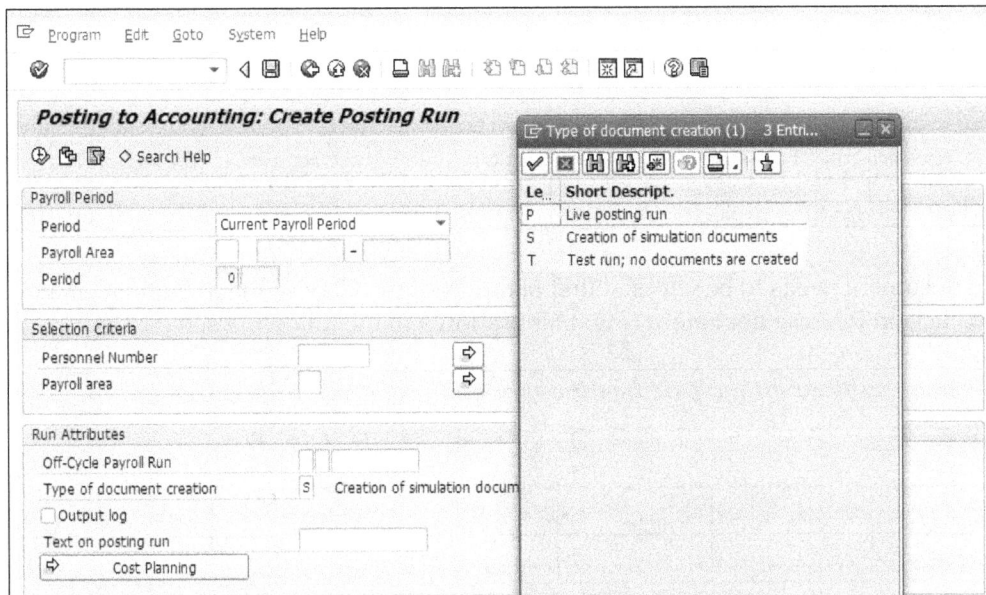

The three different statuses available are as follows:

- **P**: This refers to a live posting run
- **S**: This refers to the creation of simulation documents
- **T**: This refers to a test run; no documents are created

The following screenshot demonstrates this:

Click on **Personnel Numbers** and a new **Posting to Accounting: Document overview** window will open. This is shown in the following screenshot:

Posting to Accounting: Document overview

Document	CoCd	Pstng Date	Typ	Run Number	Status	User name	Created on	Time
☑ 0000004383	3000	02.12.2005	PP	0000003019	Incorrect	KARTHIK	05.03.2014	21:10:01

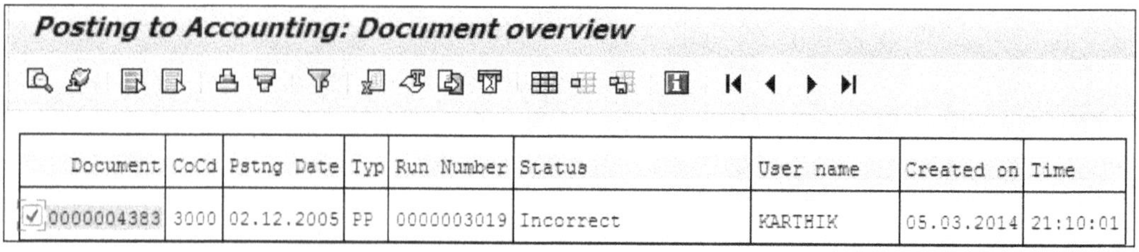

The document needs to be released first before posting. Choose the document created and click on **Release document** (*F9*). This is shown in the following screenshot:

Posting to Accounting: Document overview

Document	CoCd	Pstng Date	Typ	Run Number	Status	User name	Created on	Time
✓ 0000004367	2800	28.05.2012	PP	0000002988	Created	--- _ _	15.06.2012	14:09:14

Release document/s ☒

Do you want to release the selected documents for posting ?

Yes	No

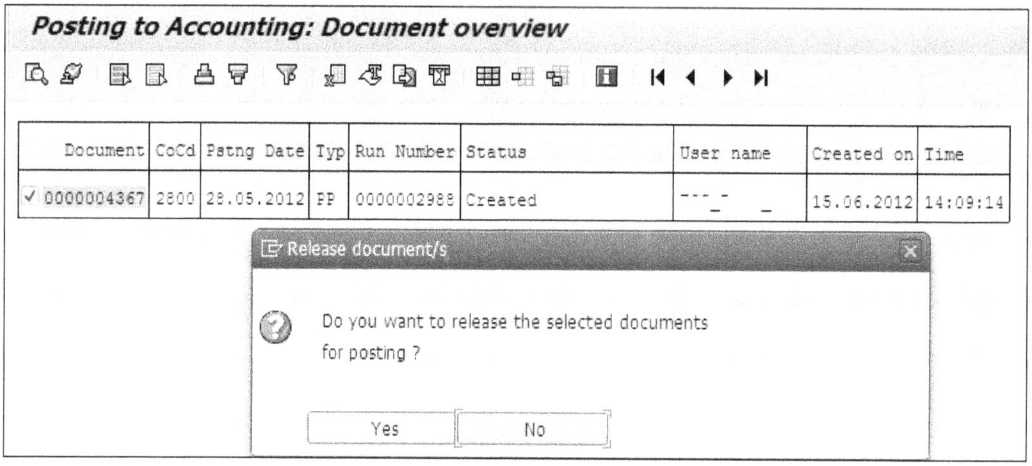

Click on **Yes** and note that the **Status** is changed to **Released**. This is shown in the following screenshot:

Posting to Accounting: Document overview

Document	CoCd	Pstng Date	Typ	Run Number	Status	User name	Created on	Time
0000004367	2800	28.05.2012	PP	0000002988	Released		15.06.2012	14:09:14

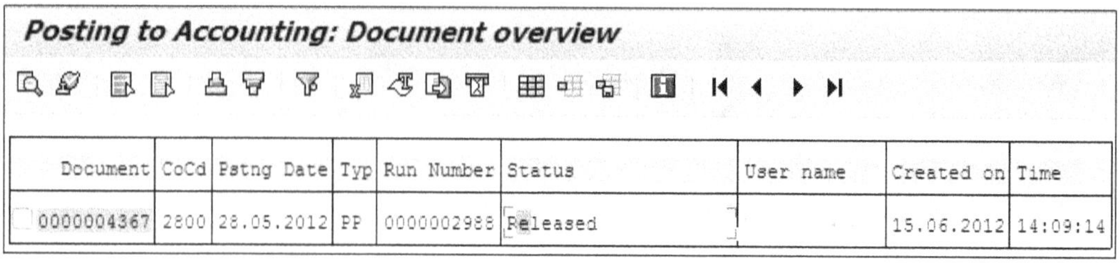

The posting runs can be displayed via the PCP0 T-code.

Different statuses of a posting run

The finance posting run can have the following statuses:

Fixed value	Text
31	This refers to the creation of documents
50	This refers to the posting of documents
61	This refers to the reverse document that is created

Summary

In this chapter, we attempted to clear the notion that payroll is complex. After reading this chapter, you should be comfortable configuring the Payroll submodule. We covered important payroll-related infotypes. We also covered the functionalities of payroll schema and PCR.

In the next chapter, we will closely look at configuring the **Talent Management** submodule and explore the standard functionalities provided by SAP.

7

Talent Management and Development Configuration

The Personnel Development component is an extension of the OM component. It deals with personnel engagement and development activities. The personnel development component comprises the following:

- Qualifications/requirements
- Appraisal systems
- Career and succession planning
- Development plans

The Personnel Development submodule enables us to plan and implement training measures to enhance the professional development of the personnel. The settings made in the following submodules also have an impact on the Personnel Development submodule:

- Organizational Management
- Compensation Management
- Training and Event Management

Basic settings – Personnel Development

The PD view **Infotypes per object type** can be controlled by navigating to **SPRO | Personnel Management | Personnel Development | Basic Settings | Maintaining Infotypes**, as shown in the following screenshot, or via the SM30/31 T-code in the T777I table:

The **No Maintenance** indicator controls settings if the infotype can be maintained via basic transaction such as PP01. In the standard system settings, some infotypes have the **No Maintenance** checkbox flagged, but if we would like to maintain them through the PP01 transaction code, then the **No Maintenance** (T777I-MAINT) flag needs to be removed.

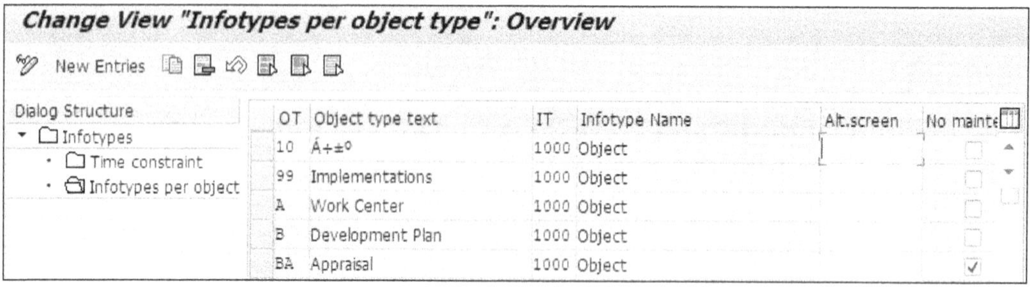

Change View "Infotypes per object type": Overview

New Entries

Dialog Structure	OT	Object type text	IT	Infotype Name	Alt.screen	No mainte
▾ ☐ Infotypes	10	Á+±º	1000	Object		☐
• ☐ Time constraint	99	Implementations	1000	Object		☐
• ☐ Infotypes per object	A	Work Center	1000	Object		☐
	B	Development Plan	1000	Object		☐
	BA	Appraisal	1000	Object		✓

Customer-specific settings for PD-related infotypes can be maintained by navigating to **SPRO | Personnel Management | Personnel Development | Basic Settings | Maintaining Infotypes**, as shown in the following screenshot, or via the SM30/31 T-code in the T77CD table.

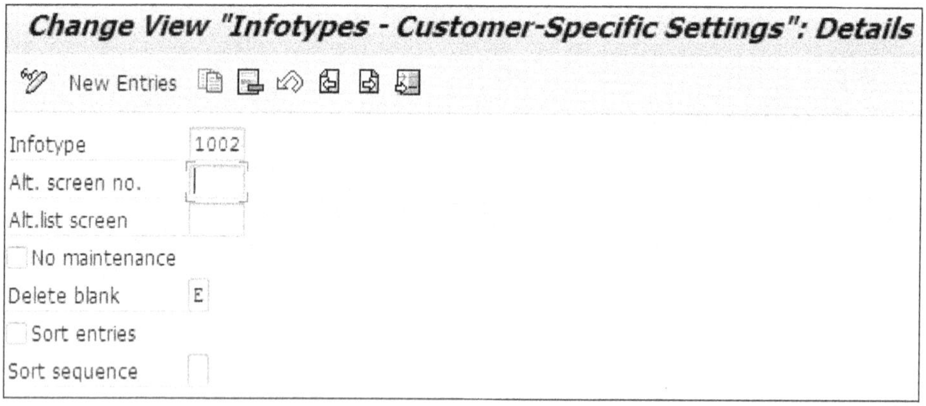

Change View "Infotypes - Customer-Specific Settings": Details

New Entries

Infotype	1002
Alt. screen no.	
Alt.list screen	
☐ No maintenance	
Delete blank	E
☐ Sort entries	
Sort sequence	

The customer-specific settings can be defined in the table for PD infotypes.

If we are not going to use the standard screen 2000, an alternate screen number can be defined. The screen number 2000 is usually the default screen for infotypes and only has different screen numbers as the default for certain country-specific infotypes.

- If we are not going to use the standard list screen number 3000, an alternate screen number can be defined

- The maintenance of the infotype via the PP01 TCD can be controlled by checking the **No Maintenance** flag

- In the case of language specific infotypes, the **delete blank** switch lets us know how blank lines can be processed. The three options available are as follows:
    - E: blank lines are only deleted at the end
    - A: all blank lines are deleted
    - Blank lines are retained

We can also sort the infotype in sequence by flagging the **Sort Entries** flag. We can sort it based on the following settings:

Sort sequence	Description
	In the ascending order by subtype and in the descending order by "from" date
1	In the descending order by "from" date and in the ascending order by subtype
2	In the ascending order by subtype and in the ascending order by "from" date
3	In the ascending order by "from" date and in the ascending order by subtype

We can specify whether an infotype is maintained only for a particular country such as the USA, for example, by navigating to **SPRO | Personnel Management | Personnel Development | Basic Settings | Maintaining Infotypes**, as shown in the following screenshot, or via the SM30/31 T-code in the T77NI table.

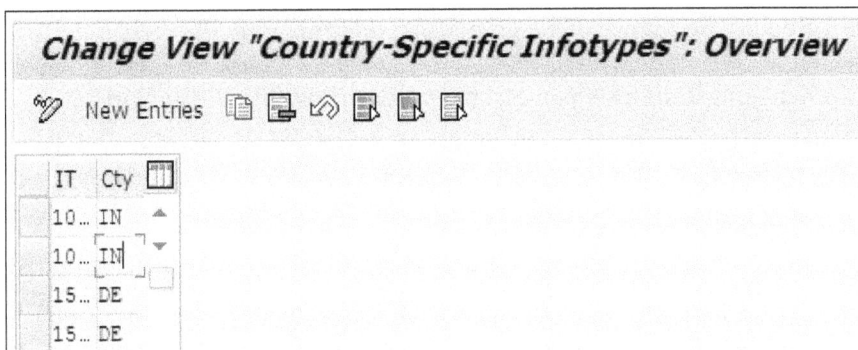

The time constraint for each object type can be set by navigating to **SPRO | Personnel Management | Personnel development | Basic Settings | Maintain Relationships | Define Time Constraint Depending on Target Object Type**, as shown in the following screenshot, or via the SM30/31 T-code in the T77ZR table:

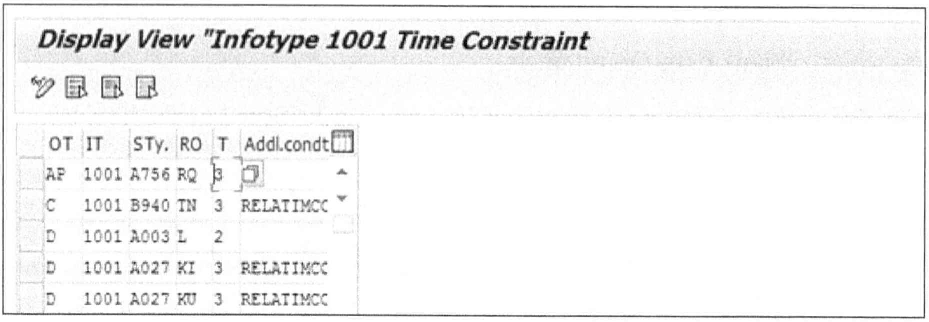

The standard TC settings are as follows:

TC class	Description
0	This may only exist once
1	This exists without gaps
2	This exists with gaps
3	This is available as often as required

The different languages supported in the PD submodule can be displayed by navigating to **SPRO | Personnel Management | Personnel development | Basic Settings | Specify Sequence of Languages Available** or via the SM30/31 T-code in the T778L table. The standard sequence of languages is **German**, **English**, **Spanish**, **Dutch**, **French**, and **Italian**, as you can see in the following screenshot:

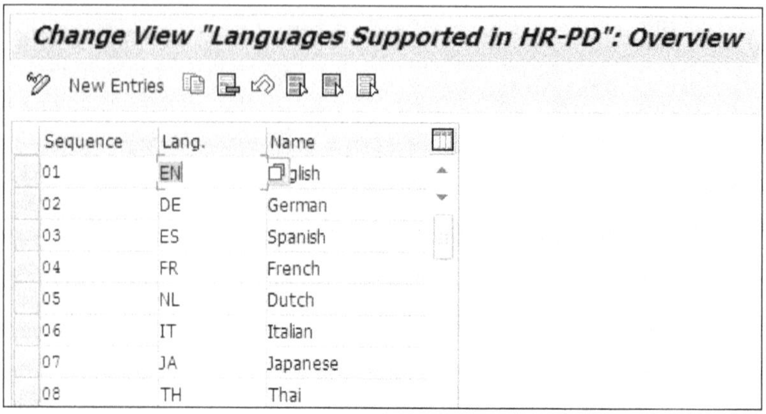

This useful tool provided to check the consistency of installation can be accessed by navigating to **SPRO | Personnel Management | Personnel development | Basic Settings | Tools | Check Consistency of Installation**, as shown in the following screenshot, or via TCD OOCH. They can also be accessed by navigating to **Report | RHCHECK0**.

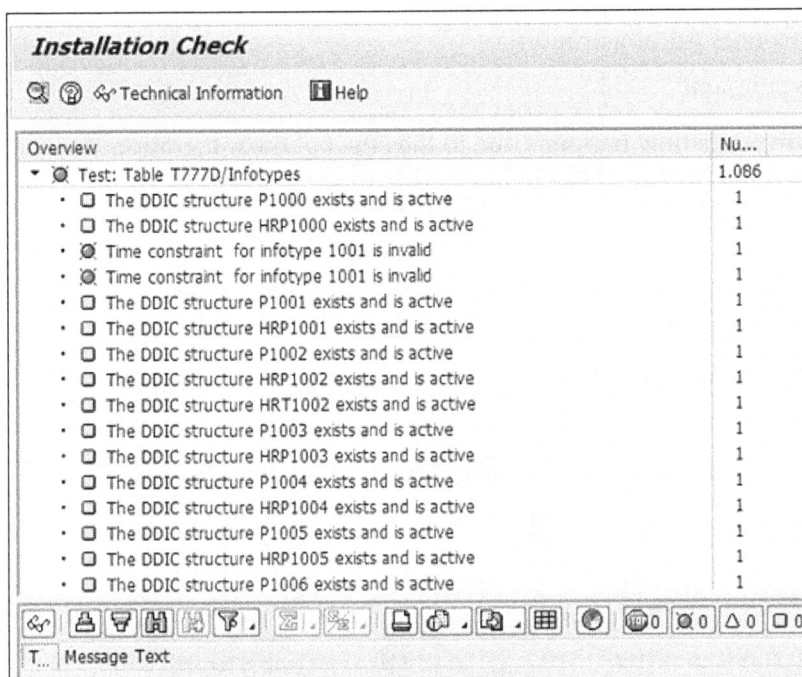

The infotypes that the change documents need to be captured can be defined by navigating to **SPRO | Personnel Management | Personnel development | Basic Settings | Activate Change Documents**, as shown in the following screenshot, or via the SM30/31 T-code in the T77CDOC_CUST table. In the standard settings, the table is empty and we can activate the change document functionality for infotype, subtype, object type, and plan version.

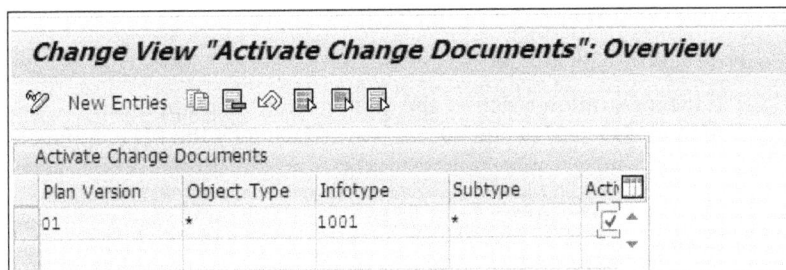

Integration aspects with other submodules of HCM

There is a tight integration between the following submodules of **Human Capital Management (HCM)**:

- Personnel Administration
- Recruitment

The following data flow happens due to the effect of the integration:

- Qualifications are transferred from personnel administration.
- Qualifications are transferred from recruitment.
- Appraisals are transferred from personnel administration. We can use the OOPD transaction code for setting the control features.

The **HR Master Data** view is as shown in the following screenshot:

The integration helps in using the qualifications from the PD submodule, instead of from the 0024 infotype (Qualifications).The appraisal system in the PD submodule can be used instead of the 0025 (Appraisals) infotype. This table is maintained by navigating to **SPRO | Personnel Management | Personnel development | Integration | Set up Integration with Personnel Admin. and Recruitment** as shown in the preceding screenshot, or via TCD OOPD.

> If the integration is active, the qualifications and appraisal maintained in 0024 and 0025 are overridden by the PD component.

To import the qualification and appraisal maintained in the PA submodule and recruitment component, the following reports are used:

- The **RHQINTE0** report transfers the personnel data stored in 0024 (PA infotypes) to the same object ID in T574A. The data stored in PA0024 is then deleted.

- The **RHQINTE1** report transfers the applicant data stored in 0024 (PA infotypes) to the same object ID in T574A. The data stored in PA0024 is then deleted.

- The **RPIT25APP** report is a useful report to convert the 0025 infotype data to the appraisal system of personnel development. We can also delete the entries in PA0025 using this report after conversion.

These reports can be accessed by navigating to **SPRO | Personnel Management | Personnel development | Integration | Transfer Qualifications from Personnel Administration**.

Master data for the Personnel Development component

There are four major activities that can be performed. This depends on whether the modules already implemented are used. The activities are as follows:

- Organizational plan maintenance
- Scales
- Qualifications catalog
- Careers

If we have the OM module implemented, then we need not perform the organizational plan maintenance step. If the OM component is implemented, the organizational plan maintenance need not be performed separately.

The active integration of PD components will allow us to define the scales, qualitative or quantitative. Examples of quality scales can be as follows:

- Expert
- Beginners

Some recommendations while creating qualitative scales are as follows:

- Define less than 20 proficiencies for a scale
- At least one proficiency must be created for a scale

Examples of quantity scales can be 100 percentage, where 1 is the lowest proficiency and 100 is the highest proficiency.

The scales are defined by navigating to **SPRO** | **Personnel Management** | **Personnel Development** | **Master Data** | **Edit Scales**, as shown in the following screenshot, or via the SM30/31 T-code in the V_T77SK table.

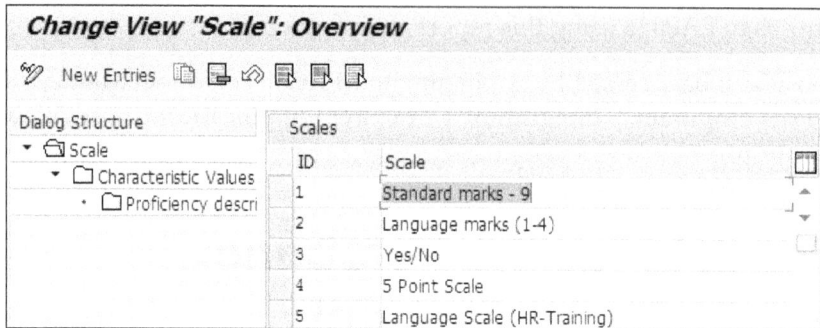

We define, for example, a 5-point scale, and the system prompts us to choose whether it's qualitative or quantitative, as shown in the following screenshot:

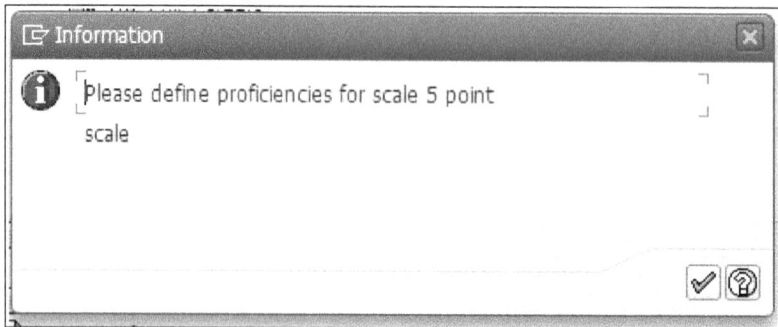

The proficiencies are defined by choosing **Quality scale** or **Quantity scale**.

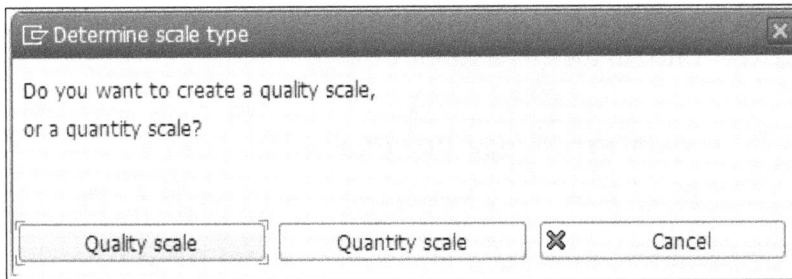

The characteristic values are defined by navigating to **SPRO | Personnel Management | Personnel Development | Master Data | Edit Scales | Characteristics Values**, as shown in the following screenshot, or via the SM30/31 T-code in the V_T77SP_1 table.

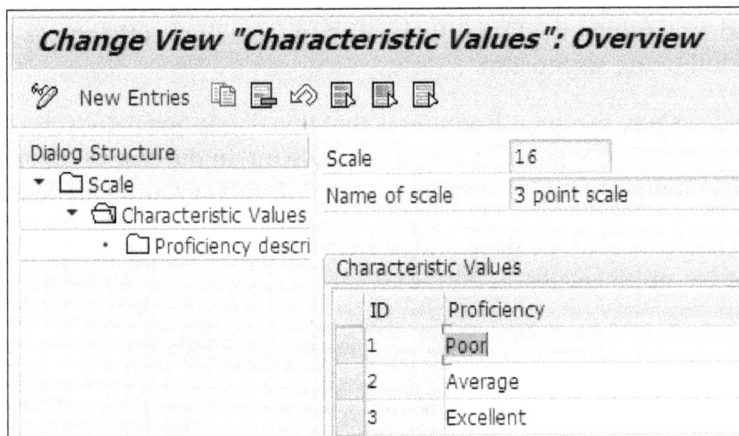

The qualification catalogue

The qualification catalog lets us define the qualification or proficiency in which the employer is interested. The qualification groups and qualifications together make a qualification catalog. The qualification catalog can be defined by navigating to **SPRO | Personnel Management | Personnel Development | Master Data | Edit Qualifications Catalog**, as shown in the following screenshot, or via TCD OOQA.

A qualification catalogue can be edited by selecting **Functional/Technical** (qualification) under **SAP Skills** (qualification group), as shown in the following screenshot. The proficiency description of the qualification defined in the appraisal catalogue can be edited in the qualification catalog.

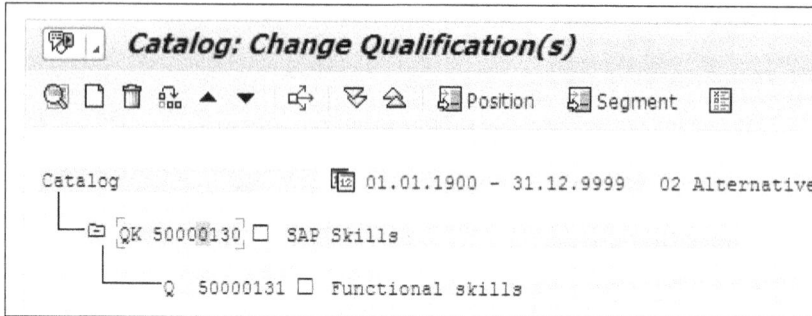

The inherited proficiency descriptions should be displayed for the object and feature. It is controlled by flagging the **Default** checkbox under the **Proficiencies** tab, as shown in the following screenshot.

In the standard system, the default setting is that this flag is normally activated. This implies that the proficiency descriptions of the scale (or, in the case of qualifications, the proficiency descriptions of the corresponding qualification group) will be displayed.

The **Default** checkbox shall be deactivated to create or display an individual description of the proficiencies.

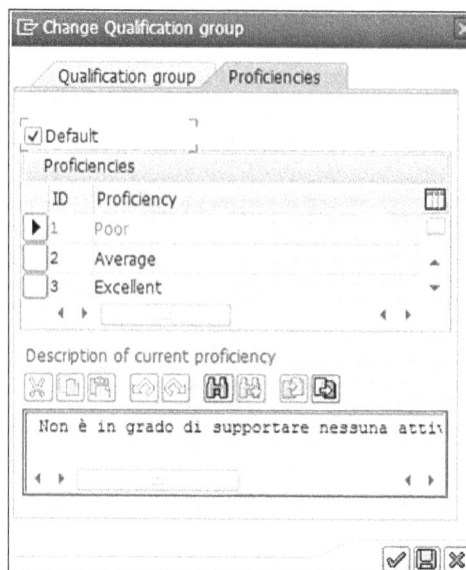

The qualification group (object type QK) is assigned a proficiency scale. It is also used to structure the qualification catalogue. The qualifications, on the other hand, cannot be directly inserted into catalogues; they must be mapped via the qualification group. The validity period and deficiency meter can be assigned to qualifications. The qualification catalogue can be uploaded using **LSMW** (**Legacy System Migration Work Bench**), along with the qualification group, qualifications, and proficiencies. The proficiencies against each position level are normally uploaded via **Batch Data Collection** (**BDC**). The validity or the depreciation meter is maintained by clicking on the additional data table for each qualification, as shown in the following screenshot:

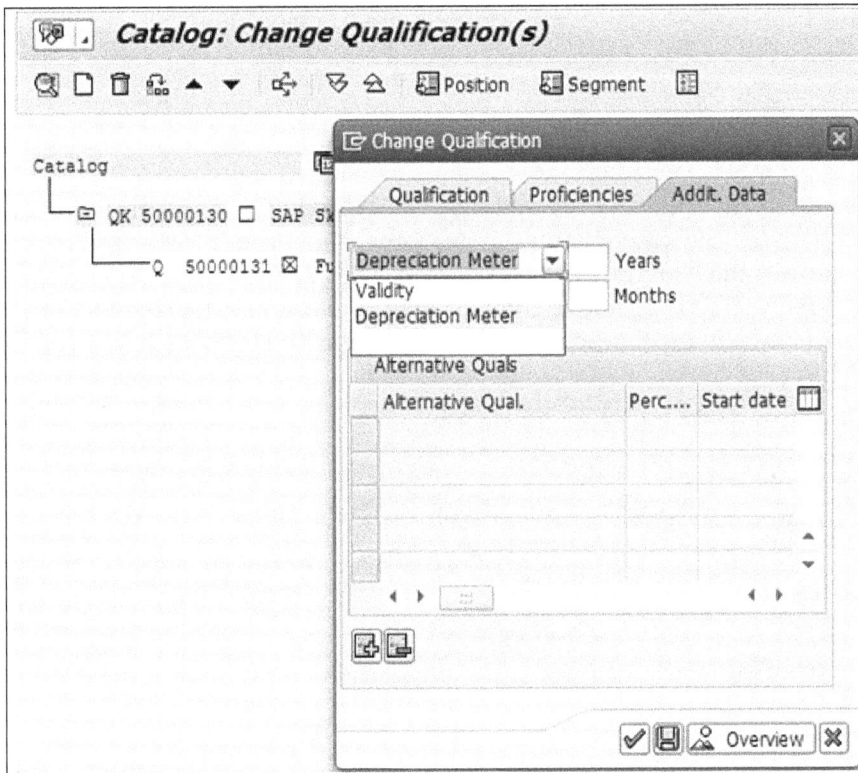

The **Where-used** (*Ctrl + Shift + F3*) functionality, shown in the following screenshot, is useful to find the relationships of the qualification group object type:

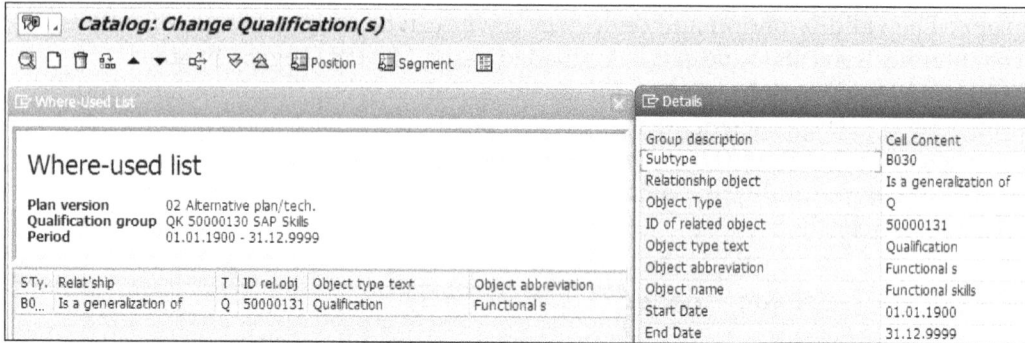

Career maintenance

The applicable path within an organization can be defined via careers. One career can contain up to 9,999 career items. Career items are normally arranged bottom up. Items high up in the hierarchy come at the top. They are defined by navigating to **SPRO | Personnel Management | Personnel Development | Master Data | Edit Careers**, as shown in the following screenshot, or via TCD OOQ4. Changing a career is a customizing activity in SPRO.

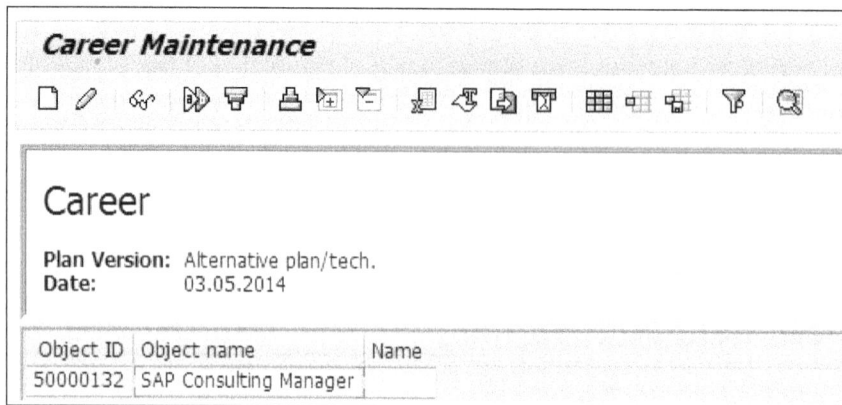

Functions in Personnel Development

Personnel Development functions such as profile view, control parameters, selection criteria, and specifying the vacancy infotype are some features in a PD component. The profile view lets us define a view for each object type. It comprises of a number of subprofiles. The profile view can be defined by navigating to **SPRO | Personnel Management | Personnel Development | Functions | Define Profile View** or via the SM30/31 T-code in the T77PP_VIEW table. The profile view lets us define the views (headers and subprofiles) such as qualifications, potentials, and dislikes for an object type P, as shown in the following screenshot:

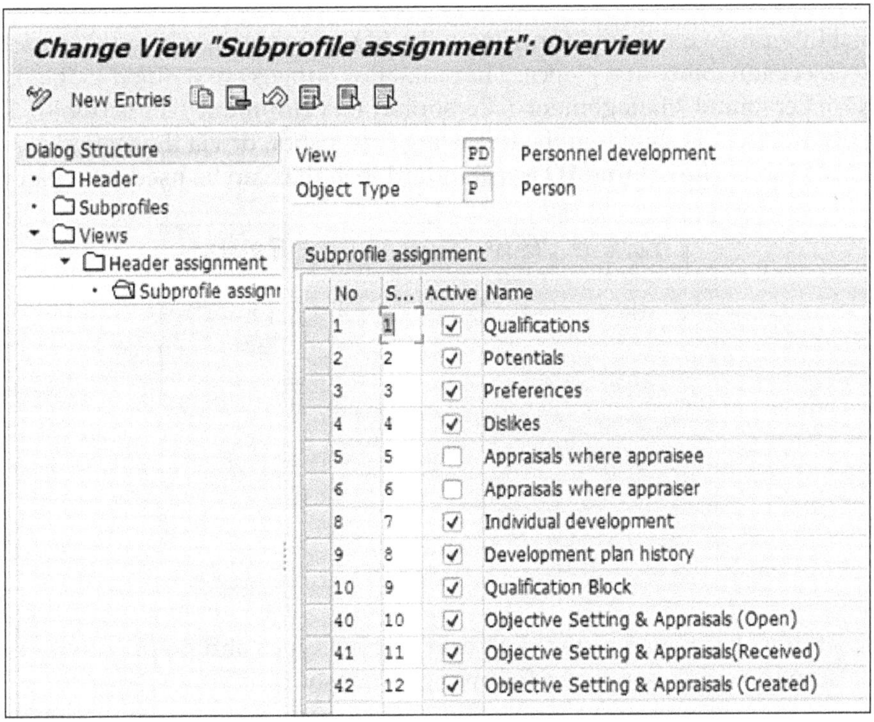

The control parameter function in V_T77S0 lets us define the features mentioned in the following list. They are defined by navigating to **SPRO | Personnel Management | Personnel Development | Functions | Set Up Control Parameters**.

- Maximum number of entries in the hit list
- Handling over qualification
- Activating the qualification bundle

The following values are maintained for the standard settings switches:

Group	Sem abbreviation	Value	Description
QUALI	MAXEN	20	Maximum number of entries in the hit list
QUALI	OVERQ	1	Valuation of over-qualification
QUALI	QBUSE		Use qualifications bundle
QUALI	QPROZ	100	Replacement percentage for alternative qualification
QUALI	SHORT		Code in qualifications catalog

The suitability range is a useful function in the PD component, which helps users identify object suitability at a glance. The suitability ranges are defined by navigating to **SPRO | Personnel Management | Personnel Development | Functions | Define Suitability Ranges**, as shown in the following screenshot, or via the SM30/31 T-code in the T77CS table. The column **ID** is a standard icon that can be used to depict ranges.

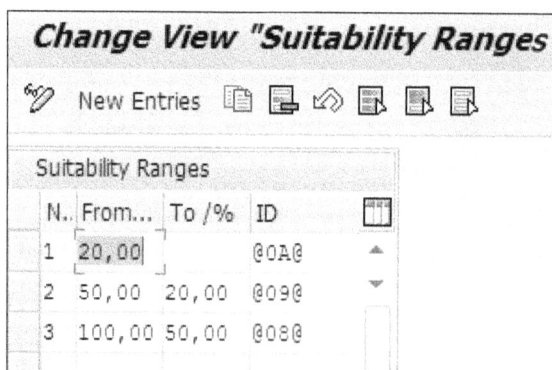

The infoset must be created with the AP and P object types and mapped with the PDVFINE scenario, as shown in the following screenshot:

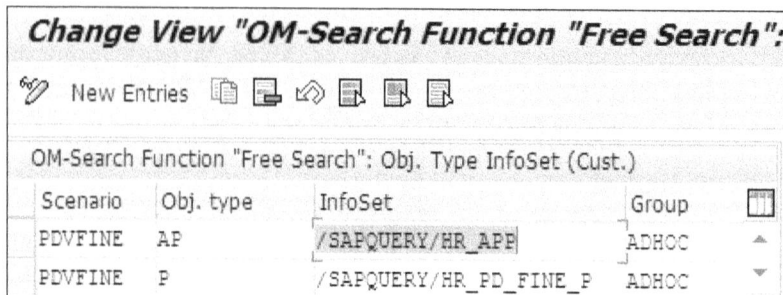

The standard system settings have the PDVFINE scenario defined for the AP and P object types maintained in T77OMAHQ_FUNCARS, as shown in the following screenshot:

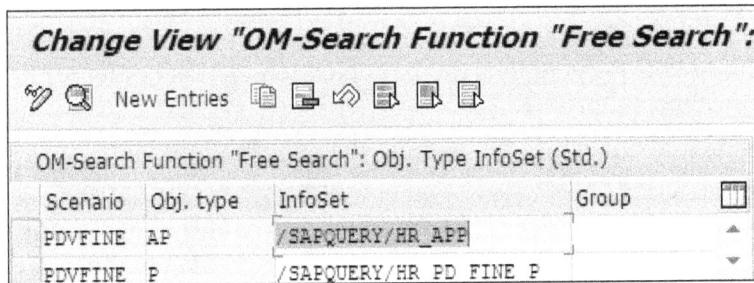

This infoset can be seen in the sq02 TCD, as shown in the following screenshot:

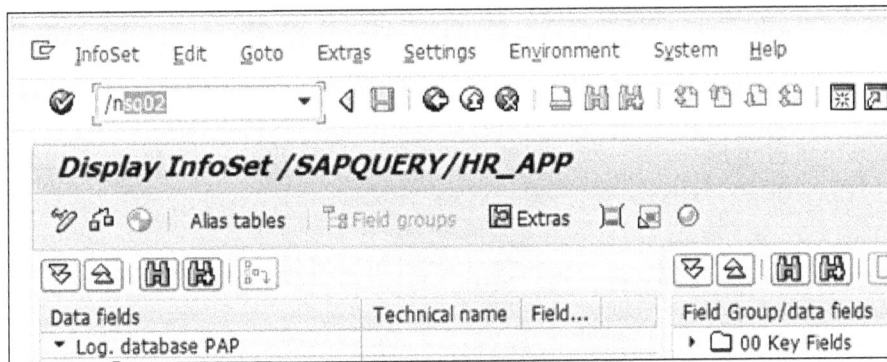

We can specify whether the vacancy infotype needs to be maintained in 1007 or not by navigating to **SPRO | Personnel Management | Personnel Development | Functions | Activate/Deactivate "Vacancy" Infotype**. If the PPVAC PPVAC switch in the T77SO table is set at 0, then integration with recruitment is inactive, as shown in the following table:

Group	Sem abbreviation	Value	Description
PPVAC	PPVAC	0	1007I cannot be maintained
PPVAC	PPVAC	1	The vacant position is indicated by 1007I and is maintained for Personnel Development

Standard tools in the PD component

There are some standard tools provided in PD components to perform the following functions:

- Requirements for positions can be copied to position holder's qualification subprofile

- Mass data maintenance for creating the qualifications subprofile

  They can be accessed by navigating to **SPRO | Personnel Management | Personnel development | Tools | Copy Requirements Profiles to Position Holder(s)**, or via **SPRO | Personnel Management | Personnel Development | Tools | Qualifications Profile: Mass Data Maintenance**.

Development plans

The individual development plan status is defined to identify the current progress of the business event planned. The status can be defined by navigating to **SPRO | Personnel Management | Personnel development | Development Plans | Define Development Plan States**, or via the SM30/31 T-code in the T77BZ table. In the standard system, the following settings are defined:

State	State of development plan
1	Planned
2	Current
3	Completed
4	Completed unsuccessfully
5	Completed successfully
6	Not carried out

The development plan catalog contains the development plan group and development plan, and they can be maintained by navigating to **SPRO | Personnel Management | Personnel Development | Development Plans | Edit Development Plan Catalog**, as shown in the following screenshot:

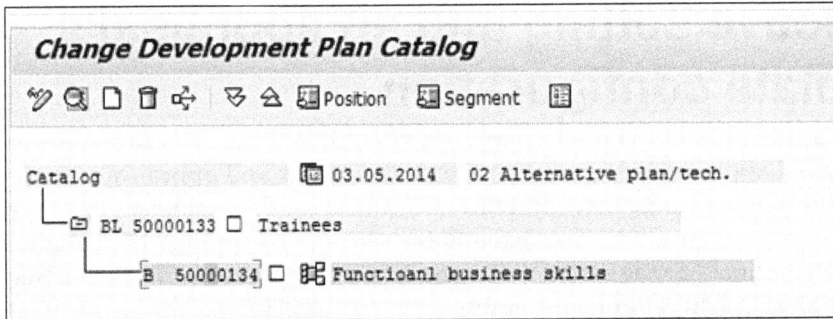

The development plan contains subactivities, and the following object types can be included as items in a development plan:

- A: This is the work center
- BS: This is the appraisal model
- C: This is the job
- D: This is the course type
- DC: This is the curriculum type
- F: This is the location
- O: This is the organizational unit
- S: This is the position

We can also define the following information for the development plan:

- Duration in months, days, or years
- Notes for items
- Specify whether an item is mandatory, as shown in the following screenshot:

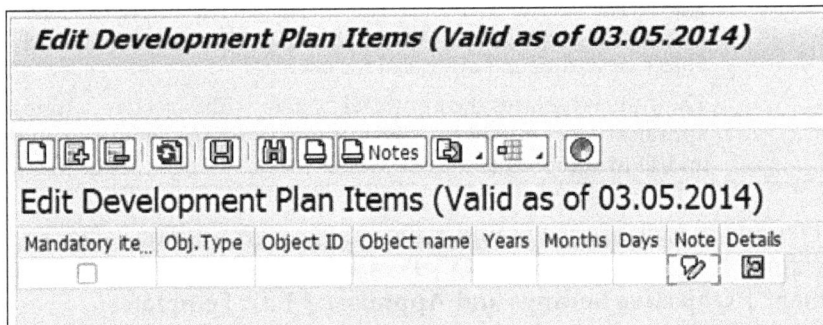

Objective setting and an appraisal's template configuration

The basic settings need to be set up in a way that determines whether we are going to use the old appraisal system or the objective settings and appraisal system component. To replace the new system, we need to set the system switch, as shown in the following screenshot. The system table settings are defined by navigating to **SPRO | Personnel Management | Personnel Development | Objective Settings and Appraisal | Edit Appraisal Catalog** or via the OOHAP_SETTINGS_PA TCD, as shown in the following screenshot:

Change View "PA: Settings": Overview

Documentation

System Switch (from Table T77S0)

Group	Sem. abbr.	Value abbr.	Description
HAP00	REPLA	T	place Old Appraisal System with New
HAP00	RFCSE	B3TCLNT800	RFC Destination in SEM System

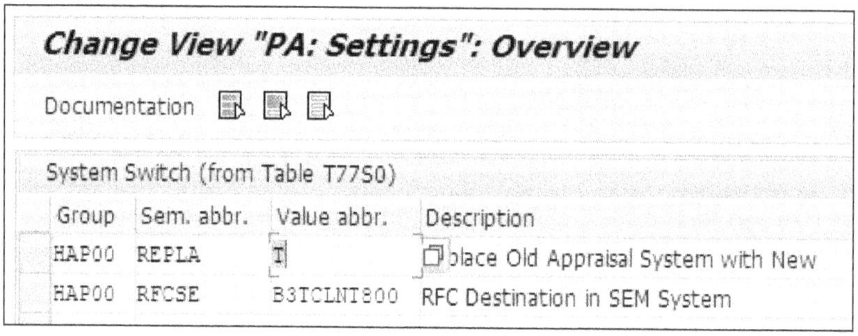

The possible values that can be defined for the switches are explained in the following table:

Value possible	Description
	Retain the old appraisal system
X	The system replaces the appraisal system with objective settings and appraisal subcomponents.
T	The system replaces the appraisal system with objective settings and appraisal subcomponents. It also has an impact on the TEM submodule. For business event processing, the system offers the function of objective setting and appraisal for users.
A	The system replaces the appraisal system with objective settings and appraisal subcomponents. The settings also have an impact on the PD and TEM submodules.

Appraisal templates will be created under the category group. The category group is defined by navigating to **SPRO | Personnel Management | Personnel Development | Objective Settings and Appraisal | Edit Templates**.

The appraisal template includes the following elements:

- Category (appraisal) group
- Appraisal category
- Appraisal template
- Criteria group
- Criterion
- External element

Category groups let us define the object types, status, authorized persons, and workflow events. They also include appraisal documents for the objective settings and appraisals' applications.

An appraisal category groups different appraisal processes, for example, the 360-degree appraisal process.

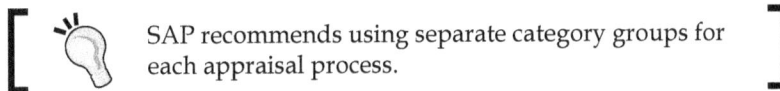

> SAP recommends using separate category groups for each appraisal process.

An appraisal template lets us define specific appraisal documents. It is always assigned to a category. It is quite simple to create an appraisal template for an appraisal process. The standard templates delivered by SAP can be used instead of creating a new one.

A criteria group follows the appraisal template. An individual characteristic in an appraisal document that needs evaluation is referred to as a criterion. The standard system delivers the following categories:

- 360-degree feedback
- Standard appraisal
- Objective setting

The following are delivered as standard templates:

- Objective setting
- Performance appraisal

Category group creation

The category groups use the object types such as P that are chosen during the appraisal form creation. The object types included in **Allowed Object Types** control the selection during the appraisal form creation process, as shown in the following screenshot:

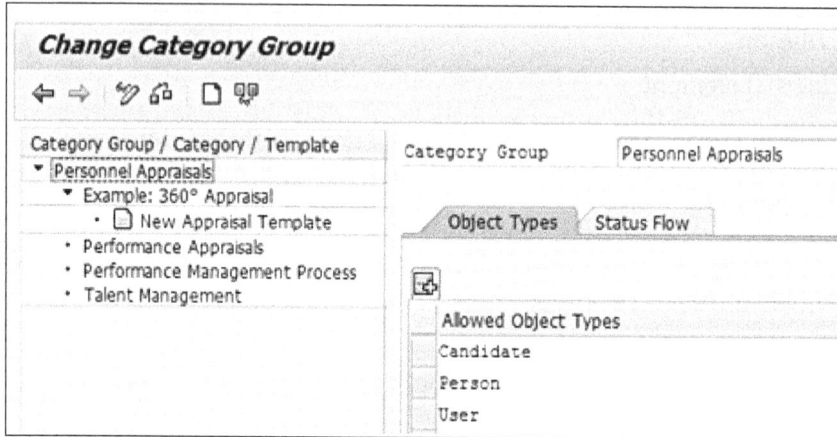

The status that needs to be included in the appraisal template is included in the **Status Flow** column. The status that is mentioned at the **Category Group** level applies to the category and template as well. The selected flag controls whether the status can be used or not, as shown in the following screenshot:

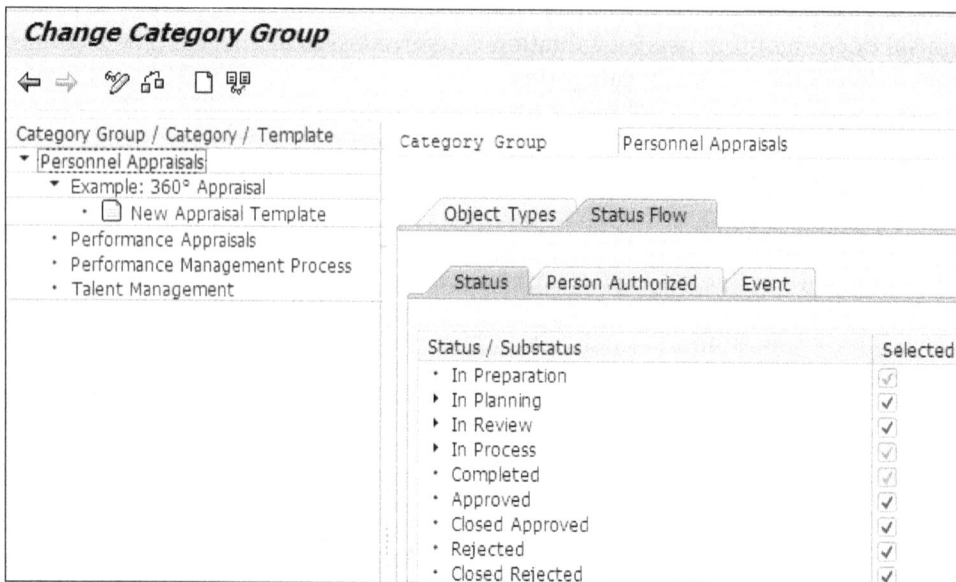

The people authorized to access the appraisal template and the status are defined in the **Person Authorized** tab, as shown in the following screenshot:

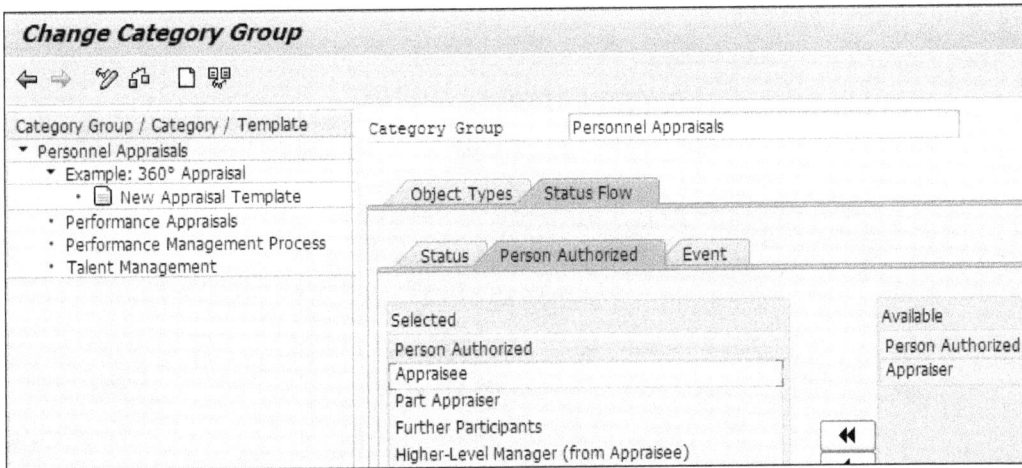

As an additional function, the workflow templates can also be added in the appraisal template. The workflow can be triggered based on the events setup, as shown in the following screenshot:

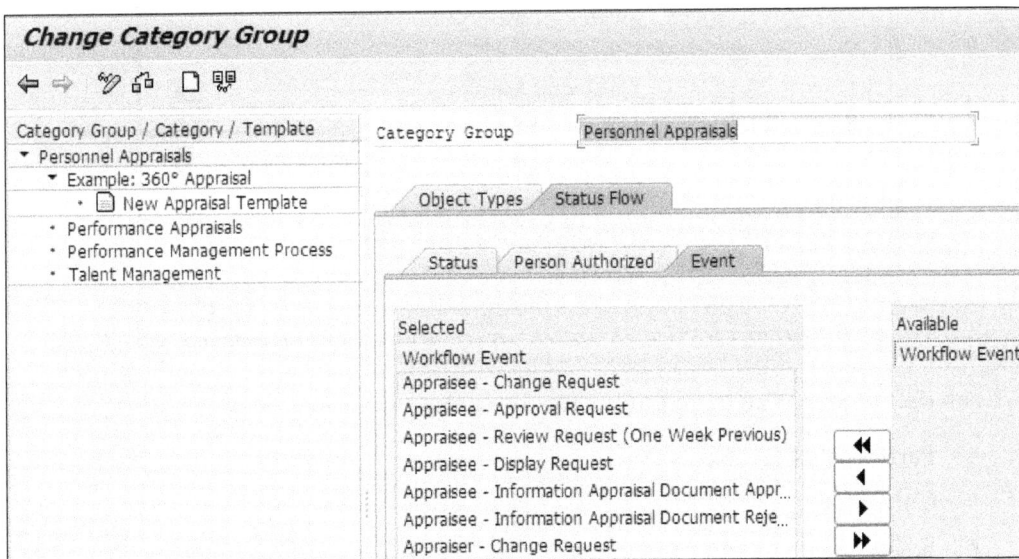

Category creation

We can create a new category by right-clicking on the category group, as shown in the following screenshot:

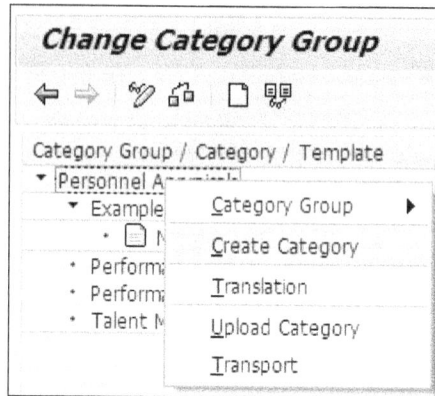

We will have an option to choose from the pop-up screen.

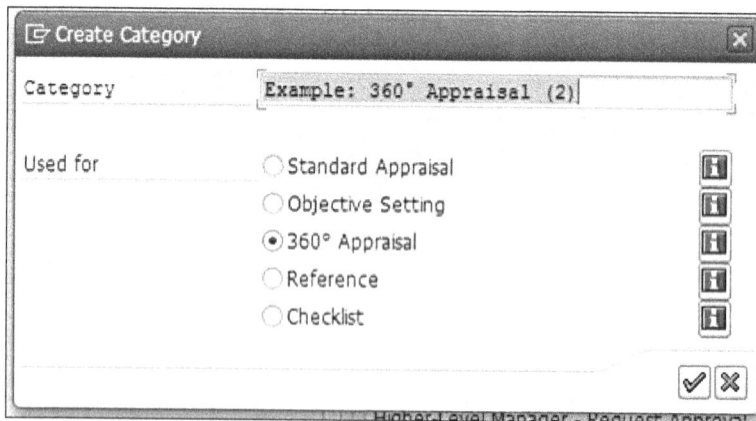

We can define the following columns for the category:

- **Participants**
- **Columns**
- **Roles**
- **Value Lists**
- **Enhancements**
- **Status Flow**

The text and type of participants can be defined in the **Participants** tab, as shown in the following screenshot. The text is displayed as a label, and if no text is maintained, the system displays a validity period.

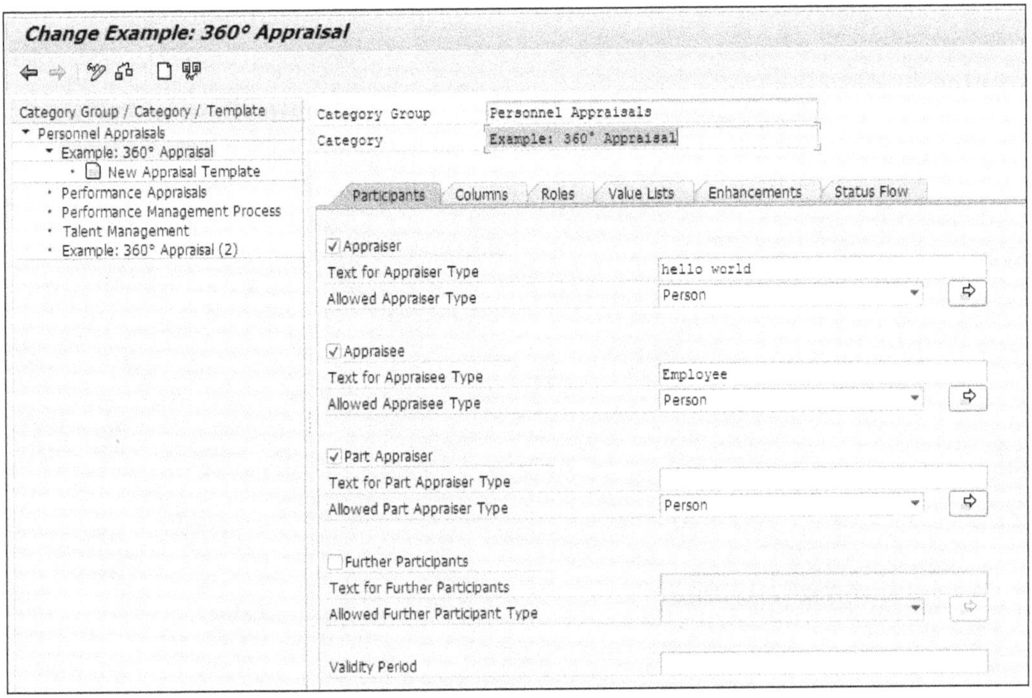

The list of columns can be defined in the appraisal template level, as shown in the following screenshot:

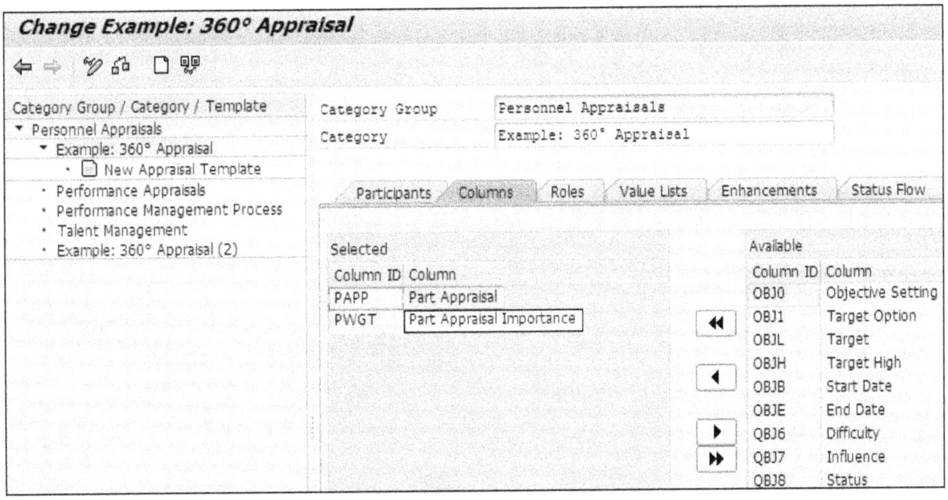

The final list of roles can be defined in the appraisal template level, as shown in the following screenshot, and is mainly for partial appraisal purposes:

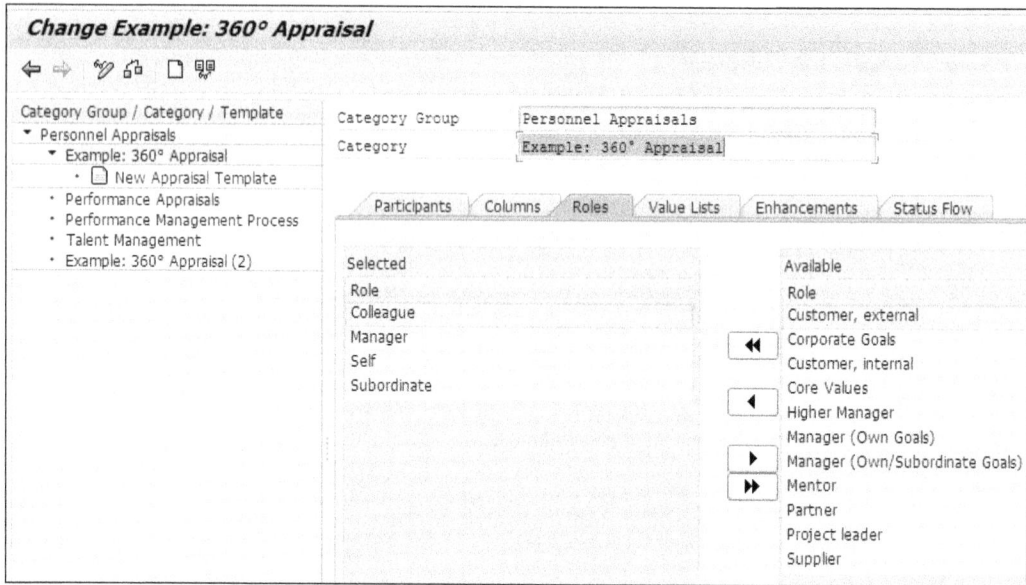

The scales can be defined in the appraisal template level in the **Value Lists** tab:

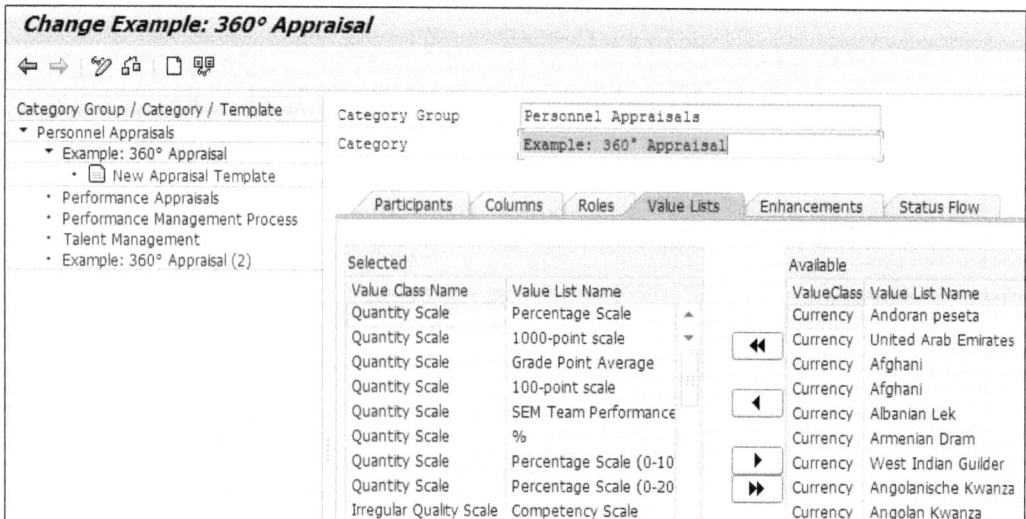

If we are going to use any enhancements in the appraisal, the template level can be defined in the **Enhancements** tab, as shown in the following screenshot. The enhancement is a technical activity and can be performed by the technical consultants.

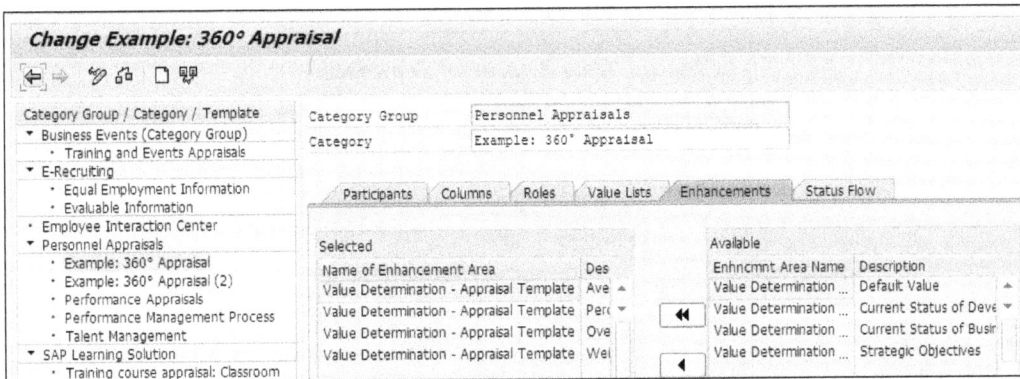

The person authorized to access the appraisal template and status flow of events can be defined in the **Status Flow** tab, as shown in the following screenshot:

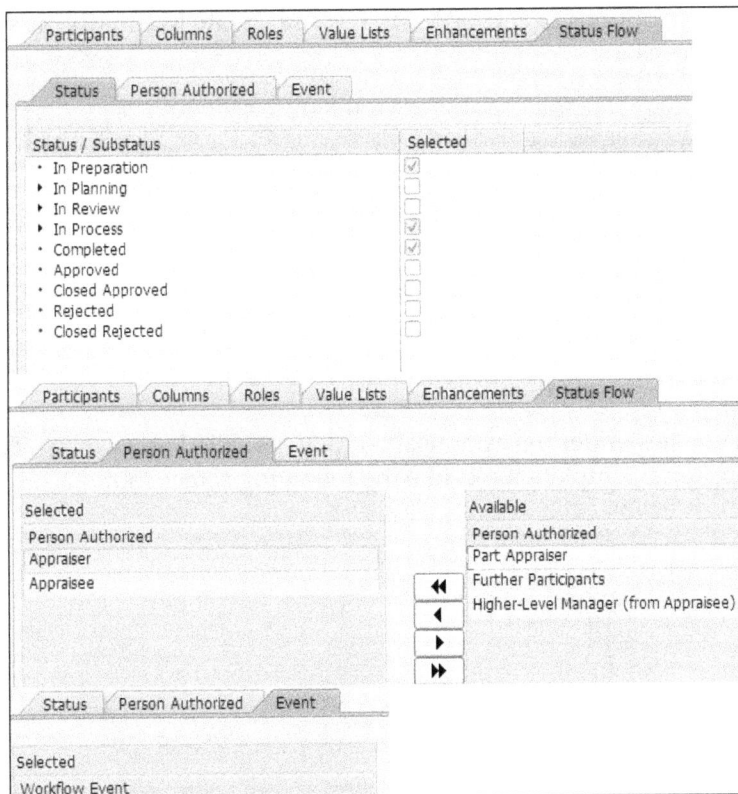

Steps to create an appraisal template

We need to right-click on the category and choose **Create Template**, as shown in the following screenshot:

Here, we will have options to choose from. Choose **Create Manually**, as shown in the following screenshot:

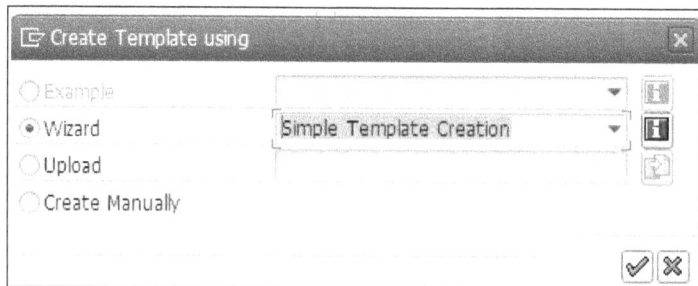

Each item that comes under the appraisal template is called an element. The overall view of the appraisal template looks like the following screenshot:

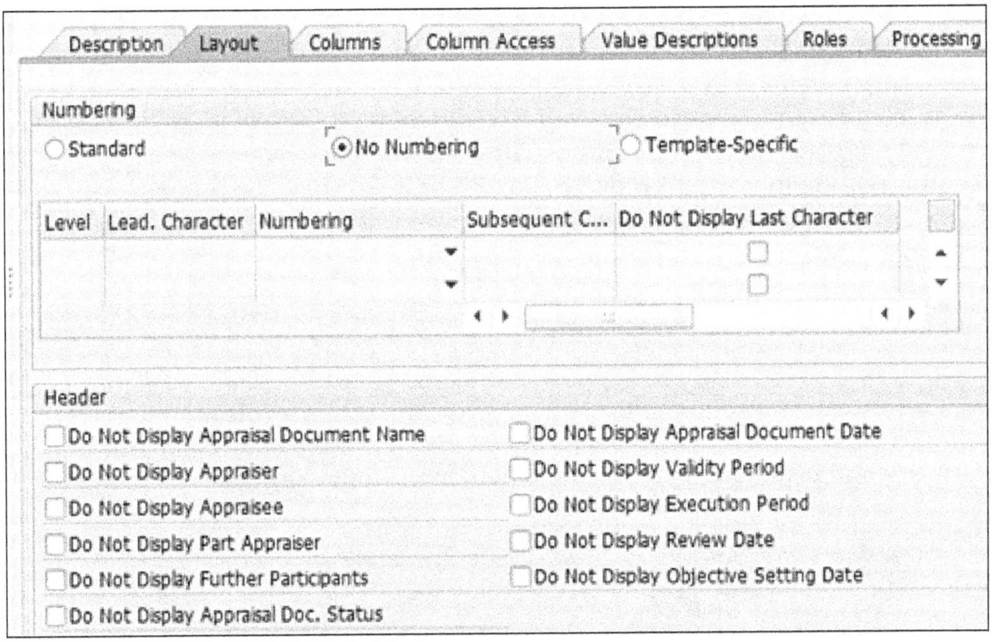

The description that needs to be shown after the header is defined can be done under the **Description** tab. The setup for numbering and appraisal document headers is controlled in the **Layout** tab, as shown in the following screenshot:

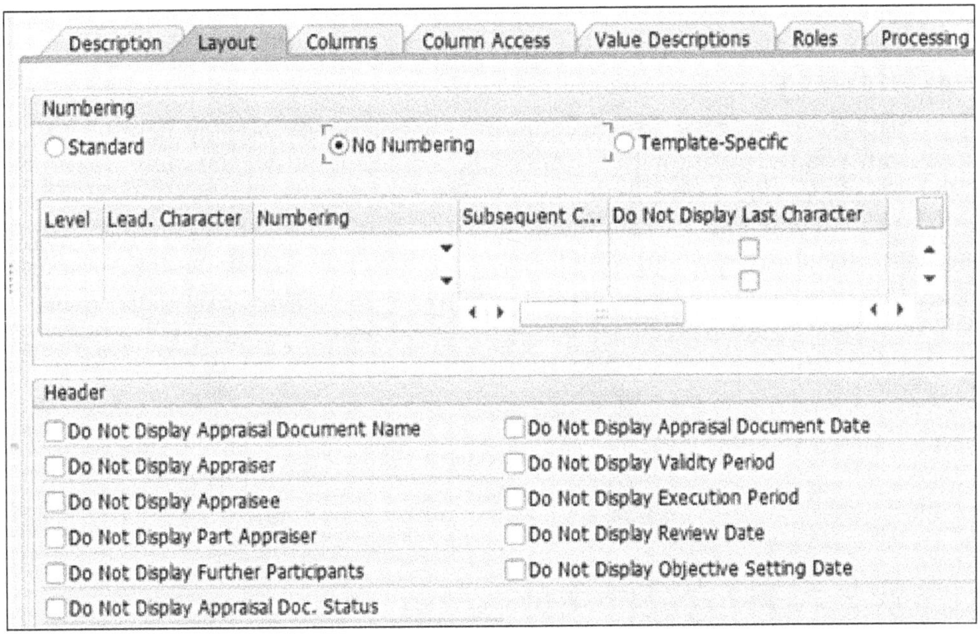

The unchecked header details will be displayed in the appraisal document. The enhancement can also be defined in the template in the further block. The column owner setup is defined in the **Column Access** tab. The different statuses such as display, change, and hide can be set up. The different statuses that can be used in the appraisal template are set in the **Status Flow** tab. The push button can be defined for each process, and the workflow event can also be defined for the process.

> The OSS note *Target function: FAQ - 1549085* is a useful note for reference.

In all the standard reports, the appraisers and appraisees are defaulted. The appraisees are defaulted not at the person level but at the organization unit level. To avoid this, VC_T77HAP_CATEGORY can be used to remove the allowed appraiser type, which is O, and maintain the type P, as shown in the following screenshot:

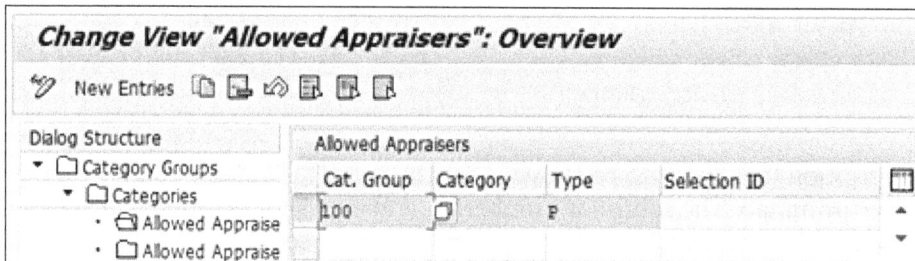

Summary

In this chapter, you learned how to configure the Personnel Development component. You learned how to maintain the important master data required for the Personnel Development component. We only focused on PD and did not cover the **Talent Management/Development** suite for the purpose of this chapter. We covered the basic settings required for configuration and learned about the important master data maintained in PD. We also learned how to create appraisal templates based on corporate goals and corporate or team values.

8
Training and Event Management Configuration

The **Training and Event Management (PE)** component offers a variety of features that help a company plan and administer their employees' training courses. It also helps companies keep a track by recording the knowledge and skills acquired by employees that can be used in real-time practice. The TEM submodule enables us to plan and manage business events; we can also book, prebook, and cancel events using this component. In this chapter, we will learn to set up event catalogs and integration aspects with other modules such as time management and material management. Although SAP Learning Solution is based on Training and Event Management, we are limiting our learning only to TEM (PE). To use the SAP Learning Solution functionality, its add-on must be installed on the system. **Learning Solution (LSO)** is a portal-based solution and is activated by installing the add-on. **Success Factor (SF)** is making a wave in the Talent Management space, and we hope to cover it in a separate book.

The following topics will be covered in this chapter:

- The basic settings of TEM
- Integration aspects of TEM
- Configuring Business Event preparation

The basic settings in TEM

The plan version is defined to maintain a different simulation of the plan, and this has been covered in the previous chapters. The plan version is defined by navigating to **SPRO | Training and Event Management | Basic Settings | Plan version maintenance | Maintain plan version**.

We can set up the number ranges as plan version dependent or independent, and it is maintained by navigating to **SPRO | Training and Event Management | Basic Settings | Number Range Maintenance | Set Up Plan Version-Independent Number Assignment**. If the NUMRG COMP switch is set to X, then the number can be assigned across different plan versions. The internal and external number ranges can be defined by navigating to **SPRO | Training and Event Management | Basic Settings | Number Range Maintenance | Define Number Ranges for Objects** or via the transaction code, OONR. The new number range object, HRTEM_REFN, has been introduced in Training and Event Management for number range reference objects for external operators. These are useful for the following functions:

- Requesting material in the Material Management submodule
- Billing and activity allocation of business events in the sales and distribution (SD) and cost accounting (CO) modules

The factory calendar holidays can be linked to the TEM submodule by navigating to **SPRO | Training and Event Management | Basic Settings | Control Options for Days Off | Specify Factory Calendar**. The SEMIN ORTCA switch needs to be set with the default factory calendar ID. This serves as a control feature for holidays that are defined for the enterprise.

Integration aspects in the Training and Event Management module

TEM modules support integration with many submodules such as the following ones:

- Time management
- Material management
- Budget management
- Billing and activity allocation
- Appointment calendar
- Mail connection
- SAP knowledge provider

Time management integration allows us to define the incompatible absence or attendance types with a particular business event type function. The PLOGI TIME switch needs to be activated, and its value needs to be X for the integration to be active. The different attendance types are defined for attendees and instructors along with a mandatory minimum percentage of attendance. We define the settings by navigating to **SPRO | Training and Event Management | Integration | Time Management | Specify Attendance Types**.

Group	Semantic abbreviation	Description
SEMIN	AINST	Attendance type for instructor in T554S
SEMIN	APART	Attendance type for attendance in T554S
SEMIN	TIMEP	Minimum percentage attendance

If materials required for a particular event are available in the material management module, they can be integrated to TEM. There is a wizard that helps us integrate the MM and TEM modules. The control parameters maintained in T77S0 are activated only after the wizard has successfully completed. If we want to activate the MM functions, we need to choose **Yes** from the wizard options, as shown in the following screenshot:

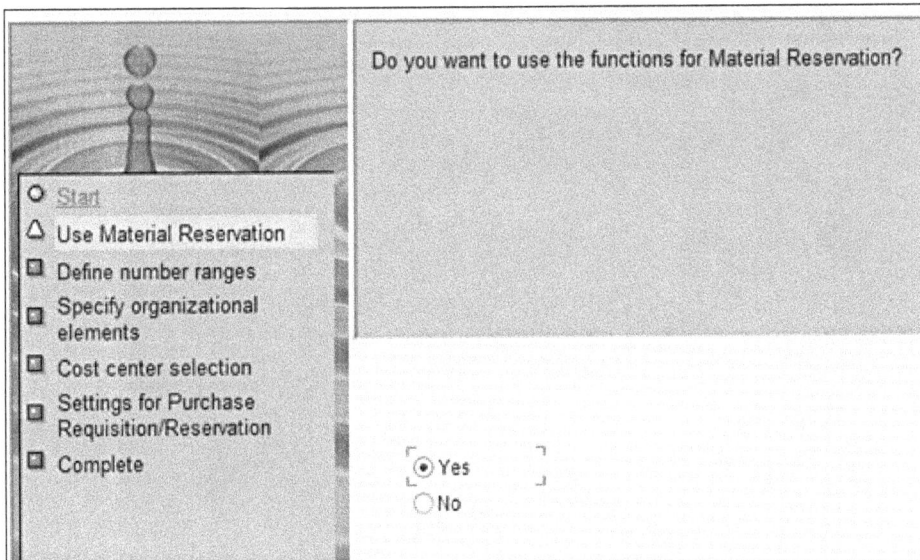

The wizard then helps us assign the number ranges to the next step, and the plant location, storage area, and controlling area details can be input in the wizard. The wizard then allows us to assign the document type and movement types. Documents are simply purchase requisitions in the MM module, and hence, the default document type NB is reserved for purchase requests from the TEM module. The movement of goods is controlled in MM as movement types, so when a request comes from TEM for issuing goods, then the movement type goods issue (GI-201) for cost center is supported. The customizing setting is completed after filling in all the integration details with MM, and we get a message to click on and complete the process to save the settings.

Name	Value
Plant	6650
Storage location	0002
Controlling area	2000
Document type	NB
Transaction type	201

The ones shown in the following screenshot are not standard values:

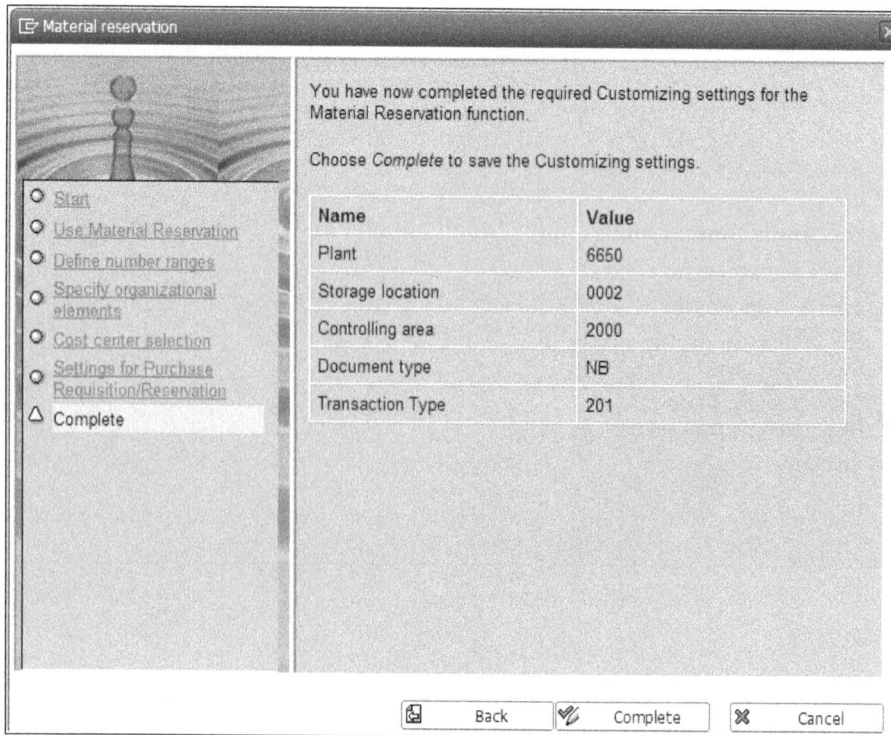

The SEMIN MAT switch must be set as 1 for the activation to be switched on, and it's defined by navigating to **SPRO | Training and Event Management | Integration | Material Management | Integration Yes or No?**. The integration is usually deactivated by default, and it needs to be activated by changing the standard settings.

The controlling area, plant, and storage location are defaulted by navigating to **SPRO | Training and Event Management | Integration | Material Management | Specify Organizational Elements**. The default value is assigned in T77S0 for the following groups and semantic abbreviations:

Group	Semantic abbreviation	Description
PPINT	PPINT	Default value for controlling area
SEMIN	PLANT	Plant for material administration
SEMIN	STORE	Storage location for material administration

The document types and movement types are defaulted by navigating to **SPRO | Training and Event Management | Integration | Material Management | Specify Control Elements**.

Group	Semantic abbreviation	Description
SEMIN	DOCTY	Purchase requisition (document type)
SEMIN	MOVTY	Reservation: movement type

The budget allocated versus the measurement of the cost incurred for training events can be defined if the **Organizational Plan** component (**PA-OS**) is active and if it is defined by navigating to **SPRO | Training and Event Management | Integration | Budget Management | Specify Budget Currency**. The currency is mapped via this node or via the SM30/31 T-code in the V_T7PM2 table. The budge types and their attributes are defined by navigating to **SPRO | Training and Event Management | Integration | Budget Management | Define Budget Type and Attributes**, as shown in the following screenshot, or via the SM30/31 T-code in the V_T7PM3_B table:

Change View "Budget Types": Overview

Budget type group   03   Training and Event Management

Budg.type	Budget type name	Mon.budget	Unit	Unit name	Allocat.
0001	Budget Training	☐	DEM	Full-time equivalent	✓
4101	KR Training budget	✓			✓
CYD		✓			✓
T&E	Training and Events	✓			✓

The default of the budget type group is 03, that is, **Training and Event Management**. Some of the other groups are as follows:

- 01: This is **HR Funds and Position Management**
- 02: This is **Compensation Management**
- 03: This is **Training and Event Management**
- 04: This is **Organization Management for Public Services**

The budget periods can be defined by navigating to **SPRO | Training and event management | Integration | Budget Management | Specify Budget Period** or via the table V_T7PM9_B. The start date, end date, and key date are defined in the table.

We can integrate SAP knowledge providers such as document management service, content management service, text retrieval, and information extraction. We can do this by navigating to **SPRO | Training and event management | Integration | SAP Knowledge Provider**.

Configuring a business event preparation/event catalog

The configuration of business event preparation will help set up master data for the Training and Event Management components such as resources. It also helps in setting up the hierarchical structured business event catalog. We start setting up the cost items; basically, the cost items represent the costs incurred by the business events. It is also required for transferring costs to cost accounting and also for determining price proposal. Cost items are defined by navigating to **SPRO | Training and Event Management | Business Event Preparation | Define cost items** or via the SM30/31 T-code in the T77KB table. Cost items help us store the costs for resources, resource types, business events, and business event types. The cost items have a provision for defining the cost as follows:

- Attendee
- Time unit
- Business event

We can also state whether the cost is relevant for transfer to accounting, and if yes, we have them mapped to the controlling area and cost element, as shown in the following screenshot:

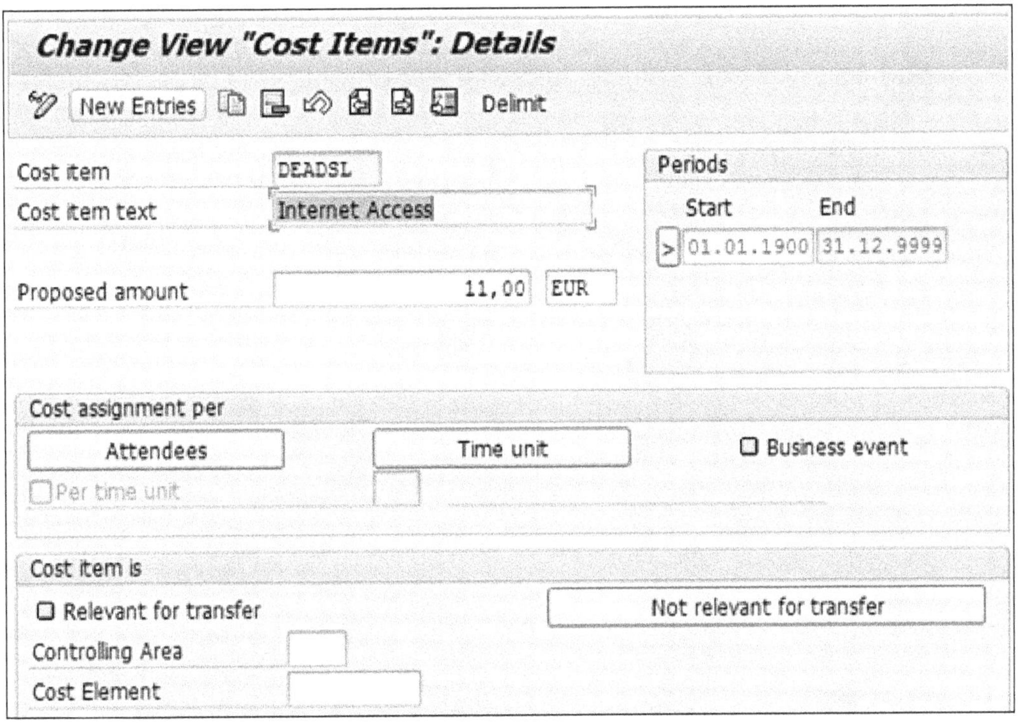

Time schedule

We can define the time schedules for each business event, say, the duration of training sessions such as one full day and with different day segments. Day segments allow us to define the schedule or break it up into three different blocks.

Day schedule and time segment are defined by navigating to **SPRO | Training and Event Management | Business Event Preparation | Define Time Schedule/Day segment**, as shown in the following screenshot, or via the SM30/31 T-code in the T77AM/T770A table:

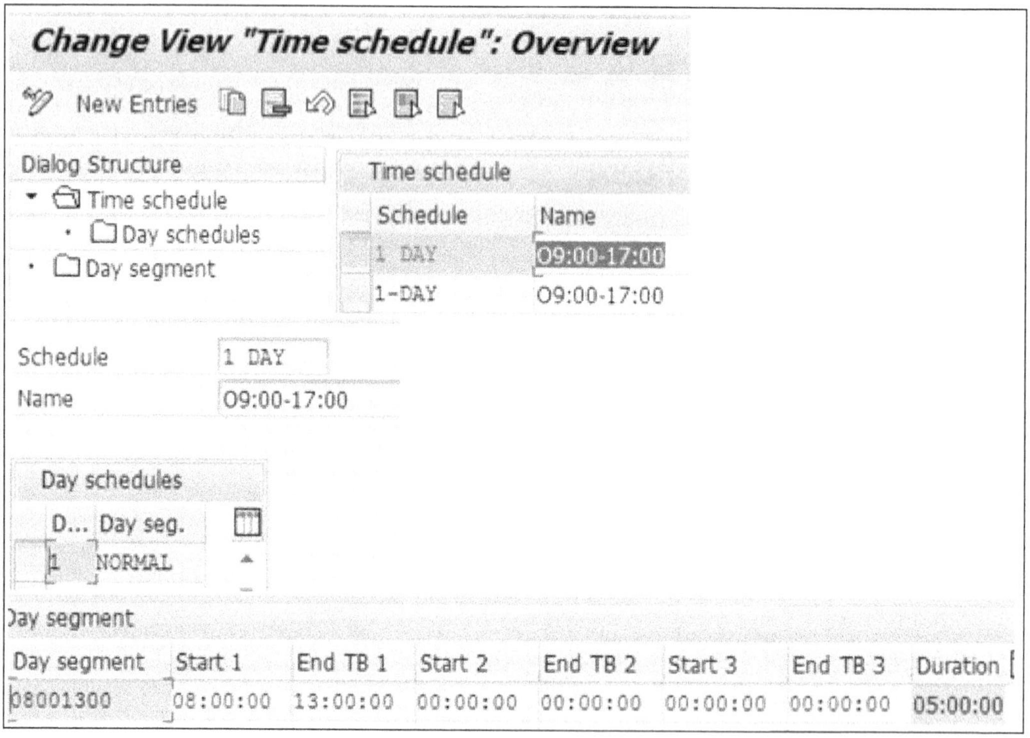

Physical location

The physical location of the rooms can be maintained by navigating to **SPRO | Training and Event Management | Business Event Preparation | Create Building Address** or via the SM30/31 T-code in the T777A table. The business event locations can be maintained by navigating to **SPRO | Training and Event Management | Business Event Preparation | Location | Business Event Location Switch**.

The **SEMIN ORT** switch must be activated for using the business event locations. When an event is created, locations can be assigned, and they are defined by navigating to **SPRO | Training and Event Management | Business Event Preparation | Location | Create Location**, as shown in the following screenshot. We can also capture the following details when the locations are defined:

- **Site-Dependent Info**
- **Address**
- **Further information**

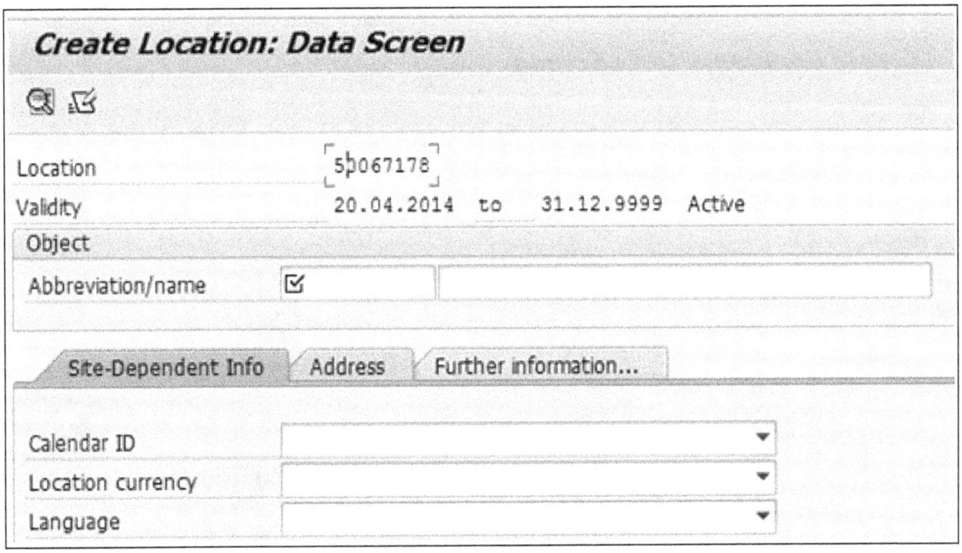

Internal or external organizers conducting the business event can be defined by navigating to **SPRO | Training and Event Management | Business Event Preparation | Organizers | Specify Organizer Types**. The standard organizer types are company (U object type), organizational unit (O object type), customer (KU object type), and interested party. The SEMIN VTYP1 switch must be assigned the relevant object type.

External organizers of business events are defined as companies, while internal organizers are defined as organization units by navigating to **SPRO | Training and Event Management | Business Event Preparation | Organizers | Create Company**, as shown in the following screenshot. We can set up a company in TEM as follows:

- It can set as an organizer of a business event type
- It can be set as an organizer of a business event
- It can be set as independent external organizers conducting events
- It can also be assigned to an external instructor or attendee

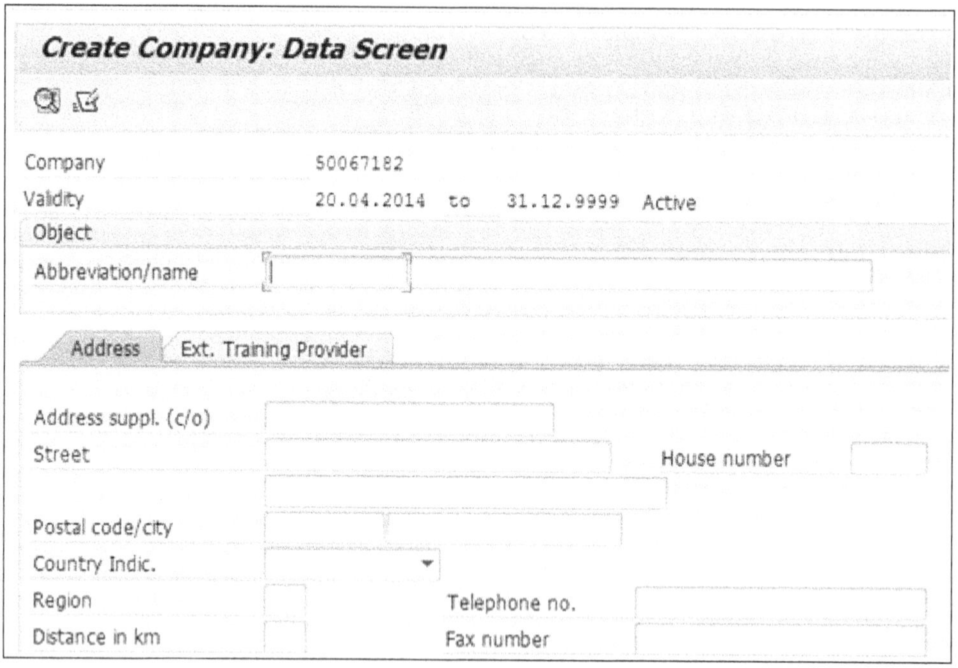

The internal organizers of an event are set up by navigating to **SPRO | Training and Event Management | Business Event Preparation | Organizers | Create Organizational Unit**. Internal organizers are of object type o and need not be defined if they are already defined in OM.

The business event group helps set up the event catalog and is defined by navigating to **SPRO | Training and Event Management | Business Event Preparation | Create Business Event Group**. The business event group has the following details captured:

- General description
- Relationship

- The business event type serves as a blueprint from which the date of a particular business event is generated. We can also schedule a business event type to take place at a particular time and date. We can maintain the following infotypes for business event type **Description**:
  - Time schedule model
  - Capacity
  - Prices
  - Relationships
  - Validity period

An internal and external price for the event type can be maintained. While the internal prices are a user's activity allocation purpose, the external is used for billing purposes.

The following screenshot shows the **Relationships** tab:

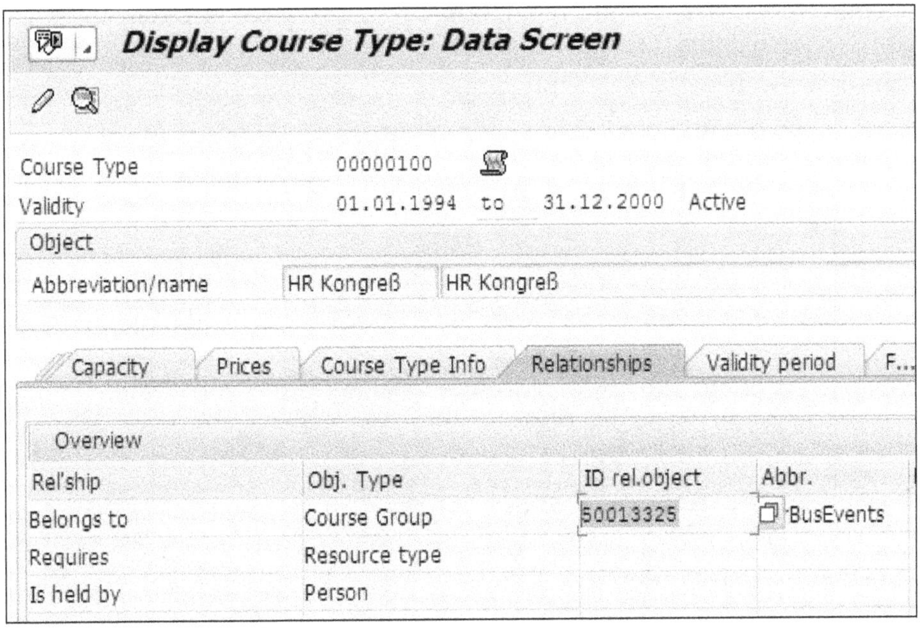

The validity period is used as a depreciation meter. The capacity function plays a vital role in the following features:

- Bookings
- Resource selection
- Price proposal

It also allows us to define the minimum, optimum, and number of attendees of a particular business event type permissible. The schedule model is defined in the time schedule that can be mapped. We can activate or deactivate integration with time management in the **Course Type** info tab. It also controls the availability check for the attendees.

> If the **Do Not Display Business Event Type** indicator is flagged in the intranet, then the business event type won't be displayed in the **Employee Self-Service** (ESS) or portal view of TEM.

Master data

SAP allows us to define all the master data related to TEM in one step with the catalog feature. The objects are displayed in the hierarchical form if they are already set up in individual objects' steps in the **Implementation Guide**. This feature can be explored by navigating to **SPRO | Training and Event Management | Business Event Preparation | Maintain Master Data via Catalog**, as shown in the following screenshot:

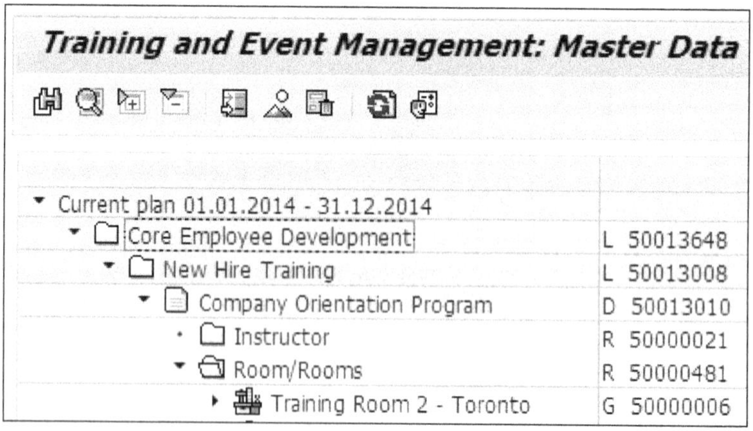

The relationships between object types can be established by clicking on the **Create Relationship** option (*Ctrl + F10*), as shown in the following screenshot:

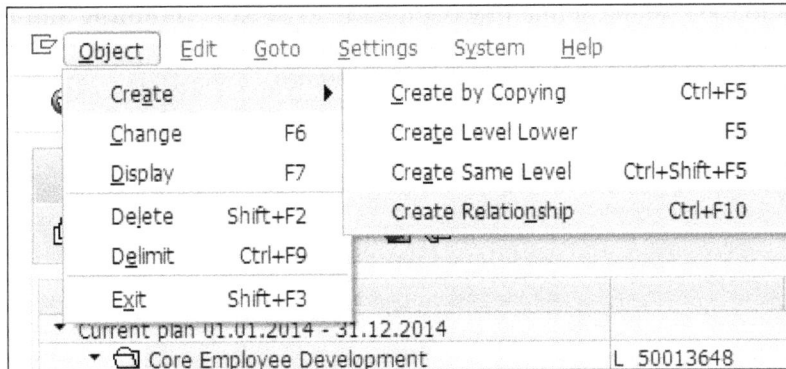

We can create objects and relationships for the following using this catalog:

- Location
- Company
- Organizational unit
- Resource type
- Room
- External instructor
- Other resources
- Business event group
- Business event type

Resource management

Resource management allows us to define the resources such as rooms, instructors, materials, and they can be defined by navigating to **SPRO | Training and Event Management | Business Event Preparation | Resource Management | Create Resource Type**, as shown in the following screenshot, or via TCD OORT:

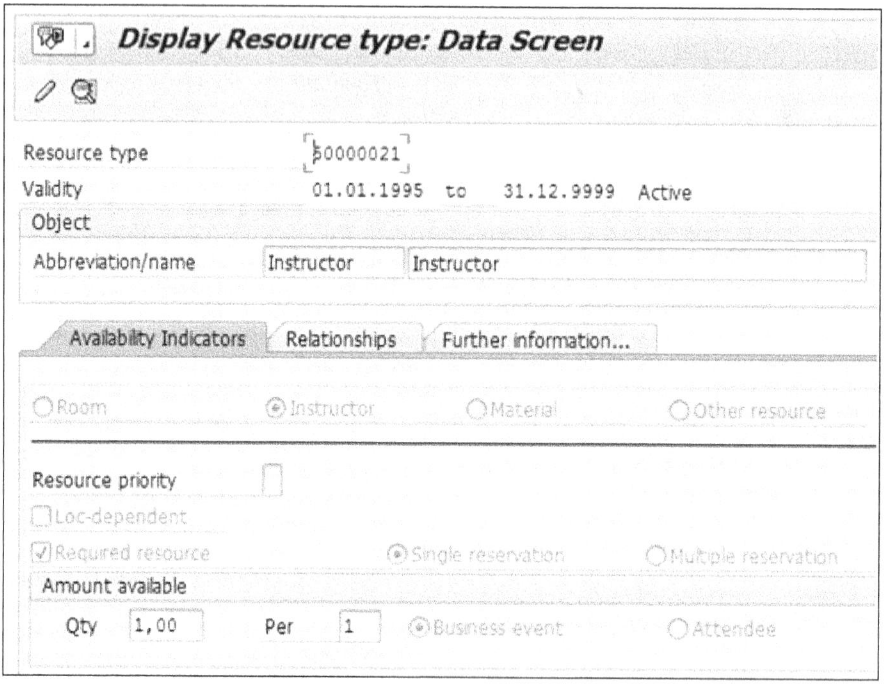

To have direct access to resource reservation tables in TEM, the user exit needs to be assigned in SEMIN RESOC. It is assigned by navigating to **SPRO | Training and Event Management | Business Event Preparation | Resource Management | Control Elements**. By default, the standard functional module, RH_ALLOCAT, is assigned in the system table.

The three types of resources that are normally distinguished are as follows:

- Room
- External instructors
- Other resources

The three type of resources are defined by navigating to **SPRO | Training and Event Management | Business Event Preparation | Resource Management | Resources | Create Room**.

The object type (G) room is defined, and the following can be mapped when a room is defined as a resource:

- Capacity

- Address

- Cost

- Relationships such as the **Belongs to** location

The object type (H) can be defined and the following relationship can be mapped when an external person is created:

- Address

- Mail address

- Relationships such as the **Belongs to** location or **Is instructor for** business event type

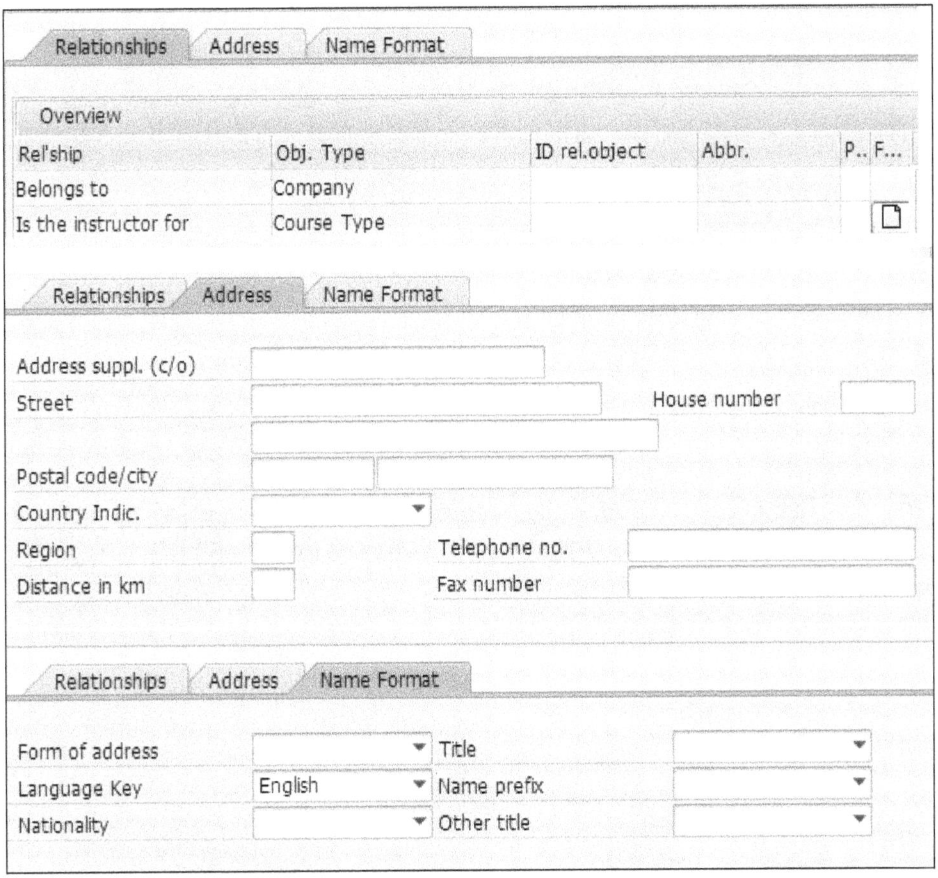

The other resource (G) can be defined, and the following relationships can be established:

- Costs
- Relationship **Belongs to** location and the **Is a specialization of** resource type

The object type (VE) can be used to lock resources in TEM. TEM doesn't have the feature of creating a relationship between resources and services. Services are defined by navigating to **SPRO | Training and Event Management | Business Event Preparation | Resource Management | Resources | Locking Resources | Create Service**. The SEMIN ENQVE switch can have the object ID assigned to it to have the service locked. It is assigned by navigating to **SPRO | Training and Event Management | Business Event Preparation | Resource Management | Resources | Locking Resources | Specify Service for Lock Administration**.

The control elements for business event execution can be defined by navigating to **SPRO | Training and Event Management | Business Event Catalog | Control Elements**.

Group	Semantic abbreviation	Text
SEMIN	FORCA	Business event preview: period in days
SEMIN	KAP	Standard capacity
SEMIN	PFORC	Planning period

The standard system, as shown in the preceding table, has the following values assigned and can be changed if required:

- FORCA: 90
- KAP: 99
- PFORC: 360

The FORCA switch is used to define the business event preview period time frame. The KAP switch is used to define the attendee's capacity, while the PFORC switch defines the planning period.

The business event catalog

The list of events is available as a catalog, and the control elements are defined in the system table with the standard settings, as follows:

Group	Semantic abbreviation	Value	Text
SEMIN	FORCA	90	Business event preview: period in days
SEMIN	KAP	90	Standard capacity
SEMIN	PFORC	360	Planning period

The value in the SEMIN FORCA switch indicates the period (in number of days) in which a business event exists. The start date is the system date when an event is booked via the PV00 TCD, and the end date is determined by the value set in SEMIN FORCA.

The following screenshot shows **Book Attendance**:

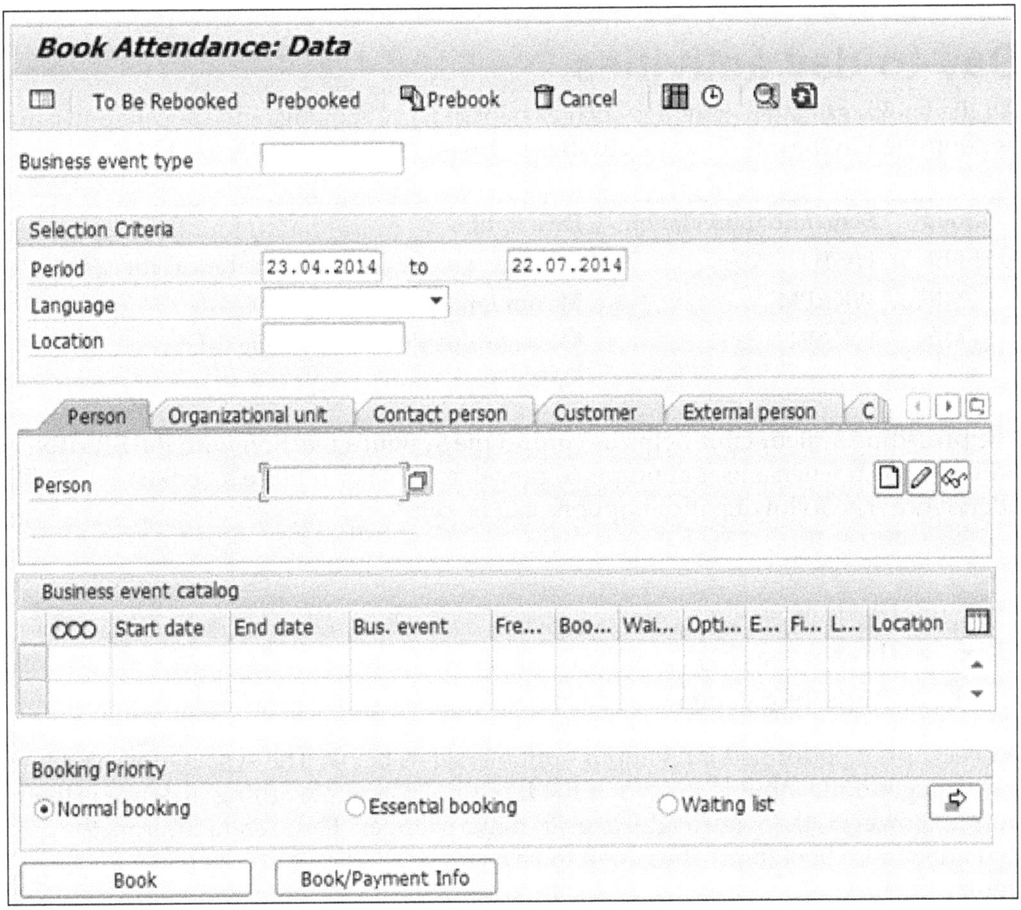

The value set in SEMIN KAP is the maximum capacity for a event. The value set in SEMIN PFORC is used for the planning period. This is used when a business event is created, as shown in the following screenshot, using the PV10 or PV11 transaction code:

Create Business Event with Resources: Initial Screen

📩 Data Screen   🗋 🖉 ⌖ 🔠 Selection Group   🔍

Business event type		
Business event		
Planning period	23.04.2014	– 18.04.2015

Day-to-day activities

All the booking-related activities such as booking, prebooking, and cancellation can be controlled in the day-to-day-activities settings.

Group	Semantic abbreviation	Description
SEMIN	HISTO	Message type for changes to historical attendances
SEMIN	WKAPM	Maximum waiting list capacity
SEMIN	WKAPT	Message type when the waiting list capacity is exceeded

The preceding system table helps us control the system's reaction with the **SEMIN HISTO** switch when a user attempts to cancel, rebook, or replace a booked attendance. The following input options can be set:

- No entry
- E: This is an error message
- W: This is a warning
- I: This is information

A check is not performed if the input option is set as blank. The system doesn't allow any changes if the input is set as E. If the input is set as W, a warning message is the output; however, the system allows us to make changes. The system informs the user that attendance booking is attempted to be changed. It allows you to make a change in the system.

The `SEMIN WKAPM` switch helps control the number of attendees per business event. The `SEMIN WKAPT` switch helps set the reaction messages when the waiting list booking is exceeded. The various input options allowed are as follows:

- `No entry`
- `E`: This is an error message
- `W`: This is a warning
- `I`: This is information

If we would like to have the system read the business event catalogs while prebooking attendees, then the `SEMIN OFFER` switch must be set to `1`. The standard values are as follows:

- `0`: System doesn't read the business event catalog
- `1`: System reads the business event catalog

Booking

The attendee type control option lets us determine the type of attendees that appear on the screen for prebooking, rebooking, replace, and cancel options. The system lets us choose a maximum of six attendee types under Sort in the range of `01` to `06`. The sort sequence function, however, doesn't allow us to hide certain attendee types. There are details that are entered for the attendee types. They are defined by navigating to **SPRO | Training and Event Management | Day to day activities | Booking | Specify Attendee Type Control Options**, as shown in the following screenshot or via the `SM30/31` T-code in the `V_T77R3_1` table:

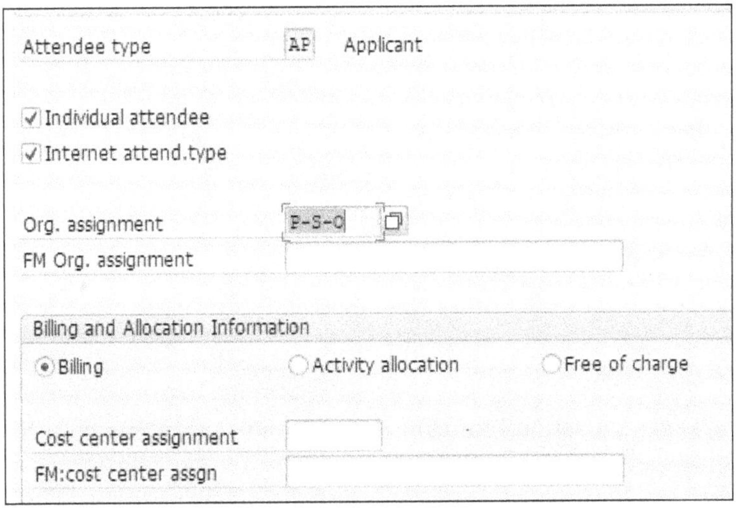

The following options can be set for the attendance or participant type:

- Individual attendee
- Relevant for the Internet
- Organizational assignment
- Function module—organizational assignment
- Billing and allocation information
- Cost center assignment
- Function module—cost center assignment

If the participant doesn't belong to a group, the flag can be set. If the attendee type is included during maintenance in the Internet application, the flag needs to be set for relevance for the Internet. The evaluation path can be mentioned to determine the attendee's organizational assignment. We can also make use of the function module if the evaluation path is not to be used. The settlement type can be set for settling the costs for the participant of attendee's type. If we do not want to mention the cost center, we can specify the function module for determining the cost center assignment of the attendees.

The booking and prebooking attendees check can be performed by navigating to **SPRO | Training and Event Management | Day to day activities | Booking | Attendee Checks**, as shown in the following screenshot, or via the SM30/31 T-code in the V_T77KV_1 table:

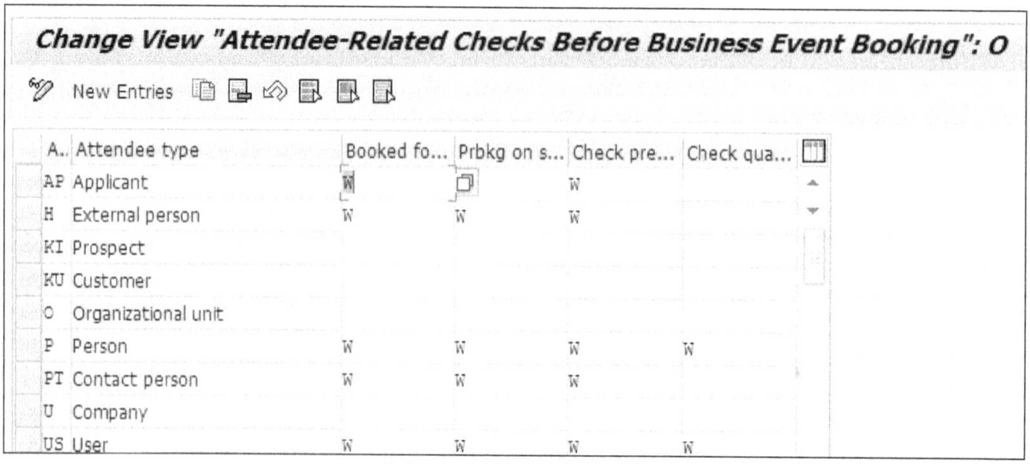

Change View "Attendee-Related Checks Before Business Event Booking": O				
🖊 New Entries 📋 🗐 ⟁ 📑 📑 📑				
A.. Attendee type	Booked fo...	Prbkg on s...	Check pre...	Check qua... ▥
AP Applicant	W	⬜	W	▲
H External person	W	W	W	▼
KI Prospect				
KU Customer				
O Organizational unit				
P Person	W	W	W	W
PT Contact person	W	W	W	
U Company				
US User	W	W	W	W

System reactions can be defined for some booking and prebooking in the form of message output.

Some of the checks, such as the following, can be set up:

- Check for bookings of the same business event type
- Check for prebookings of the same business event type
- Check for a prerequisite business event
- Check attendee's qualification

Standard output messages that can be set for the preceding fields are as follows:

- `No check`
- `E`: This is an error message
- `W`: This is a warning
- `I`: This is information

The time conflicts when the attendance booked can be controlled via the system table (`T77S0`), or the the switch needs to be set as follows:

Group	Semantic abbreviation	Description
SEMIN	TEREF	Message type for attendance/instructor function conflict
SEMIN	TETEI	Message type for attendance/attendance conflict

The settings for fee handling can be controlled by navigating to **SPRO | Training and Event Management | Day to day activities | Booking | Fee Handling**.

Group	Semantic abbreviation	Description
SEMIN	CCDCT	Dialog module cost maintenance for bookings
SEMIN	CCOST	Switch for special event costs for bookings

> The standard system settings have `RH_PRICES` as function modules and `CCDCT` and `CCOST` are set as 1.

The priority for booking can be set by navigating to **SPRO | Training and event management | Day to day activities | Booking | Booking Priorities**.

Group	Semantic abbreviation	Description
SEMIN	MAXMU	Maximum priority for essential booking
SEMIN	MINWL	Minimum priority for waiting-list booking
SEMIN	NPRIO	Default priority for normal booking

The parameter that we define for the switch is defined from 00 to 99. The number set is considered as the priority.

The control options for canceling attendances can be defined by navigating to **SPRO | Training and Event Management | Day to day activities | Canceling Attendance | Control Options**, as shown in the following screenshot.

This control feature allows us to do the following activities:

- We can specify the relationship for the cancellation where applicable
- The default value for the cancellation fees can be specified
- The move-up procedure for waiting list bookings can be specified

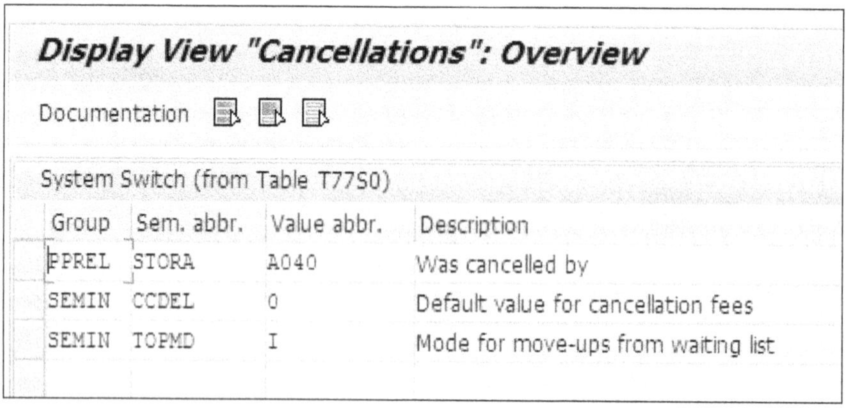

The text for attendance cancellation can be defined by navigating to **SPRO | Training and Event Management | Day to day activities | Reasons for Attendance Cancellation**, as shown in the following screenshot, or via the SM30/31 T-code in the T77CAR table:

Reas.	Reason for cancellation of attendance	Cancel %	Free of ch
1	Attendee cancels attendance booking	50	☐
2	Organizer cancels attendance booking		☑
3	Prerequisites not fulfilled	30	☐
4	Supervisor rejects booking request	50	☐
5	Employee cancels attendance booking	100	☐
6	Employee didn't show up	100	☐

The cancellation percentage fee can be defined, and the indicator for attendance/cancellation can also be set.

Recurring activities

The activities pertaining to business event dates are defined in the nodes of recurring activities. We can firmly book or cancel business events via the SEMIN FIXRV control switch. We can define it by navigating to **SPRO | Training and Event Management | Recurring Activities | Firmly Booking/Canceling | Control Options**.

0 indicates that the attendance or participation cannot be canceled unless it is rebooked.

1 indicates that attendances can be cancelled and the waiting list can be left empty.

We can define the different reasons for event cancellation by navigating to **SPRO | Training and Event Management | Recurring Activities | Firmly Booking/Canceling | Reasons for Event Cancellation**, as shown in the following screenshot, or via SM30/31 in the T77CR table. In the standard system, the following reasons are maintained, and if required, they can be changed:

- The required minimum number of attendees not reached
- The resources flagged as "required" are not available
- The training room is not available
- The instructor is not available

Change View "Reasons for Cancellation of Business Event": Overview

🖉 New Entries 🗋 🖫 🕼 🖫 🖫 🖫

Reas.	Reason for cancellation of event
1	Minimum bookings not reached
2	Required resources not available

Follow-up processing

The actions that need to be carried out post the business event for attendee type is defined by navigating to **SPRO | Training and Event Management | Recurring Activities | Follow-up Processing**, as shown in the following screenshot, or via the SM30/31 in the V_T77KV_2 table. This results in the deletion of the relationship 025 ("is attended"), and a relationship between the attendee and business event type (relationship 034 "attended") is created.

A.	Attendee type	Transfer quals	Del. BE/A rel.	Rel.BE type/Att
AP	Applicant	☐	☐	☐
H	External person	☑	☐	☐
KI	Prospect	☐	☐	☐
KU	Customer	☐	☐	☐
O	Organizational unit	☐	☐	☐
P	Person	☑	☐	☐
PT	Contact person	☐	☐	☐
U	Company	☐	☐	☐
US	User	☑	☐	☐

Change View "Business Event Follow-up Actions": Overview
New Entries

We can set the flag to mention that the qualification can be transferred to the participant or attendee subsequent to the business event.

> Read the online SAP support (OSS) note 538446 — data redundancies.

TEM contains plenty of standard reports such as resources and business events that can be accessed via a dynamic information menu. They can be accessed by navigating to **SPRO | Training and Event Management | Information Systems | Integrate Customer-Specific Reports**, as shown in the following screenshot, or via the PVDM TCD:

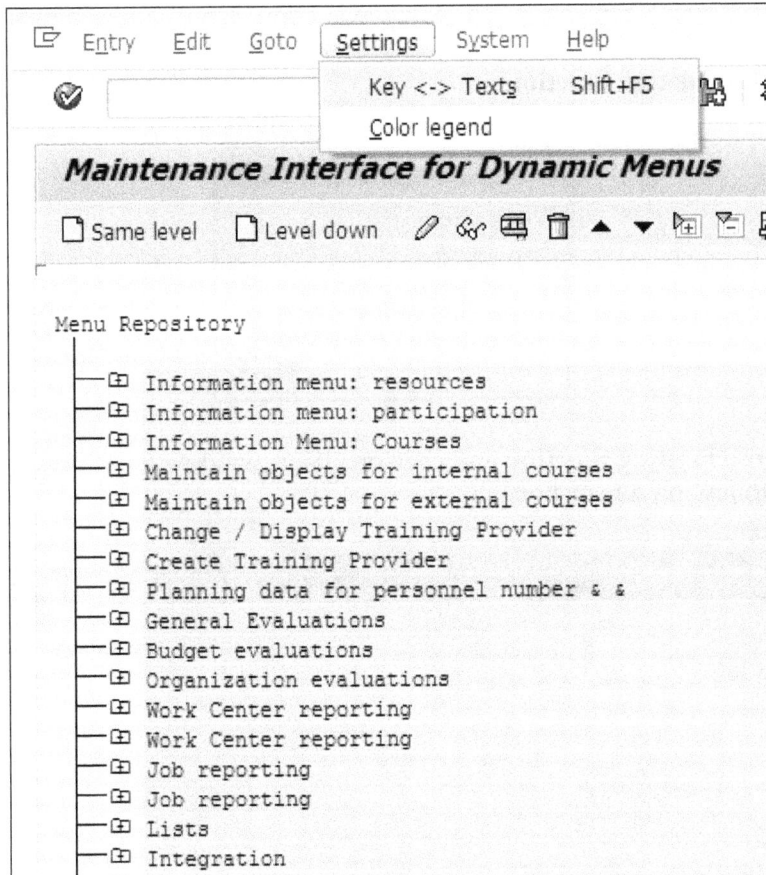

We can choose the keys <, >, or *Shift + F5* to display or hide the text. We can also integrate our own reports by performing the following steps:

1. Choose the service from the menu repository and click on level down (*Ctrl + Shift + F1*). The system lets us choose from the following three options:

    ° **New submenu**

    ° **New function**

    ° **Existing function**

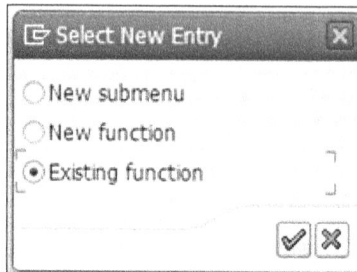

2. Choose **Existing function** and click on OK. A window will open, as shown in the following screenshot:

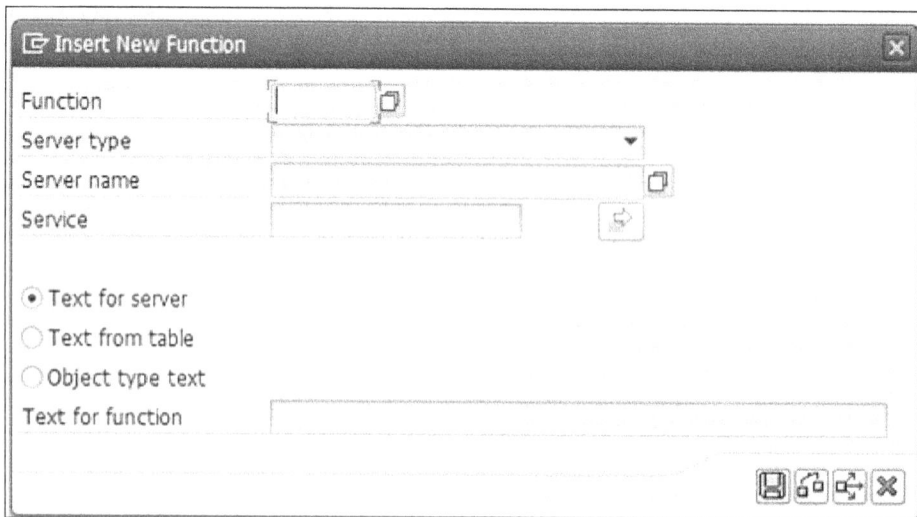

3. In the dialog box that appears, enter the following details such as the name of the function, and **Text for server** and **Text for function** auto populates, as shown in the following screenshot:

Employee Self-Service (ESS)

The control elements for integration with ESS is set up by navigating to **SPRO | Training and event management | Employee Self-Service (ESS) | Set Up Control Elements for ESS**.

Group	Semantic abbreviation	Description
SEMIN	INPRI	Booking priority for Internet
SEMIN	REQUE	Event generation in web transactions
SEMIN	WEBST	Cancelation reason for employee in ESS (PV8I)

The reasons for cancellation are stated in the T77CAR table. This can be used when the event is cancelled in ESS (PV8I).

> PV8I cannot be called via Easy Access, and if you try to do so, the system will throw a **Transaction PV8I cannot be called in the Easy Access Menu; see long text** message.

Summary

In this chapter, we have learned to configure the Training and Event Management (PE) submodule. We have only focused on TEM and not covered LSO for the purpose of this chapter. We have learned about the important master data maintained in the TEM submodule. We also learned how to integrate our own reports in the information menu.

In the next chapter, we will explore travel management configuration.

9
Travel Management Configuration

The Travel Management module covers all the activities surrounding travel. In this chapter, we will cover the important configuration steps for three areas of Travel Management: raising a travel request, planning travel, and settling travel expenses. We will also learn to configure the following important Travel Management functions:

- Planning a trip
- Booking a trip
- Settling expenses incurred for the trip in detail

Travel Management – features and functions

The standard functionalities of SAP Travel Management are equipped to plan a travel destination, book travel trips, settle expenses via payroll or finance, and also transfer the expenditure data to other modules such as controlling, payroll, and fund management.

The overall process of the Travel Management module is shown in the following screenshot:

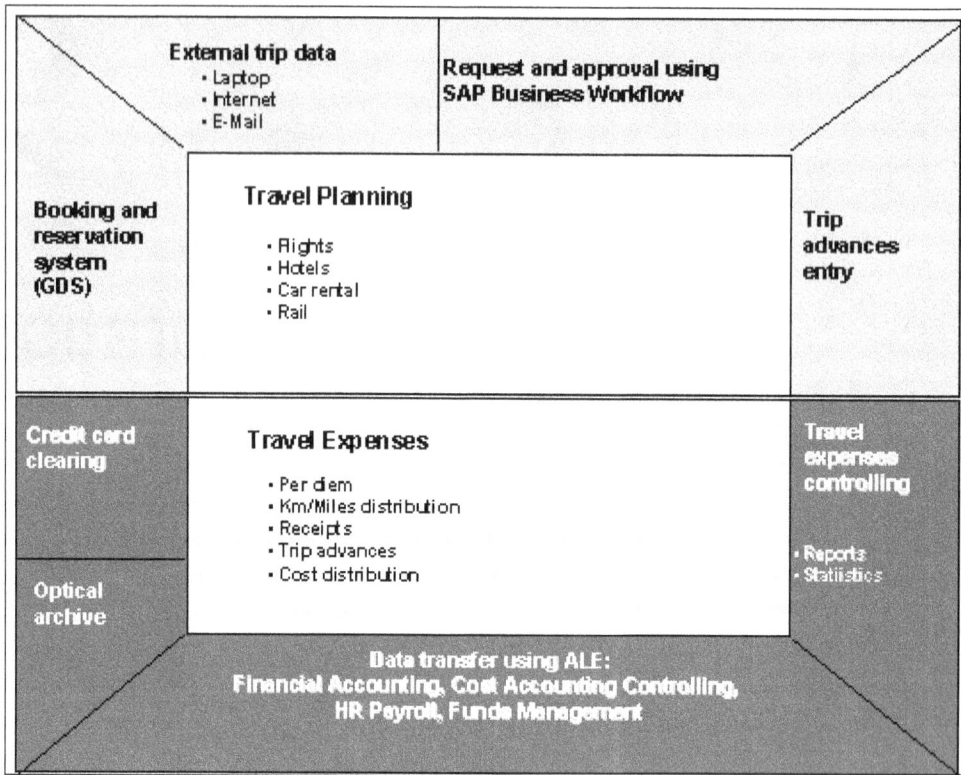

Source: `https://help.sap.com/saphelp_erp60_sp/helpdata/en/6e/6bf037f1d6b302e10000009
b38f889/content.htm`

Travel Management has tight integration with other modules such as SAP ERP Financials and the SAP Human Capital Management module.

Basic settings for number ranges

The number ranges are defined for trip number, posting, and trip transfer documents. SAP recommends that you use the internal number assignments. Let's look at the functionality of number ranges as listed in the following table:

T-code	Functionality
SNUM	The object used to define the number range is RP_REINR. We click on **Ranges** (*F7*) and use the personnel area for which we define the "from" and "to" intervals.

T-code	Functionality
PR10	This T-code is similar to SNUM. The only difference is that we don't use the object; instead, we use the personnel area for which we define the "from" and "to" number ranges.
PR11	Trip transfer document number ranges are defined using this T-code.
PR12	Number ranges for posting runs is defined via this T-code.

The number ranges are defined by navigating to **SPRO | Financial Accounting (New) | Travel Management | Set up trip number ranges**.

> Travel Expenses is an important component. The Travel Expense component can also be used independently of Travel Requests and Travel Planning.

Master data required for Travel Management

All the three areas of Travel Management use the same master data that is maintained in the following three areas:

- Travel Request
- Travel Planning
- Travel Expenses

The following infotypes are mandatory for booking Travel Planning:

- The 0001 (Organizational Assignment) infotype
- The 0002 (Personal Data) infotype
- The 0017 (Travel Privileges) infotype
- The 0006 (Addresses) infotype
- The 0017 (Travel Privileges) infotype
- The 0027 (Cost Assignment) infotype
- The 0009 (Bank Details) infotype

We have covered all the infotypes, but the 00017 (Travel Privileges) infotype is used in the previous chapters. Let's look at the features of the 0017 (Travel Privileges) infotype. This is shown in the following screenshot:

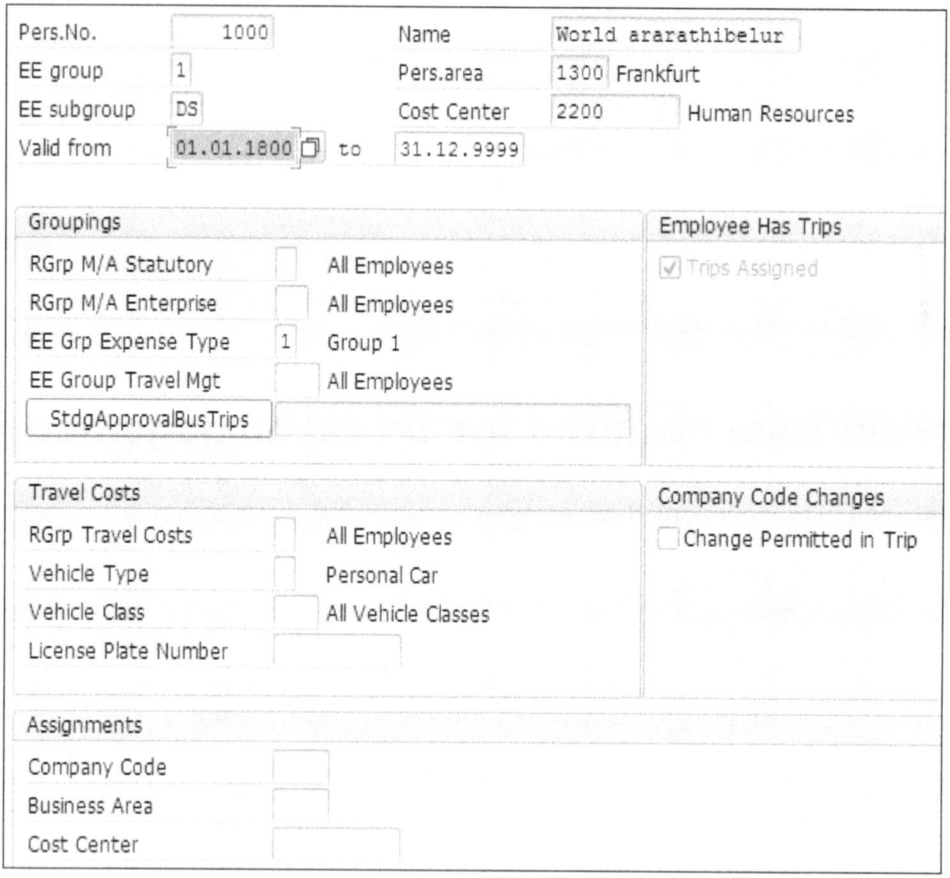

Pers.No.	1000		Name	World ararathibelur
EE group	1		Pers.area	1300 Frankfurt
EE subgroup	DS		Cost Center	2200 Human Resources
Valid from	01.01.1800 to	31.12.9999		

Groupings

RGrp M/A Statutory		All Employees
RGrp M/A Enterprise		All Employees
EE Grp Expense Type	1	Group 1
EE Group Travel Mgt		All Employees
StdgApprovalBusTrips		

Employee Has Trips

☑ Trips Assigned

Travel Costs

RGrp Travel Costs		All Employees
Vehicle Type		Personal Car
Vehicle Class		All Vehicle Classes
License Plate Number		

Company Code Changes

☐ Change Permitted in Trip

Assignments

Company Code	
Business Area	
Cost Center	

Let's closely look at the features of the different fields contained in the following `0017I` table:

Fields	Description
Reimbursement group for meals/ accommodations: this is statutory	Grouping of employees for whom the same statutory or travel provisions are applicable
Reimbursement group for meals/ accommodations: this is enterprise-specific	Grouping of employees for whom the same trip provisions are applicable, for example, senior directors, directors, managers, and so on

Fields	Description
Employee grouping for the Travel Expense type	Grouping of employees for whom the same Expense type trip is applicable
Employee Grouping for Travel Management	Grouping of employees for whom Business Trip Management is fulfilled
Reimbursement Group for travel costs	Grouping of employees for whom travel cost is applicable
Vehicle type	Classification of vehicles such as car, flight, and so on
Vehicle class	The vehicles can be classified based on their model, price, and so on
License plate number	The license plate numbers of company-owned cars or private cars can be captured in this field
Company code	Profit and loss statements are captured via different company codes assigned
Business area	A separate area of operations is represented via business area
Cost Center	Distribution of costs can be based on physical location, for instance
Indicator for recorded trips	When the trip data is recorded or changed, this is flagged and the RPRFLDEL report can be used to reset the settings
Company code change	If this is flagged, the company code can be changed when the business area is entered

Important transaction codes

The important transaction codes required to work on the Travel Management module are as follows:

T-code	Description
TRIP	Travel Manager is used to request, plan, enter, and settle a business trip
PR03	Trip advances can be created using this T-code
PR05	The Travel Expenses manager dialog screen creates trip expenses and settles and approves a business trip
PRAP	Trips can be approved using this T-code
PREC	Trip data can be settled via this T-code
PRFI	Using this T-code, we can create a posting run

T-code	Description
PRRW	Posting run is managed via this T-code
F.02/F-53/FBCJ/F110	Payment of expenses to employees (treating employee as vendors) is managed via this T-code
PRAA	Vendor master records from HR are created/changed/blocked using this T-code
XK03	Using this T-code, we can check whether the vendor has been created

Travel Request configuration steps

The overall process of Travel Management, which includes requesting a trip, planning a trip, and settling expenses incurred for the business trip, can be diagrammatically represented as follows:

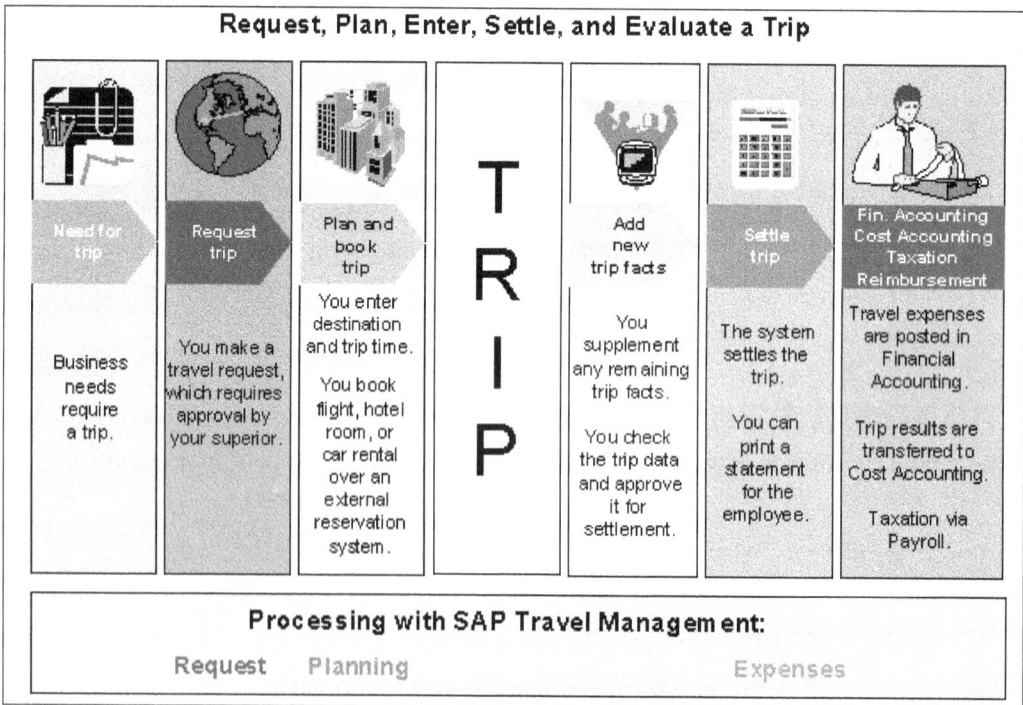

Source: http://help.sap.com/saphelp_erp60_sp/helpdata/en/26/
fddaabb7dd11d194c600a0c92946ae/content.htm

We will learn to configure the three phases that SAP has provided. Let's closely look at the Travel Request phase and the configuration steps required for the same. The possible combinations of the Travel Management module functioning could be shown in the following table:

Module	SAP Combinations
HR (Payroll) and Accounting	SAP Travel Management and Payroll and a tight integration of the Finance module
HR and the Travel module	SAP Travel Management and the HR module
Working together with Accounting and having a separate HR system	SAP Travel Management and Finance Accounting
Operate without HR and Accounting	SAP Travel Management

We will see how Travel Request uses services with the help of the **Web Dynpro Advanced Business Application Programming (ABAP)** user interface. Web Dynpro is a proprietary web application user interface technology developed by SAP AG and exists in Java and the ABAP stack. The Web Dynpro is a **user interface (UI)** platform that is used to build the portal screen. The data is fetched from the backend and displayed in the frontend portal. The standard field labels and length of the fields are controlled by the business object that is used to build them. The backend field label and length remains the same while in the portal side; it can be changed based on the logic. The functionalities are as follows:

- Enhancements made to standard Web Dynpro UI elements
- Enhancements for standard methods in different standard components

The Travel Request module can include the following information:

- This module refers to date and time of the trip requested
- This module refers to reasons for the trip and travel destination
- If there are any additional destinations, they can also be specified
- This module includes advances for the business trip planned
- The additional cost center can also be included
- There is a provision that includes comments when the trip request is created
- The different travel request mediums (such as rail, train, flight, and so on) can be included
- The estimated cost of the trip can be captured

The trip can be requested or booked through different sales offices by grouping the employees via external reservation system.

The employee grouping is defined by navigating to **SPRO | Financial Accounting (New) | Travel Management | Travel Request | Travel Request ESS | Other travel services | Define Groupings for Access to External Reservation Systems** or via the SM30/31 T-code in the V_TA200_FIND table.

The standard services can be defined and used in Travel Request in the Web Dynpro ABAP UI. They are as follows:

- Flight
- Hotel
- Rental car
- Train
- Ferry
- Helicopter
- Airport shuttle

The keys for services other than the standard ones such as flight, hotel, and so on is defined by navigating to **SPRO | Financial Accounting (New) | Travel Management | Travel Request | Travel Request ESS | Other travel services | Define Other Travel Services** or via the SM30/31 T-code in the V_TA20C/V_TA230S table.

> For PNR integration, the checkbox needs to be flagged and the **Business Add-In (BADI)**, FITP_TRAVEL_PLANNINGFITP_TRAVEL_PLANNING, can be implemented.

We can assign a sales office, reservation system, and logical system to certain groupings of employees/users using the TRVOF feature. It's defined by navigating to **SPRO | Financial Accounting (New) | Travel Management | Travel Request | Travel Request ESS | Other travel services | Assign Groupings for Access to External Reservation Systems**. The TRVOF feature helps assign the following parameters to the employees based on the following grouping:

- Reservation system
- Logical system
- Sales office
- RFC destination

The prerequisites for setting up this feature are the technical access groupings we defined in the previous table.

The estimated costs and different mediums of travel are defined by navigating to **SPRO | Financial Accounting (New) | Travel Management | Travel Request | Travel Request ESS | Define Travel Mediums and Estimated Costs to Be Approved** or via the SM30/31 T-code in the V_T706_REQ_CAT table. The travel medium defined is a four-digit alphanumeric code, and it has the following options to choose from:

- Type
- Category

There are two indicators that can be used and have specific functionalities, as shown in the following table:

Indicators	Functionalities
To be approved	Travel medium is shown in the Travel Request under accommodation types and travel mediums.
Enter estimated costs	This flag, if set, will allow the user to define the costs as a separate field. The functionality is only available in the Web Dynpro ABAP UI.

If the **Enter Estimated Costs** field needs to be only used as a display option, then the **Display Only** field needs to be flagged. This is shown in the following screenshot:

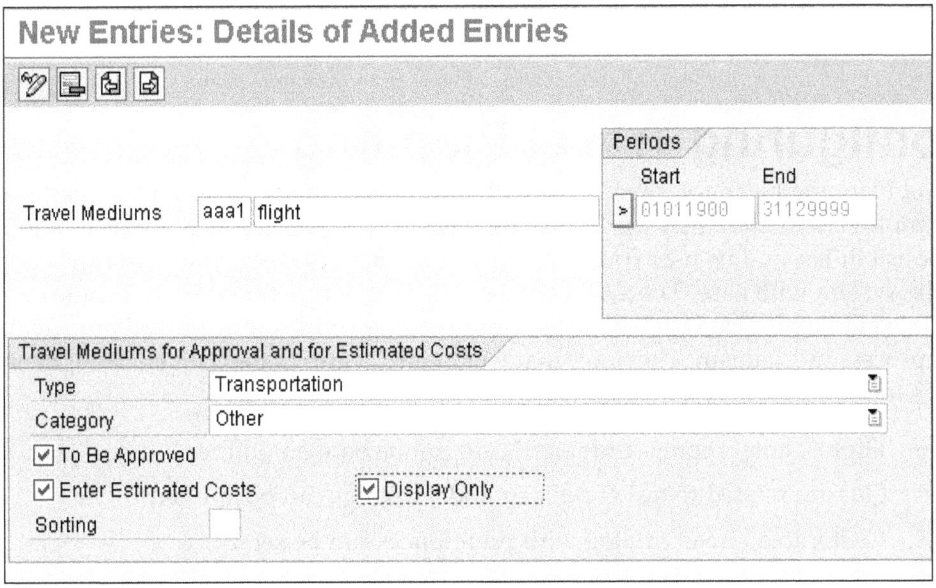

BADIs are technical activities performed by technical consultants. There are some BADIs that can be used for enhancements, and they are listed in the following table:

BADI name	Description
GET_ESTIMATED_COSTS	This is used for assigning default values to estimated costs
CHECK_ESTIMATED_COSTS	This is used for the entry of estimated costs

There are many standard forms delivered by SAP for Travel Request and Travel Planning, and they can be configured via the Adobe builder form of SFP T-code.

The standard forms are presented in the following bullet list:

- FITP_REQUEST_FORM
- FITP_PLAN_FORM
- PTRV_EES_FORM
- PTRV_EXPENSE_FORM

It is recommended that you copy the standard form and rename it "Z", with the name in customer space provided.

The TRVFR feature is used to execute the request form, and it is defined by navigating to **SPRO | Financial Accounting (New) | Travel Management | Travel Request | Forms | Set Up Feature TRVFR for Request Form**.

Configuring Travel Planning

Travel Planning has tight integration with online booking services and is hassle-free for employees to plan their trip and book their tickets. It gives its employees a lot of responsibilities, and its user friendly interface ensures that even novices can work on the system with ease. The SAP business work flow functionality that comes with the Travel Planning component adds cost advantage with standardized approval and process mechanism. There are many standard features that can be used; they are as follows:

- Flights, hotel rooms, and rental cars can be booked online
- Queries related to travel policies and bookings can be applied
- Customized hotel catalog with preferences can be set up
- Agreements made with travel service providers can be viewed and agreed upon
- A traveler's personal preferences can be requested automatically online

- Flexible reports for analysis purposes

- Tight integration with the Travel Expenses module for settling expenses incurred during the trip

The Travel Planning module supports integration with **global distribution system (GDS)** that helps in providing seamless connectivity with travel service providers. There are standard service providers that provide access to hotels, flights, train connections, and rental car offerings. Some of them are as follows:

- Galileo

- Amadeus

- Deutsche Bahn Corporate Portal

- Using a **Net Weaver Exchange Infrastructure** (XI) connection is possible with low-cost carriers and hotel reservation system such as **Sabre**

- HRS

- BIBE

There are some prerequisites that have to be fulfilled to use the features of the Travel Planning functionality. They are as discussed in the following points:

- An agreement must have been signed by the client for using the reservation system, as we would need an interface to connect with the system and a unique user ID must have been provided for the system

- There has to be a network connection that has to be set up for the reservation system and SAP to communicate with each other

The code of identification that we discussed earlier has to be provided and entered in SAP customizable tables by navigating to **SPRO | Financial Accounting (New) | Travel Planning | Master Data | Technical Control Parameters for Travel Planning | Sales Offices and Queues | Sales Offices** or via the SM30/31 T-code in the TA20SUBSCRPT table. This is shown in the following screenshot:

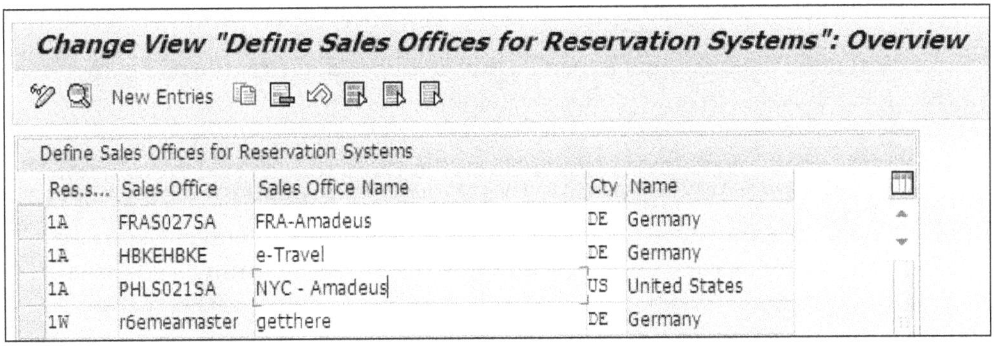

Res.s...	Sales Office	Sales Office Name	Cty	Name
1A	FRAS027SA	FRA-Amadeus	DE	Germany
1A	HBKEHBKE	e-Travel	DE	Germany
1A	PHLS021SA	NYC - Amadeus	US	United States
1W	r6emeamaster	getthere	DE	Germany

The general description of the external reservation system that is going to be interfaced with SAP is defined by navigating to **SPRO | Financial Accounting (New) | Travel Management | Travel Planning | Master Data | Technical Control Parameters for Travel Planning | External Reservation Systems | Define Reservation Systems** or via the SM30/31 T-code in the V_TA21P_R table. This is shown in the following screenshot:

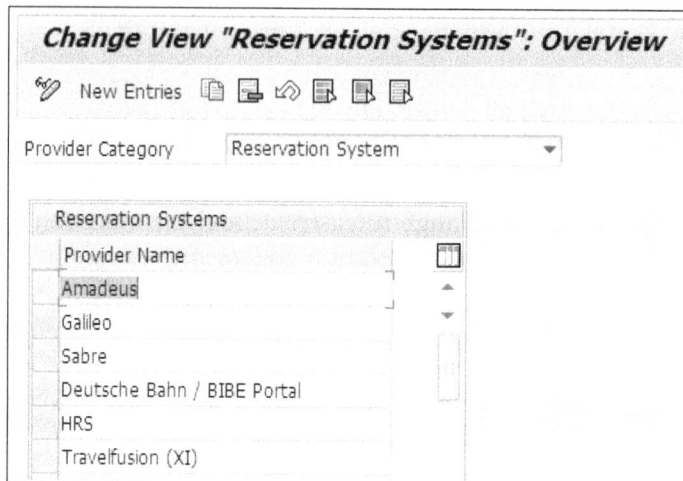

The logical systems for each of the reservation systems are defined by navigating to **SPRO | Financial Accounting (New) | Travel Management | Travel Planning | Master Data | Technical Control Parameters for Travel Planning | External Reservation Systems | Define Logical Systems for Reservation Systems** or via the SM30/31 T-code in the V_TA20LOGGDS table.

The logical systems could be as follows:

- A unit testing client
- A quality testing client
- A production system

The technical table that contains the SAP code is mapped to provide code, and as a rule, it is advisable to not change the standard settings. The standard entries containing hotel areas (domain FTPD_HOTEL_AREA) and transportation options (domain FTPD_HOTEL_TRANSPORT) are included in the standard system, and it is recommended that you not change them. The codes are defined by navigating to **SPRO | Financial accounting (New) | Travel Management | Travel Planning | Master Data | Technical Control Parameters for Travel Planning | External Reservation Systems | Assign SAP Codes to Specific Codes for Reservation Systems** or via the SM30/31 T-code in the TA20GDS_CODES table.

The travel preferences of each personnel between the reservation system and SAP system is established by navigating to **SPRO | Financial Accounting (New) | Travel Management | Travel Planning | Master Data | Technical Control Parameters for Travel Planning | External Reservation Systems | Synchronization of Travel Preferences with External Reservation**. Synchronization, however, is not supported by all the providers. Some of the providers such as Amadeus and Galileo/Apollo are supported, while Sabre is not supported currently.

There is a standard BADI provided by SAP to compare travel preferences of personnel providers with global data service providers. The FITP_PREFERENCE_DATA BADI enables us to send data to the reservation system based on your personnel preferences.

> RFTP_SYNCHRO_PREFRFTP_SYNCHRO_PREF is a handy program used for sending the preferences from HR infotypes to the reservation system.

In the following steps, we define the sales office and IDs. The IDs are useful when interfacing with the reservation system.

The sales offices are defined by navigating to **SPRO | Financial Accounting (New) | Travel Management | Travel Planning | Master Data | Technical Control Parameters for Travel Planning | Sales Offices and Queues | Sales offices | Define Sales Offices** or via the SM30/31 T-code in the V_TA20OFFICE2 table. If it's a virtual office, then there is a flag that can be checked; this flag serves as an indicator.

The physical address of the sales office can be accessed by navigating to **SPRO | Financial Accounting (New) | Travel Management | Travel Planning | Master Data | Technical Control Parameters for Travel Planning | Sales Offices and Queues | Sales offices | Specify Addresses of Sales Offices** or via the SM30/31 T-code in the V_TA23OFFICE_ADR table.

The sales office that we defined earlier needs to be connected to the reservation system via a log on ID. The following are the prerequisites for this step:

- We must have defined the reservation systems and logical systems
- We must have defined the sales offices
- We must have defined the log-on data (identification indicators) for the reservation systems such as Amadeus, Galilieo, and so on

The functionality of queues allows seamless connection with the sales offices and SA Travel Planning component. It also allows all the sales offices to access the booking code **PNR** centrally with ease. It helps to sort booking and determine price, and the modification of booking can also be accomplished. The prerequisites for defining the queues for sales offices are as follows:

- The reservation system must have been defined
- The logical system must have been defined
- The sales office must have been defined

The queues are defined by navigating to **SPRO | Financial Accounting (New) | Travel Management | Travel Planning | Master Data | Technical Control Parameters for Travel Planning | Sales Offices and Queues | Queues | Define Queues of Sales Offices** or via the SM30/31 T-code in the TA20Q table.

In the following customizable table, we can define the activities of sales offices such as price determination, short-term booking, and so on. We can assign the queue activities so that we can control the activities that can be performed by the travel centre.

There is FITP_CUST_QUEUEING BADI, which associates associating sales office queues with a particular travel plan.

The prerequisites for defining the queue categories are as follows:

- The reservation system must have been defined
- The logical system must have been defined
- The sales office must have been defined
- The queues of the sales office must have been defined

The queue categories are defined by navigating to **SPRO | Financial Accounting (New) | Travel Management | Travel Planning | Master Data | Technical Control Parameters for Travel Planning | Sales Offices and Queues | Queues | Define Queue Categories** or via the SM30/31 T-code in the TA20Q_CAT table.

The sales office's activities are defined by navigating to **SPRO | Financial Accounting (New) | Travel Management | Travel Planning | Master Data | Technical Control Parameters for Travel Planning | Sales Offices and Queues | Queues | Define Sales Office Activities** or via the SM30/31 T-code in the V_TA230A table.

The standard entries in SAP are as follows:

- **B**: This refers to bookings
- **E**: This refers to urgent bookings

- **F**: This refers to booking price, which is already determined
- **M**: This refers to booking modifications
- **P**: This refers to the determination of price
- **T**: This refers to ticket issues

For the reservation system and SAP Travel Planning component to interface between each other, there has to be a **Remote Function Call** (**RFC**) set up; this is a technical activity. The RFC serves as a connection between SAP and the SAP gateway. The SAP gateway acts as a bridge between SAP and GRS. The landscape of the server is graphically represented, as shown in the following screenshot:

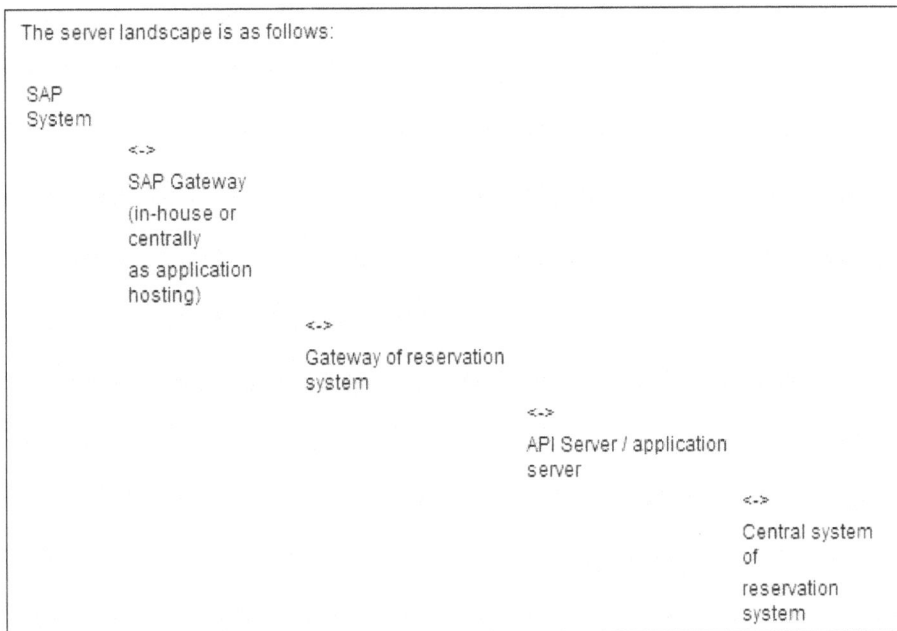

```
The server landscape is as follows:

SAP
System
          <->
          SAP Gateway
          (in-house or
          centrally
          as application
          hosting)
                       <->
                       Gateway of reservation
                       system
                                    <->
                                    API Server / application
                                    server
                                                 <->
                                                 Central system
                                                 of
                                                 reservation
                                                 system
```

It's defined by navigating to **SPRO** | **Financial Accounting (New)** | **Travel Management** | **Travel Planning** | **Master Data** | **Set up RFC Destinations for Interfaces to External Systems**.

The grouping of external reservation systems and other travel service categories are covered in the following configuration nodes:

By grouping, we can enable the user to book trips based on the different sales offices and reservation systems. The grouping is defined by navigating to **SPRO** | **Financial Accounting (New)** | **Travel Management** | **Travel Planning** | **Master Data** | **Technical Control Parameters for Travel Planning** | **Access to External Reservation Systems** | **Define Groupings for Access to External Reservation Systems** or via the the SM30/31 T-code in the V_TA200_FIND table.

The enterprise level service categories are defined by navigating to **SPRO** | **Financial Accounting (New)** | **Travel Management** | **Travel Planning** | **Master Data** | **Technical Control Parameters for Travel Planning** | **Access to External Reservation Systems** | **Define Travel Service Categories**. The standard codes provided by SAP are as follows:

- **F**: This refers to flight
- **C**: This refers to car rental
- **H**: This refers to hotel

In addition to defining the standard service categories, SAP also provides other travel services such as ferry. We define these services by navigating to **SPRO** | **Financial Accounting (New)** | **Travel Management** | **Travel Planning** | **Master Data** | **Technical Control Parameters for Travel Planning** | **Other travel services** | **Define Other Travel Services** or via the SM30/31 T-code in the V_TA230S table.

The Travel Planning component has the functionality of defining the enterprise-level geography that is normally covered in trips and characteristics of travel service providers. We will cover them in detail when we define the **International Air Transport Association (IATA)** locations and service provider's details that form the master data for the employee to choose from.

The **IATA** locations are defined by navigating to **SPRO** | **Financial Accounting (New)** | **Travel Management** | **Travel Planning** | **Master Data** | **Geographical Situation** | **IATA locations** | **define IATA locations** or via the SM30/31 T-code in the V_TA21L table.

The geographic characteristics are defined by navigating to **SPRO** | **Financial Accounting (New)** | **Travel Management** | **Travel Planning** | **Master Data** | **Geographical Situation** | **IATA locations** | **Define Geographical Facts of IATA Locations** or via the SM30/31 T-code in the V_TA21L_1 table.

The characteristics such as country, region, and so on are very useful when trip rules are mentioned. SAP standard entries have provided states as regions for some of the following countries:

- Argentina
- Australia
- Brazil
- Canada
- U.S.

SAP has the functionality of defining the synonyms for airports, and we can also assign a single destination to multiple IATA locations. The synonyms for airports, hotels, and car rentals can be defined by navigating to **SPRO | Financial Accounting (New) | Travel Management | Travel Planning | Master Data | Geographical Situation | Synonyms for Hotel Locations | Define Synonyms for Airports** or via the SM30/31 T-code in the TA23L_F table.

When a travel plan is created and when the trip destination is entered, for example, Sweden is the destination and corresponding IATA locations can be displayed in the selection screen for the availability of the flight.

The synonyms for hotels are defined by navigating to **SPRO | Financial Accounting (New) | Travel Management | Travel Planning | Master Data | Geographical Situation | Synonyms for Locations | Define Synonyms for Hotel Locations** or via the SM30/31 in the TA23L_H table. These are very useful for the travel plan when it is queried for hotel reservation and availabilities.

The synonyms for car rentals can be defined by navigating to **SPRO | Financial Accounting (New) | Travel Management | Travel Planning | Master Data | Geographical Situation | Synonyms for Locations | Define Synonyms for Car Rental Locations** or via the SM30/31 T-code in the TA23L_C table.

We can also define the IATA locations within the countries and cross-country regions as well. They are freely definable in customizable tables, and they are defined by navigating to **SPRO | Financial Accounting (New) | Travel Management | Travel Planning | Master Data | Geographical Situation | Regions | Define Regions Within Countries** or via the SM30/31 T-code in the V_TA21R_1 table.

The IATA locations can be mapped to the regions that we defined by navigating to **SPRO | Financial Accounting (New) | Travel Management | Travel Planning | Master Data | Geographical Situation | Regions | Define Assignment of IATA Locations to Regions Within Countries.** The prerequisite is that the IATA code must have been defined.

The travel service provider's details and its characteristics are defined in the following steps. We can store details such as costs for the flights, hotels, car rentals, and so on. We define it by navigating to **SPRO | Financial Accounting (New) | Travel Management | Travel Planning | Master Data | Travel Service Providers | Flights | Define airlines** or via the SM30/31 T-code in the V_TA21P_F table. Specific airline programs such as frequent flier can be defined by navigating to **SPRO | Financial Accounting (New) | Travel Management | Travel Planning | Master Data | Travel Service Providers | Flights | Define Customer Programs of Airlines** or via the SM30/31 T-code in the V_TA21PF_F table.

We can also define the hotel service providers, their classes, and different programs they offer by navigating to **SPRO | Financial Accounting (New) | Travel Management | Travel Planning | Master Data | Travel Service Providers | Hotels | Define Hotel Chains** or via the SM30/31 T-code in the V_TA21P_H table.

There are some standard entries available for room rates via the Amadeus reservation system. It also depends on the providers; they can store their own rates according to their company policy. We can see the following standard entries maintained via the Amadeus reservation system:

- CON (conventional rate)
- COR (company rate)
- FAM (family rate)
- GOV (statutory rate)
- MIL (military rate)
- PKG (package rate)
- PRO (promotion rate)
- RAC (standard rate)
- SRS (senior citizen rate)
- STP (stopover rate)
- TUR (tourist rate)
- TVL (rate for travel industry)
- WKD (weekend rate)

The standard entries via the Amadeus reservation system can be accessed by navigating to **SPRO | Financial Accounting (New) | Travel Management | Travel Planning | Master Data | Travel Service Providers | Hotels | Define hotel rates** or via the SM30/31 T-code in the V_TA21H table. The room classes are defined via the SM30/31 T-code in the V_TA21HO table or by navigating to **SPRO | Travel Management | Travel Planning | Master Data | Travel Service Providers | Hotels | Define room classes**.

The car rental service provider's details can be maintained by navigating to **SPRO | Financial Accounting (New) | Travel Management | Travel Planning | Master Data | Travel Service Providers | Car Rentals | Define car rental companies** or via the SM30/31 T-code in the V_TA21P_C table. We can also define the customer programs and classes similarly how we defined for rooms and flights via the SM30/31 T-code in the V_TA21PF_C and V_TA21CA table.

The Travel Planning components also have the functionality of defining the agreements between travel service providers and customer programs such as frequent flier. They can be defined by navigating to **SPRO | Financial Accounting (New) | Travel Management | Travel Planning | Master Data | Travel Service Providers | Define Agreements Between Travel Service Providers on Customer programs** or via the SM30/31 T-code in the V_TA21PFA table.

Any questions regarding the Travel Planning or Travel Expenses that need to be addressed by a concerned person can be defined by navigating to **SPRO | Financial Accounting (New) | Travel Management | Travel Planning | Master Data | Define Contact Persons**. We can define all the credit card providers' details by navigating to **SPRO | Financial accounting (New) | Travel Management | Travel Planning | Master Data | Define Credit Card Providers for Travel Planning**. It's a two-character code followed by long text. We can keep the entries in the following V_T706_CCOMP table:

ID	Name of the credit card company
AX	American Express
MC	MasterCard

Any negotiations we have with the travel service providers can be stored in SAP. This feature is useful during the reservation of travel services such as flights, room bookings, and so on. The negotiated rates and discounts for airlines can be maintained by navigating to **SPRO | Financial Accounting (New) | Travel Management | Travel Planning | Rates and Discounts | Airline rates and discounts | Define Airfare Rates** or via the SM30/31 T-code in the V_TA20NEGOF_2 table. The mandatory parameters for defining the airline rates are as follows:

Field	Mandatory
Provider	Yes
Validity period	Yes
Fare type	Yes

There are optional fields that might / might not be maintained in the table, and they are shown as follows:

Field	Optional
Price information	Yes
Flight direction	Yes
Flight cabin class	Yes
Start and destination locations	Yes

Similarly, we can also maintain the discounted rates of other service providers such as hotel bookings by navigating to **SPRO | Financial Accounting (New) | Travel Management | Travel Planning | Rates and Discounts | Define Enterprise-Specific Hotel Rates** or via the SM30/31 T-code in the V_TA20NHC table.

The different parameters based on which the rates are defined, are as follows:

- Geographical area
- Location
- Hotel chain or chain of hotels
- Validity period

The car booking can be maintained by navigating to **SPRO | Financial Accounting (New) | Travel Management | Travel Planning | Rates and Discounts | Car Rental Rates** or via the SM31/31 T-code in the V_TA20NCR_2 table.

SAP also has the provision of maintaining the internal trip policies and procedures that can be mapped to SAP using the 0470 (Travel Profile) infotype. This infotype contains the special rules that govern a group of employees, for example, a board of directors being given a special flight and room. If the 0470 infotype is not maintained for an employee, the trip rules are automatically applied via the TRVCP feature, as shown in the following screenshot:

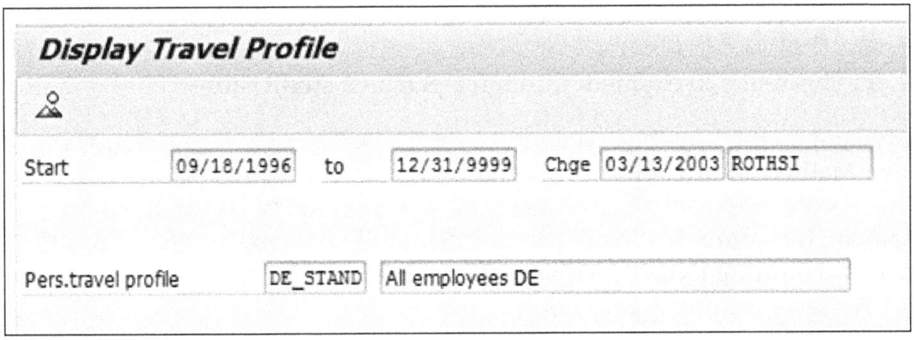

If the 0470 (Travel Profile) infotype is not maintained, the system will check the TRVCP feature.

SAP has the functionality of maintaining the trip rules for the following travel service providers:

- Flight
- Hotel
- Rental car
- Rail

Some of the categories based on which the trip rules are defined, are as follows:

- Travel service category providers such as flight bookings, room bookings, and so on
- Travel locations such as IATA locations, regions, and so on
- Class of the service (first class, for instance)

The trip rules and travel policies are maintained for flights, hotels, car, and rails by navigating to **SPRO | Financial Accounting (New) | Travel Management | Travel Planning | Trip rules and profiles | Trip and Class rules | Trip and Class rules for flight/hotel/car rentals**.

The mode of payment for travel plan can be maintained by navigating to **SPRO | Financial Accounting (New) | Travel Management | Travel Planning | Process control | Payment Method**. SAP delivers standard payment methods that can be supported; these methods are as follows:

- **C**: This refers to payment through a corporate credit card
- **R**: This refers to an invoice
- **B**: This refers to payment by cash
- **P**: This refers to payment through a personal credit card

The payment method can be executed via the TRVCC Assign Groupings for Payment Method feature. The other control parameters such as details of building a store in the `0032I` table needs to be shown in PNR; only then can we maintain the address in the `TA20BUILDING` table or by navigating to **SPRO | Financial accounting (New) | Travel Management | Travel Planning | Expert View | Assign Building Addresses**.

Configuring Travel Expenses

After the trip is completed, the Travel Expenses report is completed by the employee with the supporting documents. The Travel Expense report is then sent for approval. This again can be automated with the workflow settings. The system determines the Travel Expenses results and also determines the amount to be reimbursed for the travel expenses incurred by the employee. The expenses are always transferred to the Finance module by posting to finance module and then to controlling. The settlement of the amount can happen in any of the following ways:

- This can happen via a check
- This can happen via payroll accounting
- This can happen via financial accounting
- Bank transfer to the employee's bank account via **Data Medium Exchange (DME)**

The first step in Travel Expense is to define the trip provision variant. It helps us to determine the specific applicable policies based on validity areas such as private or public sector using the travel expense accounting method. The trip provision variant is defined by navigating to **SPRO | Financial Accounting (New) | Travel Management | Travel Expenses | Master Data | Control Parameters for Travel Expenses | Define/Delete/Restore Trip Provision Variants** or via the `SM30/31` T-code in the `V_T706N` table. This is shown in the following screenshot:

Change View "Names for Trip Provision Variants": Overview

New Entries

Names for Trip Provision Variants

TrProv.Var	Name
01	German accounting
02	Swiss Accounting
03	Austrian collective agree
07	Canada Travel Accounting
08	British Accounting
10	US accounting (docs)

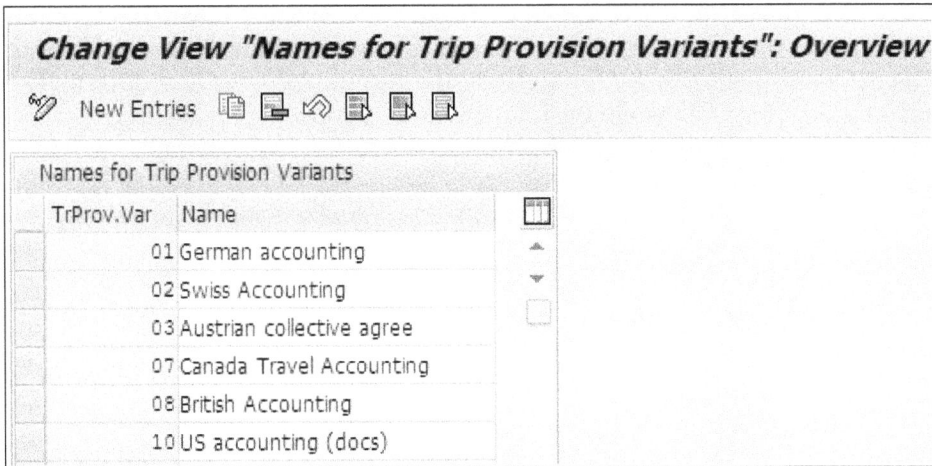

Two trip provision variants must be defined if there is a requirement for representing two different valid areas in one system. If different verticals, industries, or countries have different sets of accounting principles, then we need to have multiple variants set up. This is shown in the following table:

Country	Tax-free reimbursement	Trip provision variant	Description of trip provision variant
XX	Media industry	90	Media industry accounting principles
XX	Manufacturing	91	Manufacturing industry principles

The TRVCT feature is used to execute the trip provision variant based on the organizational requirements. It is defined by navigating to **SPRO** | **Financial Accounting (New)** | **Travel Management** | **Travel Expenses** | **Master Data** | **Control Parameters for Travel Expenses** | **Assign Organizational Areas to Trip Provision Variants via Feature**.

The global settings for each trip provision variant enables us to set the applicability of the payroll based on country grouping and its wage type validity. The currencies and input tax applicability can also be controlled in this customizable table. The different methods for converting the recipient currencies to trip currencies can also be controlled.

We can set the global settings options by navigating to **SPRO | Financial Accounting (New) | Travel Management | Travel Expenses | Master Data | Control Parameters for Travel Expenses | Define Global Settings** or via the SM30/31 T-code in the V_706D_B table. This is shown in the following screenshot:

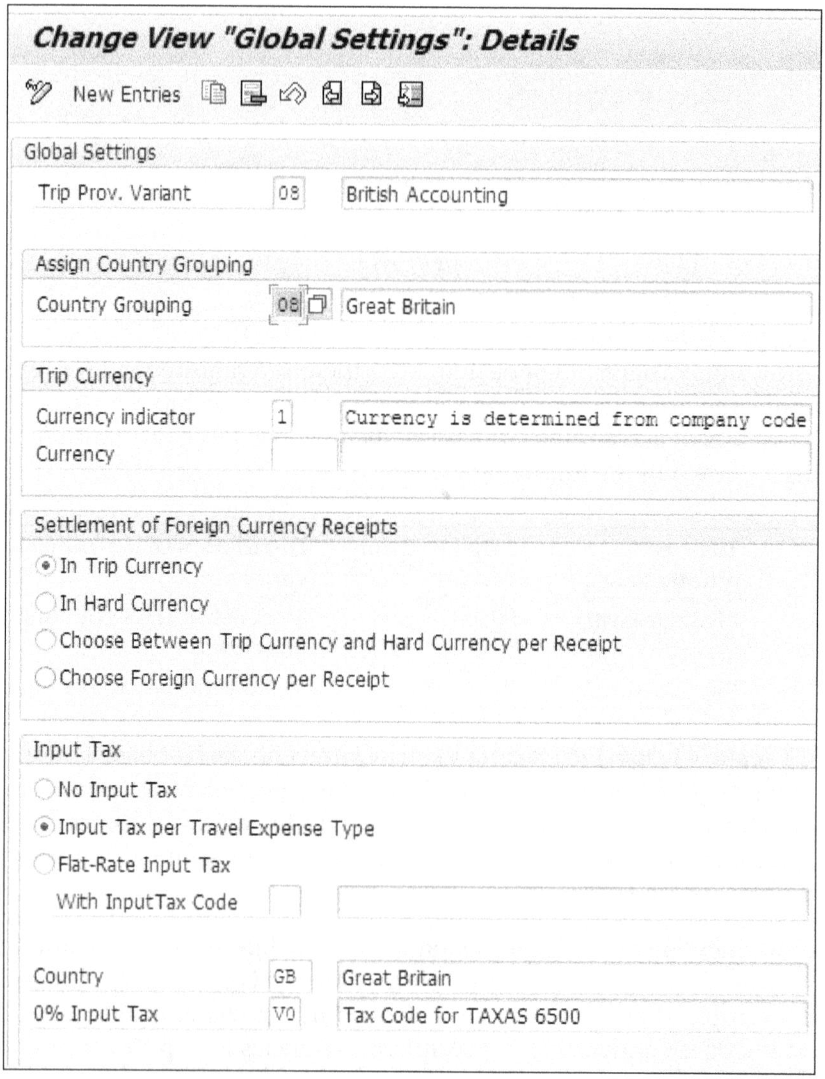

The valid entry values for control parameters for cost accounting that can be maintained, employee-wise, in the master data in 0017I (travel privileges) is set up by navigating to **SPRO | Financial Accounting (New) | Travel Management | Travel Expenses | Master Data | Control Parameters for Travel Expenses | Control Parameters for Travel Privileges**.

The grouping configurations such as reimbursement groups for travel costs, statutory meals and accommodation reimbursement groups, employee grouping for Travel Expense types, and employee groupings for Travel Management are all defined to be maintained in the master data of each employee in the 0017 infotype. We have seen this infotype in the *Master data required for Travel Management* section in this chapter.

The control parameters for trip data is defined by navigating to **SPRO | Financial Accounting (New) | Travel Management | Travel Expenses | Master Data | Control Parameters for Travel Expenses | Control Parameters from Trip Data**. The prerequisite is that the trip provisions variant must have been defined. The statutory trip types and trip activities types are also defined in the control parameters from the trip data nodes.

The Travel Expense type serves as a conduit for capturing travel expenses for a business trip and settling expenses incurred for travel. The expenses based on individual receipts or per diem are defined based on the trip provision variant. The expense types such as breakfast, flight, laundry, and so on are defined by navigating to **SPRO | Financial Accounting (New) | Travel Management | Travel Expenses | Master Data | Travel Expense Types | Create Travel Expense Types for Individual Receipts**. This is shown in the following screenshot:

The maximum amount for each expense type, for example, 30 USD for breakfast, can be defined by navigating to **SPRO | Financial Accounting (New) | Travel Management | Travel Expenses | Define Maximum Rates and Default Values for Expense Types** or via the SM30/31 T-code in the V_T706B2 table. SAP recommends that you set the end date to 31,129,999. It also helps to restrict the changing and delimiting of the end date.

We define the Expenses types for per diem or flat rates by navigating to **SPRO | Financial Accounting (New) | Travel Management | Travel Expenses | Create Travel Expense Types for Per Diems/Flat Rates** or via the SM30/31 T-code in the V_T706B1_A table. This is shown in the following screenshot:

We can define for each travel provision variant, only if combination from one of the three options of accounting of both the individual receipts and per diem/flat rates is available. This is possible by navigating to **SPRO | Financial Accounting (New) | Travel Management | Travel Expenses | Travel Expense Types | Define Per Diem/Flat Rate or Individual Receipt Reimbursement** or via the SM30/31 T-code in the V_T702N_J table.

The travel position variant is a dialog window and looks as shown in the following screenshot:

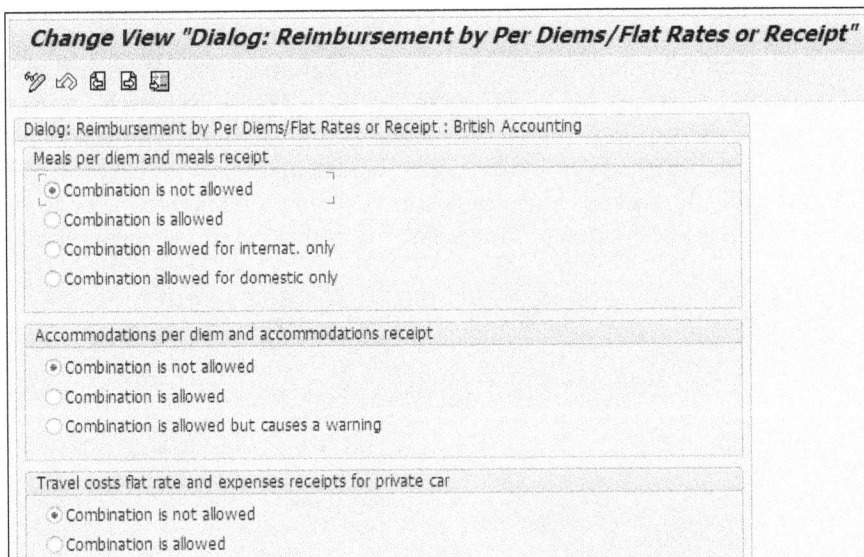

For the purpose of credit card expense settlement, the credit card companies' details must be maintained. This will enable us to assign credit cards to the Travel Expense types in SAP. This is defined by navigating to **SPRO | Financial Accounting (New) | Travel Management | Travel Expenses | Master Data | Credit Card Clearing | Define Credit Card Companies**. Some standard abbreviations that SAP has provided are as follows:

- **AX**: American Express
- **DC**: Diners
- **MC**: MasterCard
- **TP**: Airplus
- **VI**: Visa

The payment of the amount that needs to be reimbursed can happen in the following ways:

- Travel advance
- Credit card clearing
- By check
- Through payroll accounting
- By bank transfer to the employee's bank account

The data of travel expenses, and wage types are stored in the ROT cluster tables, and we have to define the wage types for each expense type for settlement. These wage types serve as an interface between accounting and travel. We will define the travel expense wage types for individual receipts and per diem/flat rates by navigating to **SPRO | Financial Accounting (New) | Travel Management | Travel Expenses | Wage Types for Interfaces | Assign Wage Types to Travel Expense Types for Individual Rec** or via the SM30/31 T-code in the V_T706B4 table. There will be first wage type and second wage type that needs to be defined for expense type, where the tax free share of the expense amount is stored, while the taxable part of expense amount is stored in wage type two. This is shown in the following screenshot:

Similarly, wage types are assigned to flat rate or per diems by navigating to **SPRO | Financial Accounting (New) | Travel Management | Travel Expenses | Wage Types for Interfaces | Assign Wage Types to Travel Expense Types for Per Diems/Flat** or via the SM30/31 T-code in the V_T706B4_A table.

To transfer the travel accounting results to the finance system, we have to set up symbolic accounts. A symbolic account serves as an interface between wage types; this is very important in travel accounting and for accounts in financial accounting. There are two important steps that need to be performed; they are as follows:

- Assigning wage types to symbolic accounts
- Assigning symbolic accounts to expense accounts in financial accounting

We execute the preceding steps by navigating to **SPRO | Financial Accounting (New) | Travel Management | Travel Expenses | Transfer to Accounting | Define Assignment of Wage Type to Symbolic Account** or via the SM30/31 T-code in the V_T706K table. This is shown in the following screenshot:

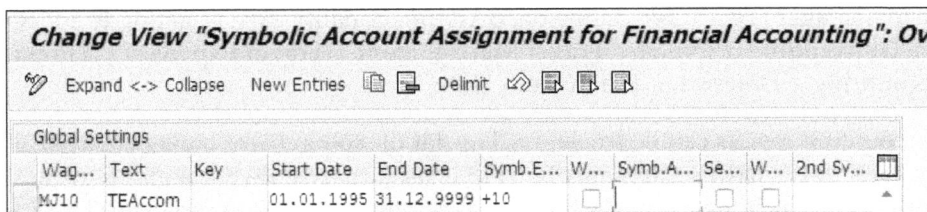

Change View "Symbolic Account Assignment for Financial Accounting": Ov

Expand <-> Collapse   New Entries 🗋 🗐 Delimit 🗐 🗐 🗐 🗐

Global Settings

Wag...	Text	Key	Start Date	End Date	Symb.E...	W...	Symb.A...	Se...	W...	2nd Sy...
MJ10	TEAccom		01.01.1995	31.12.9999	+10	☐			☐ ☐	

The sign below the symbolic account has a specific meaning, as shown in the following table:

Sign	Significance
+	A positive amount is posted to debits of the G/L account
-	A positive amount is posted to credits of the G/L account

The symbolic accounts are then assigned to the expense account by navigating to **SPRO | Financial Accounting (New) | Travel Management | Travel Expenses | Transfer to Accounting | Conversion of Symbolic Account to Expense Account** or via the PRT3 T-code. It is very important to understand the meaning of the following groups:

- **HRT**: This is used to identify travel expense postings: expense accounts

- **HRP**: This is used to identify travel expense postings: customers/vendors/ clearing account

The following screenshot demonstrates the FI configuration:

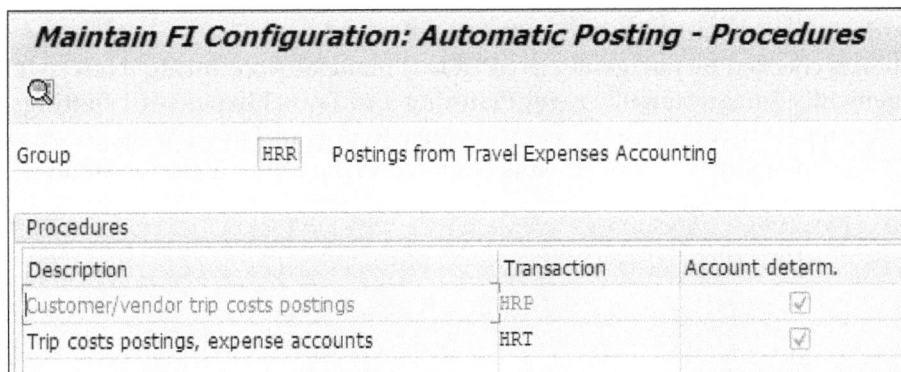

Maintain FI Configuration: Automatic Posting - Procedures

🔍

Group   HRR   Postings from Travel Expenses Accounting

Procedures

Description	Transaction	Account determ.
Customer/vendor trip costs postings	HRP	☑
Trip costs postings, expense accounts	HRT	☑

When we double-click on the procedure and enter the chart of account, we will now be able to assign the G/L account number.

If the travel expenses are reimbursed using different vendors, then SAP has the functionality only if the status icon is included in the travel expense manager (PR05) and trip manager (TRIP). We define the SAP functionality by navigating to **SPRO | Financial Accounting (New) | Travel Management | Travel Expenses | Transfer to Accounting | Determine FI Payment Date**.

The accounting results can be transferred as flat file to payment banks via DME. The house bank needs to be set up, and TRVHB is used to execute the house bank and the account from which the expenses have to be reimbursed to the employee. This can be done by navigating to **SPRO | Financial Accounting (New) | Travel Management | Travel Expenses | Transfer to Data Medium Exchange**.

Integration aspects with other application components

We will learn two important integration aspects; one is the integration of Travel Planning and Travel Expenses that enable us to transfer data from Travel Plan to Travel Expense reports, and the other one is transferring travel accounting results to payroll. There are activation steps required for using Travel Manager, Travel Planning, and Travel Expenses. For the Travel Manager, there are three components available that can be flagged, and they are explored as follows:

- Create Travel Requests
- Plan a business trip
- Create travel expense report

For each trip provision variant, we have to activate the components that are active in the TRIP T-code, backend, and the Web Dynpro portal interface. The SAP standard has three components activated for all the trip provision variants. The activation is checked by navigating to **SPRO | Financial Accounting (New) | Travel Management | Integration of Travel Planning and Travel Expenses | Settings for travel manager Activate Request/Plan/Expense Report in Travel Manager** or via the SM30/31 T-code in the V_T702N_O. This is shown in the following screenshot:

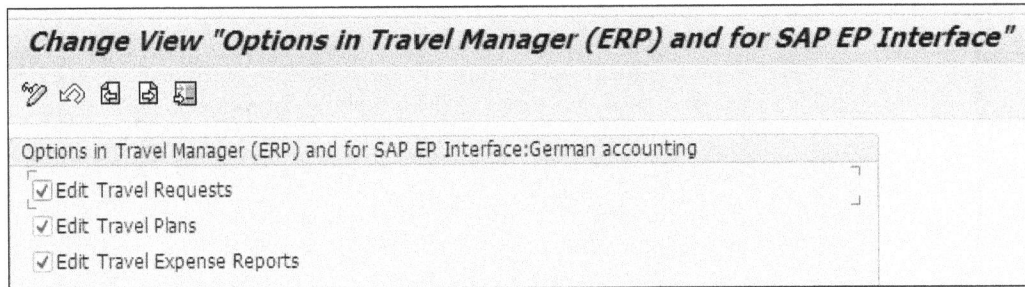

The integration aspects of Travel Planning and expenses are controlled by navigating to **SPRO | Financial Accounting (New) | Travel Management | Integration of Travel Planning and Travel Expenses | Activate Integration | Travel Planning | Travel Expenses** or via the SM30/31 T-code in the V_706D_C table.

The travel accounting results can be transferred to payroll by performing the following steps. Travel Management and payroll can be run in the same logical system or different systems and can interfaced using the **Application Link Enabling (ALE)**. To have the integration active between payroll and travel in subschema, **GREI** must be activated in the payroll schema, for example, G000 (Great Britain payroll schema). This is shown in the following screenshot:

For integration between travel and payroll, the **GREI** subschema needs to be activated. The subschema has a ASREI function that cumulates all the expenses incurred for the travel per payroll period in wage types, and the wage types are maintained in the T706B table. These values held in the wage types are posted to the finance accounting module.

PR_CHECK is a useful tool to check the customizing settings for the Travel Management submodule. We can make use of the tool to check the customizing settings of the following components in Travel Management:

- Travel Planning
- Travel Expenses (expense report)
- Geocoding
- Homepage Framework

Summary

In this chapter, we have learned the steps to configure Travel Management in detail. We have covered important infotypes pertaining to the Travel Management submodule.

In the next chapter, *Chapter 10, Building a Report Using SAP Query Viewer*, we will closely look at building reports without any ABAP or technical skills. We will have a lot of things to play around and dabble with in the next chapter for sure.

10
Building a Report Using SAP Query Viewer

SAP has provided an easy-to-use tool to build a query to meet business requirements. We don't need to know the **Advanced Business Application Programming (ABAP)** programming language to develop reports. The SAP query viewer will make this task very simple, and we will learn to transport queries across different clients.

In this chapter, we will cover the following topics:

- Building an ad hoc query using the SQ01 transaction code
- Executing a report using an ad hoc query
- Developing a report using SQVI

Building an ad hoc query using the SQ01 transaction code

The following steps need to be performed in order to build an ad hoc query:

- Create a user group using the SQ03 TCD. The prerequisite for building a query is the user group.
- Second, we create an infoset using the SQ02 TCD.
- Finally, we create a query using the SQ01 TCD.

Steps for creating the user group

The user group is a 12-character long code; SAP recommends that you use any special characters, numeric code, or characters to define the user group. There are four options available to choose from. They are as follows:

- **Create**
- **Change**
- **Display**
- **Description**

The **Create** option is used to define the name of the user group, as shown in the following screenshot. The user group is a twelve-character long code followed by its description.

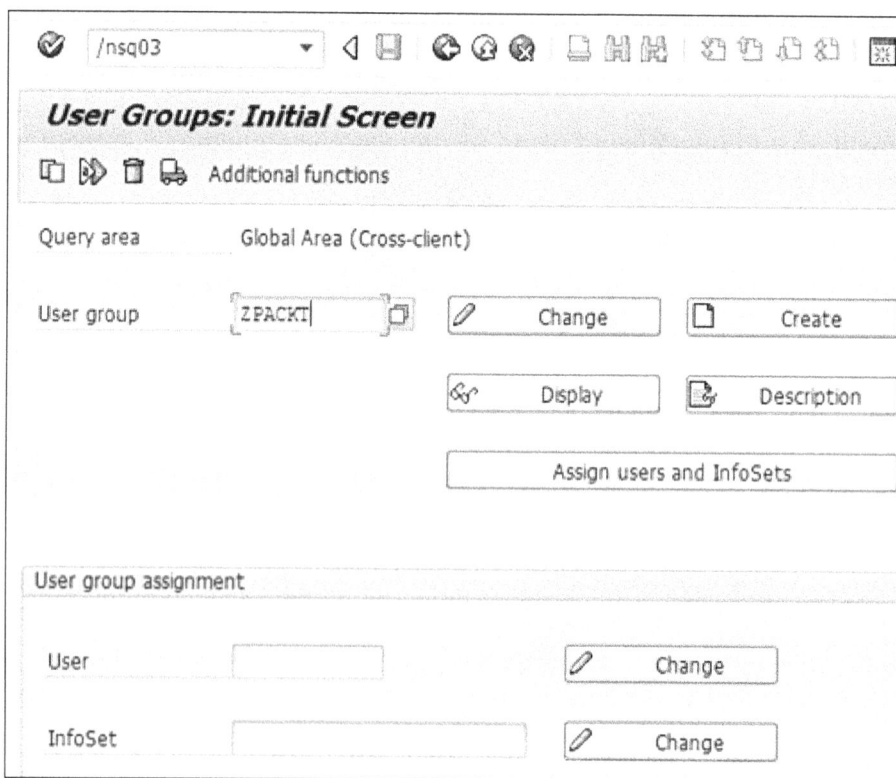

We are attempting to create a user group by the name ZPACKT; we can also change the name created by clicking on **Change**. When trying to create a query, the system will prompt us to specify the package name where it needs to be saved. Packages are technical objects in the ABAP work bench. They are normally called using the following T-codes:

- SE80: We can enter the package name, and we can access it by double-clicking on it

- SM30: This is from the V_TDEVC table/view

We will see the program listed under the $TMP package, as shown in the following screenshot:

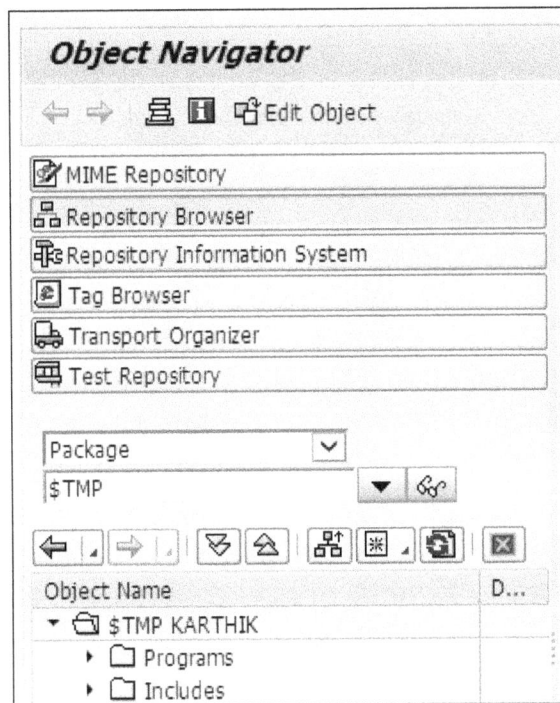

The $TMP package is only a temporary package, and a proper package name needs to be created and used in the development client. A package is created using the SE80 T-code. This $TMP package is the one we will be using when we save the user group. The table view of V_TDEVC looks like the following screenshot when we access it via SM30/31:

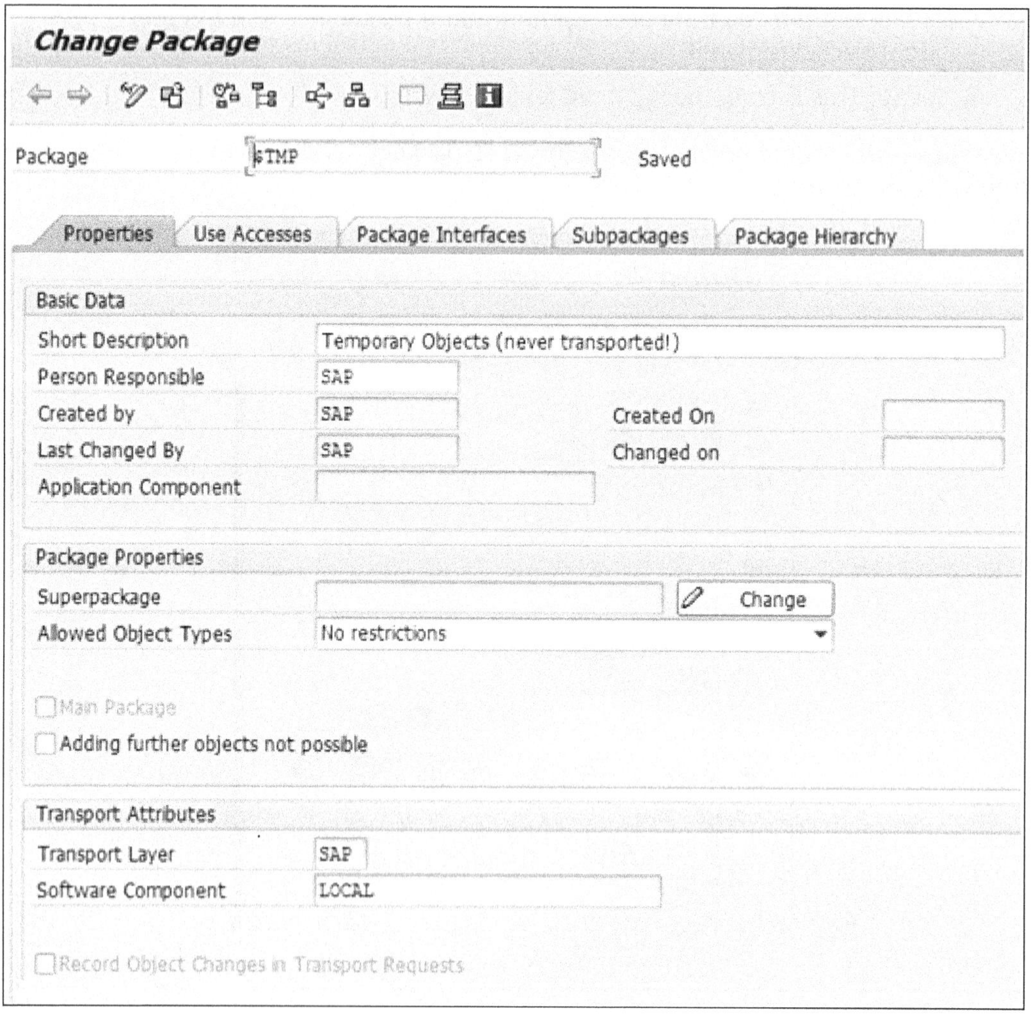

When the user group is created, the system prompts us to enter the description of the user group, as shown in the following screenshot, where we are giving it the name `Test Query`. The date and time stamp are captured for audit purposes.

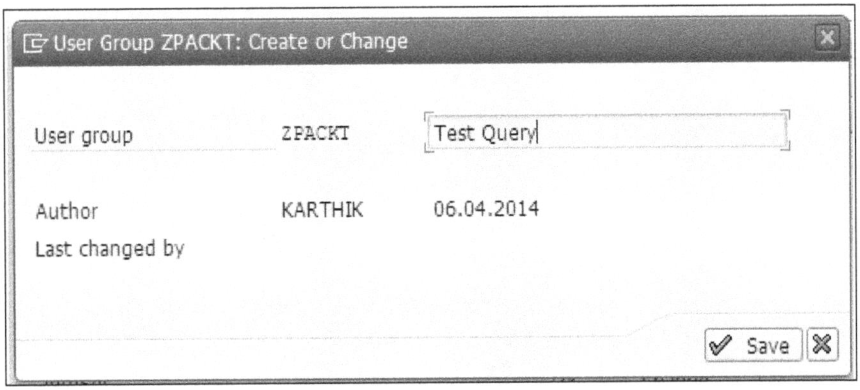

We need to click on the **Save** button. When the **Save** button is clicked on, the system prompts us to enter the package name where we would like to save the object. We will enter `$TMP`, as shown in the following screenshot. We will also go to `SE80` and see how this is getting captured in the package. We could either enter `$TMP` or click on a local object (*F7*). Both perform the same task. Then, we can use `SE80` to see how this is captured in the package.

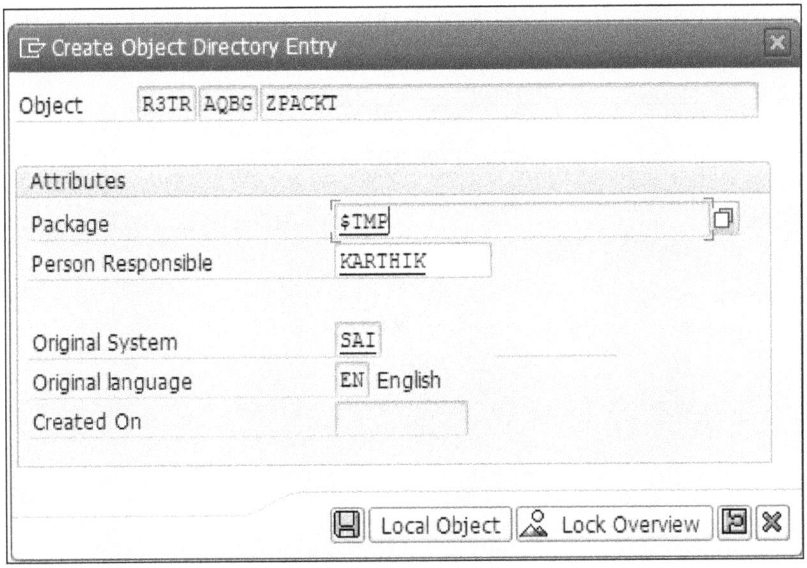

If we would like to change the package, then we can do so by navigating to **User group** | **Change Package** from the menu, as shown in the following screenshot:

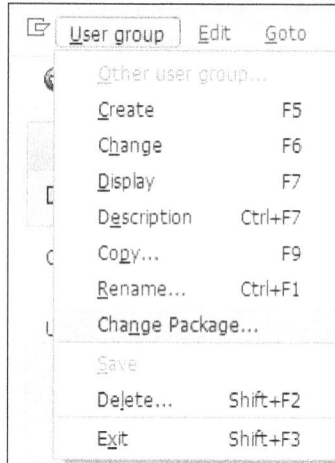

⌐	User group	Edit	Goto
	Other user group...		
	Create		F5
	Change		F6
	Display		F7
	Description		Ctrl+F7
	Copy...		F9
	Rename...		Ctrl+F1
	Change Package...		
	Save		
	Delete...		Shift+F2
	Exit		Shift+F3

The **Change Package** option helps us assign a different package if required, instead of the one already assigned.

SAP also provides options such as copying the user group created by pressing *F9* or renaming the user group by pressing *Ctrl + F1*.

The next step is to assign the usernames to the user group by clicking on the **Assign users and InfoSets** button.

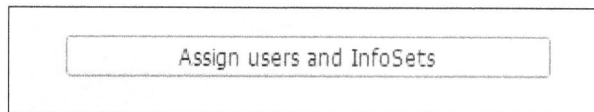

Assign users and InfoSets

The username is 12 characters in length and is assigned in order to access the user group, as shown in the following screenshot:

User Group ZPACKT: Assign Users

🗑 User   Assign InfoSets

User group   ZPACKT   Test Query

Overview

User   and Change Authorization for Queries

    KARTHIK   ✓

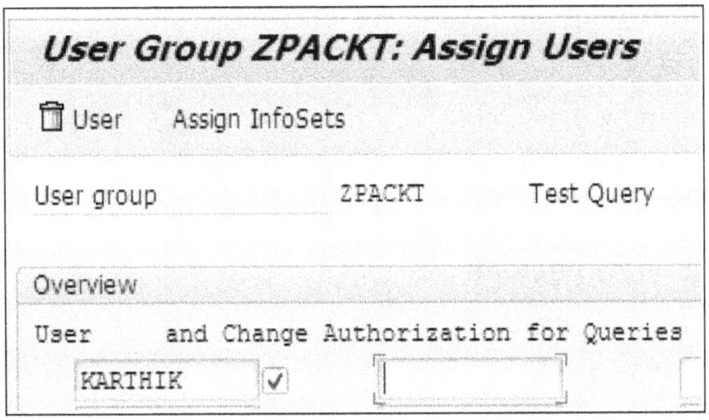

The username can also be deleted if required by clicking on the **Delete** option (*Shift* + *F2*).

Once the user ID is assigned, there will be a flag next to the username. This flag indicates that the mapping is active, as shown in the following screenshot:

User Group ZPACKT: Assign Users

🗑 User   Assign InfoSets

User group   ZPACKT   Test Query

Overview

User   and Change Authorization for Queries

    KARTHIK   ✓

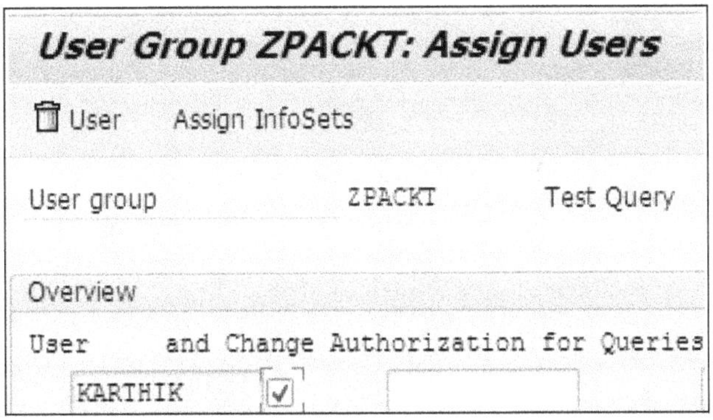

Steps for creating the infoset

The infoset is created using the SQ02 TCD by entering the infoset name and description. There are multiple options we can choose the source of data from. These options are as follows:

- **Table join using basis table**
- **Direct read of table**
- **Logical database**
- **Data retrieval by program**

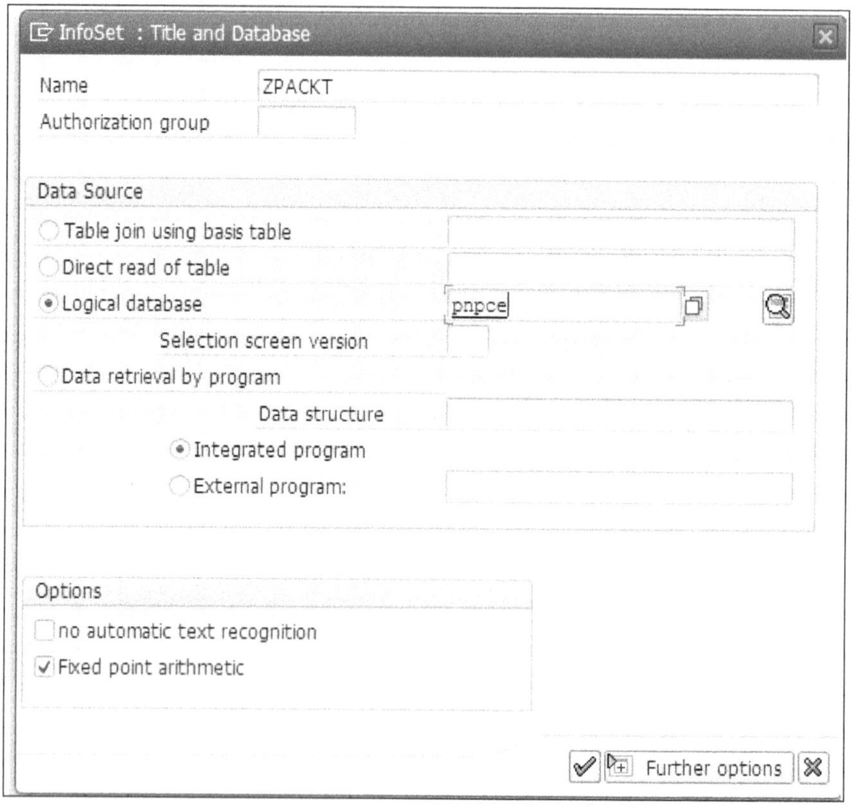

The pnpce logical database enables us to choose all the infotypes that we want to choose the input and output for. We will choose the infotypes that the data is going to be fetched from, as shown in the following screenshot:

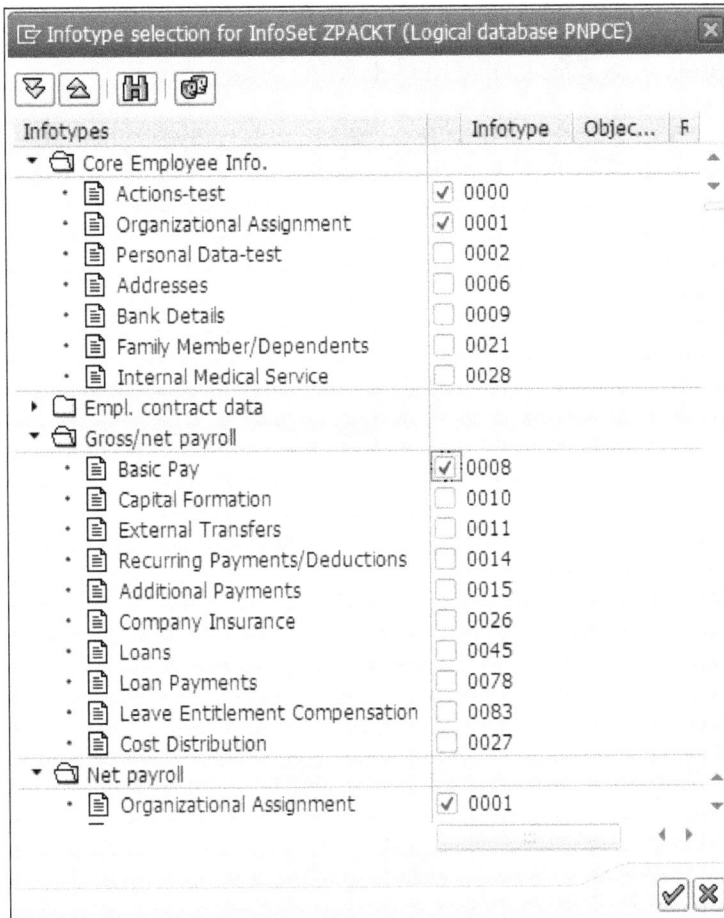

The infoset needs to be generated by clicking on **Generate** (*Shift* + *F6*). Once it is executed, the system checks the infoset and prompts a message stating that the infoset is generated at the bottom of the screen, as shown in the following screenshot:

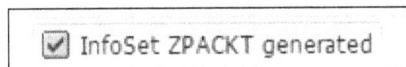

Once the infoset is created and generated, we can go to the SQ01 TCD, enter the name of the query, and click on the **Create** button. The infoset created earlier will be displayed to be chosen. This infoset has the fields from tables that are mapped using LDB PNPCE.

Steps for creating a query

The **Create Query** screen looks like the following screenshot:

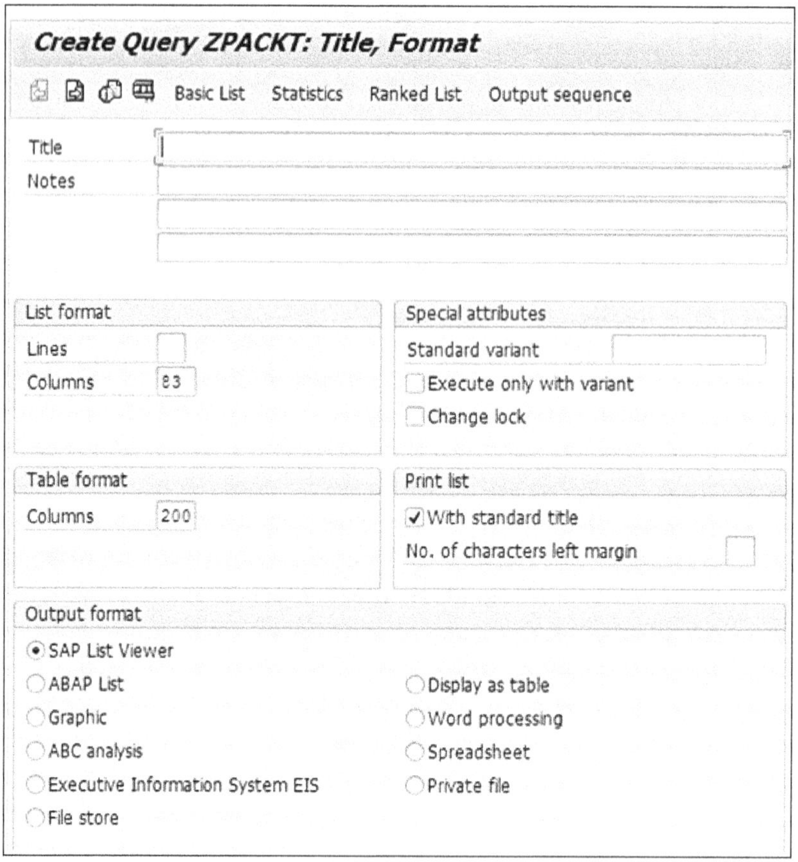

There are multiple output formats that can be chosen while creating the query. They are as follows:

- **SAP List viewer**
- **ABAP List**
- **Graphic**
- **ABC analysis**
- **Executive Information System EIS**
- **File store**
- **Display as table**
- **Word processing**

- **Spreadsheet**
- **Private file**

We need to click on **Save** (*Ctrl + S*) and then on test (*Ctrl + F8*). We can also execute the query after saving it as a variant by choosing the **Execute only with variant** checkbox. We can also lock this query from changes being made by other users by flagging the **Change lock** checkbox, as shown in the following screenshot:

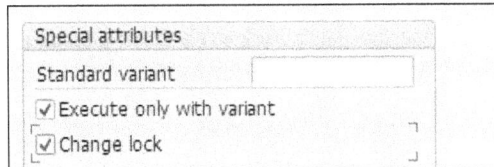

We need to go back and execute the query (*F8*) or execute it as a variant (*Shift + F5*), as shown in the following screenshot:

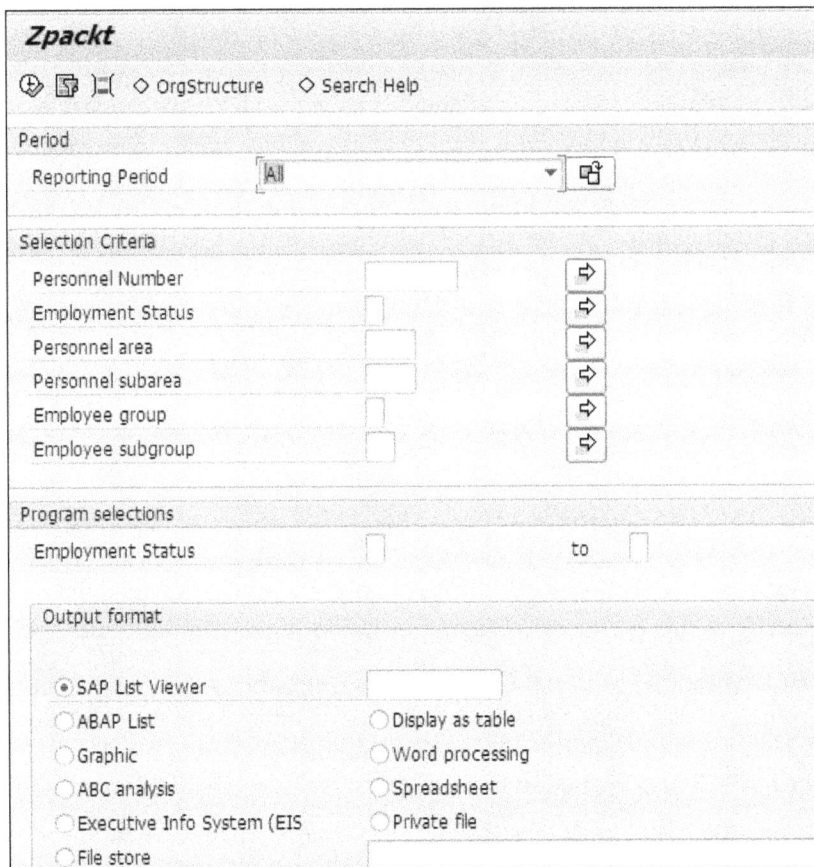

Executing a report using an ad hoc query

We will now see how we can execute a report using an ad hoc query. We will learn to use the user group and infoset that we created using the SQ03/SQ02 TCD. We can execute an ad hoc query by navigating to **SAP Easy Access | SAP Menu | Human Resources | Information systems | Reporting tools | S_PH0_48000513** or directly via the S_PH0_48000513 TCD.

When we execute the transaction code, the screen looks like the one in the following screenshot. We will have to change the **Work area** from **Standard area (client-specific)** to **Global area (cross-client)** in the **Environment** window and choose the user group that we created, for example, ZPACKT.

Environment	
Work area	Standard area (client-specific) ▼
User Group	Standard area (client-specific)
	Global area (cross-client)

> User groups get listed only when they are based on the work area assigned while creating them. We can check or change it by navigating to **SQ03 | Environment | Query Areas**.

The query area can be defaulted in the user profile by assigning the **AQW (ABAP Query area)** parameter in the user profile, as shown in the following screenshot:

Parameters		
Set/Get parameter ID	Parameter value	Short Description
SPU	X	Display confirmation prompt when leaving the transaction
UGR	01	User group (HR master data)
AQW	Global	ABAP Query: Query area

The query area contains a set of objects (user groups, infosets, queries) that are created via the SQ01, SQ02, and SQ03 TCDs. The entire gamut of SAP query functionalities can be explored with the standard and global areas. They are separate entities, and there is no relationship between the objects created in each area. We will look at the difference between the queries created in the standard and global clients now.

- **Standard area**: The queries that we create (infosets, user groups, queries) are specific to a particular client, and they are not attached to the work bench organizer. We can still transport the query, but it needs to be done manually. This query that is created in the standard area is not available across the system.

- **Global area**: The query objects that we create in the global area are available across clients, and they are connected to the work bench organizer.

The query can be assigned to a different area by navigating to **SQ03 | Environment | Query areas**, as shown in the following screenshot:

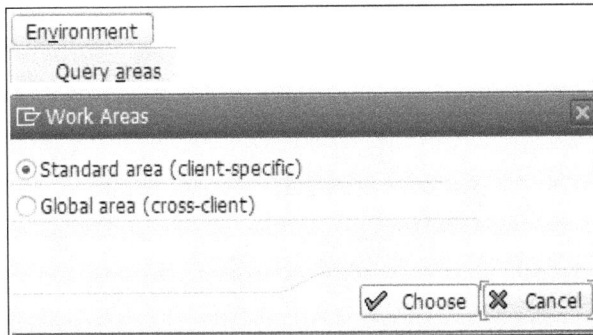

Only when we change the work area from standard to global will we be allowed to assign the user group that we created in the SQ01 TCD, as shown in the following screenshot:

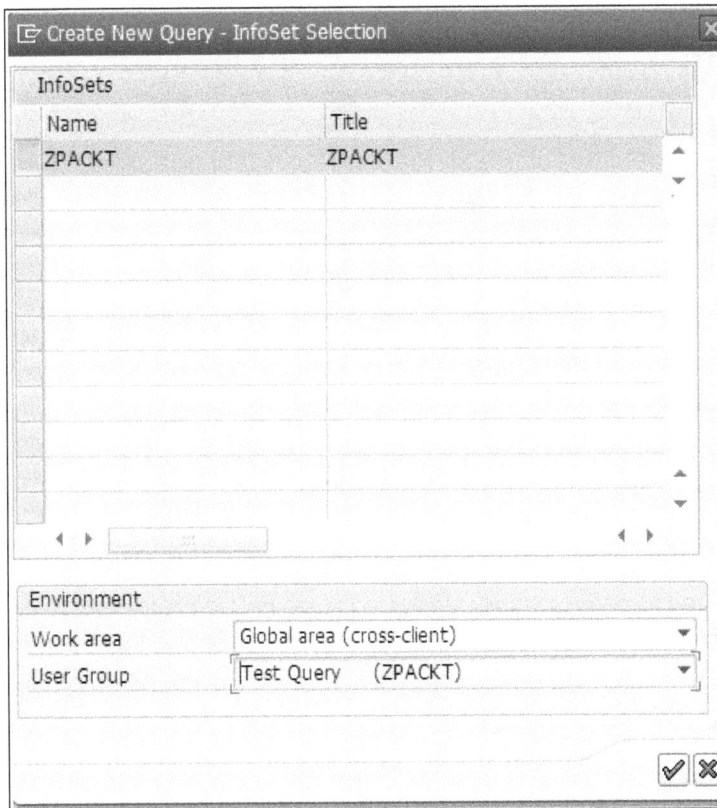

Now, the system will allow us to choose the input and output fields based on the requirement. We can also the save the query for frequent use by clicking on **Save** (*Ctrl + S*). We can enter the name and title of the query, as shown in the following screenshot:

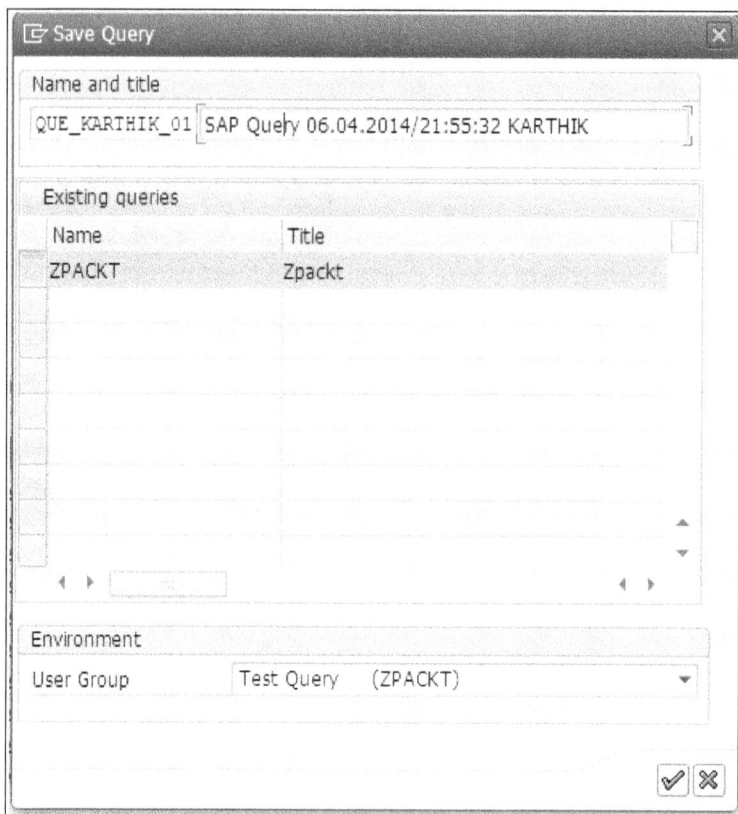

When we execute the query, the output looks like the one shown in the following screenshot:

If you noticed, the personnel number is not displayed. In order to have the personnel number displayed, we need to right-click on the column and choose the appropriate option, as shown in the following screenshot:

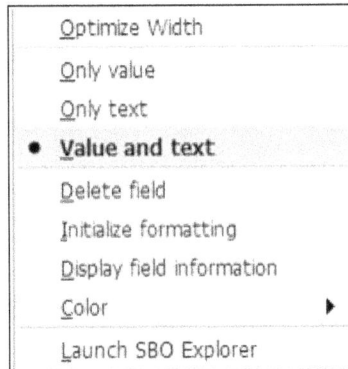

The selection in the ad hoc query allows us to change the default value, for example, 3 for **Active Employment Status**. In order to change the selection, we need to open the ad hoc query and in the main menu, click on **Extras** in the menu at the top and then click on **Switch off object selection**, as shown in the following screenshot:

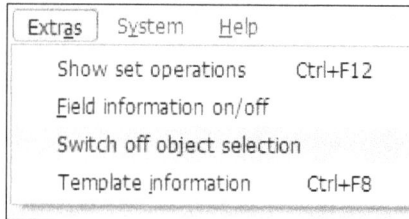

When **switch off object selection** is chosen, we will be able to right-click on the field and choose one of the three available options. When **Only text** is chosen, we see the text-selection indicator next to the field name. We can see the **Employment Status** text showing in the output, as shown in the following screenshot:

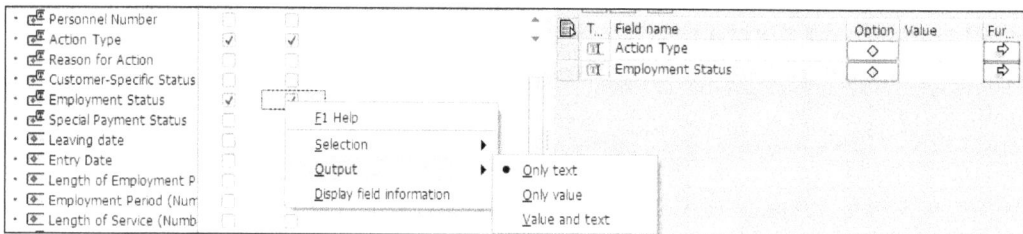

The output looks like the following screenshot with the text, as the option chosen is **Only text**:

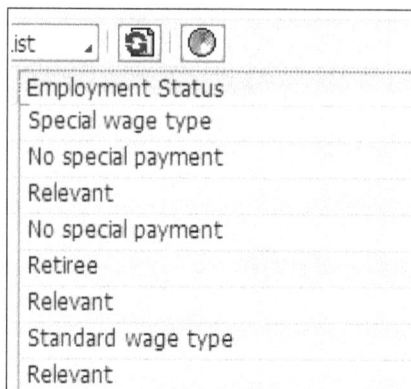

The **Hit list** button is unavailable when **switch off object selection** is selected and the same has been confirmed by SAP. We need to click on **Output** to run the report.

Frequent error messages when building an ad hoc query

We normally come across this standard error message when we create a query and click on the **Test** button:

```
No lists yet defined for query XX where XX is the query name in SQ01

Message no. AQ217
```

Analysis

By performing some analysis, we can clearly see that the XX query doesn't have the report layout specified. Neither the basic list, nor statistics, nor the ranked list have been defined for the query report layout.

Workaround

Before executing the query, we need to define the report layout (basic list, statistics, or ranked list) to fix the error. We need to define the input and output in the list, select the fields to fix this error, and execute the query, as shown in the following screenshot:

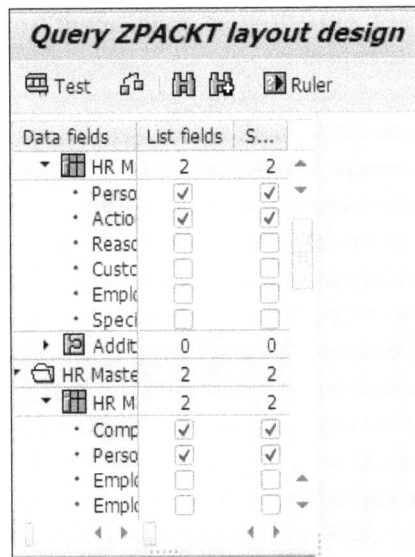

We have four options to choose from; we can click on **Basic List** and choose the list and selection fields, as shown in the following screenshot:

Change Query ZPACKT: Title, Format

Basic List   Statistics   Ranked List   Output sequence

Standard error messages are stored in the SE91 TCD.

An interesting feature to tag the T-code with the report

There is an interesting feature provided by SAP to tag the TCD to the report output. For example, we will have to maintain the employee master by simply double-clicking on the output. We will learn how this feature can be achieved by following the steps. **Report Assignment** is the feature we are discussing that makes this possible. The Report Assignment feature can be accessed via the SQ01 TCD and entering the query name (Shafiq Rehman, 2008, SCN) and clicking on **Change**.

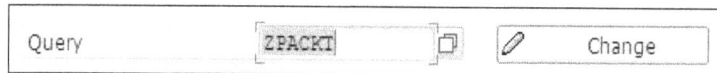

Query   ZPACKT   ⬚   ⬚   Change

The report assignment allows you to assign the TCD to the report, and can be accessed by navigating to **Goto | Report assignment** from the menu, as shown in the following screenshot:

Goto   Extras   Settings

Field selection   ▶
Basic List   ▶
Statistic   ▶
Ranked List   ▶
Saved lists...
Maintain variants...
Documentation
Trash
Report assignment
Next screen   F6
Previous screen
Back   F3

When we click on the **Report assignment**, the system populates the **Assign Reports** screen. When we click on **Insert row** (*F6*), there will be a new window to add the ABAP/4 query.

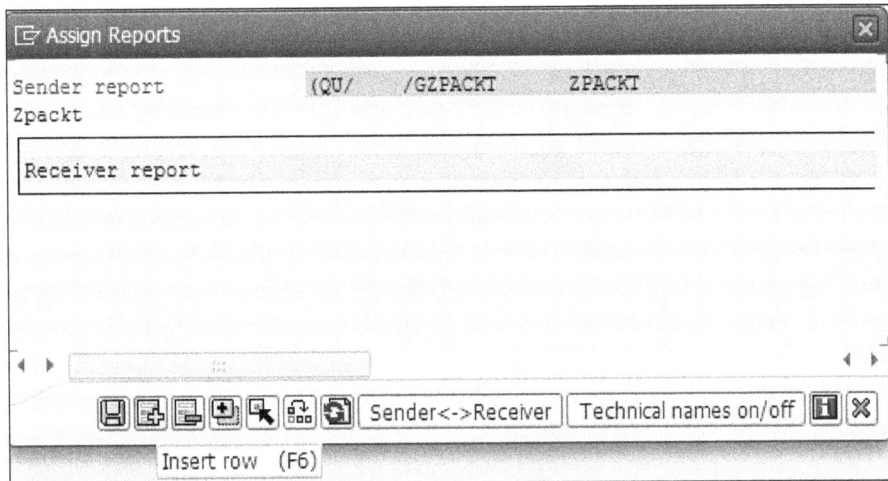

The ABAP/4 query window has the following fields for the user to choose from:

- **User group**
- **Query**
- **Variant**
- The **Global area** checkbox

We need to click on the other report type to enter the transaction code such as PA30, as shown in the following screenshot:

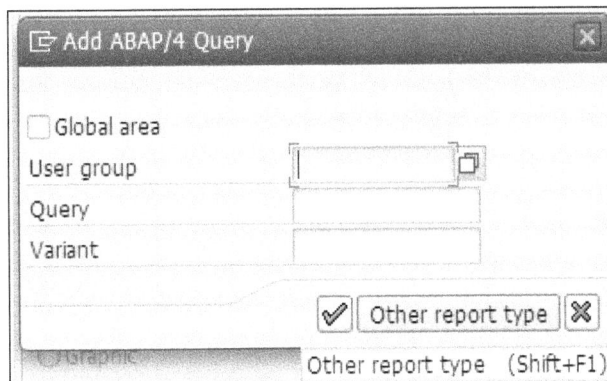

The other report type has the following report types to choose from. In our case, we are trying to assign the TCD to the report, so we will be choosing transaction:

Report type	Name
BB	Report Portfolio
BW	BW Query
QU	SAP Query
RE	Drilldown Reporting
RT	ABAP Report Program
RW	Report Writer
TR	Transaction

When we choose **Transaction**, the system prompts us to enter the TCD such as PA30, and click on the tick symbol, as shown in the following screenshot:

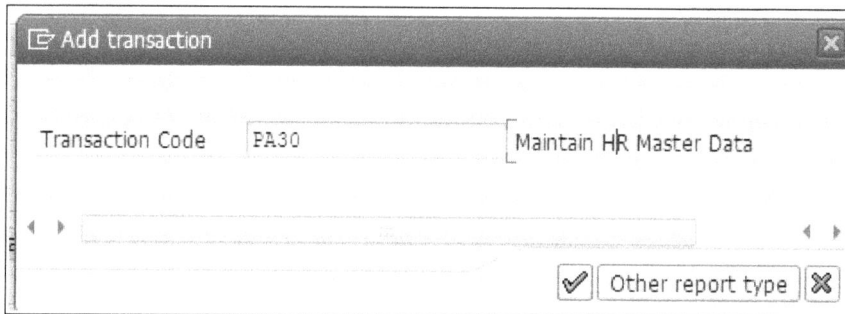

The query will now have the TCD mapped to it, so when we execute the query and double-click on the output, the system will take us to the **Master Data Maintenance** transaction (PA30).Click on **Save** (*Ctrl + S*), as shown in the following screenshot:

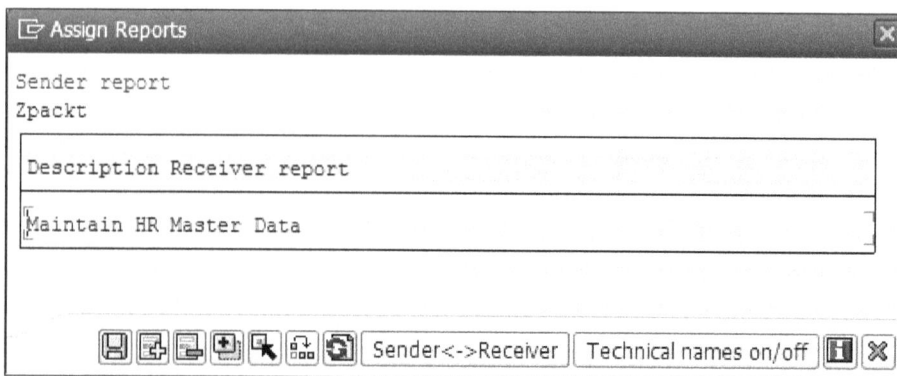

When we execute the query and double-click on the output, the system takes us to the PA30 screen. The system shows the **'Maintain HR Master Data' is executed** message at the bottom of the screen, as shown in the following screenshot. Interesting feature, isn't it?

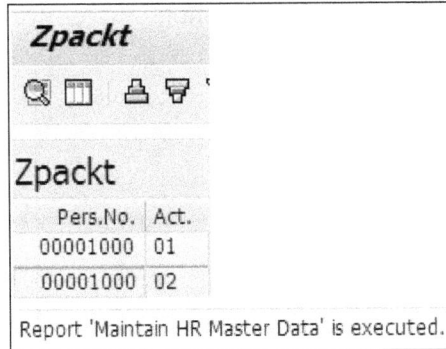

The PA30 screen will allow us to maintain the master data for the chosen personnel instantly.

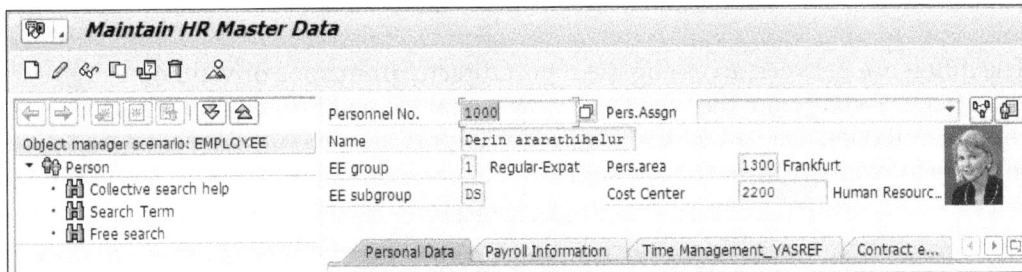

Transport a query across clients

Transporting queries across clients in the landscape is not achieved directly like in the configurable tables. We will learn the steps to transport a query. A query is transported by accessing the report by navigating to **Enviornment | Transports** (*Ctrl + F3*), as shown in the following screenshot:

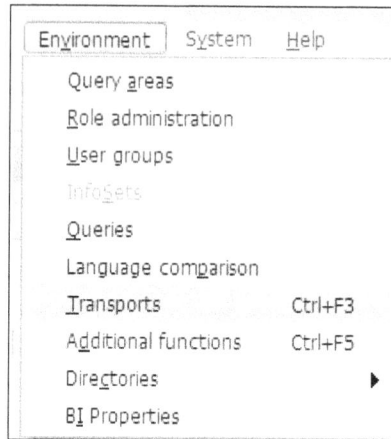

The difference between accessing the report directly from SQ02 or via the SE38/SA38 T-code from the RSAQR3TR table is that we will find the **Transport Action Selection** enabled for us to export or import the query option, as shown in the following screenshot:

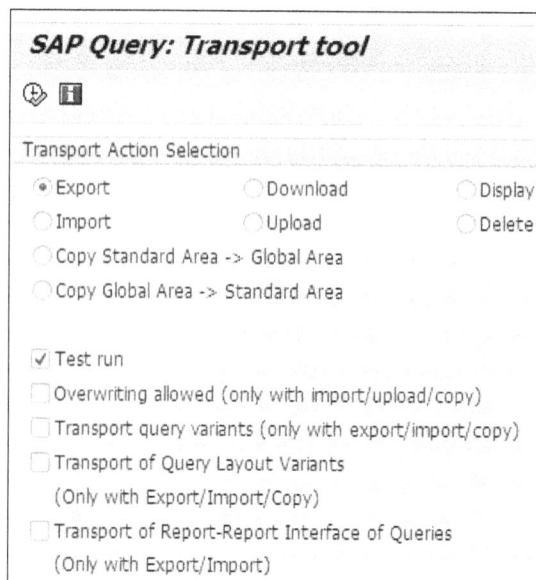

We need to choose the **Export** option and check the following boxes. It will help us generate a transport request number that can be released and referenced in the client where we would like the query to be imported.

- **Overwriting allowed**
- **Transport query variants**
- **Transport of Query Layout Variants**
- **Transport of Report-Report Interfaces of Queries**

It is mandatory that you mention the user groups, queries, or infosets from the following options provided:

- **Transport user groups**
- **Transport Infosets**
- **Transport Infosets and queries**
- **Transport Queries**

After choosing any of the options, click on **Execute**, and the system generates a transport request number that we can note down and use in the client where we would like to import the query, as shown in the following screenshot:

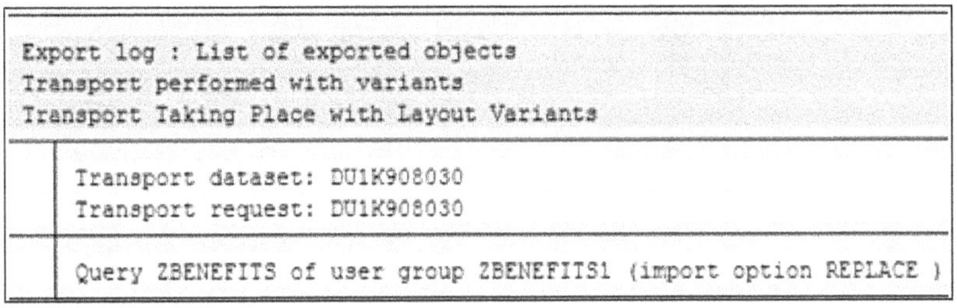

```
Export log : List of exported objects
Transport performed with variants
Transport Taking Place with Layout Variants

    Transport dataset: DU1K908030
    Transport request: DU1K908030

    Query ZBENEFITS of user group ZBENEFITS1 (import option REPLACE )
```

We need to choose the **Import** option, and the transport request number needs to be referenced in the client where we are importing the query, as shown in the following screenshot:

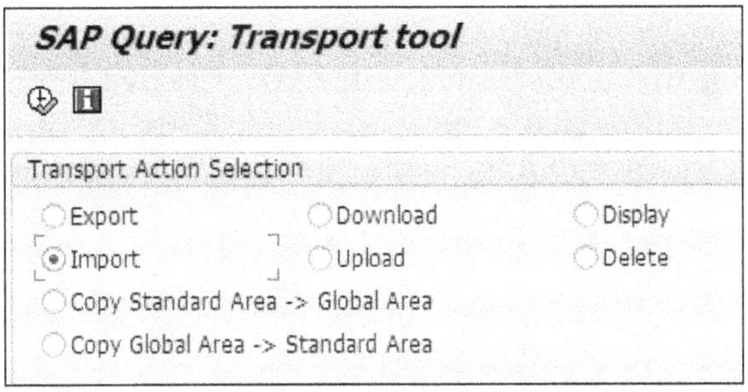

We need to refer to the transport request number in the **Datasets with imports** field.

Dataset with imports		to		⇨
☐ Delete after successful import				

Develop a report using SAP Query Viewer (SQVI)

SAP has provided a simple tool to develop reports with minimum programming knowledge. We will delve into the steps to create the reports using the SAP query viewer (SQVI) TCD. Although SQVI is simple, it is only specific to a particular user that is being tagged with it. We will also learn to convert query views to a SAP query in this section.

The query view is accessed via the TCD SQVI, as shown in the following screenshot:

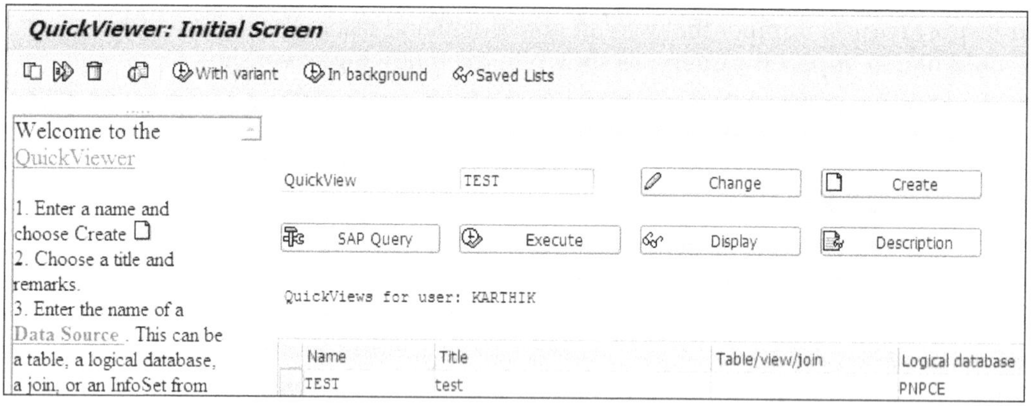

As we note from the preceding screenshot, the quick view is tagged only to the user, Karthik. Unlike the SAP query, multiple users cannot have access to the same query view.

We will assign a name to the query and click on the **Create** button. We can enter the long text in the new window that is autopopulated. There are multiple options that can be mentioned as a source of data for that query. They are as follows:

- **Table**
- **Table join**

- **Logical database**
- **SAP Query InfoSet**

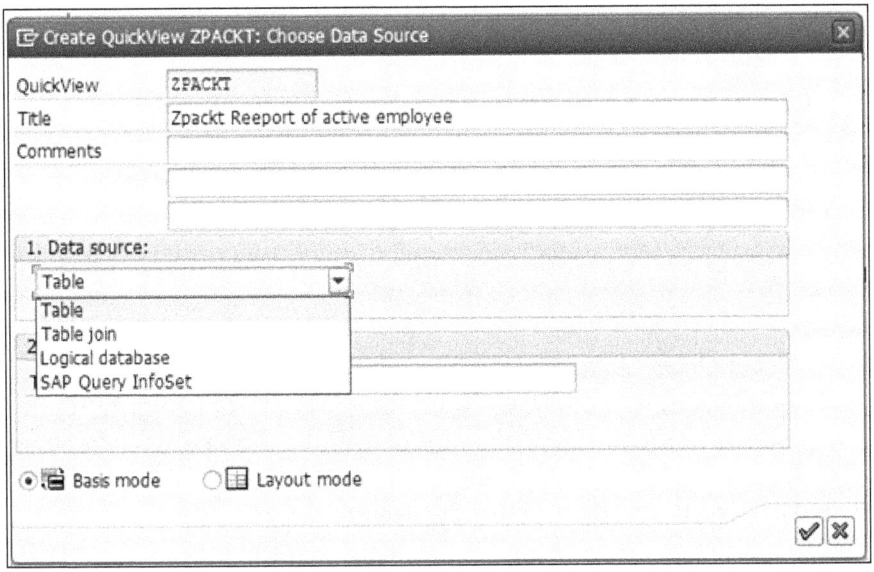

We can use **Table** as the data source and fetch output from the table used. We need to enter PA0001 in the **Table/view** field and then click on the Enter button, as shown in the following screenshot:

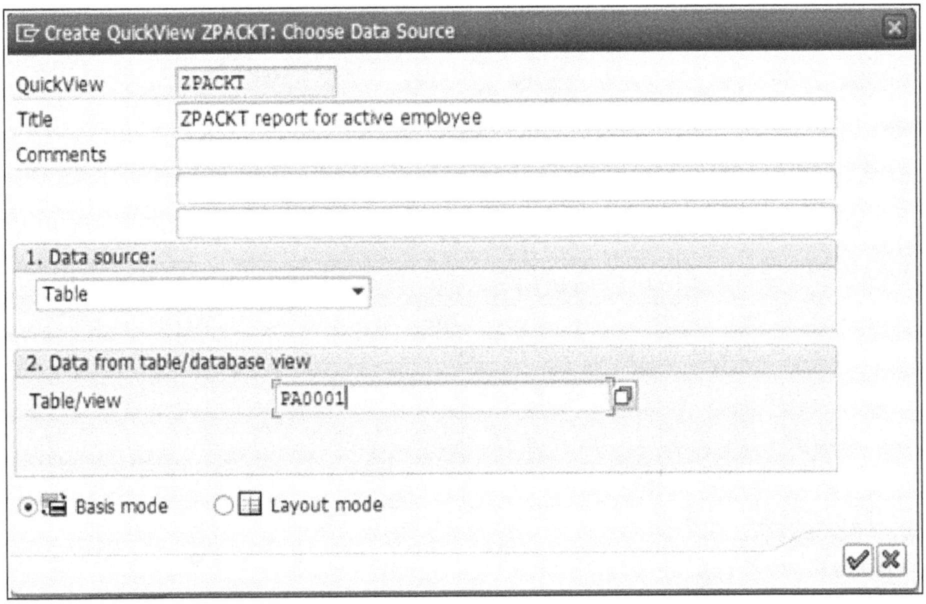

When we choose the PA0001 table, for example, all the fields related to this table are available for selection when we press *Enter*, as shown in the screenshot:

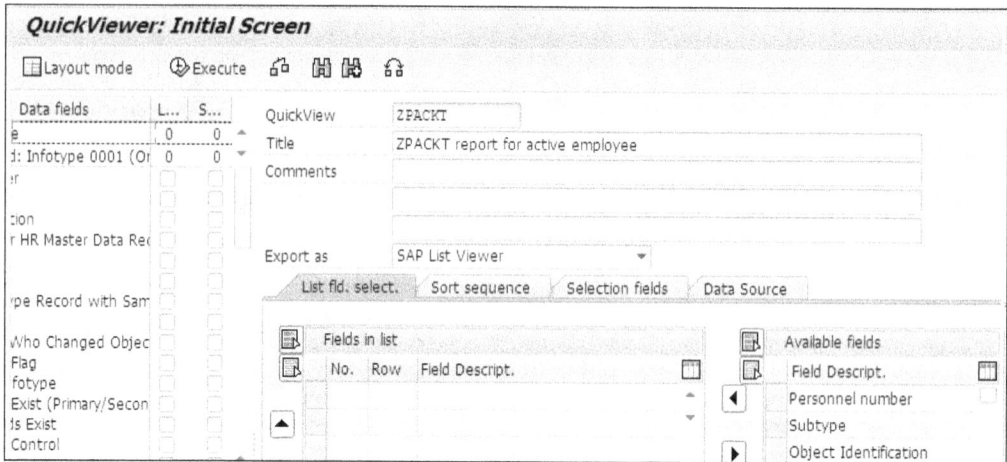

We have two options to choose from for the design:

- Basis mode
- Layout mode

The layout design has provisions to define the header text, footer text, and so on. The layout design looks like the following screenshot:

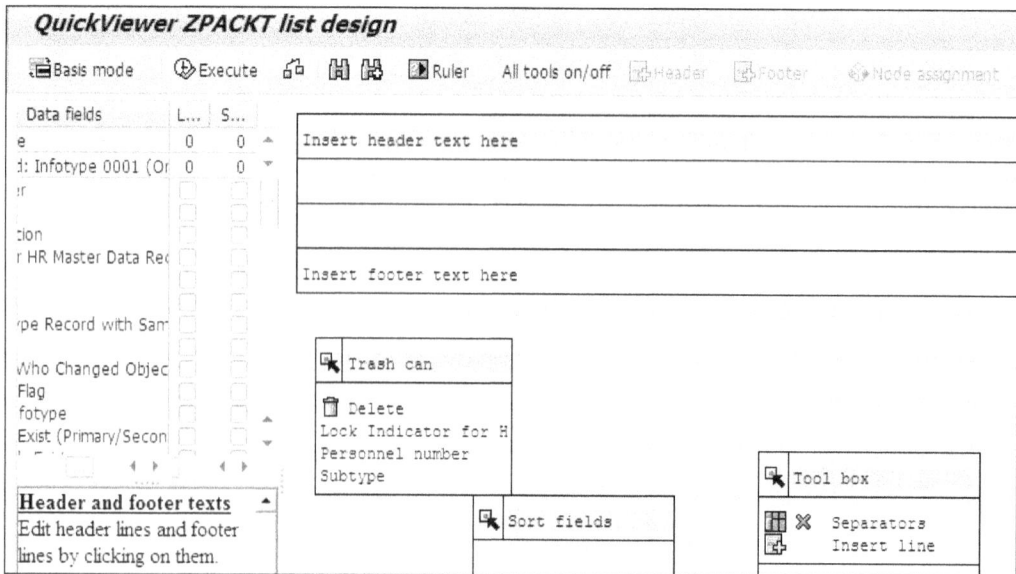

We can define the header text by double-clicking on it. We can also delete fields and move them to the trash by clicking on the **Delete** button. We can add lines by clicking on the insert line icon and dragging and positioning it in the place where we would like to add a line. The basis mode looks slightly different, and the provision to add a header and footer won't be available. The available fields are listed under the available fields' box, and we can choose the ones we would like to have as selection (input) or list fields (output). We can click on the **Insert Field** button to choose the input and output, as shown in the following screenshot:

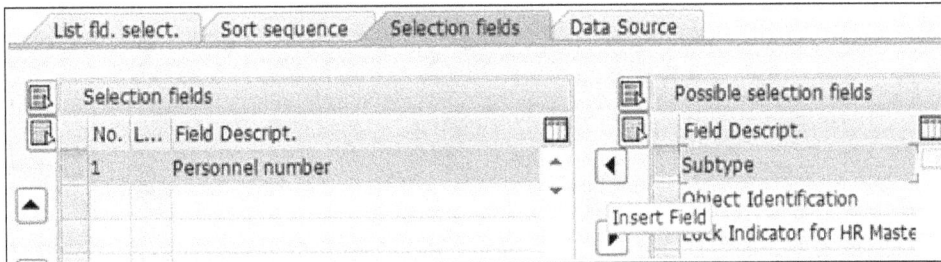

We will have four tabs in the query design, as follows:

- **List field selection**
- **Sort sequence**
- **Selection fields**
- **Data Source**

The data source gives us information about whether we have used the **Table**, **Table Join**, or **Logical** database as the source, as shown in the following screenshot:

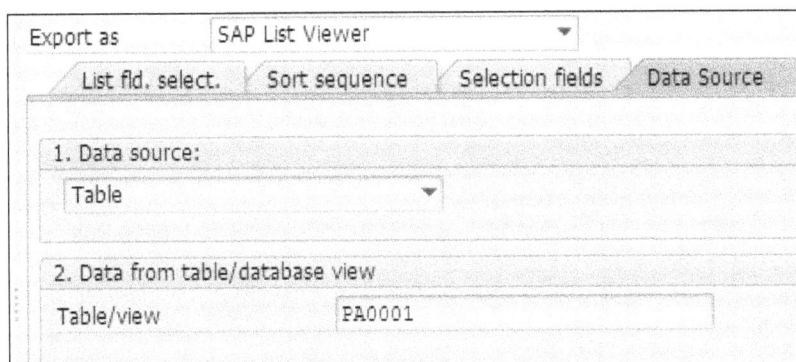

The **Selection fields** tab, as the name sounds, will have the field that will be available in the input screen of the report. The **Sort sequence** tab can be used to arrange the fields in the order of preference. The **List field selection** tab consists of the fields that we would like to have in the output. Let's say, for example, we choose **Personnel number** and **Subtype** as the selection fields, and in the output, we would like to have **Personnel number** alone. We can do this as shown in the following screenshot:

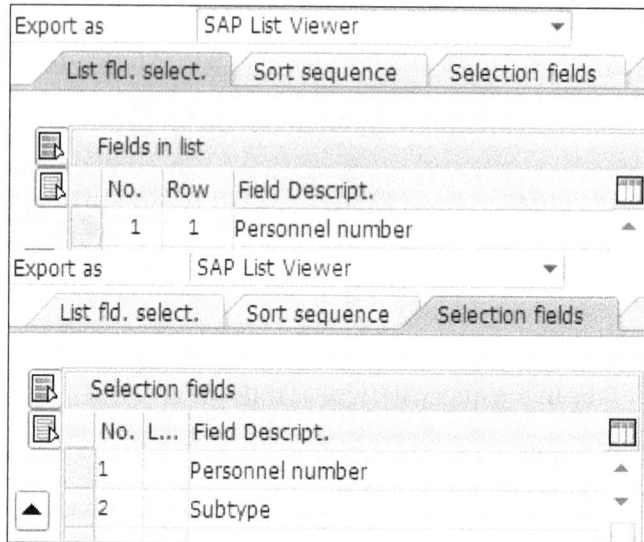

When we click on the data selection and output button (*F8*), the query that we see will have the input as **Personnel number** and **Subtype** and output as the personnel number, as shown in the following screenshot:

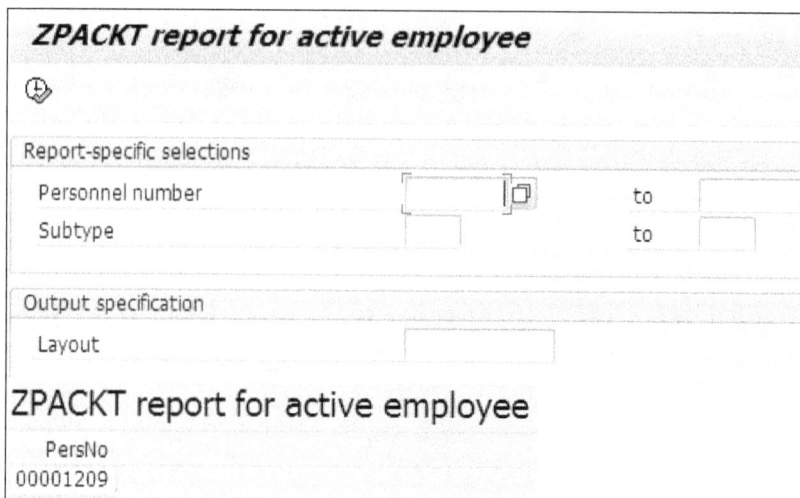

Converting the query view to a SAP query

We discussed earlier that the query view is only available for a particular user and not for all of them. We will learn how a query view can be converted to a SAP query so that all the users can run the report using the same query. We need to go to the SQ01 TCD and navigate to **Query | Convert QuickView**. We have to enter the **Quick View**, **Query**, and **InfoSet** names for the conversion, as shown in the following screenshot:

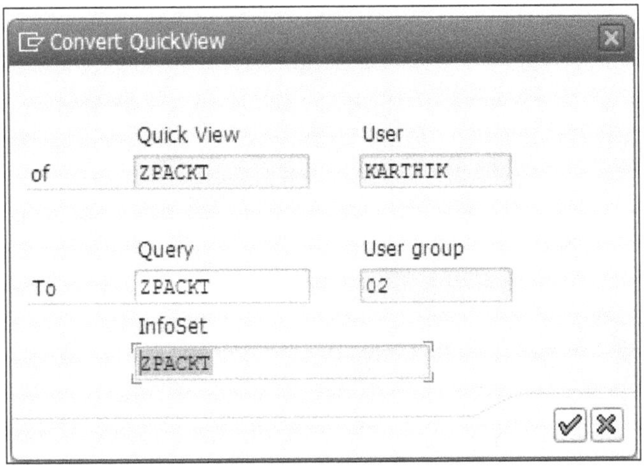

> The **Convert** quick view may be disabled from SQ01, and we have to go to **Environment | Query area | Change from Global area to Standard area (Client specific)** to have it enabled.

Summary

In this chapter, you learned to build and develop reports using the SAP query or quick view tools. You learned some tips and tricks to run the report with minimum programming skills. We got to know the difference between SAP query and quick views and how to convert the quick view to a query to be used by all users. Happy reporting!

We hope the book served as a useful reference guide to configure the SAP HCM module. The configuration steps of the core modules and a new dimension module were covered from our experiences of working on different assignments.

Index

Symbols

0000 (Action) infotype
about 110
functions 110-112
0001 (Organizational Assignment) infotype
about 112
functions 112, 113
0002 (Personal Data) infotype
about 113
functions 113
0003 (Payroll Status) infotype 197
0006 (Address) infotype
about 114
functions 114
0007 (Planned Working Time) infotype
about 114, 115
functions 114, 115
0008 (Basic Pay) infotype
about 116
functions 116
0009 (Bank Details) infotype
about 117
functions 117
0014 (Recurring Payment and Deduction)
infotype 200
0015 (Additional Payments)
infotype 201, 202
0027 (Cost Distribution)
infotype 199, 200
0267 (Additional off-cycle payments)
infotype 202
0267 (On-demand or Additional Payments)
configuration 211
$TMP package 320
/n+T-code 7
/o+T-code 7
S_AHR_61011888 T-code, Training and
Event Management submodule 14
S_AHR_61011889 T-code, Training and
Event Management submodule 14
S_AHR_61011893 T-code, Training and
Event Management submodule 14

A

ABAP/4 query window 335
Absences infotype (2001) 155
Absences Quotas
Category 157
Deduction 157
Deduction from 157
Deduction to 157
Neg. deduction to 157
nodes, configuring for 152
Quota number 157
tables, customizing for 170-176
Absence Quotas infotype (2006)
about 156, 157
generation rule configuration 176-184
generation tips 184
accounting AC system
activities 223, 224
Actions infotype (0000) 194
action type 145
activities
in accounting AC system 223, 224
in HR system 222, 223
activity status entries, SAP 135
ADDDB operation 190
Additional off-cycle payments
infotype (0267) 202

Additional Payments
     configuration (0015) 209, 210
Additional Payments infotype (0015)
  about 201
  fields 201
ADDMB operation 190
ADDWT operation 219
ADDZL operation 190
ad hoc query
  building, SQ01 TCD used 317
  used, for executing report 328-332
Advanced Business Application
     Programming (ABAP) 189, 291, 317
AMT operation 219
APPCREATE T-code, Talent Management
     submodule 14
applicant by action report 16
applicant class 42
applicant cycle
  overview 43-52
applicant data, transferring to Personnel
     Administration
  common errors 57
  integration tools 54-56
  procedure 54
applicant group 42
applicant number ranges
  changed NR status 40
  change interval 40
  display intervals 40
applicants by name report 16
Application Link Enabling (ALE) 315
appraisal category groups 247
appraisals template configuration
  about 246, 247
  category, creating 250-253
  category group, creating 248, 249
appraisal template
  about 247
  creating, steps 254-256
APPSEARCH T-code, Talent Management
     submodule 14
ASREI function 315
Attendance/Absence Data
  Multiple-Employee View report 22
Attendances infotype (2002) 155
Attendance Quotas infotype (2007) 157

Authorized Objects per
     User/Profile report 19

B

Bank Details report 24
Basic Pay configuration (0008) 206, 207
Basic Pay infotype (0008)
  about 198
  fields 198, 199
basic settings, personnel development
     component 229-233
basic settings, TEM 257, 258
Batch Data Collection (BDC) 239
Business Add-In (BADI) 292
business event preparation
  configuring 262

C

CAC1 T-code, Time Management
     submodule 11
candidate
  reasons, for rejection 44
career maintenance 240
CATA T-code, Time Management
     submodule 11
channels 40
classified advertising 39
clients
  queries, transporting across 338, 339
COLER operation 190
collective agreement
     provision (CAP) 137, 206, 207
COLOP operation 190
COM function 215
command field 5
company 118
company code 118
concepts, Organizational Management (OM)
  SPOCK 63
configuration, business event preparation
  booking 275-278
  business event catalogue 273, 274
  day-to-day activities 274, 275
  Employee Self-Service (ESS) 283
  follow-up processing 280-282
  master data 268, 269

physical location 264-267
recurring activities 279
resource management 270-272
time schedule 263
configuration, node
for Absence Quotas 152
for Work schedule rule 152
configuration, payroll
about 203
wage types 203-205
configuration, payslip 220, 221
configuration steps, PA infotypes
about 118
company code, creating 121-123
employee group, defining 126
employee subgroup, defining 126
enterprise structure components 118
executing 120-128
personnel area and
subareas, defining 124, 125
personnel structure components 119
**configuration steps, Travel Expenses
module** 306-314
**configuration steps, Travel Planning
module** 294-306
**configuration steps, Travel Request
module** 290-294
control record
about 135, 136, 196
Additional off-cycle payments
infotype (0267) 202
Additional Payments infotype (0015) 201
Basic Pay infotype (0008) 198
Cost Distribution infotype (0027) 199
functionalities 196, 197
Payroll Status infotype (0003) 197, 198
Planned Working Time infotype (0007) 198
Recurring Payment and
Deduction infotype (0014) 200
control record status
check payroll results 196
exit payroll 196
released for correction 196
released for payroll 196
COPY function 215, 218
Cost Assignment for Trip report 27

Cost Centre
about 75
creating 76
Cost Distribution infotype (0027)
about 199
fields 200
country key 133
criterion 247
Cross Application Time Sheet (CATS) 23
CUMBT function 189
**Cumulated Time Evaluation Results: Time
Balances/Time Wage Types report** 23
customization, table
for absence quotas 170-176
for Work schedule rule 162

D

daily work schedule (DWS) 165-167
Data Medium Exchange (DME) 306
Data Transfer Tools 54, 103
day type 167
Define Administrator 43
delete blank switch 231
development plan catalog 244, 245
**display absence quota
information report** 23
**Display and Create Missing Inverse
Relationships report** 19
dynamic actions
about 148
configuring 148, 149

E

employee referral program 39
**Employee Remuneration
infotype (2010)** 158
Employee Self-Service (ESS) 268, 283
employee sub group (ESG) 205
employment agencies 39
employment status entries, SAP 135
enterprise structure components
company 118
company code 118
personnel area 118
personnel subareas 119

error messages, on ad hoc query creation
about 333
analysis 333
work around 333, 334
Evaluate Careers report 25
Expert Mode
job object, creating in 80, 81
organizational unit object, creating in 78
position object, creating in 79
used, for building organizational
structure 77
used, for creating organizational structure
91-95

F

F.02/F-53/FBCJ/F110 TCD 290
features, Recruitment submodule
PAPLI 54
PRELI 54
PRELR 54
features, SAP 57-59
features, Travel Management module 285
fields functionalities, payroll area 195, 196
fields functionalities, payroll status
infotype (0003) 198
fields, schema editor
about 215, 216
D 216
Func 215
Line 215
Par1 215
Par 2 216
Par 3 216
Par 4 216
Text 216
fields, Travel Management module 288, 289
finance module
payroll processing, integrating with 221
finance posting
statuses 227
finance steps
payroll results, posting to 224-226
Flexible Employee Data report 21
folder
creating 28, 29

Functional Consultants (FC) 60
functionalities, control record 196, 197
functionalities, payroll area 194
functionalities, Travel Request module 291
functions, Personnel Development 241-243
functions, schematic payroll schema
COM 215
COPY 215
functions, Travel Management module 285

G

General Trip Data/Trip Totals report 27
generation rule configuration, Absence
Quotas infotype (2006) 176-184
generation tips, Absence Quotas
infotype (2006)
about 184
cluster tables, used in time evaluation 191
features 190
frequent error message and
workaround 185-188
functions 189
internal tables, used in time evaluation 190
operations 189
Time Management-related tables 188
tool, to check configuration settings for
quota generation 192
global distribution system (GDS) 295
Global Time Constraint
Reaction (V_T554Y) 178
GWT function 189

H

hassle-free absence quotas
generating 184-191
HCM 234
HCM submodules
integration aspects 234
Headcount changes report 21
holiday calendar 162-165
HRS operation 190
HR system
activities 222, 223
Human Capital Management. *See* HCM

I

IATA
  about 300
  locations 300
infogroups
  about 143
  configuring 143, 144
  menu type 143
infoset
  about 324
  creating, SQ02 TCD used 324, 325
infotype menu
  about 140
  configuring 140-142
infotypes, for payroll processing
  about 193
  payroll area 194
  payroll infotypes 194
Input Table (IT) 162
integration aspects, HCM submodules 234
integration aspects, TEM module 258-262
integration switches 99-101
internal postings 39
International Air Transport
        Association. *See* **IATA**

J

job fairs 39
job object
  creating, in Expert Mode 80

K

Key Data Structure (KDS) 125

L

Learning Solution (LSO) 257
line number field, schema editor
  < command 216
  > command 216
  D command 216
  I command 216
  R command 216
  Rn command 216
Logged Changes in Infotype Data 21

LSMW (Legacy System Migration
        Work Bench) 239

M

MASEX feature 190
master data, for Personnel Development
        component
  about 235-237
  career maintenance 240
  development plans 244, 245
  functions 241-243
  qualification catalogue 237-239
  standard tools 244
Master Data Maintenance transaction 336
menu types, SAP 141
MODT 169
MOLGA 13

N

Nationalities report 21
Net Weaver Exchange Infrastructure 295
node
  configuring, for Absence Quotas 152
  configuring, for Work schedule rule 152
number range assignment
  recommendations 129, 130
Number Ranges concept 81, 83
number ranges, Travel Management module
  PR10 287
  PR11 287
  PR12 287
  SNUM 286
NUMKR
  using 130
NUM operation 219

O

objective settings 246, 247
OH11/PU30 T-code, Payroll Accounting
        submodule 12
On-demand or Additional Payments
        configuration (0267) 211, 212
online recruiting sites 39
OOB1 T-code, Talent Management
        submodule 14

OOHAP_SETTINGS_PA T-code, Talent
    Management submodule 14
OOPS T-code 101
Organizational Management (OM)
    reports 19
Organizational Management (OM)
    submodule, T-code
  about 7, 8
  PO03 9
  PO10 9
  PO13 9
  PO14 9
  PP01 9
  PP03 9
  PPOCE 8
  PPOC_OLD 8
organizational objects
  relationships between 65, 66
Organizational Plan
    component (PA-OS) 261
organizational structure
  building, Expert Mode used 77
  building, methods 66
  building, Organization and Staffing method
    used 66, 67
  building, Simple Maintenance
    method used 70-75
  concept, of Number Ranges 81, 83
  Cost Centre, creating 76
  creating, Expert Mode used 91-95
  creating, multiple interfaces used 66
  elucidating 64
  job object, creating in Expert Mode 80, 81
  plan version, activating 85, 86
  plan version, maintaining 86-90
  position object, creating in Expert Mode 79
  Org unit and position, relationship 68
  relationship between Position, and Job 69
  scenarios, of using external number
    assignment 83, 84
  table configuration steps 96-98
organizational unit object
  creating, in Expert Mode 78
Organization and Staffing method
  used, for building organizational
    structure 66, 67

Organizational Assignment
    infotype (0001) 194
Organizational Management (OM)
  concepts 63
  integrating, with Personnel
    Administration 99
  tools, purpose 106
Organizational Management (OM), SAP
    standard reports 29
Organizational Management (OM), with
    Personnel Administration
  Data Transfer Tools 103
  integration switches 99-101
  tool, purpose 106
  RHINTE Reports 104, 105
Overtime infotype (2005) 158

P

P2001 function 189
P2006 function 189
PA03 T-code, Payroll Accounting
    submodule 11
PA20 T-code, Personnel Administration
    submodule 9
PA30 T-code, Personnel Administration
    submodule 9
PA40 T-code, Personnel Administration
    submodule 9
PA42 T-code, Personnel Administration
    submodule 9
PA61 T-code, Time Management
    submodule 10
PA70 T-code, Personnel Administration
    submodule 9
PA71 T-code, Time Management
    submodule 10
PA infotypes
  0000 (Action) infotype 110-112
  0001 (Organizational Assignment)
    infotype 112, 113
  0002 (Personal Data) infotype 113
  0006 (Address) infotype 114
  0007 (Planned Working Time)
    infotype 114, 115
  0008 (Basic Pay) infotype 116
  0009 (Bank Details) infotype 117

about 109
and configuration steps 110-117
PAPLI 54
Payday calendar report 24
Paydays on holidays or weekends report 24
payroll
configuring 203
Payroll Accounting report 23
Payroll Accounting, SAP standard
      reports 31
Payroll Accounting submodule, T-code
about 11-13
OH11/PU30 12
PA03 11
PC00 12
PC00_M99_CIPC 12
PC00_M99_CIPE 12
PC00_M99_DKON 12
PC00_M99_DLGA20 12
PC00_MXX_CALC 11
PC00_MXX_CDTA 12
PC00_MXX_CEDT 11
PC00_MXX_PA03_CORR 11
PC00_MXX_PA03_END 11
PC00_MXX_PA03_RELEA 11
PC00_MXX_SIMU 11
PCP0 12
PC_Payresult 12
PCXX 12
PE01 12
PE02 12
PE04 12
PE51 12
PU03 11
PUOC_99 12
payroll area
about 194
fields functionalities 195, 196
functionalities 194
payroll configuration
Additional Payments
    configuration (0015) 209, 210
Basic Pay configuration (0008) 206, 207
On-demand or Additional Payments
    configuration (0267) 211, 212
Recurring Payments and Deductions
    configuration (0014) 208, 209

wage types 203-205
payroll functions
COPY 218
PGM 219
PIT 219
PRT 219
UPD 219
WPBP 219
payroll infotypes
about 194
actions (0000) 194
Organizational Assignment (0001) 194
payroll operations
ADDWT 219
AMT 219
NUM 219
RTE 219
VWTCL 219
payroll processing
integrating, with finance module 221
payroll results
posting, to finance steps 224-226
Payroll Status infotype (0003)
about 197
fields functionalities 198
payscale type 138
payslip
configuring 220, 221
PB10 T-code, Recruitment submodule 7
PB20 T-code, Recruitment submodule 7
PB30 T-code, Recruitment submodule 7
PBA1 T-code, Recruitment submodule 7
PBA2 T-code, Recruitment submodule 7
PBA7 T-code, Recruitment submodule 8
PBA8 T-code, Recruitment submodule 8
PBAA T-code, Recruitment submodule 7
PBAW T-code, Recruitment submodule 7
PBAY T-code, Recruitment submodule 7
PC00_M99_CIPC T-code, Payroll
    Accounting submodule 12
PC00_M99_CIPET-code, Payroll Accounting
    submodule 12
PC00_M99_DKON T-code, Payroll
    Accounting submodule 12
PC00_M99_DLGA20 T-code, Payroll
    Accounting submodule 12

PC00_MXX_CALC T-code, Payroll
    Accounting submodule 11
PC00_MXX_CDTA T-code, Payroll
    Accounting submodule 12
PC00_MXX_CEDT T-code, Payroll
    Accounting submodule 11
PC00_MXX_PA03_CORR T-code, Payroll
    Accounting submodule 11
PC00_MXX_PA03_END T-code, Payroll
    Accounting submodule 11
PC00_MXX_PA03_RELEA T-code, Payroll
    Accounting submodule 11
PC00_MXX_SIMU T-code, Payroll
    Accounting submodule 11
PC00 T-code, Payroll Accounting
    submodule 12
PCP0 T-code, Payroll Accounting
    submodule 12
PC_Payresult T-code, Payroll Accounting
    submodule 12
PCR Operation
    3 operation 161
    1234 operation 162
    ADDWT operation 162
    AMT/30 operation 162
    AMT=6789 operation 162
    MULTI ANA operation 162
    ZLEN operation 161
PCXX T-code, Payroll Accounting
    submodule 12
PE01 T-code, Payroll Accounting
    submodule 12
PE02 T-code, Payroll Accounting
    submodule 12
PE04 T-code, Payroll Accounting
    submodule 12
PE51 T-code, Payroll Accounting
    submodule 12
period work schedule 167
personnel actions
    about 144
    configuring 145-148
    dynamic actions 148, 149
Personnel Administration (PA)
    Organizational Management (OM),
        integrating with 99
    recruitment, integrating with 52

Personnel Administration report 20-22
Personnel Administration, SAP standard
    reports 30
Personnel Administration submodule,
    T-code
    about 9
    PA20 9
    PA30 9
    PA40 9
    PA42 9
    PA70 9
personnel area
    about 118, 165
    factors, influencing 118
Personnel Calculation Rules (PCR)
    about 137, 216-218
    frequent error message 219
    work around 219
    writing 213
Personnel Development
    functions 241-243
Personnel Development component
    about 229
    basic settings 229-233
    master data 235-237
personnel structure, components
    employee group 119
    employee subgroup 119
    organization key 119
    payroll area 119
personnel subarea (PSA) 119, 205
PGM function 219
PHAP_CATALOG_PA T-code, Talent
    Management submodule 14
PHAP_CATALOG T-code, Talent
    Management submodule 13
PIT function 219
Planned Working Time
    infotype (0007) 198, 152-154
Plant Data Collection (PDC) 153
plan version
    about 83, 85
    activating 86
    maintaining 86-90
pnpce logical database 324
PO03 T-cold, Organizational Management
    (OM) submodule 9

PO10 T-cold, Organizational Management (OM) submodule 9
PO13 T-cold, Organizational Management (OM) submodule 9
PO14 T-cold, Organizational Management (OM) submodule 9
position object
  creating, in Expert Mode 79
PP03 T-cold, Organizational Management (OM) submodule 9
PP61 T-code, Time Management submodule 10
PPCP T-code, Talent Management submodule 13
PPEM T-code, Talent Management submodule 13
PPMOD feature 222
PPO1 T-cold, Organizational Management (OM) submodule 9
PPOCE T-code, Organizational Management (OM) submodule 8
PPOC_OLD T-code 71
PPOC_OLD T-cold, Organizational Management (OM) submodule 8
PPOME T-code 68, 69
PPSP T-code, Talent Management submodule 13
PR03 TCD 289
PR05 TCD 289
PR05 T-code, Travel Management submodule 15
PR10 TCD 287
PR11 TCD 287
PR12 TCD 287
PRAA TCD 290
PRAP TCD 289
PRAP T-code, Travel Management submodule 15
PR_CHECK tool 316
PREC TCD 289
PREC T-code, Travel Management submodule 15
PRELI 53, 54
PRELR 53, 54
PRFI TCD 289

PRFI T-code, Travel Management submodule 15
process input table. See PIT function
PRRW TCD 290
PRRW T-code, Travel Management submodule 15
PRT function 219
PSV1 T-code, Training and Event Management submodule 15
PSV2 T-code, Training and Event Management submodule 14
PSVQ T-code, Training and Event Management submodule 14
PT01 T-code, Time Management submodule 10
PT50 T-code, Time Management submodule 10
PT60 T-code, Time Management submodule 10
PT62 T-code, Time Management submodule 10
PT_CLSTB2 T-code, Time Management submodule 11
PT_ERL00 T-code, Time Management submodule 10
PTMW T-code, Time Management submodule 10
PU03 T-code, Payroll Accounting submodule 11
PUOC_99 T-code, Payroll Accounting submodule 12

Q

qualification catalogue 237-239
Qualification overview report 25
query
  creating, SQ01 TCD used 326, 327
  transporting, across clients 338, 339
queries, in global area 328
queries, in standard area 328
query view
  converting, to SAP query 345
QUOMO feature 190
Quota Correction infotype (2013) 159, 160
QUOTA function 189

R

recruitment
integrating, with Personnel
Administration 53
Recruitment infotypes
ranges 35
recruitment instruments
about 39, 40
classified advertising 39
employee referral program 39
employment agencies 39
internal postings 39
job fairs 39
online recruiting sites 39
search firms 39
used, for mapping vacant position 41
recruitment medium 41-43
Recruitment report, SAP standard
reports 29
Recruitment standard reports 15-18
Recruitment submodule, T-code
about 7
PB10 7
PB20 7
PB30 7
PBA1 7
PBA2 7
PBA7 8
PBA8 8
PBAA 7
PBAW 7
PBAY 7
Recurring Payment and Deduction
infotype (0014) 200
Recurring Payments and Deductions
configuration (0014) 208, 209
relationship type, Organizational
Management (OM)
A002 65
A003 65
A007 65
A008 65
A011 65
A012 65
B002 65

B003 65
B007 65
B008 65
B012 65
Remote Function Call (RFC) 299
report
developing, SQVI used 340-344
executing, ad hoc query used 328-332
Report Assignment feature 334
report output
TCD, tagging to 334-337
RFTP_SYNCHRO_PREFRFTP_SYNCHRO_
PREF program 297
RHINTE00 tool 104
RHINTE10 tool 104
RHINTE20 tool 104
RHINTE30 tool 104
RHINTECHECK tool 106
RHINTE Reports 104
RHQINTE0 report 235
RHQINTE1 report 235
ROUND operation 190
RPIT25APP report 235
RPTERL00 report 191
RPTERR00 report 191
RPUCTP00 report 187
RTE operation 219

S

Sabre 295
S_AHR_61011841 T-code, Training and
Event Management submodule 14
S_AHR_61011843 T-code, Training and
Event Management submodule 14
S_AHR_61011845 T-code, Training and
Event Management submodule 14
SAP
about 45
features 57-59
standard statuses 44
transport request 59-61
SAP-delivered function codes 145, 146
SAP-delivered indicators 149
SAP Easy Access window 6
SAP Plant Maintenance and Customer
Service (PM/CS) 153

SAP Production Planning (PP) and Process Control (PP/PI) 153
SAP Project Systems (PS) 153
SAP query
  query view, converting to 345
SAP standard employment status. *See* STAT2
SAP standard reports
  Organizational Management (OM) 29
  overview 29
  Payroll Accounting 31
  Personnel Administration 30
  Recruitment 29
  Talent Management 32
  Time Management 30, 31
  Training and Event Management 32
  Travel Management 32
SAP Transport Management System. *See* STMS
schema editor
  fields 215, 216
schematic payroll schema
  about 213, 214
  functions 215
SE80 TCD 319
search firms 39
SEMIN HISTO switch 274
SEMIN ORT switch 265
SEMIN WKAPM switch 275
service pack (SP) 203
Simple Maintenance
  used, for building organizational structure 70-75
SM30 TCD 319
SNUM TCD 286
S_PH9_46000434 T-code, Training and Event Management submodule 15
SPOCK 63
SQ01 TCD
  used, for building ad hoc query 317
  used, for creating query 326, 327
SQ02 TCD
  used, for creating infoset 324, 325
SQ03 TCD
  used, for creating user group 318-323
SQVI
  used, for developing report 340-344

standard function characters, SAP 149
standard reports
  about 15
  Organizational Management (OM) 19
  Payroll Accounting 23
  Personnel Administration 20
  Recruitment 15
  Talent Management 25
  Time Management 22
  Training and Event Management 25
  Travel Management 26
standard tools, in Personnel Development 244
STAT2 146
STAT2 entries 146
STATU feature 45
STMS 61
submodule configuration
  tips 129
submodule configuration, tips
  mandatory infotypes, configuring 131-139
  number range assignment recommendation 129, 130
Success Factor (SF) 257

T

table configuration, steps 96-98
Table Maintenance 41
tables
  customizing, for absence quotas 170-176
  customizing, for Work schedule rule 162
Talent Management report 25
Talent Management, SAP standard reports 32
Talent Management submodule, T-code
  about 13, 14
  APPCREATE 14
  APPSEARCH 14
  OOB1 14
  OOHAP_SETTINGS_PA 14
  PHAP_CATALOG 13
  PHAP_CATALOG_PA 14
  PPCP 13
  PPEM 13
  PPSP 13
TCD
  tagging, to report output 334-337

TCD, Travel Management module
  F.02/F-53/FBCJ/F110 290
  PR03 289
  PR05 289
  PRAA 290
  PRAP 289
  PREC 289
  PRFI 289
  PRRW 290
  TRIP 289
  XK03 290
T-code
  about 5
  accessing, via SAP Easy Access 6
  adding, to Favorites 6
  moving, to folder 28
  used, for technical screen call 7
TEM
  basic settings 257, 258
TEM module
  integration aspects 258-262
TEM (PE) component 257
Time Constraint Reaction (V_554Y_B) 178
Time Constraint (TC) class 178
Time Evaluation (RPTIME00) program 153
Time Management infotypes
  about 152
  Absence infotype (2001) 155
  Absences Quotas infotype (2006) 156, 157
  Attendances infotype (2002) 155
  Attendance Quotas infotype (2007) 157
  Employee Remuneration
    infotype (2010) 158
  Overtime infotype (2005) 158
  Planned Working Time
    infotype (0007) 152-154
  Quota Correction infotype (2013) 159, 160
  Time Quota Compensation
    infotype (0416) 161
Time Management report 22, 23
Time Management, SAP standard
  reports 30, 31
Time Management submodule, T-code
  about 10
  CAC1 11
  CATA 11
  ERL00 10

  PA61 10
  PA71 10
  PP61 10
  PT01 10
  PT50 10
  PT62 10
  PT_CLSTB2 11
  PTMW 10
Time Management T-code 30
Time Quota Compensation
  infotype (0416) 161
Time spent in each pay scale area/type/
  group/level report 20
TMSTA DEFAULT VALUE FOR TIME
  MANAGEMENT STATUS
  feature 154
Training and Event Management. *See* TEM
Training and Event Management report
  about 25, 26
  fields 26
Training and Event Management, SAP
  standard reports 32
Training and Event Management
  submodule, T-code
  about 14, 15
  PSV1 15
  PSV2 14
  PSVQ 14
  S_AHR_61011841 14
  S_AHR_61011843 14
  S_AHR_61011845 14
  S_AHR_61011888 14
  S_AHR_61011889 14
  S_AHR_61011893 14
  S_PH9_46000434 15
Training and Event Management
  T-code 32
transaction code. *See* T-code
transport request, SAP 59-61
Travel Expense component 287
Travel Expenses module
  configuration steps 306-314
Travel Management module
  about 285
  basic settings, for number ranges 286, 287
  features 285
  fields 288, 289

functions 285
infotypes, for booking Travel Planning 287
integration aspects, with other application
    components 314, 315
master data 287
TCD 289
transaction code 289
Travel Management report
about 26, 27
selection parameters 27
**Travel Management, SAP standard
    reports 32**
Travel Management submodule, T-code
about 15
PR05 15
PRAP 15
PREC 15
PRFI 15
PRRW 15
TRIP 15
Travel Management T-code 32
Travel Planning module
configuration steps 294-305
prerequisites, for using features 295
Travel Request module
configuration steps 290-292, 294
functionalities 291
**TRIP T-code, Travel Management
    submodule 15**

U

UPD function 219
user group
about 46, 318
creating, SQ03 TCD used 318-323

V

vacancy
advertising 39
handling 35-37
maintenance steps 37, 39
vacant position
mapping, recruitment instruments used 41
Variable Applicant List report 16
VARST operation 190
VWTCL operation 219

W

wage type assignment 224
wage types 203-205
Web Dynpro 291
Where-used functionality 240
work centre basic pay function. *See* WPBP
    function
Work schedule rule
about 168-170
daily work schedule 165-167
day type 167
holiday calendar 162-165
nodes, configuring for 152
period work schedule 167
tables, customizing for 162
WPBP function 219
WPBP infotype 194
WPBP-FUWPBP function 194

X

XK03 TCD 290

[PACKT] enterprise 🞽
PUBLISHING   professional expertise distilled

Thank you for buying
SAP HCM – A Complete Tutorial

About Packt Publishing

Packt, pronounced 'packed', published its first book "Mastering phpMyAdmin for Effective MySQL Management" in April 2004 and subsequently continued to specialize in publishing highly focused books on specific technologies and solutions.

Our books and publications share the experiences of your fellow IT professionals in adapting and customizing today's systems, applications, and frameworks. Our solution based books give you the knowledge and power to customize the software and technologies you're using to get the job done. Packt books are more specific and less general than the IT books you have seen in the past. Our unique business model allows us to bring you more focused information, giving you more of what you need to know, and less of what you don't.

Packt is a modern, yet unique publishing company, which focuses on producing quality, cutting-edge books for communities of developers, administrators, and newbies alike. For more information, please visit our website: www.packtpub.com.

About Packt Enterprise

In 2010, Packt launched two new brands, Packt Enterprise and Packt Open Source, in order to continue its focus on specialization. This book is part of the Packt Enterprise brand, home to books published on enterprise software – software created by major vendors, including (but not limited to) IBM, Microsoft and Oracle, often for use in other corporations. Its titles will offer information relevant to a range of users of this software, including administrators, developers, architects, and end users.

Writing for Packt

We welcome all inquiries from people who are interested in authoring. Book proposals should be sent to author@packtpub.com. If your book idea is still at an early stage and you would like to discuss it first before writing a formal book proposal, contact us; one of our commissioning editors will get in touch with you.

We're not just looking for published authors; if you have strong technical skills but no writing experience, our experienced editors can help you develop a writing career, or simply get some additional reward for your expertise.

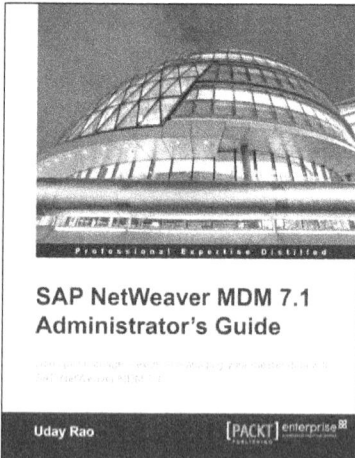

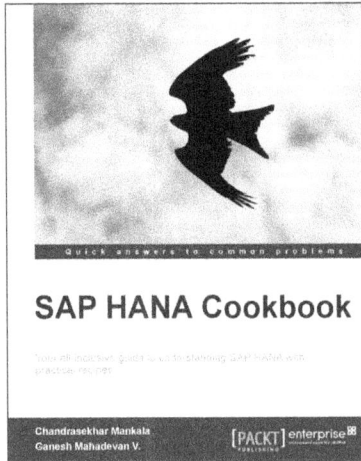

SAP HANA Cookbook

ISBN: 978-1-78217-762-3   Paperback: 284 pages

Your all-inclusive guide to understanding SAP HANA with practical recipes

1. Understand the architecture of SAP HANA, effectively transforming your business with the modeler and in-memory computing engine.

2. Learn about Business Intelligence, Analytics, and Predictive analytics on top of SAP HANA Models.

3. Gain knowledge on the process of transforming your data to insightful information using the Modeler.

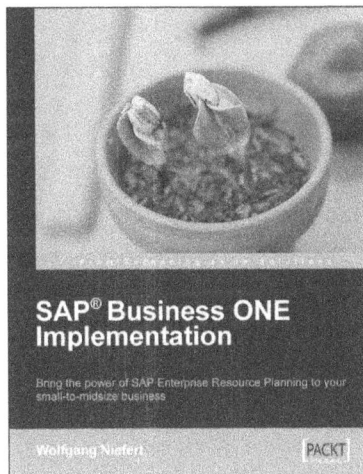

SAP® Business ONE Implementation

ISBN: 978-1-84719-638-5   Paperback: 320 pages

Bring the power of SAP Enterprise Resource Planning to your small-to-midsize business

1. Get SAP B1 up and running quickly, optimize your business, inventory, and manage your warehouse.

2. Understand how to run reports and take advantage of real-time information.

3. Complete an express implementation from start to finish.

4. Real-world examples with step-by-step explanations.

Please check **www.PacktPub.com** for information on our titles

www.ingramcontent.com/pod-product-compliance
Lightning Source LLC
Chambersburg PA
CBHW080711220326
41598CB00033B/5384